Narrative across Media

FRONTIERS OF NARRATIVE

Series Editor
David Herman, North Carolina State University

Narrative

across Media

The Languages of Storytelling

Edited by Marie-Laure Ryan

University of Nebraska Press   Lincoln and London

© 2004 by the Board of Regents of the University of Nebraska
Manufactured in the United States of America

Acknowledgments for the use of previously published material appear on page vii, which constitutes an extension of the copyright page.

Library of Congress Cataloging-in-Publication Data
Narrative across media: the languages of storytelling / edited by Marie-Laure Ryan.
p.   cm.—(Frontiers of narrative)
Includes bibliographical references and index.
ISBN 0-8032-3944-0 (cl.: alk. paper)—ISBN 0-8032-8993-6 (pbk.: alk. paper)
1. Narration (Rhetoric)   2. Mass media.   I. Ryan, Marie-Laure, 1946–   II. Series.
PN212 .N3727   2004
808—dc22
2003015225

Contents

Acknowledgments

Earlier versions or foreign language translations of some of the essays published in this volume have been published elsewhere:

David Bordwell, "NeoStructuralist Narratology and the Functions of Filmic Storytelling," appeared in Swedish translation under the title "Neostruktrualistisk narratologi och filmiska berättarfunktioner," in *Aura: Filmvetenskaplig tidskrift* 1.1 (1995): 47–57. Reprinted by permission of the author.

Justine Cassell and David McNeill, "Gesture and the Poetics of Prose," appeared in *Poetics Today* 12.3 (Fall 1991): 375–404. Copyright (c) 1991, Porter Institute for Poetics and Semiotics. All rights reserved. Reprinted by permission of Duke University Press.

Liv Hausken, "Textual Theory and Blind Spot in Media Studies," appeared in a longer version as "Tekstteoretiske utfordringer i den medievitenskaplige disiplin," in *Norsk medietidsskrift* 1 (2000): 99–113. Reprinted by permission of the author.

Peter Lunenfeld, "The Myths of Interactive Cinema," appeared in *The New Media Book,* ed. Dan Harries (London: British Film Institute, 2002). Reprinted by permission of BFI Publishing.

Marie-Laure Ryan, "Will New Media Produce New Narratives?" is an expanded version of an article published in *Frame* 16.1 (2002): 19–35. Reprinted by permission of the journal.

Wendy Steiner, "Pictorial Narrativity," is a shortened version of chapter 1 of *Pictures of Romance: Form against Context in Painting and Literature* by W. Steiner (Chicago: University of Chicago Press, 1988). Reprinted by permission of the University of Chicago Press.

Katharine Young, "Edgework: Frame and Boundary in the Phenomenology of Narrative," is a revised, slightly shortened version of chapter 1 of *Taleworlds and Storyrealms* by K. Young (Dordrecht: Martinus Nijhoff, 1987). Reprinted by permission of the author.

The work of the editor was supported in part by a fellowship from the Guggenheim Foundation.

Narrative across Media

Introduction

Marie-Laure Ryan

Narratology, the formal study of narrative, has been conceived from its earliest days as a project that transcends disciplines and media. In 1964 Claude Bremond wrote: "[Story] is independent of the techniques that bear it along. It may be transposed from one to another medium without losing its essential properties: the subject of a story may serve as argument for a ballet, that of a novel can be transposed to stage or screen, one can recount in words a film to someone who has not seen it. These are words we read, images we see, gestures we decipher, but through them, it is a story that we follow; and it could be the same story."[1] This statement has remained in theoretical hibernation for over forty years—occasionally contested by opponents of the form and content dichotomy, which it seems to imply, occasionally invoked as inspiration for concrete comparative studies, but never developed into a full-scale transmedial narrative theory. Nearly forty years later, in a period of swelling interest in both comparative media studies and narrative (the latter demonstrated by the so-called narrative turn in the humanities), the question of how the intrinsic properties of the medium shape the form of narrative and affect the narrative experience can no longer be ignored. The study of narrative across media is not the same project as the interdisciplinary study of narrative: whereas one project directs us to the importance of narrative in mostly language-based practices, the other focuses on the embodiment, that is to say, the particular semiotic substance and the technological mode of transmission of narrative. Its categories are language, image, sound, gesture, and, further, spoken language, writing, cinema, radio, television, and computers rather than law, medicine, science, literature, and history.

Even when they seek to make themselves invisible, media are not hollow conduits for the transmission of messages but material supports of information whose materiality, precisely, "matters" for the type of meanings that can be encoded. Whether they function as transmissive channels or provide the physical substance for the inscription of narrative messages, media differ widely in their efficiency and expressive power. In the words of Shlomith Rimmon-Kenan, their built-in properties "open up possibilities and impose constraints which . . . shape the narration, the text, and even the story" (160). The present collection of essays takes a close-up look at some of these constraints and possibilities—which we may call, following the psychologist J. J. Gibson, "affordances"—with a broader question in mind: what does it mean "to narrate," and what kinds of stories can be told in different medial environments?

To prepare for this journey, let me attempt to package *narrative* and *media* into transportable definitions. It is not my intent to develop a formula that captures the position of all the contributors to this volume, but in the process of working my own definition I hope to give a reasonably comprehensive view of the options that underlie my decisions. The parameters that make up this field of possibilities should provide a common denominator for the comparison of differing individual positions. The definitional considerations will be followed by a survey of some of the milestones of media studies, from which we should get a clearer idea of what needs to be done to turn its flirtation with narrative theory into a productive partnership for both parties. This introduction will not include a survey of narratology, mainly because the field is too vast to be presented in a limited space but also because several essays in this book involve a discussion of key narratological concepts: those in particular by David Herman and Wendy Steiner. For a presentation of the individual essays and an overview of the state of narrative research in each area, the reader should consult the specialized introductions to the individual sections.

Narrative: What It Could Be

The phenomenon of narrative has been explored in many terms: existential, cognitive, aesthetic, sociological, and technical. These explorations range from broad considerations about the nature of narrative to narrow definitions. The existential type (represented by Paul Ricoeur and Peter Brooks) tells us that the act of narrating enables humans to deal with time, destiny, and mortality; to create and project identities; and to situate themselves as embodied individuals in a world populated by similarly embodied subjects. It is in short a way, perhaps the only one, to give meaning to life. Through narrative we also explore alternate realities and expand our mental horizon beyond the physical, actual world—toward the worlds of dreams, phantasms, fantasy, possibilities, and counterfactuality.

Whereas existential approaches try to capture what it means for us to produce (or receive) narratives, it belongs to the cognitive approaches to describe the operations of the narrating mind. Mark Turner opens an ambitious program for both narratology and cognitive science when he writes: "Narrative imagining—story—is the fundamental instrument of thought . . . It is a *literary* capacity indispensable to human cognition generally" (4–5; emph. added). Why is narrative so fundamental to cognition? Because to notice objects or events in our perceptual environment is to construct embryonic stories about them: "Story depends on constructing something rather than nothing. A reportable story is distinguished from its assumed and unreportable background. It is impossible for us to look at the world and not to see reportable stories distinguished from background" (145). It may seem strange that a capacity as essential as narrative to cognition should be labeled literary, as if narrative were necessarily an aesthetic object and as if thought were an exclusively language-based process, but for Turner "the literary mind is not a separate sort of mind. It is our mind" (v). Turner labels the mind literary to suggest that we apply similar interpretive principles when we read a text and when we engage in the activities of everyday life.

Whereas Turner regards narrative as *the* instrument of human thought, Jerome Bruner, more cautiously, describes it as one of two fundamental ways of thinking, the other being the argumentative, or paradigmatic, mode: "A good story and a well-formed argument are different natural kinds. Both can be used as means for convincing another. Yet what they convince of is fundamentally different: arguments convince one of their truth, stories of their lifelikeness" (11). The narrative mode is the mode of the particular; it deals with "human or human-like intentions and actions and the vicissitudes and consequences that mark their course." The argumentative mode, on the other hand, "deals in general causes, and in their establishment, and makes use of procedures to assure verifiable reference and to test for empirical truth." It "seeks to transcend the particular by higher and higher reaching for abstraction" (13). It is easy to recognize in the argumentative mode the scientific way of thinking, but the domain of the narrative mode is less clear. Bruner seems to associate narrative with fictional stories when he writes that it is not judged by criteria of truth and verifiability—but where in this dichotomy should one fit such genres as history, news reports, and, above all, courtroom testimonies, which deal with the particular, and do so in an obviously narrative way, but at the same time make a very direct truth claim? In addition to regarding narrative as typically fictional, Bruner associates it with aesthetic qualities: "In contrast to our vast knowledge of how science and logical reasoning proceed, we know precious little in any formal sense about how to make good *stories*" (14). Neither Turner nor Bruner thus attempts to distinguish the properly narrative element from a group of features that yields what is certainly the most diversified, but by no means the only, manifestation of narrative: literary narrative fiction.

The aesthetic approaches deal with more concrete textual phenomena than either the existential or cognitive ones. This should, in principle, give them a better shot at a definition. But their chances at developing the formula of narrative are hampered by their integrationist stance. I call "integrationist" an approach that refuses on principle to isolate "narrativity" from other layers of meaning and from the total textual experience. This approach regards narrativity, fictionality, and literariness (or aesthetic appeal) as inseparable features. For many literary critics the quintessential narrative text is the novel, a proteiform genre that encompasses not only action-filled tales but also the psychological narratives of modernism and the plotless or self-reflexive texts of postmodernism. To the integrationist aesthetician, a satisfactory definition of *narrative* should gives equal status to Gustave Flaubert's *Madame Bovary* and Flann O'Brien's *At Swim-Two-Birds* or to James Joyce's *Dubliners, Ulysses,* and *Finnegans Wake.* One of the most extreme forms of this approach is the concept of narrative proposed by Philip Sturgess. In *Narrativity: Theory and Practice* Sturgess criticizes available attempts at defining narrative, particularly those of Gerald Prince and of the story-grammar school on the ground that they presuppose a deep-structural, preverbal armature to which the text owes its narrativity (14). For Sturgess there is no such thing as nonverbalized narrativity, nor are there nonnarrative elements in a narrative text: narrativity is a global effect toward which every single textual element conspires, and it is inseparable from the "verbal and syntactic" progress of the text. "Narrativity," Sturgess writes, "is the enabling force of narrative, a force that is present at every point in the narrative" (29). The inevitable consequence of this rather tautological definition is that narrativity becomes indistinguishable from aesthetic teleology, or, as Sturgess puts it, from the consistency with which every text uses its devices (36). Since aesthetic teleology is unique to each text, so is narrativity. For the most radical versions of the integrationist position, narrative is just too deeply entangled with the verbal fabric of the text to be definable at all.

Sociological approaches shift the focus of investigation from narrative as a text to the performance of this text as what we may call, with David Herman (in this volume) a "contextually situated practice." The study of the contexts in which narration takes place is an important project, but it is not conducive to a general definition. Even if we remain within the domain of verbal narration, the common denominator of social events as diverse as conversational gossip, the presentation of news on television, the play-by-play broadcast of a sports event, the oral performance of a traditional epic by a bard, the retelling of the plot of a movie to a friend, the confession of sins to a priest, or the writing of a novel resides neither in the concrete circumstances nor in the particular social function of the narrative act but in the context-transcending nature of this act. This leads us back to square one: for we cannot define the act of narration without defining the object created through this act.

The technical approaches are the most inclined to isolate narrativity from both context and other textual features. We may therefore call them "segregationist." By technical approaches I mean not only narratology proper, a structuralist project that recruits most of its troops from literary theory, but also work done in folklore, experimental psychology, linguistics, and discourse analysis. Since the technical approaches tend to favor language-based narrative, I propose here to examine some of the difficulties encountered by the project of defining narrative as a discourse-theoretical object. This investigation should pave the way toward a medium-free definition.

One of the main concerns of the technical approaches is the place of narrative in a comprehensive discourse theory: is it a speech act, a genre, or a type of sentence? Several theorists have proposed definitions of narrative that suggest a speech act—for instance, Barbara Herrnstein Smith, who writes, "we might conceive of narrative discourse most minimally and most generally as verbal acts consisting of *someone telling someone else that something happened*" (228). One of the basic assumptions of speech act theory, as formulated by Searle, is the relative independence of illocutionary force (a technical term for *speech act*) from the propositional content of an utterance. While the relation between illocutionary category and propositional content is governed by constraints (you cannot, for instance, mean "I will kill you" as advice or use "The weather is nice" to christen a ship), an illocutionary category cannot be entirely predicted on the basis of prepositional content. A proposition made of the subject *the dishes* and the predicate *washed* can be used to make an assertion ("The dishes are washed"), a question ("Are the dishes washed?"), a command "Wash the dishes!"), the condition for a threat ("The dishes had better be washed by noon, or you'll be in trouble"), and so on. At first sight Smith's characterization divides neatly into an illocutionary category (someone telling someone else) and a propositional content (something happened). To narrate, then, would be one of the several speech acts that one can accomplish with a propositional content of the type "something happened," but what can one do with a collection of propositions that describe events besides narrating them? And what is narrating, if not asserting these propositions either seriously or in make-believe (for example, fictionally)? The so-called speech act of narration thus turns out to be an assertion that concerns a particular type of meaning. This suggests that narrativity is a matter of propositional content, not of illocutionary force.

If narrating is not a technically distinct sort of speech act, one that stands on par with assertion, command, question, or promise, could narrative be a genre? It all depends on whether we interpret genre in an analytical or a cultural sense. (This distinction is from Dan Ben-Amos.) In the analytical interpretation, genre (or analytical category) corresponds to any kind of criterion that can be used to build a discourse or text typology. In the cultural sense, by contrast, genre designates text types not merely drawn by theorists but enjoying widespread recognition in a given community. Within the medium of language the genre system of Western cultures correspond, for instance, to traditional literary labels, such as the novel, poetry, drama, essays, and short stories. Other media also have their culturally recognized genres: comedy, action, drama, and pornography in the cinema; historical scene, landscape, portrait, and still life in painting; symphony, concerto, sonata, fantasy, intermezzo, and nocturne in music. To return to verbal texts, the notion of genre is much more problematic outside the literary sector, but a case could be made for scientific discourse, history, law, self-help books, song lyrics, and recipes as genres of contemporary Western cultures. Insofar as they form reasonably well-defined categories, cultural genres are defined by unique sets of analytical features, but a given feature can be shared by several genres: for instance, "being fictional" is common to novels and drama, while "being about past events" characterizes both history and historical novels. *Narrative,* however, does not seem to possess the recognition of a cultural genre. People go for novels, biographies, self-help, or for the subgenres romance and science fiction, but nobody would walk into a bookstore and ask for a narrative. Yet, as a property of texts, narrative enters into the definition of many genres, in combination with other features that operate further distinctions. It is, therefore, a prime example of an analytical category.

This diagnosis of narrative as a concept broader than genre—whether we call it an analytical category, discourse type, text type, or macro-genre—does not solve the problem of its definition. The description of discourse-theoretical concepts usually begins with the identification of the categories that operate on the same level, but in this case there is no consensus about what other categories provide a useful contrast: Chatman opposes narrative discourse to persuasive and descriptive; Fludernik's model comprises narrative, argumentative, instructive, conversational, and reflective ("Genres," 282); and Virtanen envisions five basic types, including narrative, description, instruction, exposition, and argumentation. Moreover, as all these authors recognize, narrative intervenes both on the macro and the micro level: a persuasive text, such as a political speech, will use narrative anecdotes; a descriptive text, such as an account of the behavior of wildlife in a certain area, will almost inevitably resort to mini-stories. Conversely, a narrative text includes description or argumentation on the micro level. A typology that resorts to the same categories on different levels is a dangerously tangled hierarchy.

Since narrative appears on two discourse levels, its macro-level manifestation could be regarded as the extension of a micro-level feature. Would it be possible to associate narrativity with small discourse units, such as a specific rhetorical or semantic type of sentence? Here the rival categories might be description (again), evaluation, generalization, commentary, judgment, argument, or metatextual comments. This interpretation of narrative supports the intuitive notion that, within a novel, not every sentence moves the plot forward. The narrativity of a text would be born by sentences that imply the temporal succession of their referents, as is the case with the evocation of events and actions, as opposed to those sentences that refer to simultaneously existing entities, to general laws, to static properties, or to the narrator's personal opinions. The degree of narrativity of a text could thus be measured by the proportion of properly narrative sentences. A fairy tale or conversational narrative of personal experience would be much higher in narrativity than a nineteenth-century novel rich in descriptions or philosophical passages, even if the latter has a more intricate plot, because a summary would retain a higher proportion of the information contained in the text.

While the idea of degrees of narrativity indeed seems promising—it enables narrative theory to recuperate most of postmodern literature—the assimilation of narrative to certain rhetorical or semantic sentence types puts excessive restrictions on the reader's representation of narrative meaning. In our mental image of a plot, expository statements ("Little Red Riding Hood was a little girl") and at least some descriptive ones ("She was

named that way because her mother made her a red cap") coexist with
propositions reporting the actions of characters. It would make no sense
to commit to memory sequences of action without including in the picture the identifying properties of the individuals involved in those actions.
Moreover, as David Herman has argued in *Story Logic* (chap. 7), narrative
is a spatio-temporal construct: it reports actions that take place in a world,
and the evocation of the spatial layout of this world requires descriptive
sentences. Explanatory and evaluative sentences are no less constitutive of
narrative meaning than state-reporting discourse: the former are needed to
make explicit causal relations between events (for example, "Grief caused
the queen to die"), while the latter are used to state the importance of
events for the protagonists ("It totally changed her life"). Without denying
the privileged connection between narrativity and action-reporting, clock-
moving sentences, we cannot, therefore, exclude a priori any kind of sentence from a text's narrative layer.[2]

   All of these attempts at fitting narrative within a formal discourse model
encounter the same difficulty: we cannot identify positively the other elements of the presumed system. Since we have a clearer intuitive idea of
what narrative is than of what it contrasts to, the Saussurean program of
defining the units of language differentially fails in this case for a lack of
neighboring elements. The alternative to regarding narrative as a member
of a linguistic paradigm is to define it as a type of meaning and to do so
in positive terms. By advocating a semantic approach, I am not denying
that narrative involves both a signified and a signifier (what narratologists
customarily call "story level" and "discourse level"), but I am making the
claim that its identity resides on the level of the signified. In contrast
to the approach that attempts to link this meaning to a specific type of
sentence, I propose to regard narrative meaning as a cognitive construct,
or mental image, built by the interpreter in response to the text. Gerald
Prince has attempted to describe this construct through an elaborate formal
grammar.[3] Here I would like to propose an informal characterization of
the representation that a text must bring to mind to qualify as narrative.

    1. A narrative text must create a world and populate it with characters
       and objects. Logically speaking, this condition means that the narra-
       tive text is based on propositions asserting the existence of individuals
       and on propositions ascribing properties to these existents.
    2. The world referred to by the text must undergo changes of state that
       are caused by nonhabitual physical events: either accidents ("happen-

ings") or deliberate human actions. These changes create a temporal dimension and place the narrative world in the flux of history.

3. The text must allow the reconstruction of an interpretive network of goals, plans, causal relations, and psychological motivations around the narrated events. This implicit network gives coherence and intelligibility to the physical events and turns them into a plot.

When a text fulfills these conditions, it creates what I shall call a "narrative script." This definition does not take into consideration what enables a narrative script to capture the interest of the audience: a complete narrative theory would need to complement minimal conditions with what discourse analysts, following William Labov, call "principles of tellability." It would also need principles of efficient presentation, such as Labov's structural analysis of conversational narration into five components: abstract, orientation, complicating action, evaluation, result or resolution, coda. But narrativity is a type of meaning that transcends aesthetics and entertainment, as anybody who has been forced to listen to a boring, self-absorbed, rambling conversational storyteller realizes. A narrative that falls flat is still a narrative.

How compatible is this formula with nonverbal forms of narrative? Rather than locating narrativity in an act of telling, my definition anchors it in two distinct realms. On one hand, narrative is a textual act of representation—a text that encodes a particular type of meaning. The definition remains unspecific about what type of signs are used to encode this meaning. On the other hand, narrative is a mental image—a cognitive construct—built by the interpreter as a response to the text. Once again, this representation may be induced by various types of stimuli. But it does not take a representation proposed as narrative to trigger the cognitive construct that constitutes narrativity: we may form narrative scripts in our mind as a response to life, which is definitely not a representation (though, of course, we experience it through cognitive processes that produce mental images). To describe these two modalities, I propose to make a distinction between "being a narrative" and "possessing narrativity." The property of "being" a narrative can be predicated on any semiotic object produced with the intent of evoking a narrative script in the mind of the audience. "Having narrativity," on the other hand, means being able to evoke such a script. In addition to life itself, pictures, music, or dance can have narrativity without being narratives in a literal sense.

The fullest form of narrativity occurs when the text is both intended as narrative and possesses sufficient narrativity to be construed as such, though the story encoded in the text and the story decoded by the reader can never be extracted from the brain and laid side by side for comparison. But the properties of being narrative and having narrativity can be dissociated in a variety of ways. The standard case of dissociation occurs when the story is so poorly presented that the audience cannot reconstrue the proper script. In this case the text is a narrative of low narrativity. I alluded earlier to the opposite case, of a life situation rationalized in narrative terms. The property of being a narrative is much more clear-cut than the property of having narrativity, but it becomes fuzzy when the text uses narrative scripts in an instrumental way—for instance, when sermons or philosophical works resort to parables and narrative examples on the micro-level or when computer games rely on story to lure the player into their world, even though the story does not form the focus of interest once the player is immersed in the strategic action. A game, after all, is not "a narrative" in the sense that a novel or a film can be. The question "Is it a narrative?" is even more problematic when the text embodies the artistic intent to both arouse and frustrate narrative desire. Many postmodern texts present themselves as bits of pieces of a narrative image but prevent the reader from ever achieving the reconstruction of a stable and complete narrative script. This may explain why narrative theory has never been comfortable with either including or excluding postmodern literature.

But, if the distinction between being a narrative and having narrativity allows the extension of the concept of narrative beyond verbal artifacts, it does not entirely solve the thorny problem of the relationship between language and narrative. It seems clear that of all semiotic codes language is the best suited to storytelling. Every narrative can be summarized in language, but very few can be retold through pictures exclusively. The narrative limitation of pure pictures stems from their inability to make propositions. As Sol Worth has argued, visual media lack the code, the grammar, and the syntactic rules necessary to articulate specific meanings. A propositional act consists of picking a referent from a certain background and of attributing to it a property also selected from a horizon of possibilities. Whereas language can easily zero in on objects and properties, pictures can only frame a general area that contains many shapes and features. To convey the idea that Napoléon was short, for instance, a picture would have to represent the height of the emperor together with many of his other visual properties, and there would be a significant risk that the spectator would be more impressed by one of the other features than by the height itself. Pictures may admittedly find ways around their lack of propositional ability to suggest specific properties (for instance, through caricature), but there are certain types of statements that seem totally beyond their reach. As Worth argues, pictures cannot say "ain't." Nor, as Rimmon-Kenan observes, can they convey possibility, conditionality, or counterfactuality (162).[4] Being limited to the visible, they are unable to express abstract ideas, such as causality. Only language can make it explicit that the queen died of grief over the death of the king or that the fox stole the cheese from the crow by fooling him into believing something that was not the case.

The narrative limitations of music are even more blatant than those of pictures, since sound waves (or tones and rhythms) are not in themselves semiotic objects. As Seymour Chatman writes, "Music offers no consistency of reference between each of its elements—notes, phrases, movements—and something else in the real or an imagined world so that we may think of the first as signifier and the second as signified" (*Coming to Terms* 8). Pure sounds can be used to evoke mental images, some of which may resemble stories, but they possess neither a context-independent, stable core of signification definable by "lexical" rules nor an immediately perceivable iconic meaning.

All of these observations seem to support the conclusion that verbal language is the native tongue of narrative, its proper semiotic support. Without denying the unsurpassed narrative ability of language, however, I would like to defend a more nuanced position. If we define *narrative* in cognitive terms, it is not a linguistic object but a mental image. While it may be true that only language can express the causal relations that hold narrative scripts together, this does not mean that a text needs to represent these relations explicitly to be interpreted as narrative. As David Bordwell and Kristin Thompson have argued, the seemingly disconnected sequence of cinematic images "A man tosses and turns, unable to sleep. A mirror breaks. A telephone rings" can become a narrative sequence if the spectator supplies common agents and logical connections (55). Brian Richardson proposes the following narrativization: "The man can't sleep because he's had a fight with his boss, and in the morning is still so angry that he smashes the mirror while shaving; next, his telephone rings and he learns that his boss has called to apologize" (170). The visual track may be unable to explicate causal relations—this is why some people who are used to books have difficulty following cinematic narratives—but what matters in this case is the spectator's ability to infer them from the text. Even purely verbal texts, which are perfectly able to say, "The queen's grief over the king's death caused her to die," usually dispense with such explanations.

Although the ability to infer causal relations is essential to narrative understanding, readers' mental images of stories could be as elliptic as the texts themselves. It seems unlikely that narratives will be internalized as fully connected networks of logical relations. The mind is notoriously capable of emergent behavior—of creating new connections and of forming new patterns of ideas in response to certain stimuli. It is much more efficient to store an incomplete version of a given narrative and to flesh it out when the need arises than to clutter memory with all the details of its logical armature. What is left out and what is included in this image depends on the individual interpreter. The complete and explicit representation of a story is an ideal, somewhat Platonic version toward which readers work, as they fill in their cognitive blueprint of the story.

A model that defines narrative as a cognitive construct remains uncommitted about what this construct is made of. Since no CAT scan can reveal the contents of the brain, we can only speculate in this domain, but cognitive research suggests that the mental representation of a story involves various types of images (the term is taken here in the broadest possible sense, as an informational pattern stored in the mind).[5] It seems safe to assume that propositions abstracted from the text, rather than reproducing it, are the dominant element, but certain aspects of narrative could be stored as words (for instance, the memorable replies of characters) or as visual images (the setting, the appearance of characters, the map of the narrative world, and some striking actions and situations, such as Emma Bovary making love to Léon in a carriage storming in full gallop through the streets of Rouen). It is not inconceivable that moods and emotions will be associated with rhythms and melodies. Conversely, pictures can be remembered either in visual terms or as propositions: we may, for instance, be able to tell that in the background of a painting is a mirror, though we cannot remember its exact shape.[6] The cognitive representation that I call narrative could thus be the mental equivalent of a "multimedia" construct. While its logical structure is probably stored as propositions, which in turn can only be translated through language, other types of images, and consequently other "mental media," enrich the total representation in ways that remain inaccessible to language. Yes, language is the privileged medium of summaries because it can articulate the logical structure of a story; yes, language all by itself can support a wider variety of narratives than any other single-track medium, not just because of its logical superiority but also because only words can represent language and thought. But this does not mean that media based on sensory channels cannot make unique contributions to the formation of narrative meaning. There are, quite simply, meanings that are better expressed visually or musically than verbally, and these meanings should not be declared a priori irrelevant to the narrative experience.

To capture the ambiguity of the relationship between language and narrative, we need to distinguish theory from practice. Theoretically, narrative is a type of meaning that transcends particular media; practically, however, narrative has a medium of choice, and this medium is language. This explains why narratology tends to treat the types of narration exemplified by novels, short stories, news, history, and conversational storytelling as the unmarked, standard manifestation of narrativity: telling somebody else that something happened, with the assumption that the addressee is not already aware of the events. But, if narratology is to expand into a medium-free model, the first step is to recognize other narrative modes, that is to say, other ways of evoking narrative scripts. What should we understand under this concept of modes? I propose to include the following pairs in what I regard as an open list. In each case the left term can be regarded as the unmarked case, because the texts that present this feature will be much more widely accepted as narrative (at least by theorists) than the texts that implement the right-hand category. To take only one example: those narratologists who define narrative as "telling somebody that something happened" exclude all instances of mimetic narrativity.

Diegetic/Mimetic: This distinction goes back to Plato's *Republic*. It is also discussed in Aristotle's *Poetics*. A diegetic narration is the verbal storytelling act of a narrator. As the definition indicates, diegetic narration presupposes language, either oral or written; it is, therefore, the typical mode of the novel, conversational storytelling, and news report. A mimetic narration is an act of showing: a "spectacle," as David Bordwell characterizes it (*Narration* 3). In forming a narrative interpretation, the recipient works under the guidance of an authorial consciousness, but there is no narratorial figure. Mimetic narration is exemplified by all dramatic arts: movies, theater, dance, and the opera. But each of these two modes can intrude into a narration dominated by the other. The dialogues of a novel are islands of mimetic narration, since in direct quote the voice of the narrator disappears behind the voice of the characters, and, conversely, the phenomenon of voiced-over narration in cinema reintroduces a diegetic element in a basically mimetic medium.[7]

Those theoreticians who regard the presence of a storyteller performing a verbal act of narration as an essential condition of narrativity recuperate mimetic narrative by ascribing these forms to a nonhuman narratorial figure, such as the ghostly "grand-image-maker" of film theory.[8] But the narrativity of mimetic forms could also be defended by regarding them as virtual stories. When we retell a play, we produce a standard diegetic narrative. The *possibility* to retell as a story would then be the condition of narrativity, and the narrativity of a given text would stand whether or not the possibility is actualized.

Autonomous/Illustrative (or ancillary): In the autonomous mode the text transmits a story that is new to the receiver; this means that the logical armature of the story must be retrievable from the text. In the illustrative mode the text retells and completes a story, relying on the receiver's previous knowledge of the plot. Halfway between these two poles is the case of a text that offers a new, significantly altered *version* of a familiar plot.

Receptive/Participatory: In the receptive mode the recipient plays no active role in the events presented by the narrative: he merely receives the account of a narrative action, imagining himself as an external witness. In the participatory mode the plot is not completely pre-scripted. The recipient becomes an active character in the story, and through her agency she contributes to the writing of the plot. This mode has been practiced for quite a while in staged happenings, "improv" theater, and scripted role-playing games (for example, Dungeons and Dragons), but it has flourished with the advent of interactive digital media. In many computer games, for instance, the user is represented in the game world through an avatar. By solving problems in the real time of the game session, she determines whether the life story of this avatar will end in success or failure or how long the avatar will live.

Determinate/Indeterminate (or actual/virtual): In the determinate mode the text specifies a sufficient number of points on the narrative trajectory to project a reasonably definite script. In the indeterminate mode only one or two points are specified, and it is up to the interpreter to imagine one (or more) of the virtual curves that traverse these coordinates.

Literal/Metaphorical: What constitutes a literal or metaphorical narration depends on the particular definition given to narrative. Whereas literal narration fully satisfies the definition, the metaphorical brand uses only some of its features. The degree of metaphoricity of a narrative thus depends on how many features are retained and on how important they are to the definition. If we conceive narrative as the mental or textual representation of a causally linked sequence of events involving individuated and humanlike agents, the following relaxations of the definitions should be regarded as metaphorical: scenarios about collective entities rather than individuals (for example, the "grand narratives" of history or the "narratives of class, gender, and race" so dear to contemporary cultural studies); narratives about concrete entities deprived of consciousness (for example, Darwin's story of evolution); and dramatizations that attributes agency to abstract objects. [9] If we want to stretch the metaphor to its limits, we can apply it to art forms deprived of semantic content, such as music and architecture. In the case of music the metaphor can be invoked to analyze the structure of the work in terms of narrative effects, such as foreshadowing and suspense, dramatic patterns of exposition, complication, climax and resolution, or even Propp-inspired narrative functions. In the case of architecture a metaphorical interpretation may draw an analogy between the temporality of plot and the experience of walking through a building. In a narratively conceived architecture—found, for instance, in Baroque churches, where the walk-through reenacts the stages of the Passion—the visitor's discovery tour is plotted as a meaningful succession of events.[10]

To sum up the previous discussion: The nature of narrative and its relation to language can be conceived in three ways. Each of them carries different implications for the project of this book:

1. Narrative is an exclusively verbal phenomenon. You cannot speak of narrative outside language-supported media (that is, media that not only include a language track but also rely on language as their principal mode of presentation). This position is incompatible with the study of narrative across media.

2. The set of all narratives is a fuzzy set. The fullest implementation of narrativiy is in its language-supported forms. The study of narrative across media is only feasible if one can transfer the parameters of verbal narration to other media. This means, generally, finding a communicative structure that involves a narrator, narratee, and narrative message, in addition to sender (author) and receiver (reader, spectator, etc.).

3. Narrative is a medium-independent phenomenon, and, though no medium is better suited than language to make explicit the logical structure of narrative, it is possible to study narrative in its nonverbal manifestations without applying the communicative model of verbal narration. The definition proposed in this introduction represents the third option. But option 2 is also compatible with a study of narrative across media, and some of the contributors to this volume implicitly or explicitly adhere to it.

What Are Media?

Ask a sociologist or cultural critic to enumerate media, and he will answer: TV, radio, cinema, the Internet. An art critic may list: music, painting, sculpture, literature, drama, the opera, photography, architecture. A philosopher of the phenomenologist school would divide media into visual, auditory, verbal, and perhaps gustatory and olfactory (are cuisine and perfume media?). An artist's list would begin with clay, bronze, oil, watercolor, fabrics, and it may end with exotic items used in so-called mixed-media works, such as grasses, feathers, and beer can tabs. An information theorist or historian of writing will think of sound waves, papyrus scrolls, codex books, and silicon chips. "New media" theorists will argue that computerization has created new media out of old one: film-based versus digital photography; celluloid cinema versus movies made with video cameras; or films created through classical image-capture techniques versus movies produced through computer manipulations. The computer may also be responsible for the entirely new medium of virtual reality.

These various conceptions of medium reflect the ambiguity of the term. The entry for *medium* in *Webster's Dictionary* includes, among many other meanings more or less irrelevant to the present study (for example, "somebody in contact with the spirits"), the following two definitions:[11]

1. A channel or system of communication, information, or entertainment.
2. Material or technical means of artistic expression.

The first definition presents a medium as a particular technology or cultural institution for the transmission of information. Media of this type include TV, radio, the Internet, the gramophone, the telephone—all distinct types of technologies—as well as cultural channels, such as books and newspapers. In this conception of medium, ready-made messages are encoded in a particular way, sent over the channel, and decoded on the other end. TV can, for instance, transmit films as well as live broadcasts, news as well as recordings of theatrical performances. Before they are encoded in the mode specific to the medium in sense 1, some of these messages are realized through a medium in sense 2. A painting must be done in oil before it can be digitized and sent over the Internet. A musical composition must be performed on instruments in order to be recorded and played on a gramophone. A medium in sense 1 thus involves the translation of objects supported by media in sense 2 into a secondary code.

In his groundbreaking work on the "technologizing of the word," Walter Ong avoids the term *medium* as a label for the various supports of language because he objects to its sense 1:

The term can give false impression of the nature of verbal communication, and of other human communication as well. Thinking of a "medium" of communication or of "media" of communication suggests that communication is a pipeline transfer of material called "information" from one place to another. My mind is a box, I take a unit of "information" out of it, encode the unit (that is, fit it to the size and shape of the pipe it will go through), and put it into one end of the pipe (the medium, somewhere in the middle between two other things). From the one end of the pipe the information proceeds to the other end, where someone decodes it (restores its proper size and shape) and puts it into his or her own box-like container called a mind. This model . . . distorts the act of [human] communication beyond recognition. (176)

If indeed communicative media were the hollow pipes that Ong caricatures, there would be little purpose in analyzing their narrative potential; any kind of narrative could be fitted into the pipe and restored to its prior shape at the end of the transfer. On the other hand, if we totally reject the conduit metaphor and the notion that meaning—in this case, narrative—is encoded, sent over, decoded, and stored in memory at the other end of the transmission line, if, that is, we regard meaning as inextricable from its medial support, medium-free definitions of narrative become untenable. What, then, would entitle us to compare messages embodied in different media and to view them as manifestations of a common semantic structure? To maintain the possibility of studying "narrative across media," we must find a compromise between the "hollow pipe" interpretation and the unconditional rejection of the conduit metaphor (which itself is a concrete visualization of Roman Jakobson's model of communication). The terms of this compromise are suggested, perhaps unwittingly, by Ong himself, when he writes that information must be fitted to the "shape and size" of the pipeline. This amounts to saying that different media filter different aspects of narrative meaning. Far from being completely undone at the end of the journey, as Ong suggests in his critique, the shape imposed on the message by the configuration of the pipeline affects in a crucial way the construction of the receiver's mental image.

Because of the configuring action of the medium, it is not always possible to distinguish an encoded object from the act of encoding. Consider the cinema: what it records are not autonomous artistic objects but a staging of action done for the express purpose of being filmed. It is the edited footage that forms the artistic object, not something that exists independently of the filming. In the live broadcasts of TV, similarly, the object to be sent is created through the act of recording itself. Moreover, if communicative media encode and decode messages, they do not strip them of any material support at the end of the journey. After being decoded by the electronic circuits in the black box, TV signals are projected on a small screen in the middle of a family room. The experience is very different from watching a film on a large screen in a dark theater, and it calls for different forms of narrative. Insofar as they present their own type of material support, channel-type media can be simultaneously modes of transmission and means of expression.

In media theory, as in other fields, what constitutes an object of investigation depends on the purpose of the investigator. Here we want to explore media in terms of their narrative power. Hence, what counts for us as a medium is a category that truly makes a difference about what stories can be evoked or told, how they are presented, why they are communicated, and how they are experienced. This approach implies a standard of comparison: to say, for instance, that "radio is a distinct narrative medium" means that radio as a medium offers different narrative possibilities than television, film, or oral conversation. "Mediality" (or mediumhood) is thus a relational rather than an absolute property. To test the thesis of the relativity of mediality with respect to narrative, let us consider the respective status of the gramophone and of daily newspapers. From a technological point of view the gramophone stands as a prototypical medium. When it was developed at the end of the nineteenth century, it did to sound what writing had done to language. Thanks to the new technology, sound could now be recorded, and it was no longer necessary to be within earshot of its source to apprehend auditory data. From a narratological perspective, however, the purely transmissive medium of the gramophone does not seem to entail significant consequences. It wasn't until the development of wireless telegraphy that a long-distance, purely auditory type of narrative was developed, namely the radiophonic play. Daily newspapers represent the opposite situation: historians of technology would regard them as a manifestation of the same medium as books, since they rely on roughly the same printing techniques, but narratologists would defend their medium status with respect to books by pointing out that the daily press promoted a new style of reporting news, which gave birth to an autonomous narrative genre. Daily newspapers also differ pragmatically from other types of communication channels in that they must be delivered regularly at twenty-four-hour intervals. The coverage of a time-consuming crisis must therefore begin before the crisis is resolved, and the daily reports lack the completeness and retrospective perspective of other types of narrative. All these characteristics suggest that newspapers indeed support a distinct type of narrativity.

Where, however, does medium end, and where does genre begin? I would suggest that the difference between *medium* and *genre* resides in the nature and origin of the constraints that relate to each of them. Whereas *genre* is defined by more or less freely adopted conventions, chosen for both personal and cultural reasons, *medium* imposes its possibilities and limitations on the user. It is true that we choose both the genre and the medium we work in. But we select media for their affordances, and we work around their limitations, trying to overcome them or to make them irrelevant. Genre, by contrast, purposefully uses limitations to channel expectations, optimize expression, and facilitate communication: tragedy must be about the downfall of a hero and use the mimetic mode of narrativity; symphonies must comprise several movements (usually four), each with a distinct mood and tempo;[12] novels must be long, and novellas must be short, and both must possess some degree of narrativity (far more for the novella). These conventions are imposed as a second-order semiotic system on the primary mode of signification. Genre conventions are genuine rules specified by humans, whereas the constraints and possibilities offered by media are dictated by their material substance and mode of encoding. But, insofar as they lend themselves to many uses, media support a variety of genres.

The diversity of criteria that enters into the definition of *medium* makes it very difficult to establish a typology of media and to draw a dividing line between *medium* and *genre*. I will nevertheless give it a try, fully aware that my decisions will not meet with unanimous acceptance. If table 0.1 helps readers refine their own notion of medium and understand the complexity of the problem at hand, it will have reached its goal, no matter how many amendments they make to my taxonomy. I propose two main criteria for classifying a form of expression/communication as a narrative medium: (1) As suggested earlier, it must make a difference about what kind of narrative messages can be transmitted, how these messages are presented, or how they are experienced. (2) It must present a unique combination of features. These features can be drawn from five possible areas: (a) senses being addressed; (b) priorities among sensory tracks (thus, the opera will be considered distinct from drama, even though the two media include the same sensory dimensions, because the opera gives music higher priority than drama); (c) spatio-temporal extension; (d) technological support and materiality of signs (painting versus photography; speech versus writing versus digital encoding of language); (e) cultural role and methods of production/distribution (books versus newspapers). Table 0.1 uses spatio-temporal extension and sensory dimension as primary taxonomic categories. These criteria seem indeed more relevant to the issue of narrativity than distinctions relative to technological support, though the latter are not negligible. The drawback of this prioritization of sensory dimensions is that a given technology or cultural channel needs to be listed twice when it is used to transmit different types of sensory data: digital writing is distinguished from multimedia applications of computer technology; silent film is distinguished from multisensory movie productions. Another problem with the division of media into temporal and spatio-temporal is that, if we apply strict criteria, the temporal column will be virtually empty. As Leonard Talmy remarks, a case could be made for putting all manifestations of writing in the spatio-temporal column, since writing requires a two-dimensional support and exists all at once for the reader (425–26). Books on tape would then be the only legitimate members of the temporal column.

Narrative Media Studies: A Very Brief History

Of the two definitions of the term *medium*—channel of communication or material means of expression—the first has been by far the more influential on the field of media studies. At U.S. universities most departments of media studies concern themselves with the cultural institutions and technologies of mass communication developed in the twentieth century: telephone, radio, TV, computer networks, and the press. As the theorist Joshua Meyrowitz observes, the majority of these studies focus on the content of the messages sent through the medium under study. Questions of social impact are primary: "Typical concerns centre on how people (often children) react to what they are exposed to through various media; how institutional, economic, and political factors influence what is and what is not conveyed through media; whether media messages accurately reflect various dimensions of reality; how different audiences interpret the same content differently; and so on." A different approach to media as instruments of mass communication has been promoted by Meyrowitz as "medium" (rather than media) theory. This approach focuses not on the content of messages but on "the particular characteristics of each individual medium or of each particular type of media. Broadly speaking, medium theorists ask: What are the relatively fixed features of each means of communicating and how do these features make the medium physically, psychologically, and socially different from other media and from face-to-face interaction?" (50). Here, again, the primary focus of studies is sociological: "On the macro-level, medium questions address the ways in which the addition of a new medium to an existing matrix of media may alter social interaction and social structure in general" (51). Working from the assumption that the development of technologies of communication is

Table 0.1. *A typology of media affecting narrativity*

Temporal			Spatial	Spatio-Temporal	
One Channel		Two Channels	One Channel	One Channel	Multiple Channels
Linguistic	Acoustic	Linguistic/Acoustic	Visual/Static	Visual/Kinetic	
Media of long-distance oral communication: Radio, Telephone Manuscript writing Printing writing in various supports Digital writing: e-mail, Internet chat, Hypertext (text-only)	Non-texted music	Songs with lyrics, Sung poetry	Painting, Sculpture, Photography, Architecture(?)	Mime, Animated graphics, Silent movies without music	Acoustic-visual (kinetic): Dance, Silent movies with live music Linguistic-visual (static): Comic strips, Artist's books, Children's books, Newspapers Linguistic-visual (kinetic): Fact-to-face oral communication Linguistic-acoustic-visual (kinetic): Cinema, Theater, TV, Opera Synthesis of all channels: Installation art, Interactive computer-mediated forms of expression: Web pages, Art CD-ROMs, Computer games, Virtual reality

one of the most decisive influences on the development of human societies, medium theorists postulate three (and more recently four) pivotal events in the history of civilization: the invention of writing; the invention of print; the development of electronic communications (TV, radio); and the development of electronic writing and computer networks. This sketch of history—inspired by the pioneering work of two Canadians, Harold Adams Innis and Marshall McLuhan—provides a solid theoretical foundation, and a vast program of research, to communicative medium or media studies.

The concentration of this book on narrative calls, however, for approaches based on the second definition. The comparative study of media as means of expression lags far behind the study of media as channels of communication in both academic recognition and theoretical maturity. We have well-developed analytical tools and methodologies relating to individual media, such as cinema, music, literature, and electronic art, but we do not have a comprehensive and widely accepted theory of the importance of the medium as material support for the form and content of message. From their origins in poetics, rhetoric, and aesthetics, semiotic media studies—as I will call this type of inquiry—have progressed bottom up rather than top down, as a series of individual case studies and not as the application of global principles. My brief overview of the field will, therefore, not be the outline of a unified theory but a sketch of some of the milestones in the emergence of medium as an object of semiotic inquiry. My preference will be given to those landmarks that bear upon the question of narrativity.

Awareness of a dimension of art and communication that translates into English as medium goes back at least to Aristotle's *Poetics*. After defining *poetry* as a "species of imitation," Aristotle mentions three ways of distinguishing various types of imitation: medium, object, and mode (2, 3).[13] Under *medium* Aristotle understands expressive resources, such as color, shape, rhythm, melody, and language (or voice).[14] He sketches a classification of art forms based on the media they use: "For example, music for pipe and lyre . . . uses melody and rhythm only, while dance uses rhythm by itself and without melody (since dancers too imitate character, emotion and action by means of rhythm expressed in movement) . . . The art which uses language unaccompanied, either in prose or in verse . . . remains without a name to the present day . . . There are also some arts which use all the media mentioned above (that is, rhythm, melody, and verse), for instance, dithyrambic and gnomic poetry, tragedy and comedy; these differ in that the former use them all simultaneously, the latter in distinct parts" (2.1, 4).

The second criterion, object, operates generic distinctions within imitations that share the same medium. Tragedy, for instance, imitates better people, while comedy depicts inferior ones. Aristotle invokes the third criterion, mode, to make distinctions between imitations that share both medium and object: "It is possible to imitate the same objects in the same medium sometimes by narrating . . . or else with all the imitators as agents and engaged in activity" (2.3, 5). Thus, tragedy and epic both deal with "better people" and do so through language, but tragedy imitates in what Plato calls the mimetic mode, while epic poetry imitates through diegesis. (I use here Plato's terminology instead of Aristotle's contrast between narrative and performing arts to avoid describing tragedy as nonnarrative.) When Aristotle claims that mode operates distinctions within the same medium, he forgets, however, that performing actors appeal to the sense of vision, while diegetic narration does not. Differences in mode inevitably entail differences in medium.

According to Aristotle, the distinction between the mimetic and the diegetic mode does not affect the general structure of plot: "The component parts [of epic plots] are the same [as those of tragedy]: it too needs reversals, recognitions, and sufferings" (10.2, 39). But, because of their distinct mode (and consequently medium), tragedy and epic poetry implement this abstract structure in different ways: "one should not compose a tragedy out of a body of materials which would serve for an epic—by which I mean one that contains a multiplicity of stories . . . [E]veryone who has composed a Sack of Troy as a whole, and not piecemeal like Euripides . . . has either failed or done badly in the competitions" (8.7, 30). Epic plots and dramatic plots can be represented by the same summary, but dramatic plots are much more tightly woven, since their temporal frame must roughly correspond to the length of the performance, while epic plots can afford to stretch out the basic structure through numerous episodes that repeat one another. Not being tied to the here and now of the stage, epic poetry has an "important distinctive resource for extending [the length of the plot]": it is able to "imitate many parts of the action being carried on simultaneously" (10.3, 39–40). By presenting plot as a structure common to dramatic and epic poetry, while suggesting that the resources inherent to the medium make a difference about what kind of subject matters can be represented efficiently, the *Poetics* outlines an agenda for the cross-medial study of narrative: to find out how the medium configures the particular realization of narrativity.

The concept of artistic medium lay dormant until the eighteenth century, when G. E. Lessing published *Laocoön: An Essay on the Limits of*

Painting and Poetry (1766).[15] Neither *medium* nor *narrative* appears in the translation of the text, but Lessing's essay offers the first detailed comparative study of the narrative power of artistic media. The title refers to a famous Greek sculptural group that depicts an episode narrated by Virgil in the *Aeneid:* the Trojan priest Laocoön being devoured by sea serpents together with his two sons. The critics of the time wondered why Laocoön expressed an almost serene resignation in the face of such a horrible death. Against those critics who invoked an ethics of stoicism or a cultural taboo against the display of male emotions in Greek society, Lessing proposes an explanation entirely based on aesthetic principles. The face of Laocoön cannot be distorted, he argues, because sculpture is a work of visual art, and the purpose of visual art is to represent beauty. We may no longer accept Lessing's association of art with the beautiful—shortly after he wrote the "Laocoön" the work of Goya began to demonstrate the artistic power of horror—but, by insisting on the visual nature of painting, the essay represents a watershed in aesthetic philosophy. The art criticism scene of the eighteenth century was very much dominated by the philosophy captured in the saying of Simonides of Ceos: "painting is mute poetry and poetry a speaking painting" (4). Taken literally—and Lessing shows little understanding for figural language—the formula blatantly ignores the sensory and spatio-temporal dimensions of the two media: painting speaks to the sense of sight, poetry to the imagination; painting is spatial, poetry is temporal. These contrasts predispose painting and poetry to the representation of different ideas: "I reason thus: if it is true that in its imitations painting uses completely different means or signs than does poetry, namely figures and colors in space rather than articulated sounds in time, and if these signs must indisputably bear a suitable relation to the thing signified, then signs existing in space can express only objects whose wholes or parts coexist, while signs that follow one another can express only objects whose wholes or parts are consecutive" (78).

The spatial dimension of its signs enables painting to represent physical beauty, because beauty is an effect that results from the harmonious combination of various parts. Poetry cannot do so: it divides what should be perceived simultaneously into discrete elements and present them one at a time to the "eye" of the imagination. Homer's use of a simple epithet— "white-armed Helen"— therefore goes farther in suggesting beauty than lengthy descriptions. Conversely, because of its temporal nature, poetry excels at the representation of actions, while painting freezes processes into a single shot: "In the one case [poetry] the action is visible and progressive, its different parts occurring one after the other in a sequence of time, and in the other [sculpture] the action is visible and stationary, its different parts developing in co-existence in space" (77).

Should we conclude that poetry cannot describe and that painting cannot narrate? Even a series of paintings, Lessing argues, would not give an adequate idea of the plot of the *Odyssey* (71). Throughout the "Laocoön" Lessing admonishes painters and poets to avoid subject matters that do not take advantage of the strength of the medium. The subtitle of the work, on the *limits* of painting and poetry, is symptomatic of a prescriptive and separatist stance. To be an artist, in the classical age, is to learn to work within the limits of the chosen medium. Yet, despite his classical restraint, Lessing does not totally lack understanding for the artistic drive to push back the limits of media. One of the few descriptive passages in poetry that meets his approval is Homer's technique of narrativized description: "If Homer wants to show us Juno's chariot, he shows Hebe putting it together piece by piece before our eye. We see the wheels and axle, the seat, the pole, the traces, and the straps, not as these parts are when fitted together, but as they are actually being assembled by Hebe" (80). The description works, because spatial vision has been transformed into temporal action.

Conversely—I reserve here for the end of my sketch the concept for which the "Laocoön" is the most famous—painting can overcome its narrative limitations (or at least push them back) by turning its spatial display into the representation of what has become known as a "pregnant moment": "Painting can use only a single moment of an action in its coexisting composition and must therefore choose the one which is most suggestive and from which the preceding and succeeding actions are most easily comprehensible" (78). The representation of a fold in a garment, so dear to Baroque art, captures the trace of a moving body: "We can see from the folds whether an arm or leg was in a backward or forward position prior to its movement; whether the limb had moved or is moving from contraction or extension, or whether it had been extended and is now contrasted" (Anton Meng, qtd. by Lessing, 92). For Lessing the most pregnant moment in a process is the one that just precedes its climax: "Thus, if Laocoön sighs, the imagination can hear him cry out; but if he cries out, it can neither go a step higher nor one step lower than this representation without seeing him in a more tolerable and hence less intense condition" (20). Elsewhere in the essay Lessing writes that painting is strictly an art of the visible, which means that it is an art of the present, but through the pregnancy of the depicted moment painting can reach into the past and the future, thereby transforming itself from an art that speaks exclusively to the senses to an art that also speaks, like poetry, to the imagination. What is represented in the fold of the garment and in the face of Laocoön is not arrested time but a virtualization of temporal movement: the passing of time is contained *in potentia* in the pregnant moment, as the tree is contained in the acorn. "To use the language of scholastic philosophy," writes Lessing, "what is not contained in the picture *actu* is there *virtute*" (100). Whereas poetry actually narrates, painting does so, when it does, in a virtual mode that leaves much more to be filled in by the interpreter. To use a pair of terms that Marshall McLuhan would propose two centuries later, we could say that poetry is a "hot" narrative medium and painting a "cold" one.

Let's fast-forward to the twentieth century. The technological explosion of the nineteenth century produced new artistic media, photography and cinema, and led to the development of a whole array of mainly transmissive media: gramophone, telephone, radio, and TV. Around 1930 the term *medium* entered language to designate channels of communication. In the midcentury two intellectual events took place that would alter the course of the humanities and lead to the birth of contemporary media studies. The first is the so-called linguistic turn in the humanities. After discovering Ferdinand de Saussure's linguistic theory, scholars working in various disciplines proclaimed linguistics to be a "pilot science" in the humanities and set out to fulfill the master's prediction that linguistics would soon be part of a general science of signs. The French version of this "science," known as "semiology," conceived its task as the extension of Saussure's conception of the linguistic sign to all areas of significations; doing semiology was, therefore, a matter of insisting on the arbitrariness of the relation between signifiers and signifieds and of discovering the system of relations—or play of differences—through which these signs acquire their phonic or semantic value. This branch eventually led to what is known as deconstruction, poststructuralism, or simply "theory," a critique of representation that originated to a large extent in a reading of media: written versus spoken language for Derrida; advertisement and photography for Barthes; TV and other mass media for Baudrillard and Virilio; the cinema for Deleuze. Meanwhile, a mainly American branch of the project known as semiotics, also joined by the Italian scholar and novelist Umberto Eco, relied on C. S. Peirce's division of signs into symbols, indices, and icons. In contrast to its French counterpart, this school did not try to impose a linguistic model on nonverbal media. In spite of their different theoretical inspiration, both schools ventured into hitherto neglected areas of signification, and both refocused the study of artistic media from the hermeneutic question "*what* does this work mean?" to the more technical issue: "*how* does it mean?" or "how does it *work*?"

The second event, which is mainly associated with the name of Marshall McLuhan (but Walter Benjamin and Roland Barthes also made significant contributions toward this development), is the emancipation of media studies from aesthetics, philosophy, and poetics. This emancipation meant the breakdown of the academic barrier between elite and popular culture. For McLuhan comic strips, advertisements, or the composition of newspaper front pages were no less worthy of "poetic" analysis than works of "high" literature. A mercurial, aphoristic thinker who loved to play with language in a way that anticipates French poststructuralist theory, McLuhan preferred puns, metaphors, parody, and the epiphanies of sudden jumps to the systematic, linear development of ideas. It is, therefore, poetic as well as philosophical justice that nowadays most people associate his name with a few catchphrases that lend themselves to free interpretation, such as "global village," "hot and cold media," or "the medium is the message."

Although the work of McLuhan defies summarization, his own interpretations of the slogan "the medium is the message" allows a glimpse into the nature and style of his contribution to media studies. In this postmodern age the interpretation of the slogan that immediately comes to mind is the self-referentiality that pervades both avant-garde art and popular culture, but McLuhan has broader phenomena in mind: "This revolution [that is, electric modes of moving information] involves us willy-nilly in the study of modes and media *as forms that shape and reshape our perceptions.* That is what I meant all along by saying the 'medium is the message,' for the medium determines the modes of perception and the matrix of assumptions within which objectives are set" (*Essential McLuhan* 188; emph. added). In his book *The Gutenberg Galaxy* McLuhan develops the idea that media affect perception and consequently thought by linking oral and written communication to different types of brain activities. The oral communication of preliterate societies relies on an "acoustic space" in which sound comes to us from all directions and in which all the senses contribute information. McLuhan associates this effect with the right side of the brain. With the development of writing technologies, emphasis shifts to the left side: now all information comes to us through an act of vision that scans the book linearly, one letter at a time.[16] This is why print culture favors logical, abstract, and controlled thought, at the expense of spatial perception and of the artistic, holistic, metaphorical, or musical types of imagination. But in the development of electronic media, which offer data to all the senses, McLuhan sees a chance to reverse what for him is an impoverishing trend for the human mind: "Today, our universal environment of simultaneous electronic flow, of constantly interchanging information, favors the sensory preferences of the right hemisphere. The First World is aligning itself, however gradually, with the Third World" (*Global Village* 56).

The second interpretation of the formula suggests, in vaguely Saussurean fashion, that media form a tightly connected system, in which every element functions through a network of connections with other media. But the relations, rather than being purely differential, consist of a chain of positive substitutions: "The 'content' of any medium is always another medium. The content of writing is speech, just as the written word is the content of print, and print is the content of the telegraph. It is asked, 'What is the content of speech?' it is necessary to say, 'It is an actual process of thought, which is in itself non-verbal' " (*Essential* 151). Or further: "The content of a movie is a novel or play or opera" (159). This statement could be taken to mean that writing is a mere translation of speech, speech a mere translation of thought, and so on. Such an interpretation would clash, however, with another of McLuhan's probes into the meaning of his own slogan: " 'the medium is the message' because it is the medium that shapes and controls the scale and form of human association and action" (152). How, then, can a medium form the content of another medium, without becoming interchangeable with it? I would suggest that McLuhan's self-interpretation ought to be read in the light of C. S. Peirce's definition of signs. According to Peirce, a sign is "anything which determines something else (its interpretant) to refer to something to which itself refers (its object), the interpretant becoming in turn a sign, and so on, ad infinitum" (303).[17] To "understand" a medium in formal and cultural terms is thus to think of another medium, which itself necessitates interpretation through yet another medium. Because "interpretation" is always a partial fit, this chain of substitutions highlights the particularities of each medium much more than it negates their differences.

It was left to much more systematic and less cryptic thinkers than McLuhan to cultivate the seeds that he casually scattered in the furrows of the new field. Walter Ong, McLuhan's one-time student and colleague, undertook a thorough investigation of the effect of the passage from oral/aural to chirographic/typographic cultures for consciousness, perception, and cultural life. More important for the present project, he reconnected media studies with literary theory by studying the impact of the material support of language on narrative form. To summarize Ong's observations: the contrast oral/written is felt in three areas: the pragmatic, or cultural, role of narrative; the shape of the plot; and the narrative themes, especially the presentation of characters. In oral cultures narrative used to be the sole vehicle of knowledge. Since stories deal with particulars, this affects the kind of knowledge being transmitted: "Oral cultures cannot generate [scientifically abstract categories], and so they use stories of human action to store, organize, and communicate much of what they know" (140). Moreover, by creating a sense of community, oral narrative "serves to bond thought more massively and permanently than other genres" (141). In his discussion of the shape of the plot Ong reinterprets the differences observed by Aristotle between epic poetry and drama in terms of the contrast oral versus written. Even though it is designed for oral performance, drama represents the written pole: "The ancient Greek drama . . . was the first western verbal art form to be fully controlled by writing" (148). The written origin of tragedy explains the carefully crafted rise and fall in tension known to drama theorists as the "Freytag triangle." Such a structuration necessitates a global overview of the plot that is only possible in a writing situation, for (as McLuhan fails to see) writing creates a space that frees the author from the linearity of language. Whereas tragedy is constructed top down by an author, epic poems are created by the storyteller bottom up, moment by moment, through the concatenation of relatively autonomous episodes: "Having heard perhaps scores of singers singing hundreds of songs of variable length about the Trojan War, Homer had a huge repertoire of episodes to string together, but, without writing, absolutely no way to organize them in strict chronological order" (143). "If we take the climactic linear plot as the paradigm of plot, the epic has no plot. Strict plot for lengthy narrative comes with writing" (144). Rather than denying plot to epic poetry, we might say, with Janet Murray, that oral epic has a multiform plot: each performance results in a particular linearization, which creates a different plot, at least within certain limits. Ong's "medial determinism" also accounts for the birth of the novel, a genre whose origin has been a topic of lively speculations among literary critics. "Print . . . mechanically as well as psychologically locked words into space and thereby established a firmer sense of closure than [manuscript] writing could. The print world gave birth to the novel, which eventually made the definitive break with episodic structure" (149). The novel comes into its own, after the eighteenth century, by developing a compromise between the loose structure of oral epic and the tight climactic organization of drama: a compromise that expands the global pattern typical of written composition to epic dimensions. In the area of characterization, finally, Ong associates oral narrative with "flat" characters who delight the reader by "fulfilling expectations copiously" (151); and written narrative with an attention to mental processes that results in the creation of unpredictable, psychologically complex individuals—what E. M. Forster called "round" characters.

Both McLuhan and Ong predicted that the advent of "the electric way of moving information" would create a cultural turning point. Electronic technology would challenge the supremacy of print as a channel of mass communication and open an alternative to the linear mode of thinking associated with writing. Thinking principally of TV, radio, and the telephone, all diffusers of talk, Ong calls this new stage in media history "secondary orality." But by the late 1980s the talk media had been supplanted, in terms of novelty, by the digital way of moving information. Reversing the trend observed by McLuhan and Ong, the development of computer networks meant to some extent a secondary literacy: e-mail, Internet chatrooms (where chatting is done by typing on a keyboard), and the World Wide Web now contend with the telephone, radio, or TV for both personal contacts and as a way to keep informed of current events.

The media explosion that followed the so-called digital revolution gave a tremendous boost to media studies. There were not only brand-new artistic media and modes of communications to investigate—hypertext, computer games, art CD-ROMs, Web pages, e-mail, chatrooms, virtual reality installations, all media that depend on digital support—but also old media to revisit. These old media did not live in a digital environment, but, as they began to use the computer as a mode of production, they were able to achieve entirely new effects. From drama to film, photography to painting, architecture to music, virtually every "old medium" has a new, digital twin, though whether or not this twin counts as an autonomous medium is a debatable question. (It will, according to the criteria adopted in this book, if it makes a difference in terms of narrative expressivity.) Moreover, by introducing new species competing for survival in what was increasingly becoming known as the "media ecology," the digital revolution placed old media in a different context, both in terms of their cultural function and in terms of how they were approached. In need of a standard of comparison, the study of digital writing turned, for instance, back to the codex book and discovered features that had until then been taken for granted: the advantage of a bound spine over loose leaves; the possibility to access pages randomly, despite the linear reading protocol of most printed texts; the escape from sequential reading offered by footnotes; and the importance of indexes as "navigational aide"—a concept that would have been unthinkable until the development of hypertext and of the World Wide Web.

Not to be left behind, literary criticism caught the medial tide wave by turning its attention to the proliferation of media in the twentieth century and on the effect of this proliferation on the literary imagination. Led by

Friedrich Kittler, John Johnston, Donald Theall, Michael Wutz, and Joseph Tabbi—the latter two editors of the collection *Reading Matters: Narrative in the New Media Ecology*—this school dedicates itself to such questions as reassessing the role of literature in a changed medial environment (a question that echoes the concerns of Meyrowitz's "medium theory"); analyzing how different technologies—manuscript, typewriter, or word processor—affect the practice of writing; and describing the new narrative techniques developed by modern and postmodern novelists (especially James Joyce and William Burroughs) in an attempt to simulate the resources of other media. But, in its tendency to read texts through the theories of Jacques Lacan, Jacques Derrida, Gilles Deleuze, Felix Guattari, and other beacons of postmodern thought, the "media ecology" school often practices a top-down approach that is alien to the spirit of the present volume: here the bottom-up movement from data to theory will receive precedence over the top-down application of ready-made theoretical models.

My last landmark in this survey of media studies develops the metaphor of media ecology—itself a transposition of McLuhan's vision of a media network—into the most ambitious account we have so far of the nature and history of both old and new media. This landmark is Jay Bolter and Richard Grusin's concept of "remediation." The authors define *remediation* as "the formal logic by which new media refashion prior media forms" (273). Every medium, they argue, is developed as an attempt to remediate the deficiencies of another medium. Remediation is thus *"the mediation of mediation:* Each act of mediation depends on other acts of mediation. Media are continually commenting on, reproducing, and replacing each other, and this process is integral to media. Media need each other to function as media at all" (55). According to the authors, this chain of substitutions describes not only the development of media but also their intrinsic function: "What is a medium? We offer this simple definition: a medium is that which remediates. It is that which appropriates the techniques, forms, and social significance of other media and attempts to rival or refashion them in the name of the real" (65). In this definition the appeal to reality functions as the end condition that puts a stop to what would otherwise be an endless recursion: at the beginning was reality; then medium 1 attempted to mediate some of its features; medium 2 remediated the deficiencies of medium 1; and so on. The narrative of progress implicit to this definition is obviously better suited to transmissive technologies than to artistic media. Given the postulation of "the desire to achieve the real" as the force that drives the process of remediation (53), it seems strange that Bolter and Grusin propose two "strategies" of remediation: one is *immediacy,* the attempt to make the medium disappear; the other *hypermediacy,* "a style of visual [*sic*] representation whose goal is to remind the viewer of the medium" (272). How could the opacity implicit in hypermediacy help the user "achieve the real"—unless it is the reality of the medium itself?

These reservations notwithstanding, the concept of remediation is a powerful tool of media analysis. The versatility of the concept is particularly useful in framing questions that fall within the concerns of transmedial narratology. Let me, therefore, enumerate some of the various possible interpretations of remediation and translate each of them into a narrative topic. In the list that follows, narrative implications are entered either as examples or as topics of investigation formulated as questions:

1. "Medical" remediation: the invention of a medium to overcome the limitations of another medium. Bolter and Grusin's examples: "writing makes speech more permanent"; "hypertext makes writing more interactive" (59).
   Narrative application: Cinema remediates the spatial limitations of drama by making the setting infinitely variable. What are the consequences of this freedom to travel on the thematic content of movies as well as on their presentational techniques?

2. Change in the technological support of a type of data. Example: the evolution of writing from manuscript to the typewriter, from the printing press to the word processor, or from clay tablets to scrolls, codex books, and electronic databases.
   Narrative application: The questions addressed by Walter Ong: how did these changes affect narrative plot? what was the role of the invention of the printing press in the development of the novel?

3. The phenomenon captured by McLuhan's formula: "The content of a medium is always another medium." This formula is literally applicable to cases such as the written transcriptions of oral performance or books on tape.
   Narrative application: Investigating the differences between actual conversation and the conventions of dialogue representation in fiction. Examining a novel as an instance of oral confession (for example, Camus, *The Fall*).

4. A medium taking over the social function of another. Example: television replacing radio as the main source of news and replacing movie houses as the main channel for the transmission of film.
   Narrative application: What happens to movies when they are made for TV? How does narration differ in radio and TV news programs?

5. The representation of a medium within another medium by either mechanical or descriptive means. Mechanical examples: the photographic reproduction of paintings, TV broadcast of classic film, the digitization of all artistic media. Descriptive examples: the verbal evocation of music; the musical depiction of a story or painting.
   Narrative application: Ekphrasis in novels (verbal description of artworks); the representation of performance arts or TV shows in movies (for example, *The Truman Show*).

6. A medium imitating the techniques of another. Example: digital manipulations of photographs that apply the "Van Gogh," the "Monet," or the "Seurat" filter.
   Narrative application: Cinematic or musical techniques in novels; literary collage; voiced-over narration in movies.

7. Absorption of the techniques of a new medium by an older one. Example: the use of digitally produced special effects in movies.
   Narrative application: What is the effect on movie plots of digital manipulation? (Possible answer: a move away from psychological drama and toward action and the fantastic.)

8. Insertion of a medium in another. Example: text in paintings, movie clips in computer games; photos in novels.
   Narrative application: How do these inserts enhance a work's ability to tell stories?

9. Transposition from a medium into another. Example (from Bolter and Grusin 273): commercial "repurposing" of products, such as the creation of a soundtrack CD, a Broadway musical, a Saturday morning cartoon, or a line of toys and actions figures out of the Disney movie *The Lion King*.
   Narrative application: This is the richest area of investigation: transpositions of novels into movies, novelizations of film or computer games, computer games based on literary works (the shooter Alice), illustrations of stories.[18]

Narrative across Media: Framing the Project

How does one do media studies? How does one do *narrative* media studies, or transmedial narratology? Here I would like to warn the fledgling field of three dangers. The first is the temptation to regard the idiosyncrasies of individual texts as features of the medium. For instance, just because many hypertext authors were influenced by postmodern aesthetics, does it mean that digital media inherently embody these ideas and that the relation is necessary? Since media present themselves only through individual texts, the problem of passing from observations gathered from the text to principles that describe the medium as a whole is one of the greatest challenges of media studies. The second danger is what Liv Hausken describes, in the concluding essay of this book, as media blindness: the indiscriminating transfer of concepts designed for the study of the narratives of a particular medium (usually those of literary fiction) to narratives of another medium. Hausken's prime example is the postulation of a narrator figure for all narratives, including those realized in mimetic media, such as film and drama. The third caveat is what I call "radical relativism." It resides in the belief that, because media are distinct, the toolbox of narratology must be rebuilt from scratch for every new medium. Radical relativism involves two types of blindness. The first is blindness to narrative universals. Many of the concepts developed by structuralism—for instance, Propp's functions, Bremond's modalities, or Greimas's semiotic square—describe narrative on a semantic level, and, though these concepts have been mainly tested on literary texts, they are not limited to verbal narrative. Radical relativism is also blind to the fact that different media often incorporate common tracks or semiotic systems. Print and electronic writing may rely on different material supports, which open different possibilities, but, insofar as they both involve language, they share many properties. Radical relativism would also prohibit what has been one of the most productive practices of narratology: the metaphorical transfer of concepts from one medium to another. To take a few examples: the optical notions of point of view, of focalization, of camera-eye narration, and of cinematic montage have provided insights into literary narrative that could not have been reached by limiting the investigator's analytical toolbox to strictly language-based concepts. Metaphorical borrowing is a standard practice in the narrative investigation of music, precisely because musical narration is itself restricted to the metaphorical mode (unless, of course, one adds a language channel).

Between medium blindness and radical relativism there is room for a diversified program of investigation. I envision this program as follows (each item on the list is followed by the name of the contributors who address it in their essay).

1. Critique the narratological models developed for literature; assess the applicability of their categories for media other than written language; when necessary, adapt these tools or develop new ones. (Aarseth, Bordwell, Cassell and MacNeill, Hausken, Herman)

2. Define the conditions under which nonverbal media can tell stories. (Steiner, Tarasti, this introduction)
3. Catalog the "modes of narativity." (This introduction)
4. Identify and describe narrative genres, devices, or problems that are unique to a medium. (Young, Freeland)
5. Explore phenomena of remediation, especially the problem of transferring a narrative from one medium to another. (Elliott, Steiner)
6. Explore "what can medium x do that medium y cannot" and ask how media can push back their limits. (Implicit in many essays, for example, Steiner, Ewert, Elliott, Rabinowitz)
7. Study the contribution of the various tracks to narrative meaning in "multimedia" media. (Cassell and McNeill, Rabinowitz, Ewert)
8. Ask if the properties of a given medium are favorable or detrimental to narrativity. (Ryan, Aarseth, Lunenfeld)

The organization of the volume reflects two choices. First, literary narrative, arguably the fullest form of narrativity, does not form the object of a special section but is treated, instead, as the implicit frame of reference of the entire collection—the standard against which the narrative potential of other media can be measured. The literary manifestations of narrative are simply too diverse to be adequately covered in two or three essays. And, second, rather than representing as many media as possible through one essay each, a policy that would give the reader a false sense of the authority and unchallenged status of the selected approach, the book restricts the breadth of its coverage to five areas—face-to-face narrative, still pictures, moving pictures, music, and digital media—in order to represent each of these areas through a cluster of articles. This policy led, unfortunately, to the exclusion of various types of performing arts—theater, mime, and ballet—but it also made it possible to give a voice to different, sometimes competing positions within a given area.

Whether we call it "narrative media studies" or "transmedial narratology," the study of narrative across media is a project from which the understanding of both media and narrative should benefit. Media studies will gain from the focus of this book on narrativity a point of comparison that should expose the idiosyncratic resources and limitations of individual media more efficiently than single-medium investigations can do, while narratology, an enterprise so far mainly concerned with literary fiction, will gain from the consideration of nonverbal forms of narrative an opportunity to rethink its object and to rejuvenate itself.

Notes

I am indebted to David Herman and Liv Hausken for useful comments on a first draft of this introduction.

1. Translation by Seymour Chatman, *Story and Discourse*, 20. The original reads: "La structure [d'une histoire] est indépendante des techniques qui la prennent en charge. Elle se laisse transporter de l'une à l'autre sans rien perdre de ses propriétés essentielles: le sujet d'un conte peut servir d'argument pour un ballet, celui d'un roman peut être porté à la scène ou à l'écran, on peut raconter un film à ceux qui ne l'ont pas vu. Ce sont des mots qu'on lit, ce sont des images qu'on voit, ce sont des gestes qu'on déchiffre, mais a travers eux, c'est une histoire qu'on suit, et ce peut être la même histoire."

2. An exception may be those sentences that deal exclusively with universals, such as "All men are mortal."

3. This formal characterization is developed in *A Grammar of Stories*. In his *Dictionary of Narratology* Prince proposes the following informal paraphrase: a minimal story is "a narrative recounting only two states and event such that (1) one state precedes the event in time and the event precedes the other state in time (and causes it); (2) the second state constitutes the inverse (or the modification, including the 'zero' modification) of the first." Prince's example is "John was happy, then he saw Peter, then as a result he was unhappy" (53). Prince also recognizes a minimal narrative: "A narrative representing only a single event: 'She opened the door'" (52). In a cognitivist framework, however, the difference between minimal narrative and minimal story tends to disappear, since the interpreter of "She opened the door" will rationalize the statement as a state (door closed)–event–end of state (door open) sequence. In Prince's model more complex narratives can be generated by combining minimal structures through embedding or concatenation.

4. As David Herman reminds me, comic strips and the cinema have developed some visual means to signal the lack of reality of an episode: in a comic strip, a different color frame may, for instance, indicate that the content of the picture is to be taken as merely imagined by a character; in a movie a gradual loss of focus or a trembling of the picture may lead us into an alternative possible world. But, if these devices are visual, they are not, strictly speaking, pictorial: they create an arbitrary code, similar in that respect to language, rather than expressing the lack of reality in an iconic manner.

5. For an overview of this research, see Ellen Esrock, *The Reader's Eye*, chaps. 4–5.

6. Ellen Esrock captures the dilemma in the following terms: "One can look at Monet's painting of a water lily, a visual stimulus, and process the experience either by creating a visual image of the lily, thereby using a visual code, or by assigning certain wordlike attributes to the image, such as 'oval shape, blurred edges, blue-green,' which is to use the verbal code. Similarly, these two codes can be deployed with verbal material. One can process the phrase 'a host of golden daffodils' by forming a mental image of flickering fields of light, or by forming

some kind of verbal-abstract representation of word meanings pertaining to a field of yellow flowers" (96). In the case of verbal coding I would like to add: one can remember the exact words together with the meanings or store only what Esrock calls "verbal-abstract representations of word meanings." These are what I call "propositions."

7. Bordwell also suggests that there are mimetic theories of the novel and diegetic theories of cinema (3). The common advice to novelists "show, don't tell" betrays a preference for the mimetic mode, while the attempt to locate a narrator in any type of movie constitutes a diegetic approach.

8. As postulated by authors such as Metz and Chatman.

9. An example of a narrative that attributes agency to inanimate objects is this description of his field by the mathematician Keith Devlin: "Mathematicians deal with a collection of objects—numbers, triangles, groups, fields—and ask questions like, 'What is the relationship between objects x and y? If x does thus to y, what will y do back to x?' It's got plot, it's got characters, it's got relationships . . . a bit of everything you can find in a soap opera." Quoted in *Denver Post*, January 9, 2001, 2A.

10. This idea of architecture as a "narrative art" is developed by Celia Pearce, *Interactive Book*, 25–27.

11. *Webster's Ninth New Collegiate Dictionary* (Springfield MA: Merriam-Webster, 1991).

12. These rules have been relaxed in the twentieth century.

13. The first number refers to the section in Aristotle's *Poetics* in which the text appears, the second to the page number of the translation from which I am quoting.

14. *Medium* is obviously a term introduced by the translator, since the root of the word is Latin and not Greek. Other translators (for example, I. Bywater in the Oxford edition) use *manner*. The Greek text, "he gar ton en heterois mimeisthai e to hetera e to heteros," tacks different endings on the word *hetera* (other) to suggest the three kinds of differences. A literal translation would read: "for [they differ] in imitating *in different things* (= medium) or *different things* = object) or *by different ways* (= mode)." The use of *medium* to translate "in different things" is consistent with a conception of medium as material support. (I am indebted to Cynthia Freeland for these clarifications.)

15. I use "Laocoön" to refer to Lessing's essay, *Laocoön* to refer to the statue, and Laocoön to refer to the Greek character.

16. Since McLuhan equates visuality with linear scanning of alphabetic characters, he is not bothered with placing media such as painting, cinema, or TV in the nonvisual category: "This is a major hang-up in all the confusion between TV and movie form, for example. TV is 'non visual' as Joyce understood from careful analysis" (letter to Donald Theall, qtd. in Theall 219).

17. The number in parentheses refers to a paragraph in Peirce's text, in conformity with the standard way to quote Peirce.

18. Cases 5, 6, 8, and 9 are the objects of a type of investigation currently practiced under the name *intermediality.* Werner Wolf provides a detailed typology of all the phenomena that fall under the scope of this concept. Wolf's concept of intermediality also cover a phenomenon that does not easily fit within Bolter and Grusin's theory of remediation: the presence of multiple semiotic and sensory channels in an artistic form.

References

Aristotle. *Poetics.* Trans. and intro. Malcolm Heath. London: Penguin Books, 1996.

Baudrillard, Jean. *Simulacra and Simulations.* Trans. Sheila Faria Glaser. Ann Arbor: University of Michigan Press, 1994.

Ben-Amos, Dan. "Analytical Categories and Ethnic Genres." *Genre* 2 (1969): 275–302.

Bolter, Jay David, and Richard Grusin. *Remediation: Understanding New Media.* Cambridge: MIT Press, 1999.

Bordwell, David. *Narrative in the Fiction Film.* Madison: University of Wisconsin Press, 1985.

Bordwell, David, and Kristin Thompson. *Film Art.* 3d ed. New York: McGraw-Hill, 1990.

Bremond, Claude. *Logique du récit.* Paris: Seuil, 1973.

Brooks, Peter. *Reading for the Plot.* New York: Random House, 1984.

Bruner, Jerome. *Actual Minds, Possible Worlds.* Cambridge: Harvard University Press, 1986.

Chatman, Seymour. *Story and Discourse: Narrative Structure in Fiction and Film.* Ithaca: Cornell University Press, 1978.

———. *Coming to Terms: The Rhetoric of Narrative in Fiction and Film.* Ithaca: Cornell University Press, 1990.

Esrock, Ellen. *The Reader's Eye: Visual Imaging as Reader Response.* Baltimore: Johns Hopkins University Press, 1994.

Fludernik, Monika. "Genres, Text Types, or Discourse Modes? Narrative Modalities and Generic Categorization." *Style* 34.2 (2000): 274–92.

Gibson, J. J. "The Theory of Affordances." *Perceiving, Acting, and Knowing.* Ed. R. E. Shaw and J. Bransford. Hillsdale NJ: Lawrence Erlbaum Associates, 1977.

Herman, David. "Parables of Narrative Imagining." *Diacritics* 29.1 (1999): 20–36.

———. *Story Logic.* Lincoln: University of Nebraska Press, 2002.

Innis, Harold A. *Empire of Communications.* Toronto: University of Toronto Press, 1972.

Johnston, John. *Information Multiplicity: American Fiction in the Age of Media Saturation.* Baltimore: Johns Hopkins University Press, 1998.

Kittler, Friedrich A. *Literature, Media, Information Systems.* Ed. John Johnston. Amsterdam: G+B Arts, 1997.

Labov, William. *Language in the Inner City: Studies in the Black English Vernacular.* Philadelphia: University of Pennsylvania Press, 1972.

Lessing, Gotthold Ephraim. *Laocoön: An Essay on the Limits of Painting and Poetry.* Trans. and intro. Edward Allen McCormick. Baltimore: Johns Hopkins University Press, 1984.

McLuhan, Marshall. *Essential McLuhan.* Ed. Eric McLuhan and Frank Zingrone. New York: Basic Books, 1996.

McLuhan, Marshall, and Bruce R. Powers. *The Global Village: Transformations in World Life and Media in the Twenty-first Century.* New York: Oxford University Press, 1989.

Metz, Christian. *Film Language. A Semiotics of the Cinema.* Trans. Michael Taylor. New York: Oxford University Press, 1974.

Meyrowitz, Joshua. "Medium Theory." *Communication Theory Today.* Ed. David Crowley and David Mitchell. Stanford CA: Stanford University Press, 1994. 50–77.

Murray, Janet. *Hamlet on the Holodeck: The Future of Narrative in Cyberspace.* New York: Free Press, 1997.

Ong, Walter J. *Orality and Literacy: The Technologizing of the Word.* London: Methuen, 1982.

Pearce, Celia. *The Interactive Book: A Guide to the Interactive Revolution.* Indianapolis: Macmillan Technical Publishing, 1997.

Peirce, Charles Sanders. *Collected Papers.* Vol. 3. Ed. C. Hartshorn, P. Weiss and A. W. Burkes. Cambridge: Harvard University Press, 1931–58.

Prince, Gerald. *A Grammar of Stories.* The Hague: Mouton, 1973.

——. *Dictionary of Narratology.* Lincoln: University of Nebraska Press, 1987.

Richardson, Brian. "Recent Concepts of Narrative and the Narratives of Narrative Theory." *Style* 34.2 (2000): 168–75.

Ricoeur, Paul. *Temps et récit.* 3 vols. Paris: Seuil, 1983, 1984, 1985.

Rimmon-Kenan, Shlomith. "How the Model Neglects the Medium: Linguistics, Language, and the Crisis of Narratology." *Journal of Narrrative Technique* 19.1 (1989): 157–66.

Searle, John. *Speech Acts.* London: Cambridge University Press, 1969.

——. "The Logical Status of Fictional Discourse." *New Literary History* 6 (1975): 319–32.

Smith, Barbara Herrnstein. "Narrative Versions, Narrative Theories." *On Narrative.* Ed. W. J. T. Mitchell. Chicago: University of Chicago Press, 1981. 209–32.

Sturgess, Philip J. M. *Narrativity: Theory and Practice.* Oxford: Clarendon Press, 1992.

Talmy, Leonard. "A Cognitive Framework for Narrative Structure." *Toward a Cognitive Semantics.* Cambridge: MIT Press, 2000. 2:417–82.

Theall, Donald. *Beyond the Word: Reconstructing Sense in the Joyce Era of Technology, Culture, and Communications.* Toronto: University of Toronto Press, 1995.

————. *The Virtual Marshall McLuhan*. Montreal: McGill-Queen's University Press, 2001.

Turner, Mark. *The Literary Mind*. Oxford: Oxford University Press, 1996.

Virtanen, Tuija. "Issues of Text Typology: Narrative—A 'Basic' Type of Text? *Text* 12.2 (1992): 293–310.

Wolf, Werner. *The Musicalization of Fiction: A Study in the Theory and History of Intermediality*. Amsterdam: Rodopi, 1999.

Worth, Sol. "Pictures Can't Say Ain't." *Studies in Visual Communication*. Ed. and intro. Larry Gross. Philadelphia: University of Pennsylvania Press, 1981.

Wutz, Michael, and Joseph Tabbi. *Reading Matters: Narrative in the New Media Ecology*. Ithaca: Cornell University Press, 1997.

1. Face-to-Face Narration

Face-to-face narration: the phrase is almost, but not entirely, synonymous with oral storytelling. With the invention of the telephone, radio, and television, modern technology has dissociated orality from co-presence. Most of Walter Ong's channels of secondary orality lack the live interaction between the narrator and the audience that we find in the primary type. The label "oral narrative" is therefore insufficient to capture two essential properties of face-to-face narration. The first of these properties is interactivity. It is current these days to extol the interactive narrativity of digital media, but no amount of hyperlinking can match the oral narrator's freedom to adapt his tale to the particular needs of the audience. In a conversational context the text is not delivered ready-made to the recipient but is dynamically and dialogically constructed in the real time of the storytelling event, as the narrator responds to diverse types of input: questions from the audience, interruptions, requests for explanations, laughter, supportive vocalizations, and facial expressions. The same fluidity characterizes the relation between the narrator and the audience. Since face-to-face interaction constantly renegotiates the role of the participants, every listener is, at least in principle, a potential storyteller. The second distinctive property is the multi-channel dimension of what McLuhan called in *The Global Village* (1989) (somewhat reductively) "acoustic space": face-to-face storytelling is more than a purely mental experience of language based on syntax and semantics; it is also a corporeal performance in which meaning is created through gestures, facial expressions, and intonation. The telephone may share the interactivity of face-to-face storytelling, and television may emulate the diversity of its channels, but only face-to-face narration presents both properties.

Early narratology—the body of work associated with the names of Genette, Todorov, Barthes, Greimas, Lévi-Strauss, and Propp—was too focused on the idea of narrative as a synchronic structure to pay much attention to the dynamics of its emergence from a conversational context.

Structuralist narratology does not study oral narrative genres for their transactional nature but because these genres provide purer examples than complex literary texts of the elementary structures of narrative significations. Whether it is Lévi-Strauss's analysis of the Oedipus myth in terms of kinship structures, Greimas's diagramming of folktale into semiotic squares, or Propp's dissection of Russian fairy tales into narrative functions, structuralist interest in oral narrative is exclusively focused on the level of story, at the expense of discourse strategies. It wasn't until American linguistics expanded its scrutiny from the sentence to larger units, such as text, discourse, and conversation, that the dynamic construction of face-to-face oral narrative, what may be called its "performantial dimension," began to attract attention. It is the immense merit of the sociolinguist William Labov, who studied the use of language in the African-American communities of inner cities, to have demonstrated that conversational storytelling is no less deliberately crafted than the narratives of "high" literature. Labov argued that the success of a conversational story—its ability to make a point—depends not only on the sheer tellability of its subject matter but, above all, on the speaker's ability to display narrative content properly through the use of clauses that fulfill a sophisticated pattern of rhetorical functions: abstracting, evaluating, highlighting, or providing an appropriate coda. Led by scholars such as Deborah Tannen, Deborah Schiffrin, Harvey Sacks, and Livia Polanyi, to mention only a few, the study of conversational storytelling soon blossomed into an alternative narratology. But most literary critics were too absorbed in structuralism and poststructuralism to notice this development. The literary and the sociolinguistic branches of narratology developed side by side for many years, in blissful ignorance of each other.

The first literary scholar who attempted to bridge the two traditions was Mary Louise Pratt. In her groundbreaking book *Toward a Speech Act Theory of Literary Discourse* (1977) she attacked the formalist dogma of a radical opposition between poetic (literary) and ordinary language by demonstrating the applicability of Labov's model of conversational storytelling to a selection of literary narratives. The book started a wave of attempts to link literary texts to what was quickly becoming known as "natural discourse." Pratt conceived novels as fictional imitations of nonfictional genres, such as biography, autobiography, history, diary, annotated critical edition of a poem (Nabokov's *Pale Fire*), or simply "narrative display text" (Pratt's term for conversational narratives whose point resides in their tellability). In her book *On the Margins of Discourse*, published just a year after Pratt's manifesto, Barbara Herrnstein Smith described poetry as an imitation of "natural" (that is, conversational) utterances. The most ambitious attempt to date to integrate the study of literary and oral narrative into one comprehensive model is Monika Fludernik's *Towards a "Natural" Narratology* (1996), but the quotation marks in the title signals the beginning of a certain skepticism toward the concept of natural discourse and its wholesale applicability to literary narrative; for, with their omniscient narration, stream of consciousness, jumping back and forth between different plot lines, collage techniques, jumbling of chronological sequence, or elliptical representation of events, most novels are anything but imitations of "spontaneous oral narration of past events" (Fludernik's definition of "natural" narrative [71]). Even when novels ostentatiously imitate oral storytelling, the imitation is never close enough to fool the reader into taking the text for a genuine transcription of oral discourse. If "spontaneous oral narration of past events" sets the standard of naturalness, all novels are artificial, and so are many instances of oral narration: telling well-rehearsed jokes, performing epic poetry, reporting live events in a radio or TV broadcast.

How can an integrated narrative theory avoid the Charybdis of a total dissociation of literary and conversational narrative and the Scylla of reducing one to the other? In "Principle and Parameters of Story Logic: Steps toward a Transmedial Narratology" David Herman examines what needs to be done to equip "classical" narratology, as he calls it in his introduction to *Narratologies* (1), with a toolbox capable of describing oral and written narratives in both their differences and similarities. The investigation takes the form of a comparison between an oral and a written narrative that share a common theme: the story of a shape-shifting ghost told by a young North Carolina woman to an interviewer seeking linguistic data; and Franz Kafka's classical story *The Metamorphosis*. Treating the question of the importance of the contrast between oral-conversational and written-literary-fictional narrative as a special case of the larger problem of the medium dependency of narrative, Herman begins his essay with a review of narratological positions regarding the possibility of transferring a given story from a medium to another. This review is presented in dialectical form. The thesis claims that narrative is medium independent; the anthithesis states that narratives of different media are incommensurable; the synthesis regards the medium dependence of stories as a matter of degree. Synthesis is the only conception that justifies a study of "narrative across media." At stake in all three positions is the classical narratological distinction between story and discourse: thesis takes its validity for granted, antithesis denies it, synthesis reaffirms it. [1] In its implicit view of the storytelling act as the "organization of a set of cues for the construction of a story" (Bordwell

62), Herman's approach to narrative offers a concrete implementation of the functionalist program outlined in David Bordwell's contribution to this volume. To assess the similarities and differences of oral and literary narrative, Herman investigates how a common set of narrative functions are fulfilled in each of his two examples: how do narratives represent space? How do they perform temporal sequencing? How do they assign actantial roles to characters (that is, agent, patient, and so on)? How do they anchor their storyworld in a particular context of interpretation?

The work of Katharine Young, both in general and in the essay contributed to this book, is one of the most powerful demonstrations available to date of the interactive nature of face-to-face storytelling. In "Edgework: Frame and Boundary in the Phenomenology of Conversational Narrative" Young describes this interactivity as a drawing of frames and a crossing of boundaries. The problem of framing a narrative from its context occurs in all media, but the frame is usually established once and for all through static devices, such as the columns and titles of newspaper articles, the frame of a painting, the audiovisual devices that signal the beginning and end of a feature movie, or the covers of a book. It is only in conversation that narrative must be isolated from a steady stream of signs that belong to the same medium, and it is only in conversation that frames are constructed in the real time of the narrative performance. Describing the temporal flow of conversation through a bold spatial model, Young regards narratives as "enclaves" in the realm of conversation. Since participants in a conversation do not easily concede the floor to one speaker for a lengthy period, the boundaries of these enclaves must be constantly defended or renegotiated. To participate in a storytelling event in the context of informal conversation is to move back and forth, under the guidance of the narrator but also through the initiative of the other participants, between three concentric domains: the taleword, the storyrealm, both tightly delimited territories, and the unbound realm of conversation. As Young persuasively demonstrates, it is the function of framing devices, such as prefaces and codas, openings and closings, or beginnings and ends, to mark the boundaries of these domains and to facilitate the perilous operation of their crossing—perilous because the interest and attention of the audience must be rebuilt or consolidated with any change in focus, topic or speaker.

Whereas Young focuses on the purely verbal signals that structure conversational storytelling into distinct layers—what she calls "laminations"—Cassell and McNeill's essay "Gesture and the Poetics of Prose" shows the importance of the other channel of face-to-face narration for the framing of these layers. The narrative potential of a medium or semiotic system is proportional to its ability to develop a reasonably well-defined syntax and semantics. Cassell and McNeill demonstrate that the visual channel of face-to-face narration is regulated by a sufficiently sophisticated grammar to take over or assist significant narrative functions. Using as data the oral retelling of Sylvester and Tweetie Bird cartoons by various informants, the essay distinguishes four semiotic types of gestures: iconics (gestures that depict narrative action); metaphorics (gestures that display the vehicle of a metaphor inherent to language, such as mimicking the transfer of a solid object to announce the transmission of a story); beats (gestures that index discourse structures, such as introducing a new character or summarizing the plot); and abstract pointing (deictics pointing to objects in the narrative world that are not objectively present). This gestural repertoire enables storytellers to perform an astonishing variety of narrative functions: indicating whether the narrator speaks in his own voice, or mimics a character; marking narratorial perspective (that is, indicating where the narrator is located in the taleworld); diagramming the plot by outlining character movements in the taleworld; mimicking action, thereby remediating the visual character of the cartoon; and moving in and out of the taleworld, from a properly narrative to a metanarrative or paranarrative stance. Through its efficient recycling of the classical narratological concepts of voice, perspective, and narrative levels, Cassell and McNeill's essay will leave those who have invested their scholarly reputation in the development of literary narratology with the comforting feeling that the extension of narrative analysis beyond the verbal channel of storytelling doe not need to start from ground zero.

Notes

1. Gerald Prince defines *story* through a systematic contrast to *discourse:* "The content plane of narrative as opposed to its expression plane or discourse; the 'what' of a narrative as opposed to the 'how'; the narrated as opposed to the narrating; the fiction as opposed to the narration; the existents and events represented in a narrative" (*Dictionary* 91).

References

Bordwell, David. *Narration in the Fiction Film.* Madison: University of Wisconsin Press, 1985.

Fludernik, Monika. *Towards a "Natural" Narratology.* New York: Routledge, 1996.

Herman, David. "Introduction: Narratologies." *Narratologies: New Perspectives on Narrative Analysis.* Ed. David Herman. Columbus: Ohio State University Press, 1999.

McLuhan, Marshall, and Bruce R. Powers. *The Global Village: Transformations in World Life and Media in the Twenty-first Century.* New York: Oxford University Press, 1989.

Pratt, Mary Louise. *Toward a Speech Act Theory of Literary Discourse.* Bloomington: Indiana University Press, 1977.

Prince, Gerald. *Dictionary of Narratology.* Lincoln: University of Nebraska Press, 1987.

Smith, Barbara Herrnstein. *On the Margins of Discourse: The Relation of Literature to Language.* Chicago: University of Chicago Press, 1979.

1

Toward a Transmedial Narratology

David Herman

True to their structuralist inheritance, narratologists such as the early Roland Barthes sought to use linguistics as a "pilot-science" in their efforts to develop new (and revolutionary) techniques for analyzing stories. Thus, in his 1966 "Introduction to the Structuralist Analysis of Narratives" Barthes conceived of discourse as the object of a second linguistics, a linguistics beyond the sentence, with narrative viewed as only one of the "idioms apt for consideration" in this context. Yet, in one of the great ironies of the history of narrative theory, the narratologists tried to elaborate this second linguistics on the basis of a structuralist approach to language that had already proven deficient in the broader context of linguistic inquiry (see Herman, "Sciences"). Notably, the structuralists tried to build a linguistics of discourse on the basis of models unable to account for the complexities of larger, suprasentential units of language. What is more, in founding the field of narratology, theorists such as Barthes, Gérard Genette, A.-J. Greimas, and Tzvetan Todorov focused mainly on literary narratives as opposed to instances of everyday storytelling. Barthes drew on Fleming's James Bond novels in his "Introduction"; Genette, Greimas, and Todorov used Proust, Maupassant, and Boccaccio as their tutor texts. Here emerges a second major historical irony. One of the foundational documents for structuralist narratology was Vladimir Propp's investigation of folktales rooted in oral traditions. But the structuralists neglected to consider (let alone mark off) the limits of applicability of Propp's ideas, trying to extend to all narratives, including complicated literary texts, tools designed for a restricted corpus of folktales. The result was an approach that championed the study of narratives of all sorts, irrespective of origin, medium, theme, reputation, or genre, but lacked the conceptual and methodological resources to substantiate its own claims to generalizability.

Meanwhile, in the Anglo-American tradition, one year after the publication of Barthes's "Introduction," William Labov and Joshua Waletzky published a groundbreaking article that sketched out a sociolinguistic approach to analyzing conversational narratives.[1] This approach derived from and fed back into traditions of linguistic research with which the structuralist narratologists were barely familiar. Centering around narratives of personal experience, Labov and Waletzky's model sparked a widespread research initiative still being pursued by a variety of investigators (see Bamberg for an overview). Labov and Waletzky's 1967 article (along with a follow-up article published in 1972 by Labov) established a vocabulary for labeling the components of personal experience narratives (abstract, orientation, complicating action, evaluation, result, coda). It also identified clause- and sentence-level structures tending to surface in each of these components, suggesting that story recipients monitor the discourse for signs enabling them to "chunk" what is said into units-in-a-narrative-pattern. For example, clauses with past-tense verbs in the indicative mood are likely to occur in (that is, be a reliable indicator of) the complicating action of the narrative, whereas storytellers' evaluations depart from this baseline syntax, their marked status serving to indicate the point of the narrative, the reason for its telling. More generally, Labov's model laid the groundwork for further inquiry into both the linguistic and the interactional profile of narratives told during face-to-face encounters. Conversational narratives do consist of clause-, sentence-, and discourse-level features, yet they are also anchored in contexts in which their tellers have to have a (recognizable) point or else be ignored, shouted down, or worse (cf. Goodwin 239–57).

Although it was firmly anchored in empirical models for studying natural language data, however, the sociolinguistic approach *also* lacked generalizability. Originally designed for narratives elicited during interviews, the model was manifestly incapable of describing and explaining the more complex structures found in written narratives, especially literary ones. For one thing, as Genette showed so skillfully in his brilliant discussion of Proust in *Narrative Discourse,* literary narratives characteristically rely on flashblacks, flash-forwards, pauses, ellipses, iterations, compressions, and other time-bending strategies not captured by Labov's definition of *narrative* as "one method of recapitulating past experience by matching a verbal sequence of clauses to the sequence of events which (it is inferred) actually occurred" (370). Further, noting the rise of simultaneous and prospective narration in contemporary literary works, Uri Margolin has revealed retrospective narration to be just one option within a larger system of narrative possibilities. The result is that, in literary contexts, it would be difficult to maintain that clauses with past-tense indicative verbs are the unmarked unit of narration, the baseline against which marked (that is, evaluative or point-indicating) syntax could be measured (cf. Herman, "Socionarratology"). For that matter some avant-garde literary narratives make a point of emphasizing their apparent pointlessness, throwing up obstacles in the way of readers struggling to discern a reason for the telling. Whereas generally speaking the onus of evaluation is on storytellers in contexts of face-to-face interaction, in experimental literary fictions the burden quite often seems to shift from teller to interpreter (but see Pratt 116; and my discussion here).

As even these preliminary comments suggest, research on the relations between conversational and literary narrative can only benefit from opening up lines of communication between what have emerged as distinct disciplinary traditions. With some important exceptions in recent years (for example, Fludernik, Polanyi, and Tannen), researchers studying stories have taken one or other of the two paths just traced—dichotomous paths that began to birfucate from the very inception of sustained inquiry into narrative. One path leads through literary-theoretical terrain, which encompasses narratives that vary dramatically with respect to length, genre, and degree of complexity. The other path leads the investigator toward naturalistic uses of stories in everyday communicative settings. Here the narratives encountered are, though not artful in the literary sense, nonetheless artfully adapted to the ecology of face-to-face interaction, with its moment-by-moment fluctuations in linguistic and paralinguistic signaling, its turn-taking imperatives, and what Erving Goffman characterized as its ritual constraints on processes of acknowledgment, disputation, inattention, and affirmation, stories being part of an interactional etiquette that generates a whole spectrum of potentially face-threatening and face-saving behaviors. The remainder of my contribution seeks to create new opportunities for dialogue between researchers traveling on these two paths, whose exact relations to one another have yet to be charted. One of my guiding assumptions is that the two routes pass through different areas of the same landscape, some of the areas separated more widely than others but none of them so far apart that communication between the regions is impossible.

In what follows I begin by exploring three theses concerning the more general problem of which the relations between conversational and literary narrative can be viewed as a special case. The more general problem can be posed as a question—What are the relations between narrative and its media (including spoken and written language)?—with each thesis constituting a strategy for addressing that question. At the risk of oversimplification (not to mention predictability), I present the three theses in quasi-dialectic fashion, as thesis, antithesis, and synthesis. Although it exists in stronger and weaker forms, thesis posits that narrative is medium independent and that essential properties of stories remain unchanged across different presentational formats. Antithesis construes stories as radically dependent on their media, making the distinction between spoken conversational and literary narrative a fundamental one—to the point where spoken and written versions of a story would not be "versions" at all but, instead, different narratives altogether. Synthesis posits that medium-specific differences between narratives are nontrivial but only more or less firmly anchored in their respective media; intertranslation between story media will be more or less possible, depending on the particular formats involved.

After reviewing previous scholarship affiliated with thesis, antithesis, and synthesis, I go on to outline a program for research that takes its inspiration from synthesis but extends that research paradigm in new directions. In particular, the second half of my essay outlines an integrative approach to "story logic" that I have also developed in other work (Herman, *Story* and "Story"). As I use the term, *story logic* refers both to the logic that stories have and the logic that they are. Stories *have* a logic that consists of strategies for coding circumstances, participants, states, actions, and events in the "storyworlds," that is, the global mental representations that interpreters are prompted to create when they read or listen to a narrative. Temporal relations between events, for example, can be more or less exactly specified, whereas participants can be assigned a variety of roles (Senser, Agent, Sayer, and so on) and their situation in space can be configured by way of choices between different kinds of verbs of motion. But narrative also *constitutes* a logic in its own right, providing human beings with one of their primary resources for comprehending experience and organizing interaction. The first kind of logic pertains chiefly to narrative as product, the second kind of logic to narrative as process. In particular, the logic that stories are encompasses processes of narrative communication; at issue are the ways in which people tell and make sense of stories in specific communicative contexts, that is, the methods by which narratives are deployed as contextually situated practices.

Sketching the logic that stories have and are, I compare and contrast a conversational and a literary narrative: on the one hand, a North Carolina storyteller's tale (transcribed in the appendix) about her grandfather's encounter with a shape-shifter who transforms himself from a man into a squirrel and back into a man again; on the other hand, Franz Kafka's "The Metamorphosis," a literary treatment of a different kind of shape-shift— one involving Gregor Samsa's irreversible transformation into an insect. By holding constant the problem that these narratives seek to address—

namely, characters who undergo cross-species transformations—I explore how properties of spoken and written discourse bear on the story logic of the two texts. My research hypothesis is that, although narratives in different media exploit a common stock of narrative design principles, they exploit them in different, media-specific ways, or, rather, in a certain *range* of ways determined by the properties of each medium.

Thesis: Narrative Is Medium Independent

The strong version of thesis, that all aspects of every narrative can be translated into all possible media, has not enjoyed prominence in the study of narrative. But a weaker version, that certain aspects of every narrative are medium independent, forms one of the basic research hypotheses of structuralist narratology. In effect, narratological distinctions between "story" and "discourse"—or, equivalently, the what and the way, *fabula* and *sjuzhet,* narrated and narrative—assume that the first term of each of these conceptual pairs is medium independent whereas the second is dependent on the particular medium in which a given story is conveyed. As Claude Bremond put it in his 1964 article "Le Message narratif," "any sort of narrative message (not only folk tales) . . . may be transposed from one to another medium without losing its essential properties: the subject of a story may serve as an argument for a ballet, that of a novel can be transposed to stage or screen, one can recount in words a film to someone who has not seen it" (qtd. in Chatman, *Story* 20). Similarly, in distinguishing between story, text (= discourse), and narration, Shlomith Rimmon-Kenan characterized " 'story' [as] a succession of events, 'text' [as] a spoken or written discourse which undertakes their telling" (3). As a mental construct independent of any medium, story constitutes "the narrated events, abstracted from their disposition in the text and reconstructed in their chronological order, together with the participants in those events" (*Narrative* 2).

Barthes, in his "Introduction," reframes the medium-independence thesis in a manner that reveals its Saussurean-Hjelmslevian heritage. Noting that there has been, from Aristotle on, "a periodic interest in narrative form," Barthes remarks that "it is normal that the newly developing structuralism should make this form one of its first concerns—is not structuralism's constant aim to master the infinity of utterances [*paroles*] by describing the language [*langue*] of which they are products and from which they can be generated [?]" (80). Correlatively, since the narrative *langue* targeted by structuralist analysis is not "the language of articulated language— though very often vehicled by it—narrative units will be substantially independent of linguistic units" (91). To use Hjelmslevian parlance, one of the hallmarks of classical narratology is its attempt "to disengage a form from the substance of the narrated content, a specific narrative form" (Rimmon-Kenan, *Narrative* 6). Thus, Gerald Prince argues that, because narratives and nonnarratives can center around the same topics and develop the same general themes, the substance of the content side does not define narrative ("Aspects" 50–51; cf. Chatman, *Story* 22–26). Further, since both narratives and nonnarratives can be expressed in one and the same medium, neither the form nor the substance of the expression side is definitive of story. What defines narrative, rather, is the form of its content side, that is, the way a sequence of (medium-specific) cues must be structured for it to encode a narratively organized (but non-medium-specific) sequence of participants-in-events.

The medium-independence thesis carries with it methodological consequences, in effect determining what counts as "data" that can be used to illustrate narratological theories. For example, an assumption about the medium independence of story is arguably what motivates Prince's use of constructed examples as evidence for his claims about narrative (see Prince, *Grammar,* "Aspects," and *Narratology*). If the form of the content is the real target of narrative analysis, then the substance of the content, which encompasses the themes and ideas treated in a narrative, is not centrally important, and constructed examples can be used to advance claims with as much validity and reliability as claims based on naturally occurring narratives, whether spoken or written. Even among analysts who argued early on for the medium independence of story, however, there was some hesitation over the *degree* of medium independence involved. For instance, whereas Chatman argued that "narrative discourse consists of a connected sequence of narrative *statements,* where 'statement' is quite independent of the particular expressive medium" and there is "no privileged manifestation" of story in one medium as opposed to another (*Story* 25, 31), he also acknowledged that "verbal narratives express narrative contents of time summary more easily than do cinematic narratives, while the latter more easily show spatial relations" (25). Such considerations eventually induced Chatman ("Directions") to question the autonomy of story with respect to print and film narratives, given that cinema draws on two information tracks (visual and auditory) instead of just one. Indeed, for some theorists considerations of just this sort provide evidence for antithesis—namely, the view that narrative is not just partly or secondarily dependent on its media but, rather, radically and primarily dependent.

Antithesis: Narrative Is (Radically) Medium Dependent

The basic intuition underlying antithesis is that every retelling alters the story told, with every re-presentation of a narrative changing what is presented. In revising her own earlier position about the relations between story and text, for example, Rimmon-Kenan embraces a version of antithesis. "Instead of relegating language to a position external or irrelevant to narrative structure," she writes, "we may perhaps reverse the perspective and consider it *the determining factor* of that structure" ("Model" 160; emph. added). Rimmon-Kenan now argues that the semiotic format of a narrative, the nature of the medium in which it is realized, determines the relations between text and story in a given case (162). To invoke C. S. Peirce's theory of signs, dance affords possibilities for creating iconic relations between sequences of physical movements and sequences of events in a storyworld; written narrative, possibilities for creating conventional relations between linguistic units and storyworld events; and conversational narrative, possibilities for creating both iconic and conventional relations via utterances and gestures. Further, the narrative-determining force of sign systems stems from their being not only media of expression but also resources for (inter)acting (160). Thus, in Barbara Herrnstein Smith's critique of structuralist narratology the medium-dependence antithesis informs her argument that stories, which are always told *by* someone *to* someone (else), should be viewed as socio-symbolic transactions instead of inert, preexistent structures. Insofar as narratives are acts, doings more than things, stories will inevitably unfold differently across different tellings. Structuralist theories about an autonomous and invariable structure, or "story," are therefore, from this perspective, a token of residual Platonism—of a predeconstructive desire to hold on to unchanging essences amid stories-in-flux (but see Prince, "Narratology" 167).

Linguists investigating the relations between spoken and written discourse have developed arguments analogous to those advanced by Rimmon-Kenan and Herrnstein Smith. Wallace Chafe, for instance, has outlined differences between the activities of speaking and writing that imply, in turn, differences in the way spoken and written "texts" (in Rimmon-Kenan's sense) might encode a story (41–50). Whereas spoken language is relatively evanescent, written language is relatively permanent and transportable; whereas spoken language is relatively fast, writing is produced more slowly; whereas conversations tend to be spontaneous, writing is typically deliberate or "worked over"; whereas speaking affords language users the fullest possible exploitation of prosody (pitches, pauses, changes of tempo and timbre, and so on), written language is impoverished in this respect. Meanwhile, theorists working in the conversation-analytic or eth-nomethodological tradition have interpreted narrative as a situated prac-tice, all storytelling acts being uniquely tailored to specific circumstances that they also help constitute (Schegloff; cf. Garfinkel). In other words, nar-ratives are, from a conversation-analytic perspective, fragments of behavior by which both tellers and recipients collaboratively display their under-standing of—as well as create—the socio-communicative logic of a context for interaction. As interactional achievements that also enable interaction itself, stories are necessarily particularized; hence, retellings produce not different versions of the same story but new narratives-in-contexts.

If thesis has difficulty accounting for the ways in which narratives are shaped by their telling, antithesis struggles to capture the intuition that stories have a "gist" that can remain more or less intact across fairly dramatic shifts in context, style, degree of elaboration, and so on. Constancy of gist is quite high in near-verbatim recountings, but even the most bizarre parody depends for its effect on commonalities between the source text being parodied and the parodic target text (Genette, *Palimpsests*). Synthesis predicts, however, that at some threshold the shift of contexts will be so extreme as to result in a different narrative; the gist of a story can be lost in a retelling, which then shades off into the telling of another narrative.

Synthesis: The Medium Dependence of Stories Is a Matter of Degree

Positing that differences between narrative media are gradient (more or less) rather than binary (either . . . or), synthesis suggests that stories are shaped but not determined by their presentational formats. Rather, synthesis con-strues narratives as variably anchored in expressive media characterized by different degrees of intertranslatability. According to synthesis, what Chatman described as constraints on the intertranslatability of print and cinematic narrative would need to be situated within a broader system of analogous constraints, including those affecting the translation of, say, an English-language narrative into Japanese; the presentation of *The Iliad* in pantomime; or the (doomed) attempt to market *My Dinner with André* action figures, as portrayed in Christopher Guest's film *Waiting for Guffman* (1996).

Inquiry into this wider system of contraints on narrative remediation is beyond the scope of the present essay.[2] Instead, my aim is to characterize that portion of the system that bears on the commonalities and contrasts between spoken and written narratives—more specifically, between conversational and literary narratives, nonfictional as well as fictional. Work done under the auspices of synthesis provides an initial point of entry into the relevant region of the constraint system at issue; to put the matter the other way around, researchers who argue that spoken and written narrative can be located on a continuum or scale, instead of exemplifying distinct categories, are rejecting both the medium-independence thesis and the medium-dependence antithesis in favor of some version of synthesis.[3] For proponents of synthesis, despite nontrivial differences between everyday storytelling and literary art, instances of the narrative text type that fall into these two classes show a relatively high degree of intertranslatability. Other instances, by contrast, would have to be grouped into less intertranslatable classes—for example, operatic narratives as compared with narratives conveyed through silent film.

In the (socio)linguistic tradition Deborah Tannen is one of a number of theorists who have developed a scalar model of spoken and written narrative (cf. Polanyi, "Literary"). Tannen suggests that "strategies that have been associated with orality grow out of emphasis on interpersonal involvement between speaker/writer and audience, and . . . strategies that have been associated with literacy grow out of focus on content" ("Introduction" xv). Accordingly, it is possible to situate narrative discourse on "an oral/literate continuum, or, more precisely, a continuum of relative focus on interpersonal involvement vs. message content" (Tannen, "Oral/Literate" 15). Tannen's continuum assumes that there is a functional equivalence—that is, intertranslatability—between involvement-oriented and content-oriented features in spoken and written narrative. Thus, as Tannen ("Strategies") shows, the more the involvement-oriented features included in written narrative, the more successfully it remediates the functional profile of oral narrative. Relevant features include high concentrations of detail or imagery; use of the active instead of the passive voice; parallel (that is, list-like) constructions rather than embedding or hypotaxis; and use of direct quotation of storyworld participants. Tannen's position can be aligned with synthesis insofar as it begins with the premise that distributions of involvement-oriented or content-oriented features shape the sort of story told; anchors those features in particular media; but then explores the extent to which one medium can appropriate, or approximate, features associated with another medium. Tannen's approach can be reconstrued as arguing that there are relatively few (and relatively weak) constraints on the redistribution of both sets of features across the boundary between spoken and written narratives—a boundary that must therefore be viewed as variable and open rather than fixed and impermeable.

Likewise, in the narratological tradition Monika Fludernik has advanced a scalar model based on a version of synthesis. Focusing on conversational and literary narrative specifically, Fludernik detects a continuum that links the foregrounding of narrative experientiality in everyday storytelling with the experiential modes of narration prominent in the realist and modernist novel (*Towards* 92 / ff.). Further, she identifies a set of features surviving from natural narrative into much contemporary fiction, including the use of a narrator figure, who often provides moralizing and evaluative commentary; the storyteller's empathetic identification with and self-distancing from storyworld participants; and mimetic impersonation via various styles of discourse representation (57 / ff.). In parallel with Tannen, Fludernik assumes not the identity but, rather, the intertranslatability of such features across natural and literary narrative. Hers is not a general claim about processes of remediation vis-à-vis all narrative formats but, instead, an investigation of the extent to which features prominent in two particular formats might be functionally equivalent.

As should already be apparent, carrying synthesis forward will necessitate an integrative, cross-disciplinary approach to narrative analysis—one that takes into account developments not only in literary and cultural theory but in other, neighboring research traditions as well, including linguistics, ethnography, sociology, and cognitive science. In the sections that follow, I hope to make a small contribution to this important program for research. In particular, I explore why some aspects of narrative lend themselves particularly well to redistribution along the continuum linking features of spoken and written discourse, whereas other aspects prove more resistant to such remediation.

Extending Synthesis: Story Logic in Conversation and Literature

My strategy for extending synthesis is to examine in more detail some of the principles governing story logic, together with the parameters for their use across media (in this case, conversational and literary narrative). To reiterate: in referring to story logic, I mean to suggest that stories do not merely have but also constitute a logic, narratives being not just semiotic structures but also strategies for structuring and thereby making sense of experience—for problem solving in the broadest sense. I shall explore each of these dimensions of story logic in turn, studying how they manifest themselves in narratives centered around characters who undergo quite startling, difficult-to-understand transformations. More specifically, radical transformative processes are at work in both Kafka's account of the transmutation of Gregor Samsa into a dung beetle in "Die Verwandlung" ("The Metamorphosis") and in TS's story of the shape-shifting squirrel/man (see appendix).[4] Each story charts a causal-chronological sequence in which characters take on a hybridized physical form, blending human attributes with those of insect and animal species, respectively. Yet, besides their use of different media, there is also a generic contrast between the two narratives: Kafka's text is explicitly fictional, whereas TS's story purports to be a factual (if supernatural) account of what her grandfather experienced in the past.

At the heart of each narrative, however, is the same problem—namely, how to make sense of a transformation by which a character becomes a member of a different species. Given that narrative is a primary resource for building causal-chronological patterns—that is, sequences of events linked not just by temporal succession but also by relations of cause and effect— the problem of accounting for characters' metamorphoses would seem to be one for which stories are ideally suited. But the issue that arose during my discussion of synthesis resurfaces in this context as well. Assuming that conversational and literary narratives do in fact draw on shared principles of story logic to address such fundamental problems as how to track characters across shifts of shape, to what extent do differences between the two media result in variable use of the principles in question? More precisely, how commensurate is the range of ways story logic can be used in conversational storytelling as compared with the range of ways it can be used in literary narratives?

The Logic That Stories Are: Communicative Strategies for Storytelling

The first dimension of story logic to be considered—the logic that stories are—involves the place of narrative within the broader logic of communication. Of concern here are features of narrative that enable storytellers as well as fiction writers to accomplish communicative aims in particular discourse environments, the ecologies of talk in which their narratives unfold. Along these lines, note that TS's story of the shape-shifter is not a conversational narrative plain and simple, that is, a story told by a discourse participant to peers who have in turn prompted the telling of those stories during the normal give-and-take of informal interaction. TS's account of the shape-shifter is a tale that forms part of a larger sequence of stories told in response to a relatively decontextualized question about supernatural occurrences—a question designed in advance of the interaction itself and posed to TS by fieldworkers who are not members of her community.

Conversely, however, the narrative profile of TS's account impinges on the discourse context in which it is embedded. Displacing a dyadic interview format marked by pairs of questions and answers, the narrative organizes a relatively monologic type of speech event, one accommodating the extensive turns at talk required for storytelling. Thus, once TS's story is under way, the interviewer (BA) passes on opportunities for interrogative or other utterances in favor of minimal forms of "backchanneling" (lines h, j, u, bb, dd, mm, vv, yy, and ccc). In addition, in a portion of the interview not transcribed in the appendix, TS and BA co-construct a story preface in which BA demonstrates her willingness to adopt the role of listener by way of explicit requests that TS "tell some stories." The preface also contains emphatic speech productions in which BA underscores her interest in and appreciation of stories in general, ghost stories in particular:

TS: 'Cause of the ^stories . . I just . . all the stories
        and my house is the world's worst
        to tell you things /inaudible word/ (laughs)

        [

BA: ^Tell some stories
        I ^love stories like that.
        ^Tell us some (claps hands) . . ^yes.

Hence, as much by what she refrains from saying as by the speech tokens that she does in fact produce, the interviewer signals that she is ceding her floor rights to the storyteller, who for her part periodically checks for permission to complete the long turn at talk required for the elaboration of her narrative.

The communicative logic of "The Metamorphosis" likewise involves a situated form of narrative practice. More than this, although Kafka's narrative is differently situated in sociointeractional space than TS's account, it represents a mode of narrative practice fundamentally continuous with the mode at work in spoken stories. In the case of literary works such as Kafka's, it is true, producers and interpreters of narrative discourse do not have to make on-the-fly assessments of a real-time storytelling situation. Yet, as Mary Louise Pratt noted, in both "natural" and literary narrative the role structure of participants in the speech situation remains similarly marked vis-à-vis "the unmarked situation among peers, in which all participants have [in principle] equal access to the floor" (113). In other words, Kafka's readers, like TS's interlocutors, assume the role of an audience ceding its floor rights to discourse producers who must as a result live up to "increased expectations of delight" (Pratt 116). In contexts of literary narrative, requests for the floor can be accomplished by a variety of textual as well as paratextual cues, for example, the publication of a story in a volume containing other texts by the author or by other fiction writers. Such cues are functionally equivalent to TS's " 'Cause of the stories . . . ."

Further, just as the story logic of TS's account both emerges from and helps constitute a larger ecology of talk, a communicative environment encompassing multiple spoken discourse genres or text types (interviews, arguments, stories) from among which participants are constantly selecting and signaling their selections, so too does Kafka's narrative at once issue from and impinge upon a wider discourse environment, one encompassing written genres as diverse as recipes, academic essays, news stories, and political speeches. Literary theorists have used the term *intertextuality* to refer the network of relations between various kinds of texts, though it is important to emphasize that the network involves relations of difference as well as similarity. Indeed, part of the richness of "The Metamorphosis" derives from the way it adopts conventions and motifs from several genres without falling comfortably into any one of them. The result is a hybridized text that combines elements of psychological fiction, fantasy, and quasi- (or perhaps anti-) religious allegory. The communicative logic of Kafka's narrative thus depends on its location in *sub*generic and not just generic space. The tale—like TS's account, for that matter—specifies highly nuanced interpretive protocols vis-à-vis other subtypes of narrative practice.

The Logic That Stories Have: Coding Strategies in Storytelling

So far, I have been discussing the logic that TS's and Kafka's narratives are. I have suggested, more specifically, that producers and interpreters of literary narrative are caught up in a sociointeractional nexus that remains anchored at essential points to the communicative dynamics of face-to-face storytelling. To rephrase this point, across spoken and written language there is a high degree of commensurability between the range of ways in which this first dimension of story logic manifests itself. There are a number of methods by which storytellers, on the one hand, and fiction writers, on the other hand, can prompt shifts into and out of narratively organized discourse; allowing for the different spans of time and space separating production and interpretation of spoken versus written narratives, stories in the two media exploit a comparable range of methods for cuing such shifts. Indeed, insofar as narrative provides a basic resource for structuring and comprehending diverse aspects of experience, it is perhaps unsurprising to find robust similarities in the *processes of narrative communication* conducted in these two media.

The question remains, however, whether the *narrative products* that result from those processes are equally intertranslatable. To address this question, which requires shifting from the logic that stories are to the logic that they have, I introduce in the sections that follow some ideas developed more fully in *Story Logic.*[5] Although the two texts under examination draw on a common stock of coding strategies, which I shall also refer to as "design principles," there are media-specific constraints on how those principles or strategies can be exploited in written and spoken discourse. In some ways the differences involved are negligible, but in other respects the constraints on remediation are significant.

In all, I discuss five sets of coding strategies that can be used to structure the storyworlds evoked by conversational and literary narratives. These include role assignments for participants; blends of states, events, and actions; temporal ordering; the configuration of entities in space; and the use of deictic expressions (*here, I, now*) to anchor storyworlds in particular contexts of interpretation.

Processes and Participants

By assigning particular roles to individuals and entities mentioned or implied in a narrative, interpreters can distinguish participants more or less centrally and obligatorily involved in what goes on from various sorts of circumstances also populating storyworlds. To adapt some of the categories of the functional grammar developed by M. A. K. Halliday: narratives can potentially encode many different types of processes, with storyworld participants taking on fluctuating roles—and relations to one another—depending on which process type predominates at a given point. Process types include (among others) the perceptual, involving the participant roles of Senser and Phenomena; the material, involving Actors and Goals/Patients; the relational, involving Carriers and Attributes; and the verbal, involving Sayers, Receivers, and Targets.

There are no a priori limitations on what process types can figure in narrative discourse, whether spoken or written. Perceptions of unusual Phenomena are as reportable as the performance of unexpected, equilibrium-disturbing Doings. Nonetheless, choices from among types of process constitute one of the coding strategies used to index (or interpret) a story as belonging to a particular narrative genre or subgenre. Epics, for example, show an overall preference for material over mental processes, whereas psychological fiction displays the opposite preference rankings. In TS's story of the shape-shifter, perceptual processes (marked, for example, by the verbs *saw* in line r, *noticed* in t, the dialect-specific variant *knowed* in ii and aaa, *see* in rr, and *looked* in tt) are intermixed with material processes (marked, for example, by *went out* in p, *was hunting* in q, *shot* in v, *fell* in w, *went* in aa, *scraped* in cc, *tried to find* in gg, *were headed* in hh, *come back* in qq, and so on) as well as verbal processes in which the squirrel/man is the Sayer (cf. *yelled* in x and ee and *screamed* in y). The grandfather and his cohort are, variably, Sensors, Actors, Targets, and, when the man/squirrel "looked at them so mean," the Patients/Goals of a process of perception that seems to have a kind of material force in its own right. It is no accident that TS, in telling a tale of the supernatural, uses story logic to create such complex blends of the mental and material (and verbal) realms. The shape-shifting event involves acts of misperception and re-perception that in turn require a rethinking of what constitutes material reality itself.

Because of its polygeneric status, Kafka's "The Metamorphosis" likewise reveals a rich blend of process types and participant roles. More than this, however, properties associated with written discourse, particularly its deliberate or "worked-over" nature in contrast with the relative spontaneity of spoken discourse (Chafe), allow producers of literary narrative to situate participants in an even denser network of process types over the course of a story's unfolding. The increased span of time separating the production of the narrative from its interpretation and, for that matter, the longer span of time allowed for interpretation of literary narratives, facilitates complex blends of various processes with their attendant participants. The complexity of these blends differs in degree, though not kind, from those afforded by stories presented in conversation. Although Kafka's tale initially foregrounds material processes, ascribing Gregor the role of an Actor attempting to get his beetle's body out of bed and explain himself to the office manager, from the very start Gregor is also involved in processes of perception, struggling to make sense of the bizarre Phenomena associated with his insectoid transformation. As the story unfolds, Gregor's role as Senser blends with his role as Goal/Patient; he becomes the target of material processes that include being shoved through the door and pelted with apples by his father, whose agency and stature increase in direct proportion with the diminishment of Gregor's own. Indeed, as an instance of figural narration—in which "third-person," or heterodiegetic, narration gets filtered through a particularized center of consciousness, or "filter"— Kafka's text evokes a storyworld in which it is sometimes difficult for readers to determine exactly how particular phenomena are being coded, whether they are projections of Gregor's mental states or else actions performed (or events triggered) by other participants in the narrated world.[6]

States, Events, Actions

Besides assigning roles to participants, narrative entails apportioning particular facets of storyworlds into *states, events* that happen without being deliberately initiated, and deliberately initiated *actions*. Differences between narrative genres can be correlated, in part, with different preference rankings for states vis-à-vis (various types of) states, events, and actions. Psychological tales, for example, show a preference for coding strategies that foreground the interior states of participants over the events that befall them or the actions that they initiate. For their part both of the narratives under examination focus on the interior states of their protagonists. TS recounts her grandfather's reactions to the size and behavior of the shape-shifting squirrel/man as well as his remorse after the shape-shifter dies—apparently from the gunshot wound inflicted on the squirrel. Meanwhile, Kafka's narrator gives expression to the unvocalized reactions of Gregor as he glimpses the mind-shattering apparition of his father cloaked in a bank attendant's uniform, his enormous boots lifted threateningly, his voice no longer the voice of one father but of all the fathers there ever were. Of course, as these remarks suggest, both of my tutor texts orient themselves not only around psychological states but also around the combinations of planned actions and unplanned events that bring those states into being.

When it comes to detailed, fine-grained representation of interior states, however, the narrative structures that are typical to spoken and written discourse again display significant differences in degree, if not kind. Again because of an increased span of time separating production and interpretation of written narratives (and also because of the individually customizable periods of time available for interpretation), deliberate, "worked-over" literary texts accommodate more extensive narration of participants' private beliefs, desires, and intentions than does conversational storytelling, whose greater spontaneity and brevity often require interpreters to do more inferential work to reconstruct such interior states. Granted, as Labov notes, tellers of personal experience narratives often evaluate—that is, signal the point of—their stories by commenting on their thoughts and feelings at the time the narrated actions and events occurred (370–75). But such "external" evaluation, in Labov's phrase, is a far cry from the paragraphs that Kafka devotes to Gregor's changing attitude toward the furniture in his room ("Verwandlung" 101–6; "Metamorphosis" 489–91).

Temporal Ordering

A broad contrast can be drawn between modes of narration in which events are assigned a definite location on a timeline and modes in which the exact sequence of events resists reconstruction—whether because it is impossible to know the order in which things happened or because (as in certain postmodern texts) the narrative represents events themselves as fuzzily or indeterminately ordered. Indeed, one of the features distinguishing between narrative genres is the method of temporal ordering that is typical or preferred in a given genre. For example, in their canonical form narratives of epic adventure display a preference for definitely ordered sequences of events. By contrast, in recounting events of which he or she has a vague or incomplete memory, a witness testifying in court and bound to say what is literally true will likely produce a narrative in which events are only partly ordered. Meanwhile, in experimental literary fictions such as D. M. Thomas's *The White Hotel* or Jorge Luis Borges's "The Garden of Forking Paths," time itself is portrayed as being bidirectional or multidirectional. "Later" events may be portrayed as causing "earlier" events (Thomas), or any given moment may be represented as occupying simultaneously an infinity of timelines, with each line corresponding to possible courses the world could take (Borges). Such texts code temporal relations between events not just as difficult-to-know but, furthermore, as intrinsically indeterminate.

Besides setting apart narrative genres, however, methods of temporally ordering events also help distinguish between narrative media. In particular, whereas the full range of methods for sequencing events can be exploited in literary narratives, conversational storytelling is marked by a default preference for determinate ordering. In taking the extended turns at talk required to tell a story, participants must work against the grain of the conversational speech exchange system, which reveals a bias toward smallest possible turn size (Sacks, Schegloff, and Jefferson). The result is that chronological as well as causal relations between situations and events have to be sketched as economically as possible—a constraint reinforced by the interpretive needs of story recipients, who must work synchronously to reconstruct the event sequences being presented. Hence, whereas preferred ordering methods in literary narratives vary by genre, event sequences recounted in conversation can be expected to show a medium-based preference for definite, fully reconstructible ordering, exploiting only a subset of the sequencing options that are technically possible in narrative.

Although a larger sample size is, of course, needed, the two narratives being considered here provide initial confirmation of this hypothesis. Events are fully ordered in TS's story of the shape-shifter. Over the course of a single day the old man stares meanly at TS's grandfather after he shoots the squirrel but before the grandfather comes back on his own to find the old man dead, his back torn open as if by the very same gunshot wound. By contrast, although it is possible to reconstruct global event sequences in Kafka's text, there are local instances of indeterminate ordering. For one thing it is not possible to determine in what order certain events occur: after Gregor's transformation, who was the first to find employment, Gregor's father or his sister, Grete? Further, at one point in "The Metamorphosis" Kafka's narrator uses a rhetorical question ("Weihnachten war doch wohl schon vorüber?' 'Christmas was already past, wasn't it?' [120; 498]) to suggest Gregor's growing inability to arrange ongoing events into a determinate series, this incapacity being itself a sign of the widening gap between Gregor and his human past.

Spatial Configuration

In addition to ordering events temporally, storytelling entails configuring places, entities, and paths of motion in space. Likewise, making sense of a narrative involves building and updating "cognitive maps" of the story-world it evokes—a process that requires situating participants and other entities in emergent networks of foreground-background relationships as well as mapping the trajectories of individuals and objects as they move or are moved along narratively salient paths. My claim in this connection is that, as was the case with temporal reference, literary narratives are free to exploit modes of spatial reference that are relatively dispreferred in conversational storytelling.

It should be stressed that the two texts under examination do rely on shared strategies of spatial reference. For example, verbs of motion provide a crucial resource for spatialization in both narratives. In English these verbs are located on a semantic continuum whose poles are *come* and *go* (Brown 108–24, 188–91; Landau and Jackendoff; Zubin and Hewitt). By encoding the directionality of movement, motion verbs express the locations of entities being perceived by narrators as well as paths taken by entities as they move or are moved from place to place. Thus, in the spontaneous spoken narratives Gillian Brown studied, verbs such as "*come, arrive, walk in* are used of entry into the space . . . which is nearest the observer . . . whereas *go, walked off/out* and *leave* are used as characters leave that space" (190). Similarly, in the story about her grandfather, TS uses motion verbs to encode the direction of the two hunters' movements along the paths that lead to and away from the shape-shifter's house. Relevant forms include *were headed to* (hh), *went* (jj), *left* (oo), *went on* (pp), and *come back* and *went around* (qq). These forms encode the shape-shifter's house as an object located at the distal end of an axis whose proximal end is the vantage point of the storyteller. ts's account thus demonstrates how motion verbs can be used to mark viewer-relative, or "projective," locations in narrative discourse (Frawley 262–73; Herman, "Spatial").

In Kafka's story, similarly, trajectories of motion unfold along a distal-proximal axis whose near end—for much of the story, at least—corresponds with Gregor's vantage point. Thus, when Gregor first emerges from his bedroom as an insect ("Verwandlung" 82–83; "Metamorphosis" 479), he sees the office manager as he "langsam zurückwich" 'slowly shrank back' toward the outer door of the apartment, whereas his mother clasps her hands together and then "ging . . . zwei Schritte zu Gregor hin" 'took two steps toward Gregor.'[7] A few moments later the narrator recounts how "der Prokurist hatte sich schon bei den ersten Worten Gregors abgewendet, und nur über die zuckende Schulter hinweg sah er mit aufgeworfenen Lippen nach Gregor zurück" 'the office manager had already turned away at Gregor's very first words, and he only looked back at him over his twitching shoulder and with gaping lips' (84–85; 480). In an effort to stop the manager from leaving and thereby compromising Gregor's position at the office, Gregor "wollte zum Prokuristen hingehen" 'intended to head toward the office manager' (85; 480); at the same instant, after leaping up and crying for help, Gregor's mother "lief . . . sinnlos zurück" 'senselessly backed away' (86; 480), in the process colliding with a table and knocking over a full pot of coffee. The story thus charts the office manager's and the mother's movements as they unfold along parallel paths leading to and away from Gregor's perspective on events.

Despite their shared reliance on verbs of motion, however, the two narratives display different preferences when it comes to using this strategy for spatial reference. As was the case with temporal reference, the differences between ways of configuring things in space can be ascribed to medium-specific constraints. Notably, in contrast to conversational storytellers, producers of written, literary narratives are at leisure to select a host of lexical variants for the modes of motion associated with *come* and *go* (or *came* and *went*). *Went*, in fact, is the most frequently occurring verb of motion in ts's narrative, despite ts's occasional use of functionally equivalent forms such as *left* and *headed to*. By contrast, Kafka's lexicon of motion includes forms such as "schob sich" 'squirmed along' (70; 472); "glitt er . . . ab" 'kept sliding down' (80; 477); "nahm einen Anlauf" 'broke into a run' (86; 481), and "drängte sich . . . in" 'jammed [himself] into' (88; 482). Although still clustering around the semantic poles marked off by *come* and *go*, motion verbs in Kafka thus encode richer representations of the *manner* in which participants' comings and goings unfold. To adapt Leonard Talmy's schema for the representation of motion events (*Cognitive* 25–69; cf. Talmy, "Semantics" and "Lexicalization"), whereas TS's conversational narrative builds detailed representations of the FACT of motion and the PATH along which it occurs, in Kafka's text readers are cued to represent a third component of motion events, MANNER, in an equally detailed way. Further research (and a larger sample size) is needed to confirm that, in literary narratives generally, writers furnish richer representations of the MANNER component of motion events than do conversational storytellers.[8]

Deictic Reference

Thus, although both literary and conversational narratives rely on shared principles for temporal ordering and spatial configuration, there are medium-specific constraints on the range of ways in which those principles can be used or implemented. Similar differences come into play vis-à-vis the use of deictic terms to attach storyworlds to particular contexts of interpretation. Those differences, however, trend in the opposite direction. In particular, in the case of spatial deictics—expressions such as *here* and *there*—conversational storytelling affords more options for anchoring texts in contexts than do literary narratives.

In designing narrative texts that will be read by interpreters separated in time and space from the contexts in which the stories are composed, literary writers have to rely on readers' basic capacity for spatial navigation and their general, stereotypic knowledge of how particular sectors of the world tend to be arranged—for example, the interior of apartments or movie theatres or classroom buildings. By contrast, conversational storytellers can use spatial deictics such as *here* and *there* in reference to a current spatiotemporal environment for talk. In other words, to help their interlocutors assign referents to such expressions, storytellers can prompt their interlocutors to draw analogies between the spatial configuration of the storyworld and that of the world in which the narrative is being told and interpreted. Hence, spoken narratives can cue story recipients to build a model of the overall spatial configuration of the storyworld by drawing not just on general "background knowledge" but also on information available in the present interactional context.[9]

Although TS's account does not contain any spatial deictics of this sort, another narrative in the corpus of supernatural tales from which TS's story is taken exemplifies the process in question. In this second conversational narrative LB is telling the interviewer, NSE, about an apparition of her dead brother.

LB: (a) And my ^brother . . . he got killed

(b) but anyway . . . I'm a tell you . . honey I seen him in the night

(c) sure as if it had just been in the daytime

NSE: (d) Yeah.

(e) Now my bedroom was . . windows is right ^there,

(f) two double windows.

(g) And I seen him when he come up ^standing

(h) just as pretty as I ever seen him in my LIFE

(i) a-standing there.

In this extract LB uses the spatial adverb *there* twice, in lines (e) and (i). Whereas the second instance refers to a storyworld-internal location, the token of *there* in line (e), which "sets up" the second occurrence, functions deictically. The first *there* is the verbal accompaniment to a gesture with which LB designates a place within the current context of interaction. More precisely, the first token of *there* serves to anchor a storyworld location to a location currently at hand; that is, the *there* in line (e) prompts LB's interlocutors to project a storyworld-external space onto a storyworld-internal space, and vice versa. The second instance of *there* in line (i) thus designates a kind of blended location, one straddling the storyworld and the world in which the story is being told and interpreted. Arguably, by superimposing mental representations associated with two discrete sets of spatio-temporal coordinates, the blend in question is richer than that achieved via spatial deictics in a literary narrative such as Kafka's. As is characteristic for literary narratives, "The Metamorphosis" prompts not a blending of coordinates but, rather, a deictic *shift* from the here and now orienting the act of interpretation to that orienting participants in the storyworld.[10]

In this essay, which focuses on elements of story logic in just two communicative media, I have managed to take only a few tentative steps toward a transmedial narratology. My chief aim has been to show that a principled study of the relations between spoken and written narrative cannot take place in the absence of a more general theory about the links between stories and their media. Attempting to extend the position I characterized earlier as synthesis, my account suggests that story logic can be thought of as a system of principles and parameters within which spoken (for example, conversational) and written (for example,, literary) narratives occupy different coordinates. The principles must be implemented, in some manner or another, for a text or a discourse to be located within the system at all—to be interpretable *as* a narrative. But the parameters for variable realization of the principles determine precisely what place within the system a particular narrative can be assigned. Thus, the story logic of a tale about shape-shifting told conversationally is bound by different constraints than those bearing on a literary tale such as Kafka's, even though the two narratives focus on similar experiences. Only barely initiated here, a project for future research is to determine just what sorts of constraints shape the communicative and representational properties of each storytelling medium, creating more or less untranslatable differences between texts with comparable content.

Appendix

This story was elicited during a sociolinguistic interview that occurred in the trailer home of PS, one of the participants in the interview and a twenty-two-year-old Anglo American female. The other participants included BA, the fieldworker, and TS, a twenty-four-year-old Cherokee female. The interview occurred on March 21, 1997, in Robbinsville, North Carolina. Robbinsville is located in Graham County, which lies in the mountainous extreme western portion of the state. For ease of reference the story has been divided into alphabetically labeled clauses. (The transcription actually features a *pair* of stories; the first focuses on the experiences of the narrator's cousin and provides an introduction or bridge to the analogous—but more meticulously recounted—experiences of TS's grandfather in the second narrative.)

TS: (a) And I've had a COUSIN . .
   (b) he was a GEORGE . .
   (c) um . . that shot an OWL . .
   (d) and it ricocheted straight off that owl
   (e) and it hit him and it killed him.
   (f) That meant that that was somebody . . .
   (g) that was in the owl.
      [
BA: (h) Are you SERIOUS?
TS: (i) They call them shape shifts
BA: (j) Uh huh . . uh huh.
TS: (k) And uh . . Grandpa told me this years ago
   (l) and he . . swears up and down he . . he's killed somebody.
   (m) And uh . . he uh . . when he was littler
   (n) he used to live in Cherokee
   (o) and there was two of them
   (p) and they went out . . .
   (q) and uh . . they was hunting for SQUIRRELS and stuff
   (r) And he saw one . . it was a pretty good-sized squirrel.

(s) He said it wasn't . . a little squirrel or nothing

(t) he noticed it was BIGGER.

BA: (u) Um hm.

TS: (v) They SHOT that squirrel.

(w) And . . they could . . when it fell

(x) he said it . . YELLED . .

(y) it screamed.

(z) And he said it from . . like from its head back on its back

(aa) it just had this . . you know the bullet just went . . right through=

                            [

BA: (bb)   Um hm.

TS: (cc) =and . . kind of scraped it open and stuff=

                    [

BA: (dd)   Um hm.

TS: (ee) =and he said that . . it YELLED going down

(ff) and they tried to find it

(gg) and they couldn't FIND that squirrel.

(hh) He said he was . . they were headed to some man's HOUSE

(ii) and he knows . . he knowed the names and everything

(jj) and he WENT to that house

(kk) and he said that MAN looked at THEM SO ^MEAN.

(ll) And he said that normally he doesn't do that=

                        [

BA: (mm)   Um hm.

TS: (nn) but he said he just looked at them . . so MEAN.

(oo) And he said that . . they left and everything

(pp) the other BOY had just went on

(qq) he said he come back and went around the house

(rr) and he sa . . he wanted to SEE . . .

(ss) what was going on

(tt) he said he looked and the man had rolled over

(uu) and he had . . blood down his back . .=

      [

BA: (vv)   Ohhhh.

TS: (ww) =and he said he was bleeding.

(xx) And he said that man died.

BA: (yy) I'll be ^darned.

     [

FSSC ts:(zz) And he said "I ^didn't mean to do that"

(aaa) he says "but I KNOWED that . . he said that . . was me."

(bbb) He said "We shot him."

BA: (ccc) /I'll be darned/

   [

TS: (ddd) And he said that was him . .
     (eee) and that's . . he was a SQUIRREL (laughs)
     (fff) And he said he'll never forget that . . you know
     (ggg) and he told us over and over about that story.

Transcription Conventions

(Adapted from Tannen, "What's"; and Ochs and others):

. . . represents a measurable pause, more than 0.1 seconds
. .   represents a slight break in timing
.   indicates sentence-final intonation
,   indicates clause-final intonation ("more to come")
Syllables with ˜ were spoken with heightened pitch
Syllables with ˄ were spoken with heightened loudness
Words and syllables transcribed with ALL CAPITALS were emphatically
       lengthened speech productions
[indicates overlap between different speakers' utterances
=   indicates an utterance continued across another speaker's overlap-
       ping utterance
/ /   enclose transcriptions that are not certain
( )   enclose nonverbal forms of expression, for example, laughter
(( )) enclose interpolated commentary

Notes

1. In this essay I use *conversational narrative* as a term more specific than *oral narrative*. Like *written narrative, oral narrative* in fact subsumes a variety of narrative modes. Hence, one of my guiding assumptions is that any study of the differences between narrative media must also take into account a broader system of distinguishing features *not* based strictly on medium—for instance, oral or spoken narrative ranges over relatively formal genres (such as formulaic epic poetry or recitations of traditional narratives) as well as relatively informal genres (such as conversational storytelling). Yet level of formality constitutes only one of the dimensions along which narrative genres (and subgenres) can be distinguished. Written narratives, for example, can be distinguished not only with respect to degree of formality (for example, news reports of a barroom brawl versus epic accounts of a heroic battle) but also with respect to degree of elaboration (jotted-down anecdotes and jokes versus full-fledged autobiographies and political satires); topic (travel narratives versus narratives of domestic life); target audience (a written narrative produced during a psychological experiment versus one embedded in a private journal entry); and so on. Thus, as used here, the terms *conversational*

narrative and *literary narrative* refer to instantiations of the text type "narrative," with a variety of factors other than medium accounting for differences between these instantiations.

2. For an investigation of some of the constraints at issue, see Genette's *Palimpsests*, especially the discussion of *transmodalization* in chap. 57 (277–82). There Genette distinguishes between *intermodal* and *intramodal* shifts as well as two subtypes of each—that is, "the shift from the narrative to the dramatic, or *dramatization,* and the reverse shift from the dramatic to the narrative, or *narrativization* . . . [along with] variations within the narrative mode and within the dramatic mode" (277–78). See also Jay David Bolter and Richard Grusin, *Remediation,* which surveys some general factors bearing on inter-adaptations of sign systems.

3. For a model positing a "categorical boundary" between everyday storytelling and literary narrative, instead of a scale connecting them, see Wolf-Dieter Stempel's study.

4. Research informing my discussion of TS's ghost story (and also, in the final section of this essay, LB's narrative) was supported by NSF Grant SBR-9616331.

5. I do not mean to give the impression that these two dimensions of story logic are wholly unrelated. Indeed, in what follows I will revert repeatedly to the ways in which the different spans of time allowed for the production and interpretation of conversational versus literary narratives—aspects, that is, of their situation in surrounding discourse—result in different distributions of preferred and dis-preferred types of narrative structure.

Further, in speaking of different spans of time and space separating the production and interpretation of written and spoken narratives, I am setting aside narratives *written* in something approximating real time in synchronized forms of electronic communication, for example, chatrooms or America Online's Instant Messenger. Even in these modes of communication, however, participants are still separated from one another in space—in all but a very few specialized circumstances.

6. Among other devices Kafka's frequent use of rhetorical questions indexes situations and events as internally focalized, marking them as the product of a reflector's efforts to perceive and interpret.

7. I have slightly modified the English translation of the first of the two German phrases quoted in this sentence

8. Preliminary support for this claim can be found in an ongoing project reported in Herman, "Corpus." The project involves an empirical study of the frequency of 20 motion verbs in a corpus of approximately 250,000 words consisting of 8 different narrative text types in two different media—that is, spoken and written discourse. With respect to medium, although the conversational narratives included in the corpus scored near the top on the measure of overall frequency of motion verbs, they scored low on the measure of how many different motion verbs were used. In turn, one can assume a positive correlation between the number of different motion verbs used and the detail with which the MANNER component of motion events is represented.

9. Here I may seem to be seconding M. A. K. Halliday's and Ruqaiya Hasan's distinction between *endophoric* and *exophoric* reference, or discourse-internal and discourse-external (that is, deictic) reference (31–37). In fact, however, I begin from the premise that all reference is in a certain sense endophoric. As Gillian Brown and George Yule have pointed out, mental representations always mediate between linguistic forms and interpretations of those forms, even when the forms in question are used as the equivalent of gestures pointing to features of an immediate context of interaction (190–222; cf. Emmott 211–12).

10. Although literary narratives does not allow for "blended" spatial deixis of this sort, narrative fictions told in the second person can in some cases create analogous effects by way of *person deixis*. More specifically, some instances of narrative *you* can create similar spatio-temporal blends by referring simultaneously (and ambiguously) to a narrator-protagonist and to a current recipient of the story, superimposing the spacetime coordinates of a storyworld-internal entity upon those of a storyworld-external entity, and vice versa.

References

Bamberg, Michael G. W., ed. "Special Issue: Oral Versions of Personal Experience: Three Decades of Narrative Analysis." *Journal of Narrative and Life History* 7 (1997): 1–415.

Barthes, Roland. "Introduction to the Structural Analysis of Narratives." *Image, Music, Text.* Trans. Stephen Heath. New York: Hill and Wang, 1977. 79–124.

Bolter, Jay David, and Richard Grusin. *Remediation: Understanding New Media.* Cambridge: MIT Press, 1999.

Borges, Jorge Luis. "The Garden of Forking Paths." Trans. Donald A. Yates. *Labyrinths: Selected Stories and Other Writings.* Ed. Donald A. Yates and James E. Irby. New York: New Directions, 1964. 19–29.

Brown, Gillian. *Speakers, Listeners and Communication: Explorations in Discourse Analysis.* Cambridge: Cambridge University Press, 1995.

Brown, Gillian, and George Yule. *Discourse Analysis.* Cambridge: Cambridge University Press, 1983.

Chafe, Wallace. *Discourse, Consciousness, and Time: The Flow and Displacement of Conscious Experience in Speaking and Writing.* Chicago: University of Chicago Press, 1994.

Chatman, Seymour. *Story and Discourse: Narrative Structure in Fiction and Film.* Ithaca NY: Cornell University Press, 1978.

———. "New Directions in Voice-Narrated Cinema." *Narratologies: New Perspectives on Narrative Analysis.* Ed. David Herman. Columbus: Ohio State University Press, 1999. 315–39.

Emmott, Catherine. *Narrative Comprehension: A Discourse Perspective.* Oxford: Oxford University Press, 1997.

Fludernik, Monika. "The Historical Present Tense Yet Again: Tense Switching and Narrative Dynamics in Oral and Quasi-Oral Storytelling." *text* 11.3 (1991): 365–97.

———. *Towards a "Natural" Narratology.* London: Routledge, 1996.

Frawley, William. *Linguistic Semantics.* Hillsdale NJ: Lawrence Erlbaum, 1992.

Garfinkel, Harold. 1967. *Studies in Ethnomethodology.* Englewood Cliffs NJ: Prentice-Hall.

Genette, Gérard. *Narrative Discourse: An Essay in Method.* Trans. Jane E. Lewin. Ithaca: Cornell University Press, 1980.

———. *Palimpsests: Literature in the Second Degree.* Trans. Channa Newman and Claude Doubinsky. Lincoln: University of Nebraska Press, 1997.

Goffman, Erving. *Forms of Talk.* Philadelphia: University of Pennsylvania Press, 1981.

Goodwin, Marjorie Harness. *He-Said-She-Said: Talk as Social Organization among Black Children.* Bloomington: Indiana University Press, 1990.

Halliday, M. A. K. *An Introduction to Functional Grammar.* 2d ed. London: Edward Arnold, 1994.

Halliday, M. A. K., and Ruqaiya Hasan. *Cohesion in English.* London: Longman, 1976.

Herman, David. "Towards a Socionarratology: New Ways of Analyzing Natural-language Narratives." *Narratologies: New Perspectives on Narrative Analysis.* Columbus: Ohio State University Press, 1999. 218–46.

———. "Corpus Linguistics and Narrative Analysis." Paper presented at the Modern Language Association Convention in Washington DC, December 2000.

———. "Sciences of the Text." *Postmodern Culture* 11.3 (2001): text-only version publicly available at <*http://www.iath.virginia.edu/pmc/text-only/issue.501/11.3herman.txt*>.

———. "Spatial Reference in Narrative Domains." *text* 21.4 (2001): 515–41.

———. *Story Logic: Problems and Possibilities of Narrative.* Lincoln: University of Nebraska Press, 2002.

———. "Story Logic in Conversational and Literary Narratives." *Narrative* 9.2 (2001): 130–37.

Kafka, Franz. "The Metamorphosis." Trans. N. N. Glatzer. *The Norton Anthology of Short Fiction.* Shorter 6th ed. Ed. R. V. Cassill and Richard Bausch. New York: W. W. Norton, 2000. 471–504.

———. "Die Verwandlung." *Gesammelte Schriften, Band I: Erzählungen und kleine Prosa.* 2d ed. Ed. Max Brod. New York: Schocken Books, 1946. 69–130.

Labov, William. "The Transformation of Experience in Narrative Syntax." *Language in the Inner City.* Philadelphia: University of Pennsylvania Press, 1972. 354–96.

Labov, William, and Joshua Waletzky. "Narrative Analysis: Oral Versions of Personal Experience." *Essays on Verbal and Visual Arts.* Ed. June Helm. Seattle: University of Washington Press, 1967. 12–44.

Landau, Barbara, and Ray Jackendoff. " 'What' and 'Where' in Spatial Language and Cognition." *Behavioral and Brain Sciences* 16 (1993): 217–65.

Lejeune, Philippe. *On Autobiography.* Ed. Paul John Eakin. Trans. Katherine M. Leary. Minneapolis: University of Minnesota Press, 1988.

Margolin, Uri. "Of What Is Past, Is Passing, or to Come: Temporality, Aspectuality, Modality, and the Nature of Narrative." *Narratologies: New Perspectives on Narrative Analysis.* Ed. David Herman. Columbus: Ohio State University Press, 1999. 142–66.

Ochs, Elinor, Carolyn Taylor, Dina Rudolph, and Ruth Smith. "Storytelling as Theory-Building Activity." *Discourse Processes* 15 (1992): 37–72.

Polanyi, Livia."Telling the Same Story Twice." *text* 1.4 (1981): 315–46.

———. "Literary Complexity in Everyday Storytelling." *Spoken and Written Language: Exploring Orality and Literacy.* Ed. Deborah Tannen. Norwood NJ: Ablex, 1982. 155–70.

Pratt, Mary Louise. *Toward a Speech Act Theory of Literary Discourse.* Bloomington: Indiana University Press, 1977.

Prince, Gerald. *A Grammar of Stories.* The Hague: Mouton, 1973.

———. "Aspects of a Grammar of Narrative." *Poetics Today* 1 (1980): 49–63.

———. *Narratology: The Form and Functioning of Narrative.* Berlin: Mouton, 1982.

———. "Narratology." *The Cambridge History of Literary Criticism.* Vol. 8. Ed. Raman Selden. Cambridge: Cambridge University Press, 1995. 110–30.

Propp, Vladimir. *Morphology of the Folktale.* 2d ed. Trans. Laurence Scott. Rev. Louis A. Wagner. Austin: University of Texas Press, 1968.

Rimmon-Kenan, Shlomith. *Narrative Fiction: Contemporary Poetics.* London: Methuen, 1983.

———. "How the Model Neglects the Medium: Linguistics, Language, and the Crisis of Narratology." *Journal of Narrative Technique* 19 (1989): 157–66.

Sacks, Harvey, Emanuel A. Schegloff, and Gail Jefferson. "A Simplest Systematics for the Organization of Turn-Taking for Conversation." *Language* 50 (1974): 696–735.

Schegloff, Emmanuel. " 'Narrative Analysis' Thirty Years Later." "Special Issue: Oral Versions of Personal Experience: Three Decades of Narrative Analysis." Ed. Michael G. W. Bamberg. *Journal of Narrative and Life History* 7 (1997): 87–106.

Smith, Barbara Herrnstein. "Narrative Versions, Narrative Theories." *On Narrative.* Ed. W. J. T. Mitchell. Chicago: University of Chicago Press, 1981. 209–32.

Stempel, Wolf-Dieter. "Everyday Narrative as a Prototype." *Poetics* 15 (1986): 203–16.

Talmy, Leonard. "Semantics and Syntax of Motion." *Syntax and Semantics,* vol. 4. Ed. John P. Kimball. New York: Academic Press, 1975. 181–238.

———. "Lexicalization Patterns: Semantic Structure in Lexical Forms." *Language*

Typology and Syntactic Description. Vol. 3. Ed. Timothy Shopen. Cambridge: Cambridge University Press, 1985. 57–149.

———. *Toward a Cognitive Semantics.* Vol. 2. Cambridge: MIT Press, 2000.

Tannen, Deborah. "Introduction." *Spoken and Written Language: Exploring Orality and Literacy.* Ed. Deborah Tannen. Norwood NJ: Ablex, 1982. xv–xvii.

———. "Oral and Literate Strategies in Spoken and Written Narratives." *Language* 58.1 (1982): 1–21.

———. "The Oral/Literate Continuum in Discourse." *Spoken and Written Language: Exploring Orality and Literacy.* Ed. Deborah Tannen. Norwood NJ: Ablex, 1982. 1–16.

———. "What's in a Frame? Surface Evidence for Underlying Expectations." *Framing in Discourse.* Ed. Deborah Tannen. Oxford: Oxford University Press, 1993. 14–56.

Thomas, D. M. *The White Hotel.* New York: Penguin, 1981.

Zubin, David A., and Lynne E. Hewitt. "The Deictic Center: A Theory of Deixis in Narrative." *Deixis in Narrative: A Cognitive Science Perspective.* Ed. Judith F. Duchan, Gail A. Bruder, and Lynne E. Hewitt. Hillsdale NJ: Lawrence Erlbaum, 1995. 129–55.

2

Frame and Boundary in the Phenomenology of Narrative

Katharine Young

Frames distinguish two ontological presentations of stories in conversation: stories as a realm of events transpiring in another space and time, which I call a "taleworld," and stories as a realm of discourse transpiring in the here and now, which I call a "storyrealm." Either of these realms is potentially available at any moment during storytelling. However, for any one participant in the storytelling event, only one will be apparent at a time. Attention shifts, whimsically or deliberately, from one realm to another. But frames inherent in the storytelling occasion also direct attention from one realm to another, so that realm shifts systematically over the course of the telling. This essay specifies the multiple frames of stories in ordinary conversation. These apparently ephemeral narratives turn out to be elaborately framed. Frames thus constitute and uncover the limits of narrative.

Frames

Gregory Bateson describes frames as metacommunication, that is, "communication about communication" (Bateson and Ruesch 209), or, in Ludwig Wittgenstein's phrase, the description-under-which an event is to be seen (198, 202, and elsewhere on "seeing-as"). An utterance, for instance, might be seen-as a story. Frames themselves are of two sorts, which Bateson distinguishes as "exchanged cues and propositions about (a) codification and (b) the relationship between the communicators" (Bateson and Ruesch 209). That is to say, on the one hand, that frames codify stories among other kind of events or that they codify kinds of stories and, on the other hand, that they invite or reveal an attitude toward the story, which illuminates the relationship between its tellers and hearers. Frames of the first sort set the realm status of an event; frames of the second sort set an attitude toward the events in that realm. For narrative events a passage of conversation can be framed in the first sense as a story and in the second sense as cruel, revealing, disingenuous, rude, clever, funny, sad, or the like. Gerald Prince has aptly named framings of the first sort "metanarrative signs," indications of what he calls the coding of discourse as narrative (115–27).

Framings of the second sort are akin to what William Labov and Joshua Waletzsky call "evaluative devices," about which they write: "The evaluation of a narrative is defined by us as that part of the narrative which reveals the attitude of the narrator towards the narrative by emphasizing the relative importance of some narrative units as compared to others" (37). Labov and Waletzsky attend only to the events the story is about; I am concerned with evaluations of the telling as well as of the tale. Thus, the telling might be comical though the events recounted in it were terrifying. Labov and Waletzsky's inattention to this difference confuses events with stories by failing to distinguish, as Erving Goffman puts it, "between the content of a current perception and the reality status we give to what is thus enclosed or bracketed within perception" (3).

The confusion between taleworld and storyrealm—between, that is to say, the events the story is about and their presentation in the form of a story—has been a problem in narrative analysis. The taleworld is a reality inhabited by persons for whom events unfold according to its ontological conventions. The storyrealm consists of tellings, writings, performances— that is, of recountings of or alludings to events understood to transpire in another realm. The status of one realm bears on but does not fix the status of the other.

Frames are metacommunications of two sorts about two sorts of event: they either set the realm status of or disclose an attitude toward either taleworlds or storyrealms. Story frames distinguish stories from other forms of discourse, such as explanations, quotations, descriptions, argumentation, commands, and so on, and from other sorts of narrative events, such as plays, games, mimes, films, or dreams; and they distinguish among such genres of narrative as myths, legends, folktales, fairy tales, tall tales, anecdotes, and personal experience narratives. Story evaluations characterize stories as good, in the sense of spicy, sharp, amusing, witty, wry, well-told, pertinent, or pointed, or as poorly told, pointless, malicious, maladroit, or boring. Frames of the events the stories are about distinguish between events in the realm of the ordinary, which might be thought of as real events, and events in other realms, which might be thought of as imaginary, such as the realms of the dead, of dreams or dramas, of science, the supernatural, or the extraterrestrial. Evaluations of events qualify them as disgusting or enchanting, romantic, adventurous, daunting, dreadful, or dreary. This inquiry therefore distinguishes among four narrative frames—frames and evaluations of the story and frames and evaluations of the events the story is about—and considers their bearing on making stories.

Boundaries

Information about differences, Bateson remarks, are stacked at the edges of events (unpublished lecture). Differences between realms are at issue at the moment of transition from the realm of conversation to the storyrealm and from the storyrealm back to the realm of conversation. It is for this reason that frames, indications of realm status, are characteristically positioned between realms, in the case of stories, between the event framed and the realm that event is framed for. Frames, therefore, do what might be called "edgework" for stories.

This characteristic positioning of frames on the edges of realms gives rise to the confusion between boundaries and frames, between, that is, the literal or physical frames that lie alongside contiguous realms and the conceptual differences they reify. Boundaries locate the literal or physical borders between realms; frames locate their conceptual limits. Events are bounded; realms are framed. Or, more precisely, events are framed as to their realm status. Boundaries occur at the same level of analysis as the events they bound: a picture frame is a material object among material objects; a story boundary consists of words among words. Setting a boundary implies a frame by separating, setting off, and tying together the events within the boundary. Maurice Natanson writes: "The act of framing, of literally surrounding a canvas with sides of wood or metal, is the astonishing sorcery of the art apprentice. To frame a picture is to separate a part of experience from its context . . . To *create*, then, is to separate, to exclude, to deny a whole by intending a fraction of that whole" (81). Defining a frame likewise implies a boundary by relating events to be conceived in one realm. But, though all boundaries are frames, not all frames are boundaries.

Frames communicate about the ontological status of other events, but they have a different ontological status from the events they communicate about. Unlike boundaries, frames do not count as parts of the event they frame. As Bateson points out: "The analogy of the picture frame is excessively concrete. The psychological concept which we are trying to define is neither physical nor logical. Rather, the actual physical frame is, we believe, added by human beings to physical pictures because human beings operate more easily in a universe in which some of their psychical characteristics are externalized" (*Steps* 188). Boundaries, then, are differences themselves, drawn along the edges of realms of events whose differences they thereby come to represent. Boundaries serve as cues, or, more closely, concrete metaphors, for conceptual frames.

Boundaries are positional: they enclose or, in the case of narrative, open and close an alternate realm of experience, the storyrealm. Frames, by contrast, are transfixual: they pervasively qualify the events they span and inform. Framing transforms into a story a possible first hearing of that speech act as conversation. The frame imputes an ontological status to events wherever they are located, rendering them constituents of a realm. By its nature a frame can lie within the same realm as the event it frames, in some other realm, or along the border between realms. So, story frames are either disclosures in the course of storytelling, remarks in the course of conversation, or bridges between realms.

The distribution of frames inside, outside, or alongside the realm of events they frame reflects their bidirectionality: frames are directed from one realm and toward another, for instance, from the realm of conversation and toward the storyrealm. The instructions they bear on how to see that other realm of events implies a realm to see the events from. Frames are frames-for tellers and hearers as well as frames-of events. As Goffman points out, "assumptions that cut an activity off from the external surround also mark the ways in which this activity is inevitably bound to the surrounding world" (249). Frames do not just enclose one realm; they specify a relationship between two. Hence, this inquiry extends attention from how stories are framed to what stories are framed for.

Edgework

In virtue of their frames, stories can be identified as a different order of event from the conversations in which they are enclaves. They constitute a storyrealm. The storyrealm, that region of narrative discourse within the realm of conversation, in turn directs attention to a third realm, the realm of the events the story is about, the taleworld. Events in the taleworld are framed by the story, itself framed by the conversation. A single event can in this way be multiply framed so that, as Goffman suggests, "it becomes convenient to think of each transformation as adding a *layer* or *lamination* to the activity. One can address two features of the activity. One is the innermost layering, wherein dramatic activity can be at play to engross the participant. The other is the outermost lamination, the *rim* of the frame, as

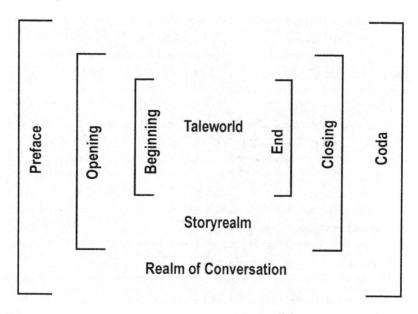

Figure 2.1. Frames that are boundaries.

it were, which tells us just what sort of status in the real world the activity has, whatever the complexity of the inner laminations" (82). This essay skips the structure of the innermost layer, the province of narrative analysis, to analyze relations among three realms: the taleworld, the storyrealm, and the realm of conversation, the province of what Goffman has dubbed "frame analysis." These realms are conceived to open out onto one another in such a way that the innermost or deepest realm is the taleworld, a realm of unfolding events and enacting characters. The next lamination, or level, is the storyrealm, the recounting of events and acts in narrative discourse. And the outermost or presented realm is the occasion of this recounting, the realm of conversation. Frames, on this analysis, orient one realm to another. (Fig. 2.1 shows these narrative laminations.)

The dynamics of the framing activity that takes place during oral storytelling will be investigated here in a corpus of stories told in the course of an evening's conversation at Algernon May's farm on Dartmoor in Devonshire, England, on Saturday, March 29, 1975. This is the first of many such conversations I tape-recorded with Algy during a year's fieldwork on Dartmoor. On this occasion the stories are exchanged among five participants: Algy, who is the main storyteller; his wife, Jean; his niece Marian, a neighboring farmer, Miles Fursdon; and myself. Algy is a sprightly, sturdy, sixty-seven-year-old countryman with bright white hair and blue eyes. His wife, Jean, spare and skittish, with a long, folded face, is a painter and breeder of thoroughbred horses and greyhounds. Marian, stocky, ruddy-faced, dark-haired, works on the farm with Algy and helps Jean with the breeding. Miles, tall, lean, and dark-haired, is a young farmer and old friend of the Mays. I am a folklorist and foreigner, to follow the Devon practice of so describing anybody from outside the shire.

We talk in the dark, stone-flagged kitchen of their nineteenth-century farmhouse in the company of three dogs, a cat, and a baby lamb, being warmed and nursed by the fire. In the background the television murmurs. The Mays know I am interested in stories, and after a half-hour's conversation Algy mentions a story connected with the main house on his farm, Rowbrook, just over the hill from the farmhouse in which we are gathered. Do I know it? At this point I get Algy's permission to start tape-recording and continue from this, the first story told on this occasion and the first I have ever heard Algy tell, to the last story he tells as Miles and I are leaving an hour and a half later. In that time span thirty-three stories have been exchanged. The corpus illustrates two functional types of frames, those that mark boundaries and those that do not.

Frames That Mark Boundaries

Frames that are boundaries lie between the realms they are frames-for and the realms they are frames-of. So positioned, they point in two directions: toward the realm they frame and toward the realm they frame that realm for.

Beginnings and Ends

Labov and Waletzsky claim it is characteristic of what they call "personal experience narratives" that the sequential organization of narrative clauses in the story matches the temporal organization of events in the taleworld. Thus, "narrative will be considered as one verbal technique for recapitulating experience, in particular, a technique of constructing narrative units which match the temporal sequence of that experience" (13). Sequence is a convention for time. As Roland Barthes writes, "Time does not belong to discourse proper, but to the referent" (252). In the taleworld one event happens after another; in the storyrealm one event follows from another. Construing consecutive events as causally related gives stories their consequentiality. "The sense of closure," Barbara Herrnstein Smith writes, "is a function of the perception of structure" (4). Consider the first story that evening about three brothers by the name of French, who once lived in the main house on Rowbrook Farm. (See appendix for transcription devices.)

		Three Brothers
Opening	Algy:	The point was
		. . .
Beginning		there were
		three
		teenage
		Frenches
		sleeping in one bed over here
		in the cottage—in the oldhouse.
		Thunderstorm?
End		Father French comes down
		finds the center one
		struck
		by lightning.
Closing		Three boys in one bed = center one killed.
Closing		Tchew.

In order to arrive at its end, the story of the three brothers opens up and spins out earlier events in such a way that they orient to the death of the middle brother. The story then moves from the beginning toward that end as its completion. The appearance of consequentiality in narrative is produced by counting the last event taken from the taleworld an end and then constructing the story backward to include whatever is necessary to account for it, thus arriving at the beginning. Beginnings do not so much imply ends as ends entail beginnings. "By reading the end in the beginning and the beginning in the end," writes Paul Ricoeur, "we learn also to read time itself backward, as the recapitulating of the initial conditions of a course of action in its terminal consequences" (180). Where the sequence of events starts and finishes in the taleworld becomes the beginning and end of the story. Taleworlds do not have beginnings and ends. They are realms experienced by their inhabitants not as beginning and ending but as ongoing. The story cuts out a portion of the taleworld to recount, but the taleworld extends beyond the boundaries set in it by the story. Other events are understood to have happened before and after, as well as at the same time as, those being recounted. Beginnings and ends are introduced into the taleworld by the storyrealm, thus rendering consequential what is merely consecutive. These boundaries set up by the story in the taleworld frame events in that world for the storyrealm. They constitute, that is, instructions that the events within the boundary are to be taken in a certain relation to one another. Framing events as stories invests them with the sense of an ending. Beginnings and ends are frames-of the taleworld and frames-for the storyrealm.

Openings and Closings

The stories, unlike their taleworlds, are enclaves in another realm, the realm of conversation. Story enclaves are a different order of discourse from the conversation that encloses them, namely, a representation of events not present to the occasion. They are also a different order of event from other events likewise enclosed in conversation. They are set off from the enclosing conversation by openings and closings, which mark the entries and exits between the storyrealm and the realm of conversation. Openings and closings can also distinguish a narrative event from other enclaves in conversation. A distinction must be made between beginnings and ends, on the one hand, and openings and closings, on the other. Beginnings and ends are the points where the events are about start and finish; openings and closings are the points where the stories start and finish. Beginnings and ends create boundaries in the taleworld; openings and closings constitute the boundaries of the storyrealm.

Characteristically, openings and closings neatly bracket beginnings and ends, as in "Three Brothers," in which the opening frame, directed to the storyrealm, is tucked in next to the beginning of the taleworld and in which the closing phrases—there are two—closely follow the end. Occasionally, however, the beginning of the taleworld is used to open the storyrealm, and the end closes both realms. For instance, after Algy finishes framing a story about a Canadian film crew trying to film ferrets catching rabbits, he opens his next story about his niece, Marian, shearing a sheep by moving straight into the taleworld to describe the film crew's intentions.

Ferreting and Sheepshearing

Evaluation	Algy:	I swear it's perfectly true.
Coda		We got a fiver for that.
		((*Chuckles*))
Opening		Then the other thing they wanted to film Marian
Beginning		shearing a sheep.

Miles's story, "Foxy and the Flywheel," is followed by an evaluation of the events in the taleworld. There is no separate frame to close the storyrealm.

Foxy and the Flywheel

End and Closing	Miles:	[and he was knocked flat]
Evaluation	Algy:	[Cor, he was lucky,] wasn't he

A result of this condensation of opening and beginning as well as end and closing frames is that the story is more slightly differentiated from the conversation in which it occurs. For instance, the activities of the Canadian film crew are carried over into the story of the sheepshearing. Layering openings along beginnings and closings along ends, on the other hand, would result in a density of frames at the edges of the story, these serving to set it off more sharply from conversation.

When openings and closings are formulaic, such as "Once upon a time" and "The end," not only do they mark a discontinuity in the order of discourse, but also, by convention, they specify the realm status of the enclave as fairy-tale-like. The openings and closings of conversational anecdotes are not usually formulaic in this traditional sense, and, although they do mark discontinuities in speaking, they do not necessarily specify the realm status of the events they bound. In the story of the three brothers the opening phrase, "The point was," alerts hearers that a story is about to commence in much the same way the formulaic opening "Once upon a time" does. The phrase is technically a restart, indicating that the storyteller is picking up where he left off doing preparatory work for the story before I interrupted him to ask if I could record him. The closing phrase, "Three boys in one bed, center one killed," draws attention to and reiterates the end of the story. The formulaic closing "The end," similarly positioned just after the end of a story, likewise draws attention to what has already happened, though without repeating it. "The end" is not itself the closing event in the taleworld, though it refers to it, but the closing utterance in the storyrealm. The phrase that follows this closing, "Tchew," appears to be a form of what Goffman has entitled "expression speech," that is, utterances that convey by rhythm or intonation the feeling of a prior remark without replicating its content (527). It is the sort of utterance adults often use with infants and animals. Here the sound "Tchew" catches the quality of lightning striking, thus reiterating the end of the story in another key. Repetition appears to create a closural effect both by creating a sense of saturation with the pattern repeated and by laying an evaluative emphasis on the element to be taken as the end of the story (Smith 42).[1] The effect is produced by doubling back over and thus reversing the flow of discourse.

Besides doing closure on the storyrealm, closings direct attention inward or backward to the taleworld and forward or outward to the realm of conversation. They can signal, on the one hand, that speakers have missed the ending in the taleworld, and they can signal, on the other hand, for hearers to resume the transition property of utterance completions, which have been suspended for storytelling.[2] These storyrealm closings have been deceptively classified by Labov as codas, though they do not fulfill his own criterion that codas follow from events in the taleworld (365–66).

Storyrealm closings orient hearers to the taleworld and to the realm of conversation while providing a transition between the two. During the course of Algy's story about Marian shearing the sheep, Miles interpolates the brief supportive utterances characteristic of hearers but no remark to indicate awareness of its end, though this is marked by Algy and Marian's laughter. So, Algy follows the laughter with a storyrealm closing to which Miles responds appropriately, both by his appreciative utterance and also by the fact of taking up his turn at talk.

Sheepshearing

	Algy:	But at the end of the shearing
		this— the camera was stopped for a second
		then this huge fleece that I'd got from the
		wool merchants (*Chuckles*)
		huge thing—
		Marian throws it out, you know, as you do after shearing
		but unfortunately the—
End		the old sheep had a green mark on it and this had
		bright red
		[(((*Laughs*))])
	Marian:	[(((*Laughs*))])
Closing	Algy:	That's the only thing about that.
	Miles:	Tsh.

If beginnings and ends frame the taleworld for the storyrealm, openings and closings frame the storyrealm for the realm of conversation. Both pairs of frames bound the story. This lodgment of beginnings and ends, as well as openings and closings, on the boundaries of the story enhances its discreteness from surrounding discourse.

Prefaces and Codas

Frames in the form of prefaces and codas also lie along the edges of the story enclave but on the side of conversation. So, whereas beginnings and ends lie just inside the taleworld and openings and closings just inside the storyrealm, prefaces and codas lie just outside both, in the realm of conversation. Beginnings and ends bound the taleworlds they frame, and openings and closings bound the storyrealms they frame. Prefaces and codas bound both realms off from the realm of conversation, creating an enclosure for these alternate realities within the realm of the ordinary. Although located within the realm of conversation, prefaces frame either the storyrealm or the taleworld, and codas frame the taleworld. All three pairs of frames can operate as boundaries between the realm of conversation and either the taleworld or the storyrealm, layering or laminating themselves along the rim of the story.

Prefaces are frames preceding the opening of the storyrealm or the beginning in the taleworld that announce a new speech event by saying, for instance, "I wanted to tell you something," and sometimes also announce the realm status of the speech event as a story, as in "I've got a great story for you," or the quality of the events the story is about, as in "The most dreadful thing happened." The preface not only sets up the prospective space into which the story can be inserted into the conversation; it also hooks it back onto the conversation by intimating that that story or those events are of particular pertinence to the hearer at that juncture in the conversation. This prefatory work is critical to the organization of storytelling in conversation because it ensures that the conversation will provide a place in which the story can be completed.

Conversation consists of what sociolinguists call "utterance turns," arrangements for participants to speak alternately. At the completion of a turn, other participants will feel expected or entitled to take their own turn at talk. Sentence ends signal utterance completions (Schegloff and Sacks 236). Thus, if a speech event is going to take more than one sentence to complete, speakers must arrange to take an extended turn or risk being interrupted on completion of the first sentence (Sacks, "On the Analyzability" 344–45). Because of the sequential relationship between ends and beginnings, even the briefest story takes more than a one-sentence utterance to tell. According to Sacks:

> The consequence of that is that one produces, for what turn out to be stories, what I'll call a *story preface*. It is an utterance that asks for the right to produce extended talk, and says that the talk will be interesting, as well as doing other things.
>
> At the completion of that "interest arouser" if you like, one stops, and it's the business of others to indicate that it's okay, and maybe also that they're interested, or it's not okay, or they're not interested. If one looks at stories one finds that prefaces of this sort are present. (1992, 226)

Algy May prefaces his story of Snailly house in the following way.

Snailly House

Preface	Algy:	But you don't know probably any of the old stories
		about
		Dolly's Cott, Snailly House.

		Do you.
	Kat:	About what?

Preface	Algy:	[Never heard] anything about Snailly House.
	Kat:	[Snailly House?]
	Algy:	Yes.
		It's a—it's in the forest now but there used to be a house up there

Ticket	Kat.:	No, I didn't know that.
Beginning	Algy:	Two old women lived in it

Conversation moves from the preface to the beginning of the story in the taleworld, "Two old women lived in it," as soon as the storyteller receives an appropriate response to his request in the form of what Goffman calls a "ticket" to take an extended turn at talk, in this instance, "No, I didn't know that." Prefacing can be done neatly in three utterance turns—preface, ticket, opening—and would have been so done here if I had not been puzzled by the referents to two no longer existing houses, "Dolly's Cottage" and "Snailly House." The preface, "But you don't know probably any of the old stories about Dolly's Cott, Snailly House. Do you," would neatly have been followed by "No, I don't," thus arriving at the beginning on the third turn. If a second speaker requests a story, the work of prefacing can be accomplished in two utterance turns, that request serving as both preface and ticket. This happens when Algy's wife, Jean, asks him to tell the story of Michael, the carthorse.

Michael and the Hag

Preface and	Jean:	Tell them about um mm Harold Bluett
Ticket		darling, in Cornwall
		and uh
		[and Michael] the horse
	Algy:	[Yes]
	Jean:	(They'd like to know.)
Opening	Algy:	This is true.
Beginning		There was a great big carthorse in Cornwall got out on the common.

Prefaces can be addressed to either the taleworld or the storyrealm, arousing interest in either the events or the story. Contrast the preface to "Foxy's Cremation" with the preface to "Foxy's Surplice, the Bentley, and the Deerstalker." The preface to "Foxy's Cremation" introduces Foxy, the eccentric parson who will appear in the taleworld.

Foxy's Cremation

Preface	Algy:	But in more recent times—Miles will remember Foxy—
Ticket	Miles:	Yeah.
	Algy:	Do you?
Ticket	Miles:	Yeah.
Abstract	Algy:	Well, he—you know, took seventeen tries to get a—
		to be a
		parson

The preface to "Foxy's Surplice, the Bentley, and the Deerstalker" directs attention, instead, to the quality of the story, an attribute of the storyrealm.

Foxy's Surplice, the Bentley, and the Deerstalker

Preface	Miles:	Now I think the best— one of the best stories about Foxy is that he used to do the service at Princetown and he used to=
Ticket	Algy:	Umhm.

The use of what sociolinguists call laminator verbs, such as *think, tell, know, hear, say, dream,* and so on, can orient to the realm status of the story as a dream, a thought, a hearing, a saying, or a knowing, whether the preface orients to the taleworld or the storyrealm (Goffman 510). Appropriate tickets can be exceedingly slight, serving merely to return the floor to the storyteller in the awareness that he is embarking on an extended turn at talk.

Since prefaces arrange to suspend the transition property of sentence completions during storytelling, a difficulty can arise when the story ends and turn-taking is supposed to be resumed. Ends are not always so clearly consequent on beginnings that they are evident to hearers. The end can be reinforced or its lack remedied by closings in the storyrealm, which draw attention to the closure of the events in the taleworld. Even these may be insufficient to reinstate turn-taking. Despite, or in the absence of, such framing devices, hearers sometimes overlook or fail to display appreciation of the end of a story by taking up their turn. In such an instance storytellers can alert hearers that the story has ended with what Labov calls a coda. "Codas close off the sequence of complicating actions and indicate that none of the events that followed were important to the narrative" (365–66). A nice parity is evident between prefaces and codas: one opens up a realm the other closes down, both working from the conversational side. These conversational frames thus parallel the edgework of openings and closings on stories and of beginnings and ends on events.

An elegant alternative to dependence on such closing frames is to build into the preface information about how to monitor the story for its end. According to Sacks, "It turns out that among the jobs of the story preface is that of giving information about what it will take for the story to be over. And there's an obvious rationality to putting information about what it will take for it to be over, right at the beginning so that people can watch from there on in to see when it will be over" (1992, 228). Thus, the preface to "Bill Hamlyn and the Cable Spool" instructs hearers to monitor the story for its similarity to the story that preceded it.

Bill Hamlyn and the Cable Spool

Preface	Algy:	But then you see Hamlyn
		the contractor
		told us a very similar story

Prefaces can take the form of what Labov calls "abstracts," consisting "of one or two clauses summarizing the whole story" (363). In this instance they do not necessarily elicit tickets but only offer instructions about how to monitor the story for its end. Abstracts as prefaces are not to be understood as part of the story nor even as a replica of it in miniature but as a metacommunication, or frame, about how to listen to it (Labov 364; Labov and Fanshel 106). Algy's abstract for the story of Marian shearing sheep instructs hearers to watch for the sheepshearing as its end.

Sheepshearing

Preface as Abstract	Algy:	Then the other thing they wanted to do was to film Marian shearing a sheep
		This is in October so I said, "Oh, likely."
	Miles:	Tsa.
	Algy:	Anyhow.
Beginning		Went down to Buckfastleigh and
		got two very big Scottish fleeces.

Prefaces to invite stories from other participants quite characteristically take the form of abstracts, as in Algy's preface to Marian's story of Foxy and the cartwheel, thus indicating at once which story is being elicited and providing a ticket to tell it.

Foxy and the Cartwheel

Preface Ticket	Algy:	Tell them about—Marian, tell them about putting the mm—
		pushing the cartwheel down Meltor 'cause
		that was
		[really Foxy]

	Marian:	[Yes.]
	Algy:	[started that again.]
	Marian:	[When—when he was um]
		vicar at Leusden, he thought he'd— he'd

Codas consist of frames following the end of the events in the tale-world that are designed to link that realm of events to the conversation. They relate the taleworld to the conversation by interposing, between the story's completion and the resumption of conversation, events sequential but not consequential to the story. Thus, Labov and Waletzsky note, "all codas are separated from the resolution by temporal juncture" (40). Labov argues, "Codas have the property of bridging the gap between the moment of time at the end of the narrative proper and the present. They bring the narrator and the listener back to the point at which they entered the narrative" (366). Such codas take the form of residues, aftermaths, traces, in the present of the events recounted in the story. Marian and Algy's codas to the story of Foxy and the cartwheel exemplify this.

Foxy and the Cartwheel

Coda	Marian:	You can still see the old—old um
Coda	Algy:	[You can, down the] wood now, yeah.
	Marian:	[remnants down—]
		down in the wood.

The continuing presence of these artifacts ties the setting of the present conversation to the past realm of events. Their persistence in everyday life, of which the conversation is an aspect, appears to authenticate the story, to attest to its relevance.

Both codas and closings succeed and reiterate the end of the story, codas from within the taleworld and closings from within the storyrealm, but their relationship to the realm of conversation for which they effect these closures is quite different. The storyrealm is an enclave in the realm of conversation, one speech event within another, whereas the taleworld is a separate reality. For this reason, while codas construct continuities between disparate realms, closings discriminate contiguous realms. The boundaries of stories provide junctures for the insertion of information about ontological differences in the form of frames. (Fig. 2.2 shows the relation between the realms these frames are located in and the realms to which they direct attention.)

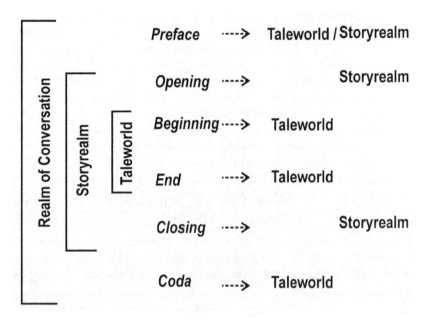

Figure 2.2. The bidirectionality of frames that are boundaries.

Frames That Are Not Boundaries

Frames that are not, or not necessarily, boundaries bear on the events in a realm but do not mark the edges of that realm of events. They are conceptual but not positional markers.

Orientations

Orientations provide information deemed necessary in order to understand what is transpiring in the taleworld. For instance, Algy tells a story about a narrow escape, which he begins with a geographical orientation.

		Algy and the Flywheel
Orientation	Algy:	Jean and I were going up a narrow lane in Cornwall
Coda		and we saw a very white-faced chap looking at us
		"Cor, thank God you're well."
		I said, "What's the matter."
		He says, "The bloody flywheel's come off."
		And he's pointing to the top of the hill.
	Miles:	((*Chuckles*))

	Beginning	Algy:	And apparently it had come down so fast it had
			jumped over this
			low lane
		Miles:	Tcha.
		Algy:	Yeah.
			End missed us
		Miles:	Tss.
		Algy:	and gone into the—
			well, miles away
			((*Chuckles*))

If Algy had not placed himself and Jean in the lane, it would not have been clear that, in jumping over it, the flywheel had narrowly missed them. (In this telling Algy has used the coda, which actually happened after the misadventure, as an abstract to rouse interest in it beforehand.) Algy has already oriented his hearers to the machines in question before he begins the story.

Algy and the Flywheel

	Algy:	But Miles
		years ago
Orientation		there used to be threshing engines—
	Miles:	Yeah.
Orientation	Algy:	steam engines.
	Miles:	Yeah.
Orientation	Algy:	Bloody good flywheels on them.
Beginning		and we were going up—
Orientation		Jean and I were going up a narrow lane.

Placed as they are around the beginning of the story, orientations provide background for the sequence of events. In this position, as Labov and Waltzky suggest, they "serve to orient the listener in respect to *person, place, time, and behavioral situation.* We will therefore refer to this structural feature as an *orientation section*" (32). Orienting remarks, explanations, or clarifications, however, can also be inserted into or after the story, directed to those particular aspects of it they are designed to elucidate. After this story it occurs to Algy that his hearers may not all realize that Cornish lanes are cut so deeply into the land by ancient usage that a projectile skimming along at ground level could fly cross the lane and miss the people in it, so he adds another orientation later on in the conversation, one that expands on the orientation to Cornwall inside the story. This orientation does not lie along a boundary of the story.

Algy and the Flywheel

Orientation	Algy:	These
		real old sunken
		Cornish lanes, you know, way down it was.
		And of course it just bounced [over]
	Miles:	[Right over] the top.

Orientations can thus transfix a narrow span of events within the sequence. In such a case, Sacks notices, "what we have is a sense of context being employed by the teller, which involved fitting to the story, in carefully located places, information that will permit the appreciation of what was transpiring, information which involves events that are not in the story sequence at that point" (1992, 274).

Orientations disclose the taleworld as a realm of events not given to hearers in the way events in everyday life are given, one for which some metaphysical constants or background expectancies are therefore made explicit.[3] The orientation to the following story locates the events in the geographical space the conversationalists are inhabiting, Rowbrook Farm, but two hundred years earlier.

Jan Coo

	Algy:	And Jan Coo.
Orientation		The one for here—Rowbrook.
Orientation		He was a boy about seventeen hundred and something
		looked after the cattle—only a youngster.

Attention to ontological differences qualifies orientations as frames even when they do not provide information about how to regard the taleworld as a whole. Sacks argues that the strategic use of such information keeps hearers attentive to how to interpret what is being told (1992, 274). Algy orients to the story of Marian shearing the sheep in this way.

Sheepshearing

Abstract	Algy:	Then the other thing they wanted to do was to film Marian shearing a sheep.
Orientation		This is October so I said, "Oh likely."
	Miles:	Tsa.
	Algy:	Anyhow.
Beginning		Went down to Buckfastleigh and got two very big Scottish fleeces.

Sheep's wool thickens over the winter and molts over the summer, so shearing is usually done in the spring when the wool is thickest. An October fleece is a fairly motley proposition. Miles, himself a farmer, is therefore alerted by the orientation to monitor Algy's story for a solution to the problem of shearing a sheep in October.

Orientations can be offered by other participants who so display just the kind of attention to the story that orientations by the teller are intended to evoke. Thus, orientations can not only insert information for understanding the story but also insert it at just the point where its teller or other participants figure the information will be needed. Its nicety of placement, then, indicates when it is to be used (Sacks 1992, 274). Orientations can be understood to introduce hearers into the realm codas then draw them out of, codas and orientations consisting of aspects or fragments of the tale-world set out in discourse beforehand and afterward. Orientations afford an angle of entry into the taleworld, an angle that can disclose a perspective on that realm. In setting up the background against which events unfold, they set up the angle from which hearers apprehend those events. They point from the context of the story to the context of the events, from hearers to hearings, and tie them together. Orientations are frames-of the taleworld and frames-for the realm of conversation, in the storyrealm, thus neatly interrelating three realms of experience. (Fig. 2.3 shows the interrelation of these three realms.)

Evaluations

The frames examined so far bear on the realm status of events and stories, on whether a piece of discourse is a story, what sort of story it is, and what sort of realm the events it recounts come from. These frames determine orders of event, in contrast to evaluations, which disclose perspectives on, attitudes toward, or feelings about events of that order. Labov describes evaluation as, "the means used by the narrator to indicate the point of the narrative, its *raison d'être:* why it was told and what the narrator was getting at" (366). He writes as if all these means were roughly equivalent. In fact, a nice distinction between the point of the story and the point of telling the story is involved. The first pertains to the relationship between events in the story and the second to the relationship between the story and the occasion on which it is told.

Evaluations of events argue that the taleworld is reportable in its own right. Labov claims, "To identify the evaluative portion of a narrative, it is necessary to know why this narrative—or any narrative—is felt to be tellable; in other words, why the events of the narrative are reportable" (370). For Labov whatever warrants their telling is inherent in the events. That quality is brought forward or marked by evaluations. The evaluations give differential weight to some events over others, especially to last events,

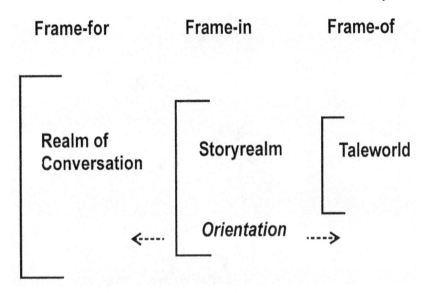

Figure 2.3. Orientations.

so that events do not just succeed one another; they come to a point. In that way the point comes to have a bearing on the end. Yet, contrary to Labov's argument, points are not ends; they are recognitions of the relation of ends to beginnings as cogent. If the end can be seen as the final element in the narrative sequence, then the point bears on the relationship among narrative elements or between these elements and nonnarrative aspects of the story. For instance, the evaluation after "Foxy's Cremation," "he'd only just got his bloody ticket," meaning he had just recently qualified as a vicar, links the orientation before the story to its end. That Foxy had some difficulty becoming a vicar makes his vagaries especially culpable. One might expect the freshly invested to take exceptional care as, according to succeeding evaluations, the bishop did.

Foxy's Cremation

Preface	Algy:	But in more recent times—Miles will remember Foxy.
	Miles:	Yeah.
	Algy:	Do you?
	Miles:	Yeah.
Orientation	Algy:	Well he—you know took seventeen tries to get a— to be a parson.

	Miles:	Did he?
	Algy:	Yeah and he
		got in on the eighteenth try.
	Miles:	Hmhmn.
Beginning	Algy:	And one of his first jobs was to—
		to—(ha) them in um t—Oh what do you call it.
	Miles:	((*Chuckles*))
	Algy:	Cremation.
		He had to chuck the ashes about, you see,
		and he went in to—
		into
Evaluation		Huccaby Church and the bloody wind blew
End		chucked them up and they went out over the wall, you see
	All:	[((*Laughter*))]
End	Algy:	[Out over the moor.]
		(Ha)
		Well that—that—
	Miles:	((*Chuckles*))
Evaluation	Algy:	he'd only just got his bloody ticket.
	All:	((*Chuckle*))
	Kat:	[Why did it—]
Evaluation	Algy:	[The bishop] was hopping mad.
Evaluation		He said, "How dare you, Foxy."

The relationships between Foxy's recent qualification, his first job, and its outcome are forms of intention, in this case of intention foiled or flawed, or what is more commonly described in literary theory as motivation.

The point appears to be lodged in the arrangement of events, whether it was inserted there by nature or teller. But it is evident that this story could be extracted from its evaluative nest and told on another occasion with a different point, one about sacred ground or botched jobs or cremations, say, rather than eccentric vicars. Clearly, though the point is introduced into the story, a narrative sequence without one would fail in some sense to be a story. The question is, does the story make the point or the point make the story? Events, it turns out, are not just tellable but tellable on occasions. It is their relevance to this occasion that is the point of the telling. Point is what connects stories to occasions. The point of the telling can, though it need not, invest itself in the point of the story. To miss the point of the story, then, is either not to see how the events in it connect together or not to see how they are relevant to the occasion of their telling.

Taleworld evaluations not only can evaluate events in the taleworld but also can specify the ontological status of those events for the occasion on which they are told. They can frame the events, that is, as real or fictitious. In this set of stories, evaluations of events as true is one of the warrants for telling them. The truth of the tale enhances the authoritativeness of the teller. In this vein Algy accompanies several of his stories with truth evaluations. They are positioned before and after as well as during the story.

Snailly House

Evaluation   Algy: This is absolutely true.

Haymen's Pit

Evaluation   Algy: That is true and you won't beat that anywhere. 'Tis absolutely gospel.

The Plough and the Hare

Evaluation   Algy: That's supposed to be true.

Ferreting

Evaluation   Algy: I swear it's perfectly true.

Truth evaluations identify the taleworld as one of those realms we call realities; the events in that realm are understood to have or have had an instantiation in space and time. Such realities are quite diverse and can include the realms of the past, present, and future; of the supernatural or the scientific; of dreams, play, and work, the realm of the dead and the realm of the gods. Evaluations of taleworlds as fictive identify them as imaginary realms, fairyland, perhaps, or hell, the supernatural or the extraterrestrial. Clearly, understandings about which realms are fictitious depend on differences in individual or cultural cosmologies. Legends, for instance, depict extraordinary events located in the geography of the ordinary. Whether that realm is seen as continuous or discontinuous with the world of everyday life depends on the skepticism or belief of teller and hearer. The displacement of extraordinary events to distant times or exotic places enhances their credibility. Thus, Algy's orientation to the legend of Jan Coo and the "piskies" (the proper Devon pronunciation of *pixies*) locates it in a realm that existed in "seventeen hundred and something," permitting hearers to perceive as unremarkable otherwise extraordinary events. He goes on to discriminate the story, "The Devil at Tavistock Inn," from the story that follows it.

The School Inspector

Evaluation   Algy: this is nothing to do with
fiction at all, this is true.

This suggests that the story of the devil, along with the stories about the piskies, the prince, and the gypsies, which also preceded it, can be regarded as fictions. The frame thus operates backward as well as forward. [4]

The evaluations observed so far are part of the storyrealm, comments by tellers and hearers on events transpiring in the taleworld. Evaluations are also located in the taleworld in the form of remarks or other indications by characters in that realm of an attitude toward the events. These "embedded evaluations," to use Labov's term, are quoted by tellers or hearers to disclose that attitude (372). Embedded evaluations characteristically transpire in the course of the events they evaluate. Here, however, Algy appends an observer's comment about the vicar's driving to give emphasis to his account of Foxy's surplice, the Bentley, and the deerstalker. Both observer and his observation are located inside the taleworld. The first embedded evaluation comments on the events and the second on their storyability.

Foxy's Surplice, the Bentley, and the Deerstalker

Algy: Somebody stopped me once,
"Who was that."
Foxy absolutely tearing down Dartmeet Hill.

Kat: (*Laughs*)

Algy: Deer—deerstalker.
Bentley with a bloody great leather strap over its bonnet and everything (*Laughs*).

Kat: (*Laughs*)

Algy: Brooom

All: ((*Laughs*))

Algy: Who on earth's that.

Embedded taleworld evaluation   "Oh," I said, "that's our local vicar," "My God," he said, "what extraordinary people you've got on" (*Laughs*).

All: ((*Chuckle*))

Algy: ((*Chuckles*))

Embedded storyrealm evaluation   "Um," he said, that's an extraordinary story."

As is evident from this transcription, laughing often counts as taking a turn, not just as a way of punctuating discourse. The utterance has the weight of evaluation. What is being evaluated can be inferred only by proximity, since laughter, unlike talk, does not carry linguistic directions to its referent.

Labov elucidates evaluations exclusively in terms of how they frame the events stories are about. They are discovered here to frame stories as well as events. Storyrealm evaluations lodge value in the story. Hearers' attention is warranted by the quality of the story, not of the events. In this vein Algy follows his story of the three brothers with the evaluation.

Three Brothers

Evaluation   Algy: Fantastic story, isn't it,
                            to strike one in a bed of three.

Harvey Sacks describes evaluations as instructions for hearing-as (1992, 286). Such instructions can be designed to preclude interactional awkwardness by disclosing the attitude of teller or hearer to the story being told. For instance, Jean May follows her husband's story about an idiot boy with an evaluation.

Not 'Xactly and the Cigarette

Evaluation   Jean: It was awfully embarrassing 'cause he always
                            used to stare at you.
                            And the horses as well.

This suggests that the rest of us hear the story as an account of embarrassment rather than, for instance, as mocking an idiot. Evaluations also provide information on how a story has been heard. Jean follows Algy's account of her own misadventures in a runaway cart with the evaluation, "Poor pony," suggesting an interpretation of the episode on her part as unfortunate, rather than courageous, and modestly circumventing compliments on her adventurousness.

Evaluations are thus of two sorts: evaluations of the taleworld and evaluations of the storyrealm. Evaluations of the taleworld focus on the events the story is about, rendering the story a transparency to another realm. Evaluations of the storyrealm focus on the telling, constituting the story a realm in its own right. Evaluations of the taleworld can be located inside that realm, in the storyrealm, or in the realm of conversation. Evaluations of the storyrealm are located in the storyrealm or the realm of conversation. (Fig. 2.4 shows the extension of evaluations from the outermost realm of conversation to the innermost taleworld.) Although they can modulate the internal dramatic structure of the story, evaluations have more general uses, which can be characterized as the management of attitudes, interest, and attention on storytelling occasions.

Narrative Laminations

The clustering of frames along the boundaries of the story accomplishes a kind of edgework for storytelling. The clustered frames give a neat parity to

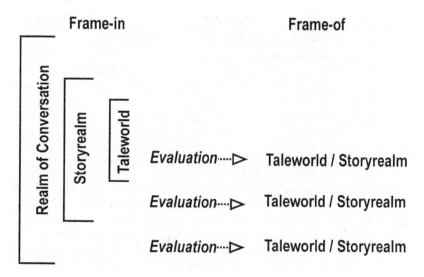

Figure 2.4. Evaluations.

the literal and ontological limits of the storyrealm. The edgework under-taken on the storytelling occasion also lends an appearance of circumscrip-tion to the events in the taleworld. The storyrealm invests boundaries in the taleworld so that events there take on some of its discretion. In reality story boundaries are not neatly fitted down over the taleworld. Events in that realm have their own boundaries. Access to the taleworld, however, is only through the story. So, apprehensions of the realm status of events in the taleworld are not contingent on experience of that realm but on its framework on the storytelling occasion.

Attention to the storyrealm implies an awareness of the occasion as performance, in the sense that it involves an undertaking by storytellers and hearers to tell and hear stories. Attention to the taleworld draws awareness away from the performer and the performance toward the events recounted by them. This tilts the occasion toward the conversational rather than the performative. During actual storytellings attention to the taleworld or storyrealm shifts over the course of a single telling and over the course of the storytelling occasion as a whole. Roughly speaking, the fixed frames move hearers from the storyrealm into the taleworld and out again; movable frames create a shifting emphasis on one or the other of those narrative realms. (Fig. 2.5 shows the shift from storyrealm to taleworld and back again.)

Algy May's story, "The Plough and the Hare," is bracketed by storyrealm

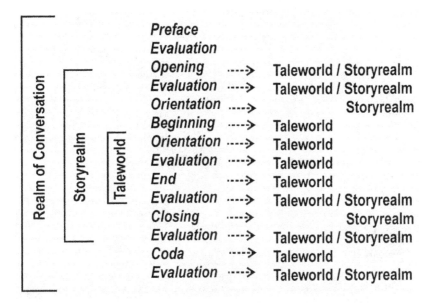

Figure 2.5. Distribution of frames over storytelling.

evaluations. Attention inside the brackets is turned to the taleworld. The story opens with an evaluation, which directs attention to its status as a story: "I like the story of . . . ." This modulates directly into orientations to the taleworld in which events transpire. Attention to the taleworld is sustained by the coda and evaluations that follow. Frames in subsequent conversation redirect attention to the storyrealm by reiterating evaluations of it. These are succeeded by evaluations and frames of the taleworld, which result in the content of that realm, hares, being taken up as a topic of conversation.

The Plough and the Hare

Storyrealm evaluation	Algy:	Now I like the story of when his old man was about seventy
Opening taleworld		
Orientation taleworld		driving a tractor,
Beginning	Miles:	((*Clears throat*))
Taleworld orientation	Algy:	ploughing [with Bill]
	Jean:	[( )]
Taleworld	Algy:	three furrow plough

orientation		You know up and down the bloody field
		and a hare got up
		and the old man
		forgot his furrow and he
	All:	[(((*Laughter*))]
Taleworld	Algy:	[took it out]
coda		right—and gave chase,
		[(((*Laughter*))]
	All:	[(((*Laugh*))]
Taleworld	Algy:	[Had a lovely furrow]
coda		right—
		following this
		hare all across the field.
	All:	[(((*Laughter*))]
Taleworld		
evaluation	Algy:	That's supposed to be true.
		. . . . .
Storyrealm	Algy:	You like that one, don't you.
evaluation	Miles:	Hm.
Storyrealm		
evaluation	Algy:	It's lovely, too.
Taleworld		Lovely straight furrows up and down
Orientation		(*Laughs*)
		You know, they'd been doing it for—all day.
Taleworld		
closing		Buuullwoom.
Evaluation	All:	[(((*Laughter*))]
	Algy:	[Away he went in top.]
Taleworld	Jean:	There's something magic about the hare,
coda		perhaps that's why—perhaps it cast a spell
		on him.

Not all kinds of frames turn up in each story, and only four kinds seem to be essential to it: a preface, the beginning and end, and some sort of evaluation. These essential frames can all be directed to the taleworld but not all to the storyrealm. A frame that can be directed to either realm is of particular interest in determining realm shift. Prefaces, for instance, can be directed to either the taleworld or the storyrealm, thus focusing attention at the outset on one or the other. Evaluations, turning up over the course of the storytelling, can closely control attention to both realms. The preface to the already discussed "Three Brothers," about practicing a story more than once, is directed toward the storyrealm, and the story's opening sustains that direction. Frames then move into the taleworld until the closing,

"Tchew," which draws away from the events to comment on them and is in that respect evaluative. Codas and evaluations by tellers and hearers, clustered together after the story, juggle attention between realms—on the one hand, earthing the events in surrounding geography and contemporary society and, on the other, charging the story with preternatural intimations. Let me quote again the story with a fuller conversational context.

Three Brothers

Storyrealm Preface	Algy:	Because you want to go through these things more than once before you start.
	Kat:	You don't— [What a silly idea.]
	Jean:	[Want some more sherry,] dear? Have some more sherry.
	Miles:	Not for me, thank you.
Storyrealm opening	Algy:	[The point was,]
	Jean:	[Would you?] ((*To Katharine*))
Taleworld	Algy:	there were beginning three teenage Frenchs sleeping in one bed over here
Taleworld orientation		in the cottage—in the old house. Thunderstorm? Father French comes down,
Taleworld		Finds the center one end struck by lightning.
Storyrealm closing		Three boys in one bed, center one killed.
Storyrealm closing		
Closing evaluation		Tchew and . . . .
Taleworld coda		One of the surivors was Herman French's father—
	Kat:	Excuse me.
	Algy:	Yeah?
Taleworld coda		other one's his uncle.
Taleworld	Miles:	Old Fred—

Coda		Fred, wasn't it.
	Algy:	Fred,
		yeah.
Taleworld coda	Miles:	Used to be up al Ollsbrim.
	Algy:	[Fred was the]
coda		
	Miles:	[Or just at the end of the] war—
	Algy:	other survivor.
		Hm.
	Kat:	That's OK. ((To Jean, refusing more sherry))
Storyrealm evaluation	Algy:	[Fantastic story, wasn't it.]
Taleworld evaluation	Marian:	[He was always a bit—]
		[He was always a bit] funny actually, wasn't he.
Storyrealm evaluation	Kat:	[It was extraordinary.]
Taleworld evaluation	Algy:	Course he was funny ((*to Marian*)).
		Damn funny.
Taleworld evaluation	Kat:	That's very strange.
		. . . .
Storyrealm evaluation	Algy:	Fantastic story, isn't it.
Taleworld abstract as storyrealm closing		to strike one in a bed of three.

The unusual layers of storyrealm frames in "Three Brothers" appears to be due to Algy's use of that story to initiate storytelling on this occasion. Part of its business is to establish the storyrealm as a speech event. Once this is accomplished, interest turns to the taleworld, which is evidenced by the framing of a later story, "Foxy's Cremation," with the taleworld frame, "But in more recent times—Miles will remember Foxy." The framework of this storytelling occasion thus replicates the framework of a single story, moving from the storyrealm into the taleworld and out again. The choice of frames can strategically manage attention to the taleworld or the storyrealm over the course of the storytelling occasion as well as during the telling of one story, thus adjudicating the ontological status of the narrative occasion in which tellers and hearers are participating.

Stories are enclaves in conversation, events in one realm bounded by another (Schutz 256). The boundaries between these realms constitute natural junctures for presenting information about their differences in the form of frames. Positioning frames between realms reiterates their dual orientation: frames are oriented to the realm of events they frame and to the realm they frame those events for. The frames-of a story, for instance, can be frames-for conversation. Frames are never of and for the same realm. They can be located in the realm they frame, as beginnings and ends are located in the taleworld or openings and closings in the storyrealm and evaluations in each. They can be located in the realm they are frames-for, as prefaces and codas, along with some evaluations, are located in the realm of conversation. Or they can be located in a third realm, as orientations to the taleworld and for the realm of conversation are located in the storyrealm. Frames do not just enclose, or open and close, one realm; they specify a relationship between two.

The taleworld, the storyrealm, the realm of conversation, indeed any realm, can engage perceivers as an ongoing reality. Framing has the capacity to detach it from that engagement; to render it subject to reflections, attitudes, evaluations; to draw perceivers back and lodge them in another realm, a realm from which they have a particular perspective on the realm they had hitherto inhabited as real. That perspective is here called a frame. In that sense frames separate as well as connect realms. To specify such perspectives on stories is to produce a phenomenology of narrative.

Transcription Devices

    Line ends   Pauses

From Tedlock

>=	Absence of obligatory pause
/	One-turn pause
Capital letters	Start of utterance
.	Down intonation at end of utterance
?	Up intonation at end of utterance
—	Correction phenomena
( )	Doubtful hearings
(Hehe)	Laughter
(( ))	Editorial comments
[ ]	Simultaneous speech, overlaps with the string similarly marked on the next or previous line

Adapted by Malcah Yeager from Shenkein

Up-down-middle   intonation

Devised by Malcah Yeager (pers. comm., 1980)

. . .   Elisions
English spelling   English speaking

Notes

1. Consider also the structuralist view that redundancy draws out pattern (Bateson, *Steps to an Ecology* 130).

2. To finish a conversation, the transition property of utterance completions must be suspended, usually by what Schegloff and Sacks call a "terminal exchange"—for instance, a leave-taking sequence (256). To reinstantiate conversations after telling a story, the transition property of utterance completions, which has been suspended for storytelling, must be reinstituted.

3. Maurice Natanson notes that Alfred Schutz used to refer to birth, death, and aging as "metaphysical constants" (198). Harold Garfinkel uses the term *background expectancies* (21).

4. Goffman describes prospective and retrospective framing (543–45).

References

Barthes, Roland. "An Introduction to the Structural Analysis of Narrative." *New Literary History* 6 (1974–75): 237–72.

Bateson, Gregory, and Juergen Ruesch. *Communication: The Social Matrix of Psychiatry.* New York: Norton, 1968.

———. *Steps to an Ecology of the Mind.* New York: Ballantine Books, 1972.

———. Unpublished lecture. University of Pennsylvania, 1973.

Garfinkel, Harold. "Background Expectancies." *Rules and Meanings.* Ed. Mary Douglas. Middlesex, Eng.: Penguin, 1977.

Goffman, Erving. *Frame Analysis.* New York: Harper and Row, 1974.

Labov, William. *Language in the Inner City.* Philadelphia: University of Pennsylvania Press, 1972.

Labov, William, and David Fanshel. *Therapeutic Discourse.* New York: Academic Press, 1977.

Labov, William, and Joshua Waletzky. "Narrative Analysis: Oral Versions of Personal Experience." *Essays on the Verbal and Visual Arts.* Ed. June Helm. Seattle: University of Washington Press, 1967.

Natanson, Maurice. *Literature, Philosophy and the Social Sciences.* The Hague: Martinus Nijhoff, 1962.

———. *The Journeying Self: A Study in Philosophy and Social Role.* MA: Addison Wesley, 1970.

Prince, Gerald. *Narratology.* The Hague: Mouton, 1982.

Ricoeur, Paul. "Narrative Time." *Critical Inquiry* 7.1 (1980): 169–90.

Sacks, Harvey. "On the Analyzability of Stories Told by Children." *Directions in Sociolinguistics: The Ethnography of Communication.* Ed. John Gumperz and Dell Hymes. New York: Holt, Rinehart and Winston, 1972. 325–45.

———. *Lectures on Conversation.* Vols. 1–2. Ed. Gail Jefferson. Oxford, Eng.: Blackwell, 1992.

Schegloff, Emmanuel, and Harvey Sacks. "Openings and Closings." *Ethnomethodology.* Ed. Roy Turner. Middlesex, Eng.: Penguin, 1974.

Schutz, Alfred. *On Phenomenology and Social Relations.* Ed. Helmut Wagner. Chicago: University of Chicago Press, 1973.

Shenkein, James, ed. *Studies in the Organization of Conversations Interaction.* New York: Academic Press, 1978.

Smith, Barbara Herrnstein. *On the Margins of Discourse.* Chicago: University of Chicago Press, 1978.

Tedlock, Dennis. *Finding the Center: Narrative Poetry of the Zuni Indians.* Lincoln: University of Nebraska Press, 1978.

Wittgenstein, Ludwig. *Philosophical Investigations.* Trans. G. E. M. Anscombe. New York: Macmillan, 1953.

3

Gesture and the Poetics of Prose

Justine Cassell and David McNeill

He who has eyes to see and ears to hear may convince himself that no mortal can hide a secret. If his lips are silent, he chatters with his fingertips; betrayal oozes out of his every pore. Therefore, the task of making conscious the most hidden recesses of the mind can be solved quite readily.–Sigmund Freud

Spontaneous storytelling is structured on multiple levels, with subtle shifts of time and space, perspective, distance between narrator and narrated, and integration of the sequential with the nonsequential—these are its fundamental dimensions. Much of this structuring, however, is carried out on the nonverbal level and is observed most clearly in the concurrent gestures of the narrator. In this essay we will explore the integration of the verbal with the nonverbal in the real-time structuring of narrative.

When we add gesture to speech, we shed light on many of the same questions that have been the focus of attention by narratologists. By adding the dimension of the hands in motion, we clarify the issue of perspective, in that speakers, by the way they use their hands, may convey where they are standing vis-à-vis the event they are narrating. We elucidate the issue of point of view as well, because the speaker's hands can make clear whether the narrator is internal or external to the narrated event and whether the speaker exists in the narrative as the speaker herself or as a narratively induced observer. In many ways gestures add another dimension to the narrative—certain aspects of events may only be conveyed in gesture and not in speech, or vice versa, or different aspects may be conveyed in each medium giving us a more complete view of the speaker's conception of the event. From one gesture to the next, depicted imagery is partially the same and is partially changed: the changes become highlighted oppositions in the structure of the narrative, strengthening our understanding of the parallels and repetitions that make up the poetics of prose.

Narrative language is thus not a two-dimensional affair with only intersecting syntagmatic and paradigmatic axes: it has a full, rounded 3D structure, one dimension of which is imagistic (both visual and kinesic and either holistic or analytic). Many of the parameters of the basic structure of literary art are conveyed in gesture in spontaneous storytelling.

Our essay aims to demonstrate this point but rests on certain premises that we had best state at the outset.

1. Narration has many properties that remain unchanged regardless of the genre. Thus, we can use storytelling from a cartoon "stimulus" but treat our conclusions as having wider generalizability. The discussion here is based on a decade-long study of the gestures that spontaneously occur during videotaped narrations by children and adults who have been shown a film or cartoon and are given the job of recounting the story to a listener.

2. Storytelling is a social activity. To be a narrator is to fulfill a recognizable social role with attendant expectations and responsibilities. There really is, and must be, a listener, since this also is an essential role in the storytelling "script."

3. Spontaneous synchronized gestures are a part of the narrative communicative apparatus as much as speech is. We are not referring here to the sorts of gestures that replace speech (known as "emblems"): the thumb-and-index-finger ring gesture that signals "okay" or the "thumbs up" gesture; or the kinds of gestures that occur in the absence of speech, for example, "word-finding gestures" made when a speaker is engaging in a word search; nor are we concerned with what might be called "propositional gestures" (Hinrichs and Polanyi), such as the use of the hands to measure a particular space while the speaker says, "It was this big." Rather, we are interested in gestures falling into four major categories (to be described in this essay) that the speaker makes, usually unwittingly, along with the verbal description of the events of a story.

4. Gestures are partial evidence for the shape of a speaker's underlying linguistic processes, in this case joining the narrator's speech to give a more complete picture of the narrative event.

Gestures of the type we describe occur only with speech and are closely linked to speech in meaning, function, and time, yet such gestures are fundamentally different from speech as expressions of meaning and pragmatic function. This difference of gestures from speech is a crucial fact that we exploit.

One might suppose that the spoken word provides the most accurate and perfect view of the events taking place at the moment of speaking. Evidence from gestures synchronized with speech reveals, however, that this is not so, that there is something more. Gestures are not merely a translation of speech into a kinesic medium. The two channels differ in fundamental ways. Speech has standards of well-formedness, is linear-segmented and combinatoric, has duality of patterning, has recurrent forms that are stable in different contexts, and is socially ratified. Gestures of the kind we will describe are the opposite on every one of these dimensions. They are not specifically organized into a socialized code. They do not constitute a separate "gesture language." They lack duality of patterning, standards of form, a lexicon, and rules of combination. Yet these gestures are symbols produced along with speech and supportive of its meaning and function. Expanding our observational net thus to include speech and synchronized gesture offers us two coordinated but distinct views of the same underlying processes of thinking-speaking-communicating. This is the essential point of our approach. It is not that gestures are uninfluenced by conventions but that the conventions that influence the kind of gestures we study are the conventions of social life in general, not specific gesture conventions. Thus, we set a conventionalized system of linguistic code elements side by side with a gestural performance that is not specifically conventionalized: this is our justification for seriously studying gesture. If language is a window into the mind, we find that it is not the only one; gesture is a second window, or, better, a second eye, and gesture and language together provide something like binocular vision and a new dimension of seeing.

Spontaneous gestures accompany many types of speech events (Rime 1983), but here we will, quite naturally, only discuss their occurrence during narrating, in which it is the case that a representation of events must be conveyed to a listener and in which the imposition of coherence of some sort—of a superordinate structure—is presumed to help the narrator construct a story and the listener to understand it.

Competent storytelling depends upon a complex interaction of cultural knowledge, cognitive representation, and linguistic skills. We use *story-telling* or *narrating* to refer to the entire set of events that make up the conveying of a story by one person to another. Each of these events is grist for the storytelling mill and may be referred to by the storyteller. That is, stories generally refer to what may be called "emplotted events":

incidents or occurrences that follow one another in a real or fictive world (for example, a character climbs up a drainpipe to reach an upper story). In addition to emplotted events, however, the stories we are concerned with also commonly contain references to the event of observing the visual text, or cartoon story ("It was a Sylvester and Tweetie cartoon" or "It was an old movie, a very bad print"), and/or to the event of the storytelling ("I'm going to tell you about a cartoon I just saw"). Reference to these "metanarrative events" often acts to indicate junctures between the parts of a story. Narrative structure is provided on the verbal and the nonverbal levels but is often more apparent on the nonverbal level (with English speakers, at any rate). Before we discuss how gesture plays a role specifically in narrative, however, let us lay out, first of all, what we mean by narrative structure and, then, what we mean by gesture.

Narratology: Stories Have Structure

The most straightforward definition of *narrative,* such as "the representation of a real or fictitious world in events or in actions which are realized through human agents in the course of a stretch of time and in a specific space" (Kloepfer 116), already presupposes a series of semiotic structures that interlock to form the textuality of a narrative. That is, events, human agents, a stretch of time, and a specific space all presuppose a macrostructure from which those elements are chosen and in which their role in the narration is specified as well as a discourse in which those roles are spelled out. This is the meaning of Jakobson's well-known statement that "the poetic function projects the principle of equivalence from the axis of selection onto the axis of combination" (358). The represented events, agents, times, and places are selected from "paradigms" of possible such structures, in order to be combined in the "syntagme" of discourse. No choice is innocent: all that takes place on the linear axis of the narrative produced in real time draws from and also participates in a larger atemporal, alinear organization that we may call simply "narrative structure." In addition, the notion of representation presupposes structure at the level of the represented (what the text refers to) and structure at the level of the representation (discourse structure). Narratology, although it often deals with individual texts, more often addresses the structure of texts or kinds of texts. And, indeed, in this essay we do not wish to stop with a definition of narrative such as that given earlier but intend to expand it in just the direction of the dimensions of underlying structure.

We'll start, however, with the dimensions listed by Kloepfer. We will depend here on a fairly pre-theoretical model of narrative that is simply composed of: (1) the features of some "real" world; and (2) their instantiation in some narrative discourse. That is, the four aspects of each event of the narrative (action, person, time, space) are present in the world and instantiated in the actual discourse. Both the "world" and the discourse have their own constituent structure. The world of narrative may be conceived of as a set of interlocking participation frameworks, in which actors participate in a given act. One participation framework is the telling of a story, and the actors are a narrator and his or her listener. Another framework is the world of the story in which, for example, a man jealously watches his wife through the slats of window blinds. The units of the participation framework are represented events, each of which is composed of actions realized by (human) agents over a stretch of time and situated in a specific space. This part of the model represents the "seemingly adirectional, atemporal, 'structural' aspect" of poetic organization—in this instance, narrative. The units of the actual discourse are clauses, the "seemingly directional, temporal 'functional' aspect . . . accomplishing the semiotic work" (Silverstein 196). In a clause each dimension of the narrative unit is represented by one or more grammatical choices. The parameters of the event or action may be marked by the verbal morphology (choice of an accomplishment or state *aktionsarten* in a verb, for example); the human agent may be marked by person on the verb and by pronouns and full-referring expressions, for example; time may be marked by verbal inflections and temporal adverbial phrases, such as "earlier that day"; and space may be marked by deictic and nondeictic locatives, such as "right here." Each choice made in the narrative framework thus is instantiated in the representing discourse by way of the speech and, as we will see, the gesture as well. For the moment we will concentrate on the speech and will discuss gestural manifestations of narrative structure in the next section.

The participation frameworks and their ensuing instantiation in discourse occur at three narrative levels: the narrative level proper, the metanarrative level, and the paranarrative level. Each of these levels concerns a different set of events that constitute the narrative act, and consequently each level specifies a different value for the parameters of action, person, time, and space.

The narrator of the stories that we study (stories told to a friend about a cartoon or movie just seen) does not fill the role of narrator throughout the storytelling process. The "narrator" is at first a viewer, face to face with a television screen on which is displayed a "visual text"—the representation in images of a particular story about Tweetie Bird and Sylvester or a murderer loose in London. After serving as the (somewhat) passive recipient of a narration, the roles are reversed, and the recipient then becomes provider of a narration, telling the story to someone who has never seen the cartoon or movie. Each role entails a situational frame, or participation framework that organizes spatial and temporal configurations of speakers and hearers and experienced sequences of events. The sequence of events that constitutes the story proper is only one of a number of sequences of events that make up the narrative. The sort of storytelling that concerns us is composed of five "event lines" (Cassell and McNeill), or "stretches of time," that make up the three narrative levels.

1. First there is the event sequence of the story: plot time (Chatman, *Story and Discourse*) or time of fiction (Genette, *Figures III*). In the cartoon Sylvester climbing up the pipe to his window is preceded by the two simultaneous events of Sylvester looking at Tweetie through binoculars and Tweetie looking at Sylvester through binoculars.

2. This story is made available by way of a visual text, which is the cartoon. In the cartoon the event of Sylvester climbing up the pipe is preceded by that of Tweetie looking through binoculars, which is preceded by Sylvester looking through binoculars. The story could be transmitted by any one of a number of media, in any one of a number of forms.

3. The viewing of the cartoon also has its own temporal sequence of actions: first the person watches a flickering screen and then sees Sylvester with binoculars in his paws.

4. The person watching the cartoon forms a representation of the visual text that is more or less transparent with respect to the sequence of events depicted in the visual text. A description of each of the actions performed by all of the actors in their original temporal order is maximally transparent, while flashbacks, or summaries such as that expressed by "There's some looking through binoculars that goes on," are less transparent.

5. Finally, there is the sequence of recounting the cartoon to a listener: the interpersonal narrative. At this point the viewer becomes a speaker and may say, "First I'll tell you who the characters are, and then I'll start the story for real."

These narrative event lines are important because all of them may equally well form the subject of the narrative that the listener hears. That is, not only the events of Sylvester chasing Tweetie Bird and then not catching him are conveyed in a narrative, but also the event of watching the cartoon and then describing it are described to the interlocutor. The event sequence of the story (1) is the narrative level of the discourse. The visual text (2), viewing (3), and representation (4) form the metanarrative level of the discourse—the part of the narrative that is about narrating. The interpersonal narrative (5) is what we are referring to as the paranarrative level of the discourse: the part of the story in which the narrator steps out and speaks in his or her own voice to the listener.

Given this, it is not enough to say that the order of the story follows the order of events, unless we specify which narrative events are being referred to and which level of the discourse (narrative, metanarrative, paranarrative) is doing the referring. Order, and the other phenomena that narratologists commonly take as objects of study (among them duration, frequency, mode, and voice [Genette, *Figures III*]) have always been difficult to isolate in the stream of discourse. In speech there is rarely a clear-cut distinction between reference to Sylvester's actions and reference to the narrator's own actions. The same linguistic devices serve. In gesture, however, distinctions are drawn between these two levels of the narrative. Likewise, distinctions are drawn between the point of view of the narrator and that of the characters. In what follows we will show how gesture, taken in conjunction with narrative speech, can elucidate these narrative phenomena in the text and in the theory.

Typology of Gestures

When people talk, they can be seen making spontaneous movements called gestures. These are usually movements of the hands and arms (although occasionally the rest of the body participates, especially so with child speakers), and they are closely synchronized with the flow of speech.

While many schemes have been proposed for categorizing gestures (for example, Freedman; Ekman and Friesen; and Kendon, "Some Relationships" and "Gesticulation and Speech"), we find that the following semiotic classification—a method that takes into account the relation of gesture forms to meaning and function—best reveals the gestural contribution to narrative discourse. We list here four major types of gesture recognized in this scheme (see McNeill and Levy) and provide examples of each. The four types are iconic, metaphoric, beat, and (abstract) deictics.

Iconics

Iconic gestures bear a close formal relationship to the semantic content of speech. That is, in their form and manner of execution they exhibit

Figure 3.1. A holistic iconic gesture with "and she dashes out of the house.".

aspects of the action or events described by the accompanying narrative discourse. Iconic gestures can be holistic or analytic. An example of the former comes from a speaker describing a character from a comic book story (fig. 3.1). As the speaker described a character leaving, saying, "And she dashes out of the house," his right hand pulled back to form a fist and then shot forward with the palm outstretched and facing down. This speaker's hand represents all of the character's body, with the arm representing the path of his movement. The gesture is holistic in that the entire character is represented as an undifferentiated whole. An example of the latter comes from the same speaker recounting another incident in the comic book story (fig. 3.2).

The narrator described a scene in which one of the characters bends a tree back to the ground by saying, "And he bends it way back" (cf. Marslen-Wilson, Levy, and Tyler, for further analysis of this narrative). As he described this event, his right hand rose upward and appeared to grip something and pull it back toward himself. In this case the speaker's hand represented the hand of the character he described. The relationship between the gesture and referent is part-part. Iconic gestures thus reveal not only speakers' memory image of an event but also their point of view toward it—whether they are participating as a character or observing the actions of another.

Metaphorics
Such gestures are like iconics in that they are representational. The pictorial content of a metaphoric gesture, however, corresponds to an abstract idea,

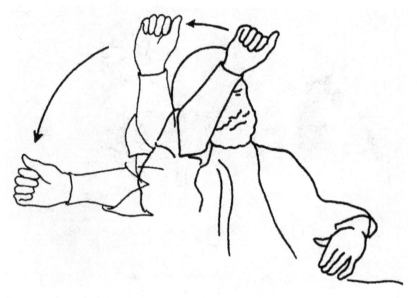

Figure 3.2. An analytic iconic gesture with "and he bends it way back."

not to a concrete object or event. A metaphoric gesture displays the vehicle of a metaphor (Richards), such as using the two hands to depict a scale of judgment when saying the verb *decide*. A wide variety of different kinds of metaphoric gestures appears during narrative discourse in which space, shape, and movement all take on metaphoric value. One specific type of metaphoric gesture that plays an important role in the framing of the narration is the "conduit" metaphoric (named after a similar linguistic metaphor [see Reddy; Lakoff and Johnson]). Some verbal examples of the metaphor, which represents information as a substance to be transferred, are "Never load a sentence with more thought than it can carry" or "This passage conveys a feeling of excitement" (from Reddy 288, 313), but in narrative discourse the conduit metaphor often appears only in gesture form. Conduit metaphoric gestures most often have the appearance of a cupped hand that seems to contain the narrative and offer it to the listener. An example is a speaker stating that he has just seen a cartoon and is about to recount it to the listener (fig. 3.3).

The speaker creates and supports with his two cupped hands an "object" that is metaphorically the cartoon and his upcoming narration. Gesture thus complements speech, adding its own metaphoric image of the narrative event.

Figure 3.3. A conduit metaphoric gesture with "it was a Sylvester and Tweetie cartoon."

Beats

Of all the gestures, beats are the most insignificant looking, but appearances are deceptive, for beats are among the most revealing of gestures for uncovering the speaker's construction of the narrative discourse. In performing beats, the hand moves with the rhythmical pulsations of speech, often achieving downward or outward strokes along with the stress peaks of the accompanying speech. Unlike iconics and metaphorics, beats tend to have the same form regardless of the content (McNeill and Levy). The typical

Figure 3.4. A beat gesture with "whenever she looks at him, he tries to make monkey noises."

beat is a simple flick of the hand or fingers up and down or back and forth; the movement is short and quick (fig. 3.4).

The semiotic value of a beat lies in the fact that it indexes the word or phrase it accompanies as being significant not purely for its semantic content but also for its discourse-pragmatic content. The beat is particularly sensitive to the momentary indexing of the larger discourse structure or narrative situation as a whole. Examples are marking the introduction of new characters, summarizing the action, introducing new scenery, and so on. Thus, beats may accompany information that does not advance the plot. With beats these events on the meta-level of discourse can be inserted

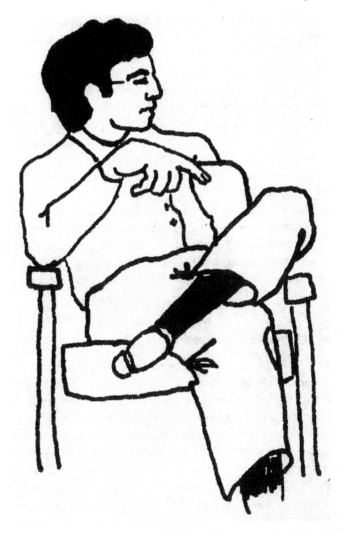

Figure 3.5. An abstract pointing gesture with "where did you come from before?" (speaker on the *left*).

into the narrative, signaling the fact that they depart from the chain of events that constitute the plot line.

Abstract Pointing

Deictic gestures, or points, have the obvious function of indicating objects around the narrator, but they also play a part in narrations in which there is nothing objectively present to point at. Although the gesture space may look empty, to the speaker it is filled with discourse entities. Deictic gestures establish in space the participants of a narrative and the participant events. An example of the former is a speaker who said, "The artist and Alice are walking by," pointing first to his right and then straight in front of him, before making an iconic gesture for walking by. An example of the latter comes from a speaker who asked his interlocutor, "Where did you come from before?" and accompanied that with a point vaguely to one side (fig. 3.5). The specific kind of abstract pointing, to be discussed later, often occurs at the beginning of new narrative episodes and scenes, in which it is the dominant gesture. In this context pointing may mark the establishment of a new focus space (Grosz).

In narrations of cartoon stories about three-quarters of all clauses are accompanied by gestures of one kind or another; of these about 40 percent are iconic, 40 percent are beats, and the remaining 10 percent are divided between deictic and metaphoric gestures. In narrating films, the proportions of metaphoric and deictic gestures increase at the expense of iconic gestures (statistics from McNeill and Levy; and McNeill).

Function of Gestures in Narratology

Different kinds of gesture appear depending on where in the narratological structure the speaker is operating at any given time. The major associations of gestures and narratological structures are summarized in figure 3.6. The chart shows the gesture situation reached by traversing the different combinations of narratological features. Note that there are missing combinations, for example, there are no iconics and no perspectives at the metanarrative or paranarrative levels. There are, however, different voices throughout the chart: a character, an observer, the narrator as a narratively created role or the narrator as herself in the experimental situation. Thus, the different gesture occurrences are genuinely distinctive additions to the narrative structure, and, by tracking them, along with speech, we can uncover the narrative structure exactly as it is being unfolded in real time.

In this section we will discuss the relationship between speech and gesture in narrative and the function that gesture may serve as a part of the narrative process. We will concentrate on how gesture marks the various elements of a story: that is, how gesture participates in the depiction of action, person, space, and time; and also how gesture participates in the processes or articulations of the discourse—that is, the role of gesture in narrative phenomena such as voice, perspective, and order that take a given set of abstract story components and realize them in a particular way, into

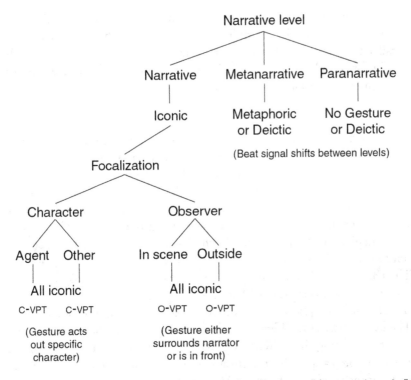

Figure 3.6. Gestures and narratological structures (c-vpt refers to "character viewpoint"; o-vpt refers to "observer viewpoint").

a particular story. We pursue this program as part of an effort to investigate the interactive aspects of narrative—the process of narrating. Attention has been paid to the linguistic devices that "allow the linguist to recognize how the narrator gradually comes to materialize his verbalization plan, how the cognitive story is organized linguistically" (Gülich and Quasthoff 175), but little attention has until now been paid to the gestural devices that achieve these ends.

Narrative Story Level

The narrative level is not an undifferentiated progression of descriptive clauses. It presents events, real or fictive, in a text order that is taken by the listener to be the same as the order of world events, but within this general iconic sequence variations of distance between events and the narrator can and do appear. Gestures have their part to play in this enrichment of the narrative line. Iconic gestures are the chief accompaniments of the narrative level, but they change depending on narrative voice and perspective and the distances implied by the different options within these parameters. In parallel, the grammatical form of speech also changes, and we see in speech itself a further illustration of iconicity, since multiple clauses are used to depict narrative distance, as is gesture.

Voice

Voice—who is narrating at the moment—is inferred from the form and space of the iconic gesture. We infer the character as the voice when the depiction is dispersed over the narrator's body in the appropriate way: the narrator's hand plays the part of a character's hand, her body the part of this character's body, and so on. The gesture enacts the character, and we infer that this character is the one who is narrating at the moment. Conversely, if the depiction is concentrated in the hand, the character being shown only as a whole in the hand, the voice is that of an observer/narrator. The narrator's body is an onlooker, and the voice is this onlooker, possibly the "omniscient observer" of fiction theory (Brooks and Warren) or the narrator herself replicating her earlier role of onlooker at the video screen. The use of space also differs for these voices, and this provides another clue to differentiating them. With the character voice the space envelops the narrator—it is a space for the enactment of the character and includes the locus of the speaker at its center. With an observer's voice, in contrast, the narrative space is localized in front of the narrator—as if it were an imaginary stage or screen—and in this space the narrator moves the relatively undifferentiated figures.

The following example illustrates both the observer and character voices. The extract begins with the observer voice (fig. 3.7), shifts to the character then back to the observer, and ends with the character once more. The voices shift back and forth in this manner, but the shifting is not, we will later show, random (o-vpt, or observer viewpoint, is the observer voice; c-vpt, or character viewpoint, is the character voice).

1. he tries going [up the inside of the drainpipe and][1] o-vpt *iconic* showing blob rising up.
2. Tweetie bird runs and gets a bowling ball
3. [and drops it down the drainpipe] c-vpt *iconic* showing Tweetie shoving bowling ball down.
4. [and . . . as he's coming up and the] o-vpt *iconic* with the right hand for a blob rising up while the left hand for the bowling ball is floating motionlessly in the upper periphery.
5. [bowling ball's coming down] o-vpt *iconic* with the left hand for the bowling

Figure 3.7. An observer viewpoint iconic gesture with "he tries going up the inside of the drainpipe."

ball coming down, while the right hand for the character floats in the lower periphery.

6. [he swallows it] O-VPT *iconic* with the left hand (bowling ball) passing inside the space formed by opening the right hand (character's mouth).

7. [and he comes out the bottom of the drainpipe] O-VPT *iconic* in which both hands place round ball into own stomach.

8. [and he's got this big bowling ball inside him] C-VPT in which both hands place round ball into own stomach.

The narrator began with O-VPT, shifted immediately to C-VPT, reverted to O-VPT again, and ended with another C-VPT. In terms of distance the narrator was at first remote from the fictive world, then inside it, then remote, and finally inside again. These are not random wobblings but apparently motivated movements to and from the narrative line to encode the degree of centrality of the event at each moment. C-VPT and near distance appeared exactly with events that are the causes and effects in the chain leading to the grand finale of the episode: the character ending up with a bowling ball inside him; this is the effect. The cause was the other character dropping the bowling ball down the pipe. These two events were narrated in close-up, as it were, with C-VPT gestures. The rest of the events are relatively peripheral, supporting this chain but not directly causes and effects (the character entering the pipe, the ball and the character at opposite ends of the pipe, and the ball entering the character are all secondary to the main causal chain), and they were marked with O-VPT gestures and far distance. All gestures are iconic, and all clauses are narrative level, but events and clauses are not equal in terms of their importance for advancing the story line, and this difference in centrality motivates changes of distance, depicted in the gesture voices of the narrative.

Statistical confirmation of this distinction between the character and observer viewpoints is contained in table 3.1, which is based on an analysis of three cartoon narrations by Church and others. Working from story grammar categories, Church and her colleagues classified story events as "central" or "peripheral": *central* meant (1) initiation of goal actions; (2) main goal actions; and (3) outcomes of goal actions; while *peripheral* meant (4) setting statements; (5) subordinate actions; and (6) responses to actions and outcomes (a further category—describing a goal—was never depicted in gestures and was rarely described in speech). Using these definitions, the two viewpoints can be shown to appear in quite different contexts: C-VPT (voice) dominates with central events; O-VPT is mainly used with peripheral events. This functional separation suggests that the character voice appears when events are salient. The narrator begins to play the part of the characters directly, and this shifts the gesture mode to the C-VPT, altering the meaning of the hands, limbs, movement, and space.

Linguistic form also encodes distance. Once we have taken note of gestural voice, we also notice that, in fact, there are co-expressive linguistic manifestations of voice as well. These linguistic manifestations, however, are not always obvious. The C-VPT tends to appear with sentences that, in their own grammatical construction, get close to the narrated action. These are simple single-clause sentences that use, where possible, active, transitive verbs. An illustration is "and drops it down the drainpipe," which

Table 3.1. *Percentage of narration events of each type*

Event Type	C-VPT	O-VPT	Uncodable	Number of Events
Central	71	24	5	66
Peripheral	6	93	1	72

was accompanied by a C-VPT gesture in which the hand appeared to grasp the ball and shove it down into the pipe. The very form of the sentence expresses the same kind of proximity to the story line. The second C-VPT gesture appeared with an intransitive verb ("and he comes out the bottom of the drainpipe") but in a simplex sentence. From this we can say that C-VPT is not simply a gestural analogue to verbal transitivity but is, rather, a manifestation of a style of narration that has its other manifestations in sentence structure and verb transitivity when the lexicon allows it.

The O-VPT conversely tends to appear with complex sentences (multiple clauses)—syntactic structures that, in their own configuration, interpose distance from the action. Distance is introduced because the action is in the embedded clause and the higher clause expresses a narrative attitude that implies an observer. In the O-VPT examples given earlier, for example, the speaker said, "he tries going up the inside of the drainpipe," in which the narrative event is going up, and this was embedded in a clause expressing the judgment of a noncharacter observer ("he tries"). Likewise, the other O-VPTs were accompanied by two subordinate clauses that interpose distance structurally between the narrator and the action ("as he's coming up and the bowling ball's coming down"). The third clause, "he swallows it," looks as if it should have been accompanied by a C-VPT gesture but was not because this was a minor outcome compared to the major outcome presented next with a C-VPT gesture ("and he comes out the bottom"). Note that the effect at this point of Tweetie's dropping the bowling ball is revealed only in the gesture.

The examples so far have presented a single voice. Dual voice was a key concept in Bakhtin's notion of dialogue, or hybrid construction, in which, for example, "the subordinate clause is in direct authorial speech and the main clause is someone else's speech" (304). In gesture a very similar situation emerges, in which two voices are simultaneously heard or seen; in the following example a character is simultaneously depicted from two viewpoints, the perspective of the character himself and the perspective of an outside observer (fig. 3.8).

1. and [he grabs Tweetie Bird . . . and as he] Hand appears to grip something at eye level (that is, C-VPT).

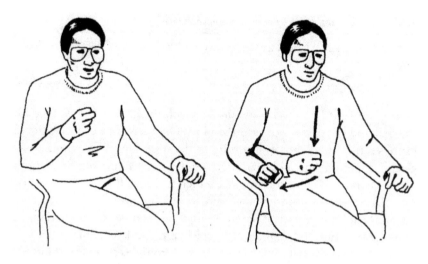

Figure 3.8. A dual viewpoint iconic gesture. The left panel shows the character viewpoint with "he grabs Tweetie Bird as he" and the right panel the dual viewpoint with "comes back down." This second gesture retains the character viewpoint while adding the observer viewpoint in the form of the downward trajectory (the speaker continued with the dual viewpoint in a third gesture and moved her hand, still in a grip, to the right to show Sylvester running away).

2. [comes back] down he lands on the ground Hand still gripping something (that is, C-VPT) plunges straight down (that is, O-VPT).

The gesture in figure 3.8 at (1) depicts grabbing Tweetie Bird from Sylvester's perspective; the concurrent sentence likewise minimizes distance with its simplex construction and transitive verb ("he grabs . . . ," and so on). The gesture at (2) continues the C-VPT of (1) while adding a downward plunge as seen from the perspective of an outside observer; this sentence also increases the distance by adopting a complex structure (subordinated under *as* in "as he comes back down . . . ," and so on). As in Bakhtin, the dual voice enables the narrator to present two narratives, two styles, two semantic and axiological belief systems, at once. We can speculate that it occurs when, as here, one voice is contrasted to the other to produce an ironic effect (in this case the observer watches the character at a moment when the character believes he has conquered, but it is a moment that actually is, as the observer knows, a prelude to disaster).

Perspective
Perspective—where the observer stands—also is revealed in the narrator's

gestures (all with an O-VPT). This is a separate question from voice; it is not who is speaking but where the narrator speaking for the observer is standing as she observes the scene. Two forms of perspective appear, the most common being the outside observer who was described in the bowling ball scene. The other is common among children but is rather infrequent with adults, and it places the observer inside the scene, a kind of resident eye that cannot participate but can see. The following examples from two different speakers present the same event from these contrasting perspectives—the first the outside observer perspective, the second the uncommon inside observer perspective.

AN OUTSIDE OBSERVER.
   1. and he tries to swing from an upper-story window of one building [right into] Tweetie's window. Blob moves from right side to left side of gesture space.

This perspective focused on Sylvester swinging from the side, apparently simulating the experience of the narrator herself watching the cartoon (the right-to-left direction of the gesture was the same as the trajectory shown in the cartoon). The syntactic structure of the utterance is again multi-clause, with the upper clause implying an observer ("he tries" is the narrator's assessment of the character's lack of success; it is probably not a description of his goals).

AN INSIDE OBSERVER.
   1. and you see him swinging down [across a rope]. Both hands clasped together move from a location in front of the narrator's right shoulder to the front and left.

From this trajectory we infer the perspective of an observer who is standing in the middle of the space that the character is swinging through and is watching him swing from rear to front. The space was thus inside the fictive world, with the narrator not as one of the characters but as a participant observer. The speaker in this framework is playing the role of a fictive entity, the narrative observer. The gesture puts the narrator right in the middle of the action, while the speech, as with other O-VPT gestures, distances him with reference to the viewing of the event with "and you see . . . ." The shift to inside observer status is apparent only in gesture, therefore.

In both examples the issue of perspective is fleshed out by reference to the speaker's gestures, with significant aspects of perspective only apparent in the nonverbal channel. In this gesture a dual viewpoint is adopted: both character and inside observer. The narrator's clasped hands represent

Sylvester's paws, while the swinging movement across space is one that only an observer could recount. This double viewpoint may stem from the ironic contrast of two axiological belief systems, the character's confidence in the triumphant swing and the observer's wry awareness of an upcoming disaster (the character smashes into a wall). The inside observer's perspective—by bringing the observer into the scene—may enhance this contrast.

Movement to Other Narrative Levels

Choices about voice and perspective are made within the narrative level proper, but a story is very rarely entirely narrated at that level (except perhaps by young children). In the same way that a narrative would be barely comprehensible if it were entirely composed of reported speech without framing clauses, a story is easier to understand when parts of its structure are made explicit. Thus, narrators move from the narrative to the metanarrative (and the paranarrative) level throughout the discourse. The shifts of level can be seen most clearly through two different gestural phenomena: the use of beats to mark movement and the semiotic value of deictic gestures found within levels.

As described earlier, the narrator of the stories that we are studying does not fill the role of narrator throughout the storytelling process. The narrator is at first a viewer, face-to-face with a television screen on which is displayed a "visual text"—the representation in images of a particular story about Tweetie Bird and Sylvester. After serving as the (somewhat) passive recipient of a narration, the roles are reversed, and the recipient then becomes provider of a narration, telling the story to someone who has never seen the cartoon. Each role entails a situational frame, or partici-pation framework (called a "framer" in Hanks), which organizes spatial and temporal configurations of speakers and hearers and experienced sequences of events. The sequence of events that constitutes the story proper is only one of a number of sequences of events that make up the narrative. The sort of storytelling that concerns us is composed of five event lines, or sequences of events. One of these event lines contains narrative information, three come under the rubric of metanarrative information, and one final event line gives paranarrative information. The importance of these different frames or event lines is threefold: (1) that particular gestures are found marking the movement between event lines; (2) that different kinds of gestures are found at each narrative level; and (3) that the gestures that are found have a different value depending on the event line in which they participate.

Gestures That Mark Narrative Movement

The following excerpt is from the very beginning of a cartoon narration by an adult speaker. It demonstrates how gestures function to indicate the kind of narrative information that is given in the clause that they accompany.

1. Um have you [seen any of the uh] Bugs [Bunny cartoons]?
                beat   *beat*

2. [Right],[ok this one][actually wasn't]a Bugs Bunny cartoon
   beat *beat*   *beat*

3. [It was one of the—the series]
      metaphoric: object in a series of objects

4. and it had [Tweetie Bird and Sylvester]
                 beat

5. [so so so you know] [the cat right]
  beat   *beat*

6. right un huh

7. and uh [the first scene you see is uh]
       iconic: window ledge

8. [this this window][with birdwatcher's society underneath it]
    iconic: window ledge   *iconic:* sign

9. and [there's Sylvester peeking] around the window
      iconic: enacts Sylvester peeking

The first clause of this narration does nothing to describe the story but does function to involve the listener; it has an interpersonal function. This participation frame is signaled by two beats. The second and third clauses still do not describe the story but classify the visual text (cartoon) as an example of a genre: the event line indexed here is the representation of the cartoon, and it is signaled by three beats. The third clause is also accompanied by a metaphoric representing the nature of the series (we will discuss this choice of gesture later in the essay). The first introduction of the protagonist of the story, Sylvester, is also indexed by a beat, at line 5.

Generally, in the flow of a narration, beats take place when the narrator withdraws momentarily from the narrative plot line and enters another participation frame either to repair a lexical item (a metalinguistic function), to introduce a new character (a metanarrative [representational] event), or to add new information about an already introduced topic in the narration (also a metanarrative function). That is, beats can be said to signal a momentary increase of distance between the narrator and the narrated event. Thus, a clause in which a beat is found often performs not the referential function of describing the world but the metapragmatic function of indexing a relationship between the speaker and the words uttered. The relationship indexed in the previous example was one of objectification: the story was being described not yet in terms of a series of events in the world but as an object with external contours. The metaphoric, then, in clause 3, appropriately depicts the story-as-object. Thus, beat gestures can signal movement between narrative levels, and between participation frames within levels, even when this movement is not consistently marked in the speech channel.

The Value of Narrative Space

We have described the gesture space in front of a listener as an active arena in which the actions of characters in a story are enacted and in which a narrative observer may be depicted as watching those actions. Another feature of the gesture space, however, is its changing semiotic value. That is, the same physical space can be, at different points during the narration, occupied by Sylvester and Tweetie Bird, by a television screen and a viewer, or by the actual narrator and her listener. These changes in value are marked by deictic gestures, which point out the participants in the current frame of interpretation. The following excerpt comes from a narration of a full-length Hitchcock movie (*Blackmail* 1929).

1. [it—it's sort of a fade-out]
   Metaphoric: fade out (curl and uncurl hand)
2. [y'know Frank obviously mad] [stalks off]
   Deictic: over right shoulder
   Iconic: stalks off
3. and then the next time we see [anyone] [involved . . .]
   Deictics: point down right
4. Frank and Al— [not Frank]
   Metaphoric: negation (closing hand)
5. [the artist] [and Alice] are [walking by]
   2 Deictics: points towards right & then center
   Iconic: walking center to left (away from Alice's space).

Several deictic gestures are found in this segment of the narration, but, although the deictics look morphologically identical, their semantic value is different with each occurrence. The first deictic gesture indicates the location of a character in the story, at the narrative level proper. Frank, whose previous position has been shown by an iconic made in center space, directly in front of the narrator, is now shown to be leaving the stage rightward in the first deictic gesture described here. The next deictic gesture, occurring in clause 3, also points toward the right (this time front and down rather than up and back), but this time the point occurs at the metanarrative level, indicating in space the position of a new scene (or new focus space [Grosz]). The metaphoric gesture for a fade-out has been made moving from the left to in front of the narrator; by contrast, the new scene is introduced to the speaker's right. It is fairly common in full-length narrations of this sort for an invisible timeline to be established in front of the narrator, with events moving forward into time from left to right. The third deictic, although it indicates the same place in space, refers back to the narrative level and to the position of two new actors, the artist and Alice. The spatialization of their position is used in the subsequent iconic, which shows the two of them leaving from the right and walking left.

Deictics also occur at the paranarrative level, as shown in the next excerpt from the very beginning of a Sylvester and Tweetie Bird narration.

   1. Well ++ [it was one of the ahm Tweetie Pie and ahm] ++ the cat ++ [cartoons][2]
       Beats
       Metaphoric: hands present cartoon to listener
   (LISTENER: Sylvester)
   2. [Sylvester] right ++
       Deictic: points at listener

In this example a deictic gesture serves to point out the participants of the interpersonal participation frame, who share a common piece of information—the name of a cartoon character.

Deictic gestures are part of the way in which narrators seem to diagram the plot structure of their story. Physical space becomes a space of referential possibilities, and any refocusing of the referent space brings out pointing. In terms of the narrative model this abstract pointing marks new characters, at the narrative level proper; new events, at the metanarrative level; and a relationship between speaker and hearer, at the paranarrative level.

Gestures at the Metanarrative Level

Within each narrative level there are characteristic patterns of gesture occurrence. In our corpus of stories, beats are evenly distributed between the narrative and the extranarrative level (a category that collapses metanarrative and paranarrative). But metaphorics and iconics show a skewed distribution: metaphorics are much more frequent on the paranarrative levels, deictics on the narrative level. Here we will therefore focus on metaphoric gestures.[3]

Metaphoric Gestures in Metanarrative

In an earlier section of the essay we described metaphoric gestures as having a representational function for ideas expressed in the accompanying speech that do not have a physically depictable form. This function is most often called into play in metanarrative speech, in which the cartoon narration may be objectified and commented on in the verbal channel and presented as an object in the gestural channel. A prototypical example comes from the beginning of a cartoon narration quoted earlier.

1. Well ++ [it was one of the ahm Tweetie Pie and ahm] ++ the cat ++ [cartoons]
   Beats
   Metaphoric: hands present cartoon to listener

The narrator here forms a largish bowl shape with his two hands and raises this bowl from his lap toward the listener. This is a conduit metaphoric gesture: the speaker presents information as if contained in a bounded object that can be passed to the listener. In this example speech and gesture work together to make clear the metanarrative level at which the narration begins. The speech presents the cartoon as an example of a type ("it was one of the"), while the gesture represents the narrator not as an observer but as the conveyor of this object, which is the cartoon.

A similar example comes from an episode boundary in a cartoon narration.

1. and . . . of course the next [develop]ment in the plot is
   Metaphoric: Both hands present an object to listener

Conduit metaphorics are frequent at these episode junctures in the cartoon. The speaker in the first example is not referring to a specific event; he is referring to the cartoon as a whole and to his upcoming narration of the cartoon—in our terms, to events in the metanarrative and paranarrative participation frames. In both of the narrative and meta- or paranarrative uses of the metaphoric gesture, time is instantiated as a bounded entity, the time of the next event in the plot line, the time of the viewing of the cartoon (as manifested in speech in a past tense verb *was*). Thus, narrators localize the various narrative times in the gesture channel.

Process metaphorics are also fairly common in narrative. The next example (fig. 3.9) also comes from the beginning of a cartoon narration.

1. Now we get into the film proper
   Metaphoric: both hands rotate toward listener

Here the narrator is concentrating on the continuity between events leading into the cartoon, as opposed to the singularity of this particular cartoon.

Gestures at the Paranarrative Level

The striking characteristic of gesture use at the paranarrative level is how reduced it is. When narrators speak as themselves, outside of a necessarily narrative situation but adopting the role of a participant in a socially defined situation of speaker and hearer, they make only a small number

Figure 3.9. A process metaphoric gesture with "now we get into the film proper."

of gestures of a restricted kind. Iconic gestures are virtually absent, as are metaphoric gestures. Deictic gestures are found, as described earlier, when they index knowledge shared by speaker and hearer. The role of deictic gestures here is to point out (so to speak) the participants of the event. Beat gestures are also found when they mark the inception of a paranarrative portion of the discourse or when they signal repairs or other metalinguistic work. This is not to say that the nonverbal channel is inactive at the paranarrative level. Gaze, for instance, plays an important role in structuring the participation of a speaker and hearer in a narrating event. Note also that outside of narrative discourse (in conversations) gestures are highly abundant. Thus, reduction of gesture in paranarrative contexts seems to be a specific clue for this level of narrative organization, opposing it to the narrative and metanarrative levels.

Conclusion

The contemporary analysis of narrative texts has in the past fifteen years begun to take place along multiple intersecting axes, such as those of perspective and mode, voice and person. But the analysis still remains in the one dimension of the temporal linearity of the text. When, by studying the concurrent gestures of the narrator, we add the nonverbal level to this picture, we find ourselves in a cross-cutting world of imagery that coexists with the linear timeline of the narrative. A written text may include hints of this atemporal structure, but in a written text it is an implied dimension and often cannot be isolated in specific linguistic structures. Rather, the underlying structure of the text must be inferred from a pattern of usage that is inherently imprecise as to locus. A spoken text, through its gestures, may make this imagery and discourse structure explicit. Gestural distinctions show the exact moment at which the narrator shifts voice and perspective and changes distance between herself and the narrative text.

We can raise the question of why gestures do these things. It is possible that gestures smooth the way for the articulatory processes of speech formation itself (Freedman), though this is not the kind of gesture aid that we have in mind. For the speaker gestures offer the advantages of an externalization of the narrator's relationship to the events being conveyed, in pure form. A speaker who wants to convey the "essence" of a story can externalize this concept in a directly sensible manner, in a gesture that creates a small, bounded, tightly contained space. The speaker's sense of the perceived centrality versus peripherality of the events in a narrative takes on concrete form in gesture voice and perspective. Narrative distance may be represented here by the actual physical distance of a narrator from the narrated. These images do not only come out of but also can have real ongoing consequences for the speaker's thoughts and, therefore, for narrative and memory. Thus, for both the speaker and the listener, gestures help to build a representation of the narration, at all of its levels, and play an important part in the "telementation" of the story.

Notes

Preparation of this article was supported by grants BNS 8211440 and BNS 8518324 from the National Science Foundation, by grants in 1981 and 1989 from the Spencer Foundation, by a 1989–90 dissertation research grant from the National Science Foundation, and by a 1989–90 dissertation grant from the Spencer Foundation. We wish to thank Anna Bosch and Laura Pedelty for commenting on the manuscript. The accurate and expressive drawings are the work of Laura Pedelty.

Table 3.2. *Frequency of gesture types in narrative contexts*

Type of clause	Iconic	Beat	Metaphoric	Deictic	None	Total
Narrative	226	134	1	25	146	543
Extranarrative	35	134	31	3	44	247
Total	261	268	43	28	190	790

1. Square brackets mark the extent of the gesture.

2. Plus signs (++) stand for pause length.

3. Table 3.2 shows the frequency of gesture types on the narrative and extranarrative levels. It was tabulated on the basis of Sylvester and Tweetie Bird cartoon narrations by six adults.

References

Bahktin, M. M. *The Dialogic Imagination.* Ed. Michael Holquist. Trans. Caryl Emerson and Michael Holquist. Austin: University of Texas Press, 1981.

Banfield, Ann. *Unspeakable Sentences.* Boston: Routledge and Kegan Paul, 1982.

Brooks, Cleanth, and Robert Penn Warren. *Understanding Fiction.* 2d ed. New York: Appelton-Century-Crofts, 1959.

Cassell, Justine, and David McNeill. "Gesture and Ground." *Proceedings of the Sixteenth Annual Meeting of the Berkeley Linguistics Society.* Berkeley CA: Berkeley Linguistics Society, 1990.

Chatman, Seymour. *Story and Discourse: Narrative Structure in Fiction and Film.* Ithaca NY: Cornell University Press, 1978.

———. What Novels Can Do That Films Can't (and Vice Versa). *On Narrative.* Ed. W. J. T. Mitchell. Chicago: University of Chicago Press, 1981.

Church, R. B., D. Baker, D. Bunnag, and C. Whitmore. "The Development of the Role of Speech and Gesture in Story Narration." Paper presented at the Biennial Meeting of the Society for Research in Child Development, Kansas City MO, 1989.

Dray, N. L., and D. McNeill. "Gestures during Discourse: The Contextual Structuring of Thought." *Meanings and Protoypes: Studies in Linguistic Categorization.* Ed. S. L. Tsohatzidis. London: Routledge, 1990.

Ekman, P., and W. V. Friesen. "The Repertoire of Nonverbal Behavioral Categories—Origins, Usage, and Coding." *Semiotica* 1 (1969): 49–98.

Freedman, N. "The Analysis of Movement Behavior during the Clinical Interview." *Studies in Dyadic Communication.* Ed. A. W. Siegman and B. Pope. New York: Pergamon Press, 1972.

Genette, Gérard. *Figures II.* Paris: Seuil, 1969.

———. *Figures III.* Paris: Seuil, 1972.

Goodwin, C., and M. H. Goodwin, "Context, Activity and Participation." *The Contextualization of Language.* Ed. P. Auer and A. Di Luzio. Amsterdam: John Benjamins, 1992. 77–99.

Grosz, B. "Focusing and Description in Natural Language Dialogues." *Elements of Discourse Understanding*. Ed. A. K. Joshi, B. L. Webber, and I. A. Sag. Cambridge: Cambridge University Press, 1981.

Gülich, Elisabeth, and Uta Quasthoff. "Narrative Analysis." *Handbook of Discourse Analysis: Dimensions of Discourse*. Vol. 2. Ed. Teun A. Van Dik. London: Academic Press, 1985.

Hanks, W. "Metalanguage and Pragmatics of Deixis." *Reflexive Language: Reported Speech and Metapragmatics*. Ed. J. Lucy. Cambridge: Cambridge University Press, 1993.

Hinrichs, E., and L. Polanyi. "Pointing the Way: A Unified Treatment of Referential Gesture in Interactive Contexts." *Pragmatics and Grammatical Theory (Papers from the 22nd Chicago Linguistics Society Parasession)*. Ed. A. Farley, P. Farley, and K. E. McCullough. Chicago: Chicago Linguistics Society, 1986.

Jakobson, Roman. "Closing Statement: Linguistics and Poetics." *Style in Language*. Ed. T. Sebeok. Cambridge MA: MIT Press, 1960.

Kendon, A. "Some Relationships between Body Motion and Speech." *Studies in Dyadic Communication*. Ed. A. W. Siegman and B. Pope. New York: Pergamon Press, 1972.

————. "Gesticulation and Speech: Two Aspects of the Process of Utterance." *The Relation between Verbal and Nonverbal Communication*. Ed. M. R. Key. The Hague: Mouton, 1980.

Kloepfer, Rolf. "Dynamic Structures in Narrative Literature." *Poetics Today* 1.4 (1980): 115–34.

Lakoff, George, and Mark Johnson. *Metaphors We Live By*. Chicago: University of Chicago Press, 1980.

Marslen-Wilson, W. D., E. Levy, and L. K. Tyler. "Producing Interpretable Dialogue: The Establishment and Maintenance of Reference." *Speech, Place, and Action*. Ed. R. Jarvella and W. Klein. Chichester, Eng.: John Wiley and Sons, 1982.

McNeill, David. *Hand and Mind: What Gestures Reveal about Thought*. Chicago: University of Chicago Press, 1992.

McNeill, David, and E. Levy. "Conceptual Representations in Language Activity and Gesture." *Speech, Place, and Action*. Ed. R. Jarvella and W. Klein. Chichester, UK: John Wiley and Sons, 1982.

Reddy, M. "The Conduit Metaphor—A Case of Frame Conflict in Our Language about Language." *Metaphor and Thought*. Ed. A. Ortony. Cambridge: Cambridge University Press, 1979.

Richards, I. A. *The Philosophy of Rhetoric*. New York: Oxford University Press, 1936.

Ricoeur, Paul. "Narrative Time." *On Narrative*. Ed. W. J. T. Mitchell. Chicago: University of Chicago Press, 1981.

Rime, B. "Nonverbal Communication or Nonverbal Behavior? Towards a Cognitive-Motor Theory of Nonverbal Behavior." *Current Issues in European Social*

Psychology. Vol. 1. Ed. W. Doise and S. Moscovici. Cambridge: Cambridge University Press, 1983.

Silverstein, M. "On the Pragmatic 'Poetry' of Prose." *Meaning, Form, and Use in Context: Linguistic Applications.* Ed. D. Schiffrin. Washington DC: Georgetown University Press, 1984.

Todorov, Tzvetan. *Les Genres du discours.* Paris: Seuil, 1978.

2. Still Pictures

What does it take for static images to evoke a story that extends over time? The need to acknowledge the narrative potential of visual media is one of the main reasons for transmedial narratology to recognize a wider variety of narrative modalities than the unmarked case of diegetic, autonomous, determinate narration. Since pictures, left by themselves, lack the ability to articulate specific propositions and to explicitate causal relations, their principal narrative option is what I call in the introduction the illustrative mode. In the words of A. Kibédi Varga, "The image is not a second way of telling the tale, but a way of *evoking* [that is, recalling it from memory] it" (204; emph. added). This statement applies not only to the vast majority of narrative paintings but also to ballet and musical compositions. It is because the spectator of the ballet *Sleeping Beauty* has a well-formed mental image of the fairy tale that she can recognize the plot in the gestures of the dancers. The same is true of religious medieval paintings or of musical compositions inspired by stories (for example, Telemann's *Don Quixote* suite). Compared to the ability to articulate new stories, illustrative narrativity is admittedly a rather weak and subordinated mode, but this does not mean that it should be dismissed as entirely parasitic. In the best of cases illustrations do not simply evoke preexisting narrative images but also create a symbiotic relation with the verbal version. Whereas they import logical relations and psychological motivation from the known story, they return visualizations, emotional coloring, or facial expressions that may provide a clue to the motivations of characters. In the most successful cases (here I am thinking of Sir John Tenniel's illustrations to *Alice in Wonderland*) the verbal and visual version blend in the mind of the reader-spectator into one powerful image, each version filling the gaps of the other.

But illustrative narrativity is not the only mode available to visual media. Silent film and pantomime can articulate simple tales, for instance, the story of a rejected lover; present-day comics strips represent original mini-dramas without using a single word; and post-Renaissance genre painting rejects traditional mythological and biblical subjects in favor of previously untold stories from everyday life. Wendy Steiner observes in her contribution to this volume, "Pictorial Narrativity," that genre scenes are usually low in tellability and that they rely on what cognitive psychologists regard as standard narrative schemata: the market script; the drinking party script; the music-making script. The familiarity of the schemata makes genre painting almost illustrative. But some works within the breed rise to a more autonomous and more interesting form of narrativity. A case in point is the painting *Breakfast Scene* by William Hogarth. The picture is actually part of a series titled *Marriage à la Mode,* but it tells a self-contained story, and it does so without relying on the verbal resources of its rather bland title. We see a couple of newlyweds in an elegant house, the man collapsed in a drunken stupor, the woman laughing, squirming, and looking very tipsy. The floor is littered with upturned furniture, and a servant is trying to clean up the mess while yelling at a debt collector who is leaving the scene with a gesture of total despair. Behind the intoxicated couple, on the fireplace mantelpiece, the bust of an elderly woman frowns her disapproval. The painter has caught the couple at the end of a night of excesses, just before they sober up and face the consequences of their irresponsible lifestyle. The tellability of the story asserts itself in an inescapable moral: these people will not live happily ever after, nor will the society that breeds and nurtures their kind.

Whether they tell or merely illustrate stories, still pictures can chose between two strategies. The technique exemplified in *Breakfast Scene* is the selection of what Gotthold Ephraim Lessing calls a "pregnant moment." Drawing on the Russian formalist distinction between *fabula* and *sjuzhet* (itself equivalent to the better-known distinction of story, the told events, and discourse, their medium-based presentation), Emma Kafalenos argues that narrative paintings compress the *sjuzhet* into a single scene, leaving it to the spectator to unfold this shot into a plot, or *fabula:* "A painting or photograph with narrative implications offers the perceiver an experience that is comparable to entering a narrative *in medias res;* we ask ourselves what has happened, what is about to occur, and where we are in the sequence of a narrative" (59). The pregnant moment technique is particularly well suited to the presentation of original stories, but the price of narrative autonomy is often a loss of determinacy. A work that defines only one point on the narrative trajectory presents the spectator not with a specific story but with an array of narrative possibilities. Every spectator will plot a different story line through the fixed coordinates of the pregnant moment, and this story tends to fray toward the edges, since the network of possibilities increases in complexity the farther one moves away from the climactic moment. It is only in cartoons without caption (*sans paroles*), a genre much more popular in French than in American culture, that the technique allows the transmission of a fairly determinate narrative: since humor resides in very narrowly definable features, the readers who get *the* point must reconstruct closely similar stories.

The other narrative strategy available to still pictures consists of dividing the picture into several distinct frames. By plotting many points on the narrative timeline, segmentation restores some determinacy to the story line. This approach prefigures the frames of moving pictures, but, instead of depending on a projector to animate the show, it uses the eye of the spectator moving from panel to panel to keep narrative time running. The reader (for the eye movement amounts to an act of reading) constructs a story line by assuming that similar shapes on different frames represent common referents (objects, characters, or setting); by interpreting spatial relations as temporal sequence (adjacent frames represent subsequent moments); and by inferring causal relations between the states depicted in the frames. The selected moments need not be pregnant, but they should be easily connectable and narratively significant: they must represent a change of state (or the lack of an expected change) that affects the goals of the characters. We associate this technique with present-day comic strips—for instance, some of the speechless graphic stories published in the *New Yorker* by the French humorist Sempé—but, as Wendy Steiner's essay demonstrates, it has been used in Western art at least since the Italian quattrocento and perhaps as early as ancient Egyptian civilization.

Steiner's essay takes us back to a time when narrative pictures had an essential cultural function to perform: they inscribed stories permanently for those who could not read. Medieval, Renaissance, and Baroque Catholic churches, and even more Russian Orthodox cathedrals, were designed to transport the faithful into the sacred space and time of biblical or hagiographic stories. Through their rich iconography churches were the site of a virtual, though spiritually live, encounter with religious figures. In order to immerse the spectator in the storyworld, pictures had to do more than illustrate: they had to take the spectator *through* storytime, as does a verbal telling. This means that they had to simulate the movement of the plot and the evolution of the narrative world by visual means. As Steiner shows in her essay, pre-Renaissance Italian paintings achieve this effect by representing several distinct moments in the plot. But, rather than creating a linear sequence of discrete frames, as do comic strips, these paintings gather the various narrative moments in a unified landscape. The frames that separate the scenes are not artificial boundaries but natural features or architectural details intrinsic to the global view captured in the painting. Since there is no room on a canvas for a large number of scenes, the moments selected have to be able to reach out toward one another. The narrativity of these quattrocento paintings thus combines the two techniques of segmentation and reliance on a pregnant moment.

In a fascinating survey of aesthetic and theoretical positions concerning the desirability and possibility of pictorial storytelling, Steiner attributes the decline of the narrative technique of quattrocento paintings to the rise of illusionism and realism, which assimilates pictorial representation to a "window on the world" and restricts the content of the window to what can be seen from a specific point of view, at a specific time. Even if the point of view is sufficiently elevated to embrace several distinct areas, the requirement of verisimilitude prohibits multiple appearances of the same figure, since an individual cannot be in several places at the same time. But I would like to suggest that the emancipation of art from religion is as much to blame for the loss of the multi-episodic narrativity of the quattrocento as the emphasis on a realistic perspective, for, when painting loses the function of bringing the Holy Scriptures to life, of immersing the spectator in a sacred reality, the picture is no longer responsible for the integrity of the story. Deprived of its spiritual dimension, narrative becomes a pretext for dramatic composition, the display of the human body in action, the representation of female beauty, and the expression of erotic desire—all of which are better realized through the depiction of a single pregnant moment.

Whether the representation of several episodes is a necessary condition of pictorial narrativity, as Steiner maintains, or whether temporal sequence can be condensed into a single pregnant scene, as Kafalenos argues, the multiple frame technique allows the representation of more complex stories and projects a clearer narrative intent than single-frame pictures. Whereas the representation of a frozen moment makes us think of a story, the paintings analyzed by Steiner invite us to attend to the dynamic unfolding of narrative time. Even so, however, their narrativity is not fully autonomous. A spectator totally unfamiliar with the biblical text would not be able to reconstruct the story of Salome from the painting by Benozzo Gozzoli that forms the focus of Steiner's essay; this spectator may, for instance, read the picture from left to right and assume that the beheading of John is the first event in the plot. After the execution Salome would present the head to her mother, Herodiad (but how could our unknowing spectator infer family relations?), and later that evening she would dance in celebration at the king's banquet. Or Salome and her mother could be grieving over the saint's death in the central scene, and the dancing Salome on the right would be hiding her sadness, while Herodiad openly mourns the beheaded saint. (She looks rather sad in the banquet scene, and her eyes are symbolically directed toward the beheading.) To the spectator already familiar with the story, on the other hand, Gozzoli's painting does much more than merely call to mind the biblical text: as Steiner demonstrates, the picture offers an original interpretation of its textual source. By creating a visual parallelism between Salome and each of the two figures in the execution scene, the painting presents the heroine as an ambiguous figure who oscillates between two roles: now dancing executioner, now kneeling victim of her mother's tyrannical desire. More than an illustration, since it actively plots a narrative trajectory, but less than an explicit and self-sufficient telling, Gozzoli's painting offers a creative retelling that deeply affects our understanding of a familiar story.

Add language to the multi-frame graphic narrative, and we have the modern comic strip, a semiotic combination vastly superior in narrative versatility (though, of course, not necessarily in aesthetic value) to the most eloquent of narrative paintings. In contrast to France, where *la bande dessinée* has long been recognized as a form of art, comic strips tend to be regarded in the United States as a genre of popular culture. Their lowbrow reputation has prevented them from receiving the theoretical attention that their unique blend of graphic and verbal signs deserves. It did not help that most comics were just that—comic—for humor has long played second fiddle in the mind of critics to "serious" (tragic, dramatic) forms of expression. It wasn't until the recent development of a new genre, the graphic novel, that the literary potential of comic strips began to receive widespread recognition. But, as Jeanne Ewert observes in her study of Art Spiegelman's Holocaust novel *Maus*, the language channel of comic strips tends to eclipse in the mind of readers and critics the contribution of the pictures. Many readers tend to rush to the next frame as soon as their eyes have scanned the text and their mind has understood the logical connection with the preceding frame.

Ewert's essay is a truly *eye*-opening reading lesson that reveals the extraordinary sophistication of Spiegelman's use of graphic elements. In Spiegelman's novel many narratological functions normally performed by language are delegated to visual items: variations in the size of the frames operate changes in narrative pace; the embedding of an image within another signal flash-forwards; the elimination of the lines that frame panels suggest an expansion of space; identical panels set wide apart create a musical effect of thematic repetition; and the visual appearance of characters—Germans are cats, Jews are mice, and Poles are pigs—functions as a literalized metaphor. Most impressive about *Maus,* as Ewert demonstrates, is how the graphic novel exploits the contrast between its two channels to create contrapuntal voices that relativize each other. Subtle visual clues may cast doubts about the reliability of the character who is currently speaking, or small graphic details may be used to introduce counterplots that play in the background of the main, verbally assisted story line. *Maus* illustrates a phenomenon that we also see at work in the musical (as analyzed in Peter Rabinowitz's contribution): a channel of lower narrative potential subtly undermining a channel with higher resources. The opposite would not work, because the channel of higher narrativity automatically represents the dominant, assertive voice and cannot therefore relativize the background story. While the cinema could in principle achieve a similar doubling of narrative voices—the background image, or even the soundtrack, telling a different story than the dialogue-supported action—the very fact that its images are moving prevents the close inspection of the visual element that *Maus* requires of its reader. In the hands of an artist like Spiegelman, less truly becomes more, as the stillness of the pictures is turned into a powerful narrative resource.

References

Kafalenos, Emma. "Implications of Narrative in Painting and Photography." *New Novel Review* 3.2 (1996): 53–66.
Kibédi Varga, A. "Stories Told by Pictures." *Style* 22.2 (1988): 194–208.

4

Pictorial Narrativity

Wendy Steiner

> Nature knits up her kinds in a network, not a chain; but men follow only
> by chains because their language can't handle several things at once.–
> Albrecht von Haller, trans. Howard Nemerov

Ariadne's thread unwinding through the labyrinth, Hansel and Gretel's
pebbles marking out the trackless woods—these and other mythic images echo von Haller's contrast between nature and human understanding.
Knowledge is a path cut through a maze, a line attempting adequacy to a
plane, a mere chain seeking dominion over a network. As such, knowledge
is necessarily incomplete, yet the drawing of lines, the chaining of links, is
the only way to reach the point at the center and to find one's way home
again.

Von Haller blames this fact on language, chainlike in the very structure
of its syntagms, and thereby he suggests another object of his analogy,
narrative. For narrative, made of language, also lives by concatenation—
both in its medium and in its temporal subject matter. Event follows event;
scene follows scene. The connection between knowledge and narrative is
apparent even in its etymology: Latin *narrare*, to tell; *gnarus*, knowing, acquainted with;, and ultimately Indo-European *gna*, to know.[1] Narrative, as
knowledge, is victimized by its diachrony yet seemingly requires diachrony
in order to be knowledge in the first place.

But if narrative in this metaphor is the chain of knowledge, painting is
traditionally the natural network—not sequence but pure configuration.
It is iconically adequate to the labyrinth of nature but incapable of cutting
through it—of functioning propositionally, Sol Worth would say, of serving as a form of knowledge. The inability of painting to include temporally
or logically distinct moments is, of course, the basis of Lessing's distinction
between the spatial and the temporal arts (*Laocoön*). It is a distinction that

explains the iconic limitations of each art: "the catalogue of Western arts is . . . a list of renunciations: with sculpture, of texture and colour; with painting, of volume; with both, of time" (Bryson xvi). One might add: with literature, of visuality and referential density. As Leonardo da Vinci put it, "If you call painting mute poetry, poetry can also be called blind painting" (*Treatise on Painting* 18).

But much as mythic imagery and neoclassical thought would support this split and its acquiescence to the impoverishment of each art, the necessity that lies behind the division is not as absolute as one might think. It is refuted most clearly by modern linguistics. The view of narrative (and language) as a mere sequence is not tenable in light of recent theory. It is the mistake of the proponents of "spatial form," who identify the novel and narrativity with pure temporal sequence and then are surprised to find other forms of cohesion in the twentieth-century novel (and elsewhere).[2] Virtually every narratologist finds narrative dependent on both its sequential and its configurational qualities.

But no similar body of theorizing is available to the visual arts. In fact, the narrativity of pictures is virtually a nontopic for art historians.[3] Not only is the concept poorly understood, but the pictures that are supposedly governed by it are now out of fashion. The last association that one would have with modern art is the adjective *narrative*, and in the formalist criticism of recent years the term has had a distinctly negative value.[4] Yet the narrative potential of the visual arts is an enormously revealing topic. As we shall discover, it can explain some of the most essential facts about Western painting and the imaginative place of art in the literary romance.

The typical art historical usage of the term *narrative painting* is very loose by literary standards. Sacheverell Sitwell (1) characterizes it as "the painting of anecdote" but applies it to what would more often be called "genre painting"—typical scenes, homely incidents, instantiations of a theme, perennial activities, and pictorial sequences such as Hogarth's *Rake's Progress*. Nancy Wall Moure uses the term not only for genre scenes but for historical and mythological subjects as well, and she contrasts it systematically to portraits and allegories. And a symposium of specialists on ancient art agreed to define *pictorial narrative* as "the rendering of specific events, whether mythological, legendary, historical, or fictional, involving recognizable personages" (Kraeling 44). It is disconcerting to note that the same term applies contradictorily to both typical scenes and specific events. But the contrastive value of the term to the allegory is interesting. It alerts us to a perennial, though largely unexplored, association between narrativity and realism.

In this essay I would like to use developments in the study of literary narrative to consider the preconditions for pictorial narrative and, once having done so, to examine the "knowledge potential" of a particular narrative painting. I realize that this is a somewhat dangerous procedure, since a theory of narrative developed for verbal art may have only a procrustean bearing on visual narrative. I hope that such will not be the case. Narratologists intend many of their notions to apply regardless of medium. Moreover, they propound a syndrome of narrative characteristics, all of which need not be in evidence for us to take a text as a narrative. One would thus be able to speak of "stronger" or "weaker" narratives according to the number and selection of these characteristics in a work. I hope to show that many of the traits producing strong literary narratives are the same as those producing strong pictorial ones but that historical developments have made strongly narrative paintings extremely rare. It is not the medium of painting but its conventions that have reduced narrativity to an apparently peripheral concern for art historians.

From a narratological point of view pictures of typical scenes and perennial activities, the sort Sitwell terms *narrative paintings,* would be considered particularly low in narrativity. As Gerald Prince points out:

> narrative prefers tensed statements (or their equivalent) to untensed ones:
> something like
> > Every human being dies
> is fine (and may well appear in a narrative) but something like
> > Napoleon died in 1821
> is better or, at least more characteristic of narrative.

Prince goes on: "If narrativity is a function of the . . . specificity of the (sequences of) events presented, it is also a function of the extent to which their occurrence is given as a fact (in a certain world) rather than a possibility or a probability. The hallmark of narrativity is assurance. It lives in certainty. This happened then that; this happened because of that; this happened and it was related to that" ("Narrativity" 74–75). It would seem clear that the genre scenes in question—typical scenes and perennial activities—lack such specificity and actuality or certainty. They are deliberately not shown as singular events; the scenes, in fact, are often not events at all but what might be termed "humanized landscapes." Indeed, Martin Meisel notes a prejudice among audiences against such specificity: "The modern view assumes, paradoxically, that realism is better served by scenes and figures whose individuality does not reach beyond generic activity, by mowers in a hayfield rather than Ruth standing amid the alien corn" (352).

The low narrativity of the genre scene also follows from its lack of what William Labov calls an "evaluation": "the means used by the narrator to indicate the point of the narrative, its raison d'être" (366). Although Labov considers the evaluation a nonessential characteristic of narrative—temporal sequence being the necessary trait—he does say that a narrative without an evaluative component leaves itself open to the withering rejoinder "So what?" "Evaluative devices say to us: this was terrifying, dangerous, weird, wild, crazy; or amusing, hilarious, wonderful; more generally, that it was strange, uncommon, or unusual—that is, worth reporting. It was not ordinary, plain, humdrum, everyday, or run-of-the-mill" (Labov 371). [5] Genre paintings explicitly present themselves as ordinary, plain, humdrum, everyday, and run-of-the-mill, and, though the insistence that we attend to the unremarkable might itself be seen as a paradoxical or witty statement—perhaps the only piece of wit proper to naturalism—nevertheless one would hardly respond to such works as narratively compelling. Indeed, they appear to be exactly the opposite of what we normally take narrative to be. Periods such as eighteenth-century neoclassicism, which elevated history painting over other genres, insisted on the representation of "significant action and strong passions" and downgraded "subject matter wholly devoid of these, such as bowls of fruit, views of countryside without human figures, portraits of unknown men and women, [and] genre scenes in which humble persons engage in trivial activities" (Fried 73). (Neoclassicism, however, did not go so far as to allow more than one episode to be represented in history paintings.)

Art historians are perhaps closer to literary usage in including the so-called conversation piece among narrative paintings, since these are specific. [6] They are a fusion of genre and portrait, showing particular people engaged in characteristic acts such as walking before their ancestral homes or playing with their children. Yet even here the activity is generic and the narrativity low. We can now understand the insistence of the ancient art symposium that an artwork render "specific events . . . involving recognizable personages" if it is to be termed "narrative" and also the common use of *narrative art* as a contrast to portrait and allegory.

So far, then, we might agree that narrativity is strongest in paintings depicting specific (though not necessarily existent) personages engaged in some singular (in both senses) act. "A story is a specific event carried out by particular characters in a particular place at a particular time," stresses one student of Egyptian art (Gaballa 5). The addition of a specific place and time introduces another of Labov's narrative components, the "orientation." Speaking of verbal narratives, he describes the orientation as that section of the narrative, often at the beginning but also placed strategically throughout, in which the text identifies "the time, place, persons, and their activity or the situation" (Labov 364). Now we would expect this kind of information to be the realm in which pictorial narrative would excel, since place, circumstance, and atmosphere are those factors for which a picture is indeed worth a thousand words. Even the less "natural" information for painting of specific names, dates, and so forth can be conveyed through iconographic symbolism, and where this is still inadequate, the painting has a title. *Judith and Holofernes, Washington Crossing the Delaware, Cupid and Psyche, The Dance of Salome*—titles provide crucial information for the orientation as well as functioning as what Labov terms the "abstract," a summary of the story.[7] The title is actually a good analogue to Labov's abstract, since the latter is a combination of narrative functions. As Labov describes it, "the reference of the abstract is broader than the orientation and complicating action: it includes these and the evaluation so that the abstract not only states what the narrative is about, but why it is told" (370). Thus, paintings do contain some of Labov's narrative structures, even if they seem far from the literary category of narrative.

The distance between paintings and literary narratives is conventionally explained by the fact that temporal sequence, what Labov calls the "complicating action," is the single most essential narrative trait. Without it there is no verbal narrativity. The insistence on temporality is part of every definition of *narrativity*, regardless of its philosophical orientation. Thus, where Gerald Prince claims in his formalist, linguistic definition that narrative is "any representation of non-contradictory events such that at least one occurs at time t and the other at time t_1, following time t" ("Narrativity," 61), Paul Ricoeur's revisionist phenomenological definition states: "I take temporality to be that structure of existence that reaches language in narrativity and narrativity to be the language structure that has temporality as its ultimate referent" (169).

But temporal reference in and of itself is not enough to qualify a discourse as narrative. The temporal events narrated must be multiple. Again, as Prince argues, "although many things . . . take time, at least some of their representations do not necessarily constitute a narrative. A fight can take a few minutes and a trip can take a few days yet neither 'There was a fight yesterday' nor 'It was a beautiful trip' constitute narratives: they do not represent the fight or the trip as a series of events but as one event; they do not recount a sequence of events . . . narrative is a representation of *at least two* real or fictive events in a time sequence" ("Aspects" 49–50). This representation of an event in terms of its temporal unfolding is what Prince calls "discreteness" ("Narrativity" 64), the division of the event into distinct, ordered parts. The chain, to be a chain, must have discrete links.

It is here, of course, that the visual arts seem least narrative, indeed, definitionally antinarrative. Virtually all post-Renaissance works—however specific or particular their action, characters, place, or time—represent an event through an isolated moment. This mode of representing temporal events as action stopped at its climactic moment, or at a moment that implies but does not show what preceded and what follows it, Lessing called the "pregnant moment." It gave rise to the literary topos of *ekphrasis* in which a poem aspires to the atemporal "eternity" of the stopped-action painting or laments its inability to achieve it.[8] Like the statement "There was a fight yesterday," ekphrastic painting and poetry refer to temporal events without being strongly narrative. Thus, one might speak of David's *Oath of the Horatii* as a powerfully historical painting without feeling that it was a particularly narrative one, although its narrativity is certainly stronger than that of a typical still life, portrait, or genre scene.

The discreteness of temporal events is still not enough to create the equivalent of literary narrativity. Events must also be susceptible to a double ordering. The narrative posits an ordering of events independent of its telling them.[9] Any change in the order of story events would thus create a different narrative,[10] although the order in which those events are told is not fixed.[11] The two orderings at issue here are the chronological order of the events referred to and the order in which they are narrated. This is the famous Russian formalist distinction between *fabula* and *sjuzet*,[12] which is the basis of virtually every subsequent account of literary narrative. Seymour Chatman names his book on narrative *Story and Discourse*—English equivalents of the French equivalents of Shklovsky's Russian terms—and states that this double ordering is definitional for narrative in any medium: "A salient property of narrative is double time structuring. That is, all narratives, in whatever medium, combine the time sequence of plot events, the time of the *histoire* ('story-time') with the time of the presentation of those events in the text, which we call 'discourse-time.' What is fundamental to narrative, regardless of medium, is that these two time orders are independent. In realistic narratives, the time of the story is fixed, following the ordinary course of a life . . . But the discourse-time order may be completely different" ("What Novels" 122). Since storytime in all but the most deviant modern narratives is tied to the chronological flow of real life, narrative can again be seen as dependent on our ideas of the extra-artistic world, which are institutionalized in art as realism.

It is just this dual temporal structuring (the order of telling versus the chronological order in the told) that has led Chatman and others to consider pictorial narrative as inevitably a contradiction in terms. "We may spend half an hour in front of a Titian, but the aesthetic effect is as if we were taking in the whole painting at a glance. In narratives, on the other hand, the dual time orders function independently" (Chatman, "What Novels" 122). Certainly, this contention would tend to reinforce Lessing's absolute split of the spatial from the temporal arts. What is seemingly missing in pictorial narrative is some way of ordering the visual medium. Even if it is clear that temporally distinct moments are being represented, if no order is indicated among them they will not function narratively. The characteristic response to such works is always that they are symbolic or allegorical. For example, Nelson Goodman describes Hans Memling's *Panorama of the Passion* as a narrative painting "without beginning or end or marked route [from one depicted scene to the next]. This pictorial organization of events of a lifetime is spatial, atemporal, motivated perhaps both by considerations of design and by regarding these events as eternal and emblematic rather than as episodic or transient" (110). Such works, then, fail in realism because they fail to pose a pictorial order against the order of events in Christ's life. They are the proverbial labyrinths, without a linear path marked through them.

Visual artists have contrived several conventions to create this double ordering. In Egyptian art the surface was often divided into separate registers, with base lines linking figures in each event or linking one event to the next; the base line established a unified plane of action distinct from the others. Figures can also be oriented so as to be looking toward the next event in a series, their eyes in effect directing the movement of ours. Another strategy is to arrange events as stages along a path (fig. 4.1): this procedure invokes the metaphor of the "path of life," the same metaphor contained in Stendhal's definition of the novel as "a mirror carried along a road." In many paintings scenes are presented as the various rooms of a building, with their order conforming to either the writing system of the culture involved—left to right and up to down in the West—or some special ordering implicit in the architectural features of the building.

Sometimes technical features of the pictorial medium support the double ordering of narrative. Architectural friezes and frescoes are often too large to be "read" all at once, so that any of the forms of division mentioned earlier can separate the various scenes of an unfolding narrative progression.

Figure 4.1. Sassetta and Assistant, *Meeting of St. Anthony and St. Paul.* Photograph ©
Board of Trustees, National Gallery of Art, Washington DC; Samuel H. Kress Collection.
Reproduced by permission of the National Gallery of Art.

The friezes on the Parthenon and the Arch of Titus are paradigmatic cases,[13] as are the Stations of the Cross fixed along the walls of cathedrals. The additive structure of diptychs and triptychs is also conducive to narrative sequence, the order in the latter often not a simple left-to-right progression but, rather, a left-to-right-to-middle sequence with the center hierarchically weighted to bear the climactic ending.

The medium most obviously suited to pictorial narrative, however, is the book. Its division into pages provides a "natural" discreteness that other pictorial media are forced to achieve metaphorically (the walls separating narrative "rooms") or arbitrarily (the frames of triptych panels or the modern-day comic strip). Kurt Weitzmann describes the historical progression of ancient narrative art as in fact culminating in the invention of the book:

> Greek artists began to line up a series of narrative representations, based either on a single hero's life or some kind of a literary unit, and taking the form of a row of metopes or of a frieze. This is the beginning of the method of the *cyclic narrative* which in the classical period was used on a rather limited scale and in the Hellenistic period developed into a *continuum narrative* whereby the individual scenes are placed in front of a unifying landscape.
>
> At the end of this long drawn-out process of binding the representational arts and literature still closer together, a new method was invented whereby a single episode was divided into several phases, so that the beholder might follow the various changes of action with the chief protagonist being repeated again and again. The result of this development is an enormous increase in the number of scenes and the formation of far more extensive picture cycles than had ever existed before. This innovation took place in the Early Hellenistic period, and the medium in which the vast expansion of narrative representations could unfold most vigorously . . . is the book . . . Thus the *art of storytelling in pictures* became inextricably linked with the history of book illumination. (83)

The structure of the book thus served as the model not only for literary narratives but for pictorial narratives as well, with their need for discreteness and ordering. Picture series such as Hogarth's *Rake's Progress, Harlot's Progress,* and *Marriage à la Mode,* which are reputedly the first picture stories in their own right independent of a previously written narrative (Witemeyer 120), would be unimaginable without the structural model of the book.

Having observed all these pictorial means for rendering events discrete, specific, and temporally successive, we still have not isolated what makes a painting narrative. It is easy to imagine pictures conforming to all these criteria that would not be interpreted as a narrative: a triptych, for example, in which one panel shows a child laughing, another a king fighting, and a third an animal eating. Each scene is discrete, each specific, and each an action, but they lack the most fundamental feature of all narratives—cohesion and, in particular, the continuity of a repeated subject. In visual narrative the repetition of a subject is the primary means for us to know that we are looking at a narrative at all.

The importance of this factor reveals once more the crucial position of realism in the semantics of narrative. For in reality a person cannot be in two places at the same time, and, therefore, if a figure appears more than once in a painting, we automatically assume that it is shown at various distinct moments. On this basis Nelson Goodman contrasts the unordered events of Hans Memling's *Life of Christ* with Jacopo del Sellaio's *Psyche*: "Here what is explicitly told takes time, and the telling has a definite order. Several incidents, with Psyche appearing in each, are shown strung across a landscape. The impossibility of the same person being in different places at the same time notifies us that difference in spatial position among scenes is to be interpreted as difference in temporal position among the events depicted. And, as with a written tale, although the whole story is presented at once, an order of telling is plainly established. The main sequence here conforms to linguistic convention . . . [going] from left to right" (105). We know that we are looking at a narrative painting because we see a subject repeated and because reality repeats only in time.

The repeated subject is equally crucial in literary narrative. As Chatman states, "a narrative may have very little or even no overt description; but a narrative without an agent performing actions is impossible" (*Story and Discourse* 34). He goes on to say that the presence of a person in a fiction does not qualify him or her as a character; instead, if he does not figure in the action of the narrative, his function is like that of the setting. With such figures "their noncharacterhood is a function of their nonreappearance" (140). To be a character is to be a recurrent subject.

Indeed, in narratives in which subjects do not recur, the reader is forced to employ interpretive strategies to connect events. Thus, Gerald Prince writes:

Given

John rode off into the sunset then Mary became a millionaire, for example, I can easily establish a strong link between the two events:

John rode off into the sunset then Mary became a millionaire because she had bet everything she owned—500,000 dollars—that he would. ("Narrativity" 72)

What the causal linkage creates here is Mary's involvement or implication in John's seemingly separate act. Mary thus becomes a repeated subject, and the events achieve narrative wholeness. Chatman goes so far as to claim that this kind of interpretive strategy is one of the hallmarks of narrative perception: "In E. M. Forster's example, 'The king died, and then the queen died of grief,' we assume that the queen was in fact the wife of that king . . . this kind of inference-drawing differs radically from that required by lyric, expository, and other genres" (*Story and Discourse* 30–31).

All genres, of course, have cohesion devices—those factors that identify old information as such, repeat it, and link it to the new. With narrative, however, the achievement of this wholeness is the active goal of the reader. This drive for cohesion and elaboration, this interpretive compulsion for both categorizing and cataloguing information under the unifying labels of characters' names, corresponds to the narrative necessity of a center of action or a subject that continues in time. In painting this narrative center resides in a literal agent, the carrier of a name.

The need for a repeated subject in narrative can be seen in historiography as well. Hayden White contrasts modes of history writing on just this basis, insisting that events merely strung together in annals and chronicles fail to bespeak their meaning, to cohere in a story form, and to close, because they are not organized around a subject. "The capacity to envision a set of events as belonging to the same order of meaning requires a metaphysical principle by which to translate difference into similarity. In other words, it requires a 'subject' common to all of the *referents* of the various sentences that register events as having occurred" (White 9, 19). The subject (an individual, a state) provides cohesion for all the diverse "predicates" of action and in doing so, allows for closure, either through the natural closure of death or political dissolution or through the story resolution of conflict.

Yet we have not isolated—even with the discovery of the importance of the repeated subject—sufficient conditions to create pictorial narrativity. In many cases a repeated figure—such as we find in M. C. Escher's lithographs—will be interpreted as a design, not as a narrative. At this point we must ask ourselves: what does it take for a painting to impart the sense of identity between repeated elements that forms the precondition for a narrative interpretation? The key lies in a realist interpretation: to read a painting narratively we must see the repeated shapes as people, their body postures as gestures, their background as a spatial environment, and the scene represented as a pregnant moment expandable into an entire temporal sequence. As I have written in connection with Escher, "it is the norms of pictorial realism that allow us to see process in pictures; without them we see mere pattern" (W. Steiner, *Colors of Rhetoric* 169).

It is worth dwelling a little on the connection between narrativity and realism. We have already seen a variety of ways in which pictorial art reveals their interdependence: the recurrent subject, who signals temporal difference; the realist norms that keep the repeated subject from being read as a design; the chronological time of the story, which is that of temporal flow in reality; the association between historical "truth" and narrative wholeness; and the tendency to read nonordered pictorial events, as in Memling's paintings, as symbols rather than narratives.

The narrative-realism connection can in fact be followed throughout the history of pictorial narrative; its elucidation is one of the chief benefits of examining narrative in the visual arts. For whereas in literary narrative the connection is hidden by its very banality, in the "unnatural" narrativity of pictorial art it is constantly obtrusive. The pregnant moment or ekphrastic painting, for example, is typically construed symbolically rather than as an attempt at storytelling. As one expert on Babylonian art states, the most favored narrative method "was allusive rather than explicit, employing the culminating scene—one group of figures, one moment of time, at the climax of a series of events—to stand for the entire story. This was undoubtedly intended to arouse in the viewer's mind recollection of the complete story, and in addition to stand as a symbol of the deeper lying ideas, beliefs, or psychical orientation of the community, as in our own society the crucifix is expected to recall the entire Passion story and also the fundamental Christian belief in the redemption of mankind by the sacrifice of Christ" (Perkins 55). In a similar pattern Frank Kermode adduces the most famous literary ekphrasis, Keats's *Ode on a Grecian Urn*, to illustrate the contrast between narrativity and ekphrastic symbolism:

> The first questions we like to ask [of a narrative] resemble those of Keats: "What leaf-fring'd legend . . . ? What men or gods are these? What maidens loth? . . . To what green altar . . . ?" There seems to be a *mythos;* these persons are acting, they seem to be trying to do something or to stop somebody else from doing it . . . and they are headed somewhere. The *mythos* appears to have the usual relation to *ethos* and *dianoia.* But Keats, and we after him, are unable to discover the plot because the arrangement of the events (*synthesis ton pragmaton*) is not such as to allow us . . . It lacks a quality we expect in imitations of our world,

where heads ache and one may be disgusted. What it lacks is intelligible sequence . . . The importance of the story on the urn, then, is that in its very difference [from our causal-temporal world] it can tell us, by intruding into our sequence of scandal and outrage, intimations not obvious but comforting. (84–85)

In Keats's poem, as in all such works, the foiling of narrativity automatically triggers symbolic interpretation. Just as art historians intuitively link narrative art to history and genre, but not to allegory, Kermode presents arrested narrative, or ekphrasis, as a tool of symbolism.

In contrast, the repetition of figures in a realistic rendering has the power to suggest narrative even when the events shown are not specific. In the high civilization of the eighteenth and nineteenth dynasties of Egypt, the "new compositional scheme developed at Amarna [brought] for the first time renderings in which the same figures appear in several different stages of an event within a coherent spatial setting . . . the new concreteness and the psychological differentiation so typical of Amarna art give the representations a narrative character even though they do not render specific events that only occurred once" (Kantor 55).

The association of narrative and realism has led historians into a chicken-and-egg debate as to the origin of "true" realism in the arts, which is traditionally accorded to the ancient Greeks. George M. A. Hanfmann argues that the development of pictorial realism in Greece through perspectival foreshortening, light modulation, and so forth gave rise to the realistic narratives of Homer. "When classical sculptors and painters discovered a convincing method of representing the human body, they set up a chain reaction which transformed the character of Greek narration" (74). E. H. Gombrich disputes this view: "I feel prompted to put forward the opposite hypothesis: when classical sculptors and painters discovered the character of Greek narration, they set up a chain reaction which transformed the methods of representing the human body—and indeed more than that . . . For what is the character of Greek narration as we know it from Homer? Briefly, it is concerned not only with the 'what' but also with the 'how' of mythical events . . . in a narrative illustration, any distinction between the 'what' and the 'how' is impossible to maintain . . . Whether he wants to or not, the pictorial artist has to include unintended information" (*Art and Illusion* 79). Gombrich concludes, "In the whole history of Western art we have this constant interaction between narrative intent and pictorial realism" (131).

This being the case, it is ironic that the institutionalization of pictorial realism in the Renaissance made pictorial narrative as we have defined it an impossibility. In a painting with vanishing-point perspective and chiaroscuro, the assumption is that we are observing a scene through a frame from a fixed vantage point *at one moment in time.* Nothing could be more foreign to Renaissance realism than the juxtaposing of temporally distinct events within a single visual field, as is commonly found in ancient and medieval art. Thus, though narrative was inextricably connected with realism, paradoxically the strict adherence to the norms of Renaissance realism precluded narrativity from the visual arts.

A symptom of this development is the use of the term *story* or *history* in Renaissance treatises on art. Alberti returns to Aristotle to urge that the proper subject of art is significant human action. But he uses *istoria* in a spatial rather than temporal sense, as a whole uniting and organizing the elements within it: "composition is that rule in painting by which the parts fit together in the painted work. The greatest work of the painter is the *istoria.* Bodies are part of the *istoria,* members are parts of the bodies, planes are parts of the members" (70). *Istoria* throughout Alberti is used more as "theme" or "composition" than as "narrated events."

Da Vinci, writing with Alberti's treatise in front of him (*On Painting* 9n, 17, 30, 117, 119), does not even mention narrativity as temporal flow but uses *narrative painting* for the stopped-action historical, biblical, or mythological scene. Everything that he says about such works is predicated, in fact, on the *absence* of temporal flow. In his chapter 58, "Conformity in the Parts of Narrative Painting," for example, he advises against the mixing of happy and sad figures in the same work, "for Nature decrees that with those who weep, one sheds tears, and with those who laugh one becomes happy, and their laughter and tears are separate" (da Vinci, *On Painting* 60). Here we have an injunction aimed at unity of effect, as if the spectator's experience with the painting were atemporal, so that he should not be called upon to register emotions that cannot be simultaneously felt or unified into a single response. Moreover, in chapter 72, insisting on the artist's diversifying the expression of faces in narrative paintings, Leonardo specifically forbids the repetition of the same figure. He attributes such repetitions to the artist's unconsciously using himself as a model for all his figures. But in enjoining him not to "make or repeat either the whole figure or a part of it, so that one face is seen elsewhere in the painting," Leonardo renders pictorial narrative impossible in terms of one of the criteria that we have established, the repetition of the subject (*On Painting* 66).

Where temporal flow is mentioned in connection with narrative art in post-Renaissance treatises, it has a contradictory quality. In the cinquecento dialogue "The Aretino" of Lodovico Dolce, for instance, Aretino goes so far as to equate pictorial *dispositio* with narrative order itself. "As for disposition", he writes, "it is necessary that the artist move from section to section following the course of time in the narrative he has undertaken to paint, and do so with such propriety that the spectators judge that this affair could not have taken place in any other way than the one he has depicted. He should not place later in time what ought to come earlier, nor earlier what should come later, but lay things out in a most ordered fashion, according to the way in which they succeeded one another." Dolce signals the literary origin of this idea in the response of Aretino's interlocutor, Fabrini: "Aristotle in his *Poetics* gave this same piece of instruction to writers of tragedy and comedy" (qtd. in Roskill 121).

Dolce's dialogue, one of the central documents in the *ut pictura poesis* argument of the immediate post-Renaissance and neoclassical periods, is as oblivious to the literal implications of its interartistic analogizing as that argument generally was. For despite the explicit mention of separate narrative episodes in his discussion of disposition, it is clear that Dolce had no such structure in mind. He is speaking of paintings in which all parts are co-temporal. Thus, in comparing him with Vasari and Alberti, Dolce's editor finds him using the terms *invention* and *disposition* as refinements on the general notion of composition (Roskill 268, 117n). " 'La inventione e la favola, o historia,' Dolce says, as if content were narrowly equivalent to the sum of the narrative elements worked in. Here Dolce's literal-minded adhesion to the sense given to *inventio* in rhetorical theory" allows artists to think of their work as narrative without its including temporally discrete moments and double ordering (269).

It is clear that both artists and theorists paid a great price for visual realism in their eradication of narrative sequence from the visual arts. Jack Greenstein has shown how central the connection had been between painting and storytelling up to the time of Alberti. He traces the background of Alberti's term *istoria* (*historia* in Latin), showing that its Greek root meant "to see or to know." (Its etymology thus leads us back to the same concept as *narration*.) In medieval thought *historia* became equated with the literal level in biblical allegory, having a meaning both true in itself and signifying other truths beyond it. Moreover, throughout its usage *historia* had signified both the events depicted and the discourse that depicted them, so that the representation of a history in any medium could be called a *historia*. "By the end of the Middle Ages, the noun *historia* and its Italian equivalents *storia* and *istoria* had taken on, as a secondary denotation, the meaning 'pictorial representation.' Under Dante's influence, *historia* became the generic name for a work of art that depicted a narrative—that is, a biblical—scene" (Greenstein 30). Like history, painting would thus present a story that is literally true and that at the same time points to truths beyond it. By extending the notion of *historia* to cover classical as well as biblical subjects, Alberti was proposing a thoroughgoing analogy between the art of painting and the creation of multilayered allegorical narratives. "The art he described was designed to produce pictures which were convincing as representations of actual events but were effective at the same time in conveying the higher significations of historia" (83).

Medieval artists, as Greenstein points out, could create this semantic richness by juxtaposing scenes to each other. But how could post-Albertian artists do so if they were limited to one scene? Greenstein describes how Andrea Mantegna contended with this problem in his *Circumcision of Christ*. Mantegna "recognized that the sacred setting used by medieval artists to bring out the sacramental significance of the Circumcision was incompatible with the representational fidelity of pictorial *historia*. Yet, to delete the sacred setting would have . . . [rent] the rite from the context that conveyed its timeless significance. To resolve this incongruity . . . Mantegna invented a *historia* that conflated the Circumcision and the Presentation in the Temple" (100–101). The details of this accommodation are not relevant to this discussion, but Greenstein's work illustrates the semantic struggle that painters were forced to take on in exchange for Albertian realism. The results of the struggle were often magnificent and carried powerful historical meanings, but these meanings resulted from different pictorial strategies than the multi-episodic narratives of pre-Renaissance art.

Arduous as it proved to be, however, the proscription against multi-episodic narrative in painting was extremely effective. Renaissance handbooks on art, as we have seen, either ignored narrativity or used it in an automatized rhetorical move as a substitute for composition. The paintings conceived at this time followed suit. Works with repeated subjects or temporally distinct events are not to be found in Italy much after 1500, when the logic of the advances in perspective, chiaroscuro, and figure modeling prevailed. The exceptions are so famous and so remarked upon that they more than reinforce the rule. They include Poussin's *Israelites Gathering Manna in the Desert* and Watteau's *Meeting in a Park*. The former "juxtaposes within the same image scenes of misery from the time before the manna was found, with scenes of youthful enthusiasm and elderly hesitation from the time after its discovery by the Israelites" (Bryson 85), while the latter contains a repeated female figure, accompanied in one appearance and solitary in the other, so that a general narrative of unhappy love is suggested. Still, the painting does not differentiate the episodes into separately zoned scenes but runs them together in a continuous landscape.

Perhaps in part as a response to even this limited loosening of temporal unity, Lessing stressed in *Laocoön* the instantaneous and, hence, unitary nature of the pictorial moment. Art theorists were profoundly influenced by Lessing. Martin Meisel writes that "nineteenth-century academic theory in England seems to have taken seriously only two books in its library: Lessing's *Laocoön* (1776) and Sir Joshua Reynolds' *Discourses* (1769–1791)" (18). Accordingly, the pronouncements of the Royal Academy frequently concerned the temporal status of the represented scene. "[Charles] Leslie and [Charles] Eastlake discuss duration as an attribute of the subject and of the finished representation, but only in its two limiting phases, the instantaneous and the permanent, zero and infinity. Neither artist challenges the idea that the frame of the painting embraces only coexistent objects and simultaneous events" (20). Thus, when John Martin exhibited his *Belshazzar's Feast* in 1821, it was criticized for combining three separate scenes in a single canvas (22). Despite the extensive interartistic connections in nineteenth-century British art that Meisel describes, the possibility that a single painting could take on the multitemporal richness of literary narrative was still ruled out. And the fact that so many periods and styles—Renaissance, baroque, neoclassical, and romantic—had felt it necessary to restate this prohibition indicates just how repressive a measure it in fact was.[14] This is not to say, of course, that post-Renaissance art is utterly nonnarrative, for historical painting as a genre contains many of the characteristics that Prince and Labov enumerate. Yet this art was weakly narrative; it proscribed multi-episodic canvases and found repeated subjects indecorous. As a result, it could imply or call to mind a narrative but not represent a narrative in all its unfolding richness.

What is crucial to note is that there is nothing inherent in the media of the visual arts to require unitemporal subjects. In fact, even the notion that vanishing-point perspective entailed the effacement of narrative sequence dawned only gradually on Renaissance painters. Between the fully realized perspective of Leonardo and medieval art, in which "the simultaneous depiction of consecutive episodes . . . was a characteristic . . . method of pictorial narration,"[15] lay a transitional period, the early and middle quattrocento. During this time painters were teaching themselves the elements of realism without as yet understanding that these techniques ideologically ruled out the narratives that they wished to paint. For this brief time in Italy realist techniques and narrative sequence came together in some extraordinary works by Fra Angelico, Filippo Lippi, Benozzo Gozzoli, and others.

Figure 4.2. Benozzo Gozzoli, *The Dance of Salome and Beheading of St. John the Baptist.* Photograph © Board of Trustrees, National Gallery of Art, Washington DC; Samuel H. Kress Collection. Reproduced by permisson of the National Gallery of Art.

Because of the special status of these early Renaissance works—between the nonrealist narrativity of the Middle Ages and the nonnarrative realism of the Renaissance—we might examine the semantic potential of narrative painting through them. It is a potential that was tapped only briefly and not reassessed until the nineteenth and twentieth centuries.

Benozzo Gozzoli is one of those artists straddling the boundary between medieval and Renaissance conventions. Bernard Berenson described him as "gifted with a . . . spontaneity, a freshness, a liveliness in telling a story that wake the child in us . . . His place . . . in spite of his adopting so many of the fifteenth-century improvements is not with the artists of the Renaissance, but with the story-tellers and costumed fairytale painters of the transition" (64).

The work of Benozzo's that I have particularly in mind is *The Dance of Salome and the Beheading of St. John the Baptist* (fig. 4.2). It is one of five predella paintings from an altarpiece whose main panel depicts the Virgin and Child enthroned. Each of the predella works, the small paintings decorating the frame below the main panel, illustrates the life of one of the saints in the main work. The contract for the altarpiece that Benozzo signed in Florence with the Confraternity of the Purification of the Virgin makes the fairly conventional relation between predella panels and central work explicit: "And the said Benozo [*sic*] must with his own hand . . . paint at the bottom, that is in the predella of the said altar-piece, the stories of the said saints, each under its own saint" (Shapley 88). Thus, the nonhistorical simultaneity of the Purification, in which the saints assemble like courtiers before the Virgin, is unraveled, so to speak, into its distinct temporal strands in the predella panels. The traditional structure of the altarpiece highlights the opposition between eternal, nonnarrative art and historical narrativity, and fittingly, every one of the predella compositions except that depicting the life of the Virgin (an echo of the atemporal main panel above it) contains two or more separate episodes.

The predella concerning John the Baptist contains three: (1) the dance of Salome on the right, (2) the beheading of the saint on the extreme left, and (3) Salome's presentation of his head to Herodias in the left-central background. The repetition of figures, so crucial to narrative recognition, is especially obvious here. Salome not only appears in both the first and third scenes with the same clothing, but her face is repeated in exactly the same profiled attitude (except for her streaming hair in scene 1). Like a cameo relief, she connects the beginning of the story with the end, and so similar is her face in each case that one wonders how to construe the fact that the same look that bewitches Herod is trained on her approving mother.

This bivalent look is all the more significant when compared to the mother's appearance in each of her two occurrences. Unlike Salome, Herodias wears different clothes and headdresses in the two scenes in which she figures. Although Salome should have been unveiled in the course of her famous dance, the painting instead uncovers the mother to reveal the harlot's red below. She looks away from her dancing daughter in scene 1 toward the cubicle where John is being beheaded. Of course, at the time that she looks he is not being beheaded, but in the simultaneity of the painting she does appear to have her eyes upon him, while her daughter, with the same colored clothing as the executioner, her arm raised in a mirror image of his arm clenching the sword, looks away from the future scene. In terms of Salome's gaze the dance's effect is the gratification of her mother in scene 3. In terms of Herodias's gaze the dance's effect is the decapitation of the saint. Although Herodias studiously looks "through" the dance into the future, she directly meets Salome's gaze in scene 3. And in that scene the kneeling Salome becomes a parody of John kneeling in prayer to his God and prefiguring the Son of that God. If Salome dancing mimics the executioner, Salome kneeling mimics the sacrificial victim. She is her own executioner. And her mother, who cradles the grotesque severed head in her lap, is a disturbing parody of the classical *pietà* or perhaps the figure of the Madonna and child with adoring saint. John's eyes, in sharp contrast to everyone else's in the painting, are closed in both his appearances. Vision, eye contact, lust, and murder are all interimplicated through the figures' eyes, but John eschews this play of worldly vice by closing his eyes and short-circuiting the visual intercourse that dominates the painting.

Like gazes, clothes create a set of symbolic connections. We have already noted the twinning of Salome and the executioner through their blue and gold attire. The association of these colors with the Virgin is again a source of irony. Herodias sheds her green mantle in the passage from scene 1 to 3, ending up in the harlot's color red, like Herod and two of his attendants in scene 1. The gold of Salome's hair and her mother's headdress in scene 3 reach a supernatural intensity in John's halo in scene 2, reflected as well in his killer's armor. If color echoing creates certain equations among characters, John's intense goldness in a sense betrays the earthly gold of the others, as do, in reverse, his "shaggy" garments next to their elegant robes.

Thus, if the central painting of the altarpiece celebrates the Purification of the Virgin, the predella panel presents John the Baptist's murder as a terrible parody of that Purification and a mocking, in fact, of the very motherhood that Mary epitomizes. Herodias—an incestuous adulteress—pimps her daughter in order to martyr Christ's precursor. The sinfulness of the mother is here instilled in the daughter, and their perfect complicity is sealed in the gratified look of the mother and the happy answering gaze of the daughter so anxious to please. I would stress that though all these interpretive possibilities are implicit in the story of Salome's dance, they are made explicit in this painting through specific pictorial techniques that depend on the repetition of characters and the copresence of temporally distinct moments.

We might at this point return to the repeated figure of Salome, whose face is so exactly echoed in the two episodes in which she appears that it might be more proper to speak of her formula there than her figure. The identity of Salome as sexual temptress and dutiful daughter immediately sets up the parodic and symbolic mechanisms that we have been noting, and, hence, the play of narrative flow and the subject's identity are crucial to the thematics of the whole painting. Salome's look in temptation is the meaning of the look of filial gratification at the end; what that beauty really meant is that severed head so proudly presented to Herodias in scene 3.

Not only does the repetition of Salome's face help us to locate the past in the present, and vice versa, but it dictates the particular meaning of that past and present, conditioning their interpretive possibilities. This procedure is important because we are dealing with a story that predates its pictorial telling and has a long interpretive history. Its story wholeness, in the sense of its having a specific beginning, middle, and end, is an accomplished fact. Moreover, it already has a prototypical principle of story wholeness available to it—that of anyone's life. This "biographical model" is the totality that links countless medieval narrative paintings into wholes: the assumption of the central figure's life as the narrative that the episodes actually rendered demarcate. Thus, Sassetta's three paintings of St. Anthony joined on a panel (*Meeting of St. Anthony and St. Paul* [see fig. 4.1], *St. Anthony Leaving His Monastery*, and *St. Anthony Distributing His Wealth to the Poor*) belong together, narratively speaking, because we automatically impose upon them an unspoken interpretive strategy that analogizes life to a plot. Benozzo, however, does not make use of this principle of wholeness; instead, he performs a virtuoso act of recounting the story of John's death. This approach was perhaps necessary, in part, because Benozzo was working in Florence, where John the Baptist was the patron saint and hence where paintings of his dramatic death abounded. The predella was thus particularly directed toward the conditions of its reception. As Paul Ricoeur writes: "As soon as a story is well known . . . retelling takes the place of telling. Then following the story is less important than apprehending the well-known end as implied in the beginning and the well-known episodes as leading to this end" (179). Not only does Benozzo allow us to read the end in the beginning, but he stamps the same likeness on the two—the likeness of Salome, however, not John.

The subject of the narrative has been shifted from John to Salome, and its point (Labov's "evaluation") has shifted accordingly, too. The lameness and inconsistency of the painting's titles illustrate this fact, the work being called variously *The Dance of Salome and the Beheading of St. John the Baptist*, sometimes just *The Dance of Salome*, and sometimes *Herod's Banquet*. These are merely the formulaic titles for paintings of the saint's death. They fail to capture the evaluative point of Benozzo's work because they fail to mention scene 3, which is the end and culmination of the story. *The Gloating over the Head* or *Filial Duty* would seem to be more appropriate titles, but even they do not do full justice to the irony palpable in the central episode. This is clearly not John's but Salome's story, though the significant event is the murder of a holy man for the basest of reasons.

By presenting his story this way, Benozzo has achieved not only a unique and powerful narrative but a narrative whose historicity competes with its aesthetic self-containment. If, as Hayden White argues, "the reality which lends itself to narrative representation is the *conflict* between desire, on the one side, and the law, on the other" ("Value of Narrativity" 16), commentators have mentioned only one side of this conflict in Benozzo's painting—desire. The figure of the dancing Salome captures everyone's attention, especially since other Florentine painters at this time were concentrating on the human figure in motion. "But the light-footed swiftness of Benozzo's figure sets it apart. There is a special freshness and eagerness in her whole body as she gracefully alights on one foot, her left hand airily resting on her hip and her right darting up in salute to King Herod" (Shapley 78). The same writer sees the composition of the painting as a reinforcement of the dance within it, which she takes as the central theme. "The weaving of the three episodes from foreground to background and then again to foreground is in perfect harmony with the dominant theme of the painting, *The Dance of Salome*" (77). From this standpoint Benozzo would appear to be recasting an event of prime historic significance into a common romance of lust, manipulation, and murder, exploiting the saint as an occasion to celebrate the beauty of a young, dancing girl—a "typical" Renaissance aestheticizing of momentous events. Indeed, Salome served just such a purpose in the nineteenth century, when she functioned as a symbol of art—oblivious to reality, morality, consequences.[16]

The shift of focus from John to Salome—and the moral bankruptcy of her desire to obey and gratify her mother—draws the painting into history in another way. Just as John the Baptist's importance was as a precursor—the one whose personal history gave way to another's and to a whole new principle of history—his story here gives way to Salome's and provides a moral meaning for her act of treachery. It lends the mother-daughter grouping in scene 3 a sinister chill that goes beyond their act of murder to the parodying of the entire system of values for which the pietà and the adoration of the child stand. Rather than settling on the close-of-a-life model that John's story offered, Benozzo implicates John's death in Salome's story and ultimately in all of sinful humankind's. In doing so, he operates in the normative historicist's fashion, sacrificing the finitude of the individual to the overarching story in which he or she figures. The significance of this merging of individual into society is marked: "we know how much Heidegger emphasizes the nontransferable character of being-toward-death and that this uncommunicable aspect of dying imposes the primacy of individual fate over common destiny in the subsequent analysis of historicality. Yet it is the primacy that the analysis of narrativity calls into question . . . After all, is not narrative time a time that continues beyond the death of each of its protagonists? Is it not part of the plot to include the death of each hero in a story that surpasses every individual fate?" (Ricoeur 188).

Much as this might sound like an argument for Benozzo as a precursor of Derrida and for the painting as an example of the infinite regress of meaning and storytelling, I have gone through this discussion of Salome's formulaic repetition and the crucial last scene in order to show the narrative potency of this work and, metonymically, of pictorial art in general. Beyond Labov's "complicating action" essential to any narrative, *The Dance of Salome* contains an extremely rich evaluative system that provides meaning and wholeness to its sequential flow and ties it to the archetypal narrative systems of both fiction and history. Moreover, this system draws in the inert details of the orientation, such as appearance and clothing, and semanticizes them, turning them into evaluative details. Prince's narrative criteria of conflict, discreteness, factuality, wholeness, gestalt-like totalizing meanings, stress on origins and ends, inversions of expectations, and desire are all to be found in this work (Prince, "Narrativity"), and not just because the literary source contains these features. On the contrary, the painting makes into a striking narrative a story that is very meagerly set forth in the Bible.

We have still not exhausted the devices for wholeness in Benozzo's work, and certainly not in pictorial art in general, and at this point I would like to interrupt the discussion of *The Dance of Salome* to examine them. We have seen the cause-and-effect relations created by the directionality of gazes, especially Herodias's, and the implication of the beginning in the end in the echoing of clothes, colors, and Salome's face. As in literary works, these metonymic and metaphoric linkages are crucial to the project of narrative wholeness. They operate on different kinds of wholes. Herodias's gaze establishes story sequence and causality: first Salome dances, and then John is executed; because of Salome's dance, John is executed. The metaphoric matchings reinterpret details. The echoing of pose and attire between Salome l and the executioner imply that to dance temptingly is to execute a saint, that allure is sin.

Allied to the metaphoric device is a strategy for wholeness that we might term "typological." In many medieval and early Renaissance paintings, for example, Giovanni di Paolo's *Annunciation* (fig. 4.3), scenes are juxtaposed because they lend meaning to one another as episodes in the Christian vision of history. In di Paolo's painting Adam and Eve are expelled from the Garden, driven by Gabriel from the left "toward" the annunciation scene in the center. The annunciation redeems the fall of man, as signaled

Figure 4.3. Giovanni di Paolo, *Annunciation*. Photograph © Board of Trustees, National Gallery of Art, Washington DC; Samuel H. Kress Collection. Reproduced by permisson of the National Gallery of Art.

by the replacement of nature by inspired architecture, of violent angel by civil angel, of nakedness by rich clothing. Thus, though there are no literally repeated subjects, the typological strategy implies that all events are unified through Christ into the story of man's fall and redemption. There are no events, in theory, that are not part of the same story. Temporal disjunction and the lack of repeated subjects are irrelevant, since all characters are versions or types of one another in a universal story that overarches all time and space.

A less ambitious version of this strategy is the biographical model, for example, Sassetta's depiction of scenes from the life of St. Anthony. We can read these episodes as a single narrative because we superimpose upon them the plot of a life, a whole in which they figure significantly, composing the totality that renders them meaningful as narrative components in the first place. The third of Sasseta's scenes (fig. 4.1) employs a special device for suggesting this wholeness—the road. The winding path is one of the devices that Nelson Goodman mentions as indicating an order of telling distinct from story order (110). And, of course, the "path of life" is a metaphor so shopworn that the picaresque novel and the painting of a life along a road hardly seem metaphoric structures at all. But the implications of this strategy in particular pictorial manifestations can be very powerful. As one commentator writes of Sassetta's *Meeting of St. Anthony and St. Paul:*

> High at the upper left, the little figure of the saint makes his appearance, passes behind a hill, meets a pagan centaur whom he rebukes and converts to an amendment of life, and finally embraces his fellow saint in greeting in the lower foreground, having passed downward in the meantime through a gloomy wood, in miniature a recall of Dante's *"selva oscura"* of the first lines of *the Divine Comedy* . . . The eye makes a journey through the imagined world of the picture; its movement in harmony with the imagery makes possible the illusion of the passage of actual time; the time-element produces a feeling of authenticity in the narrative. And the narrative finally enriches the sense of spiritual experience. (Seymour 18, 23)

The sense of sequence created by the continuity of the road is at the same time broken by the road's discontinuity. The road is interrupted by the hill, by the edge of the painting near the centaur episode, and finally by the dark wood. It returns, however, in a great sweep across the bottom of the painting where the saints embrace. The road thus functions as an analogue for the narrative flow of the painting itself and the embattled life of the holy man.

No temporal flow can be narrated through anything but broken episodes, which must be connected by some interpretive strategy. Just as the connecting path is made whole in the meeting of the saints at the bottom, so the episodes themselves are resolved in that meeting. We begin with the isolated figure of St. Anthony; then find him meeting his spiritual opposite in the centaur; and finally see him joined in an embrace with his spiritual like, St. Paul. It is as if the whole aim of the holy life, as presented in this picture, is to pass from isolation through conflict to love. The structural properties of the pictorial composition, including the broken path, reinforce this meaning. Such an interpretation seems particularly defensible, given the anachronistic "Gothic style" of Sassetta's painting, which is narrative not only in repeating its central figure in temporally distinct episodes but also in making little attempt to combine those episodes into an integrated landscape. "A charming storyteller, [Sassetta] chose to ignore the recently discovered rules of perspective and methods of rendering form realistically."[17] This deliberate eschewing of spatial unity in the interests of narrative continuity was still an unthreatening possibility for late-medieval narrative art.

The winding path was obviously a doomed narrative strategy, however, for any painter intrigued by the burgeoning techniques of pictorial realism in the early quattrocento. If one were to adopt this realism with its requirement of spatial coherence, how could one indicate the discreteness of the separate events composing the narrative? It is at this point that the multicompartmented building becomes so important as a structuring device for narrative, for it is full of discrete simultaneous units, and, with all its right angles, it is also ideal for the virtuoso treatment of perspective, light, and volume.

Indeed, the conception of narrative as a procession through the rooms of a building has a long and impressive currency. The word *stanza,* of course, means "room." And one might see in the building the contrast between the spatial and temporal arts themselves. A building is as spatial as anything one can imagine, with its floor plan and facades each present to us in a single moment of perception. At the same time, its perception involves temporality, since one cannot see all of its three-dimensionality in one moment. The experience of walking through a building, of being a participant in it rather than an external observer, is a temporal progression from stopping place to stopping place, these ordered by structures significantly called "passages" and hall-"ways."

The competition between path and building as narrative symbols in the quattrocento transition is apparent in the mixed metaphor employed by Cennino Cennini, author of *The Craftsman's Handbook,* a work that sounds particularly old-fashioned next to Alberti's nearly contemporary *On Painting.* Cennino, metaphorically torn, advises the aspiring artist: "Mind you, the most perfect steersman that you can have, and the best helm, lie in the triumphant gateway of copying from nature" (15). As Cennino's editor notes, "He seems to have had some half-formed conception of his course of study as an architectural layout, with steps rising and gates opening; but this is confused with ideas of journeys, by land and, as here, by sea" (Cennini, ed. n. 1). In Cennino's confusion, I believe, we see the passage from one aesthetic paradigm to another. The building is the archetypal symbol of the structure. It changes a narrative into a simultaneity, makes temporal order problematic, and thus serves as the natural transition to the purging of temporal flow from painting altogether. By the late quattrocento and the cinquecento not only multi-episodic but multi-roomed buildings have become rare in European painting.

But in the transitional period the building had a multitude of narrative fictions. Not only did rooms serve to demarcate episodes, but often inside was contrasted to outside for just this purpose. In the *Annunciation* di Paolo develops the contrast between outside and inside into potent narrative symbols. In the Expulsion on the left, nature is rendered flatly, as if it were a tapestry pattern; the Annunciation itself takes place in a self-consciously (if faultily) perspectival interior; on the right Joseph sits before a fire in a somewhat naturalistic courtyard, the "cubicle-space" used by Giotto and the Sienese before 1350. This ability to shift and choose styles of space is a remarkable aspect of late-medieval painting (Seymour 16). The medieval, heraldic handling of the Expulsion renders it a scene "of the past," "of the passé," in fact, for the announcement being made in the center will reinterpret that moment and redeem the pathetic outcasts. Accordingly, the Annunciation is set in a discontinuous interior whose space is inconsistent in every sense with the space on the left. Joseph on the right, warmed by the fire and sheltered by the Dove, is simultaneous with the Annunciation scene and, hence, continuous with the architecture that encloses it. But he is cut off from that scene both by a wall and a convention. His rendering belongs to the not-quite-contemporary conventions of the previous century, and the contrast between the shared punishment of the "first parents" on the left and the separate, unequal status of the redemptive parents on the right is striking.

In *The Dance of Salome* Benozzo also uses architectural framing to divide his episodes. Unlike Hans Memling's *Panorama of the Passion,* in which episodes of the life "populate" the buildings of an entire city, Benozzo's scenes occupy what appears to be a single room with antechambers. His faulty perspective—whether intentional or not—helps give the impression that all the action is simultaneous. Herodias 3, for example, appears to be sitting almost beside Herodias 1, especially because her recessed figure is, if anything, larger than her earlier standing self. The recession into deep space of scene 3, marked by the lozenged ceiling, suggests recession in time—into the future. And the cutting off of the execution from its cause in scene 1 and its effect in scene 3, by the peculiar little chamber with only a single wall, is significant. It is the ugly reality that interprets Salome's two attractive poses: dancing temptress (executioner) and kneeling donor (victim). The play of continuity and separation achieved by the architectural setting again both establishes the temporal displacements and shows the implication of one event in another. Temporal flow itself is semanticized.

Yet the ordering of events remains problematic. Discussing this painting, Seymour Chatman describes the order at "face value": "Salome dances for Herod in the right-most section of the painting, and a later event—a soldier holding the sword over John's head—occurs in the leftmost portion. It is in the middle that the final event occurs, Salome presenting the head to her mother" (*Story and Discourse* 34). The ordering, if one reads the picture like a written text (from left to right), would thus be 2–3-1. But since Benozzo's events do not all occur on a single plane, one could just as easily "read" the painting as occurring on two registers, a foreground with the ordering 2–1 and a background with the third scene. Moreover, as I stated earlier, though scene 3 as a whole is more centered than either of the others, the figure of the dancing Salome in scene 1 is dead center in the painting. The ambiguity as to center—tempting dancer or unnatural mother—is in keeping with the ironic and symbolic meanings already discussed. The fact that we cannot specify the order of telling without ignoring either the stressed depth of the third scene or the actual left-right orientation of the scenes on the picture plane is an interesting addition to this ambiguity. The interchangeability of end and beginning, their competition for semantic centrality, and the self-enforced blindness of Salome and her mother to the outcome of her dance are all suggested by the problematic ordering of episodes in this architectural simultaneity.

Thus, Benozzo's painting fulfills in virtually every respect the requirements not only of a narrative but of a strong narrative. It has an order of telling distinct from the order of happening. Its episodes have discreteness, wholeness, and evaluative point. It manages to suffuse all its elements with narrative power, so that they imply a meaning greater than themselves.

Still, in the gradual transition from medieval to Renaissance conventions signaled by the shift from path to building, the fate of narrativity in painting is apparent. The next step is to integrate the whole building temporally as well as spatially, so that the viewer becomes the orientation point for the appearance of everything in the picture. At that moment the perceptual wins over the narrative in painting, not to cede place again until the late nineteenth century.

We might return to our original metaphor of network and chain, noting that painting at a certain historical moment was faced with a choice. It could express its knowledge potential either as distinct stages of action and understanding or as an atemporal configuration. It chose the latter. The mutual exclusivity of identical repetition and realist norms was certainly never a part of Renaissance orthodoxy—quite the contrary, in fact. And yet this mutual exclusivity was the logical outcome of the Renaissance model of painting. In assenting to the restrictions of the perceptual model, visual artists split picture from narrative, space from time, and cohesion from sequence in an attempt to ensure adequacy to reality. Conventional as we know Renaissance realism was, its lack of iconic adequacy to reality lies less in what it represented than in what it excluded. For certainly reality, from any viewpoint, is pervaded by temporality. To equate reality and its representation, realism, with atemporality is to destroy the logical basis of realism—the concept of identity as a repetition traversing time.

Notes

1. In "Social Dramas and Stories about Them" Victor Turner writes: " 'Narrate' is from the Latin *narrare* ('to tell') which is akin to the Latin *gnarus* ('knowing,' 'acquainted with,' 'expert in') both derivative from the Indo-European root *gna* ('to know') whence the vast family of words deriving from the Latin *cognoscere*, including 'cognition' itself, and 'noun' and 'pronoun,' the Greek *gignoskein*, whence gnosis, and the OE p.p.*gecnawan*, whence the Mode 'know.' Narrative is, it would seem, rather an appropriate term for a reflexive activity which seeks to 'know' (even in its ritual aspect, to have gnosis about) antecedent events and the meaning of those events. " One might compare *history*, from the Greek *historia*, "a learning or knowing by inquiry, an account of one's inquiries, narrative, history," and *histor*— "knowing, learned, wise man, judge" (*Oxford English Dictionary*). (67)

2. See Frank. Formalists such as Shklovsky have unwittingly contributed to this belief by associating the chronological chaining of represented events with necessity and the narrative manipulation of this order with art. Thus, to tell a "natural" story is to follow time as in a chain; to tell an artful story is to rearrange the links into a configuration. But the identification of art with what is added to chronological sequence is certainly not uniform among the formalists and is belied by the theories of virtually every narratologist. See P. Steiner 115–16.

3. Among the few extended discussions of narrative art are Brilliant; Marin; and Meisel.

4. John Canaday wrote, for example, that "with *The Slave Ship* Turner's development toward a final abstract statement of romantic emotionalism was nearly complete. The title of the picture still clings to literary associations not inherent in the painting as an independent work of art, and it is with a kind of disappointment that we discover the narrative incident in the foreground right, where a shackled leg disappears into the water, surrounded by devouring fish. This bit of storytelling appears as an afterthought, a concession to popular standards in a picture that was not only complete without it but is reduced from grandeur by its inclusion" (96).

5. Note the similarity of Labov's notion to Alberti's stress on the importance of the pictorial commentator, "who admonishes and points out to us what is happening there; or beckons with his hand to see; or menaces with an angry face

and with flashing eyes, so that no one should come near; or shows some danger or marvelous thing there; or invites us to weep or to laugh together with them. Thus whatever the painted persons do among themselves or with the beholder, all is pointed toward ornamenting or teaching the *istoria*" (Alberti 78.)

6. For a discussion of this subgenre, see Witemeyer III.

7. See Fisher, "Entitling," for a discussion of titles in the arts.

8. I discuss this more fully in *Colours of Rhetoric* (41–48).

9. Barbara Herrnstein Smith ("Narrative Versions") would consider it fallacious, however, to speak of the priority of a story to its telling.

10. Labov unaccountably confuses the order of the story with the order of its telling in his distinction between free and narrative clauses (360–61). He claims that a change in the placement of a narrative clause will lead to a semantic alteration in the narrative, whereas a change in the placement of free clauses will not, since these refer to general events or states of affairs. Even narrative clauses, however, can appear in different orders without the narrative meaning's being changed when prepositions and conjunctions indicate the priority of events narrated later to those earlier, and vice versa. It is only a change in the *story* order that would produce a different narrative.

11. Nelson Goodman has argued for limits to the discourse distortion of story order. When these limits are transgressed, he claims, we no longer have a narrative. I would amend this position as follows: there is no limit to the discourse distortion of story order in narrative; however, not every presentation of a story is a narrative. The presence or absence of narrativity is a function of factors other than mere ordering.

12. As formulated by Viktor Shklovsky.

13. These works are cited by Joseph Kestner (104).

14. Norman Bryson has criticized the commonly held belief, which I am here endorsing, that the Albertian system held sway until postimpressionism. He claims that this "is a prejudice 'of the left' and concerns a mythical continuity: that 'Quattrocento' space reigns unchallenged from Giotto until Cézanne" (Bryson 89). In light of my argument it might be more accurate to speak about quattrocento time/space, which does seem to have remained remarkably consistent in its overall traits for the four-hundred-year period in question.

15. National Gallery of Art (Washington DC), gallery notes to *Scenes from the Life of Saint John the Baptist,* by the Master of the Life of Saint John the Baptist, Kress Collection no. 1147, Gallery 1.

16. On the legend of Salome and the principle of art for art's sake, see Zagona.

17. National Gallery of Art (Washington DC), gallery notes to Sassetta's paintings from the *Life of Saint Anthony,* Kress Collection, nos. 817, 818, and 404, Gallery 3.

References

Alberti, Leon Battista. *On Painting.* Trans. John R. Spencer. New Haven CT: Yale University Press, 1956.

Berenson, Bernard. *The Italian Painters of the Renaissance.* Ithaca NY: Phaidon, 1952.

Brilliant, Richard. *Visual Narratives: Storyelling in Etruscan and Roman Art.* Ithaca NY: Cornell University Press, 1984.

Bryson, Norman. *Word and Image: French Painting in the Ancien Régime.* Cambridge: Cambridge University Press, 1981.

Canaday, John. *Mainstreams of Modern Art.* New York: Holt, Rinehart and Winston, 1956.

Cennini, Cennino d'Andrea. *The Craftman's Handbook.* Trans. Daniel V. Thompson Jr. New York: Dover, 1933.

Chatman, Seymour. *Story and Discourse.* Ithaca NY: Cornell University Press, 1980.

———. "What Novels Can Do That Films Can't (and Vice Versa)." *On Narrative.* Ed. W. J. T. Mitchell. Chicago: University of Chicago Press, 1980. 117–36.

da Vinci, Leonardo. *Treatise on Painting.* Vol. 1. Trans. and notes A. Philip McMahon. Princeton NJ: Princeton University Press, 1956.

———. *On Painting.* Trans. Carlos Pedretti. Berkeley: University of California Press, 1964.

Fisher, John. "Entitling." *Critical Inquiry* 11 (1984): 286–98.

Frank, Joseph. "Spatial Form in Modern Literature." *The Widening Gyre: Crisis and Mastery in Modern Literature.* New Brunswick NJ: Rutgers University Press, 1963.

Fried, Michael. *Absorption and Theatricality: Painting and Beholder in the Age of Diderot.* Berkeley: University of California Press, 1980.

Gaballa, G. A. *Narrative in Egyptian Art.* Mainz-am-Rhein: Verlag Philipp Von Zabern, 1976.

Gombrich, E. H. *Art and Illusion.* Princeton NJ: Princeton University Press, 1960.

Goodman, Nelson. "Twisted Tales; Or Story, Study, and Symphony." *On Narrative.* Ed. W. J. T. Mitchell. Chicago: University of Chicago Press, 1980. 98–116.

Greenstein, Jack Matthew. "Historia in Leon Battista Alberti's *On Painting* and in Andrea Mantegna's *Circumcision of Christ.*" Ph.D. diss., University of Pennsylvania, 1984.

Hanfmann, George M. A. "Narrative in Greek Art." *Narration in Ancient Art: A Symposium.* Ed. Carl H. Kraeling. Chicago: Oriental Institute, 1955.

Kantor, Helen J. "Narrative in Egyptian Art." *Narration in Ancient Art: A Symposium.* Ed. Carl H. Kraeling. Chicago: Oriental Institute, 1955.

Kermode, Frank. "Secrets and Narrative Sequence." *On Narrative.* Ed. W. J. T. Mitchell. Chicago: University of Chicago Press, 1980. 79–98.

Kestner, Joseph. "Secondary Illusion: The Novel and the Spatial Arts." *Spatial Form in Narrative.* Ed. Jeffrey R. Smitten and Ann Daghistany. Ithaca NY: Cornell University Press, 1981. 100–128.

Kraeling, Carl H., ed. *Narration in Ancient Art: A Symposium.* Chicago: Oriental Institute, 1955.

Labov, William. *Language in the Inner City.* Philadelphia: University of Pennsylvania Press, 1972

Lessing, Gotthold Ephraim. *Laocoön: An Essay on the Limits of Painting and Poetry.* Ed. and trans. Edward Allen McCormick. Baltimore: Johns Hopkins University Press, 1984.

Marin, Louis. *Études sémiologiques. Écritures, peintures.* Paris: Klinsieck, 1971.

Meisel, Martin. *Realizations: Narrative, Pictorial and Theatrical Arts in Nineteenth-Century England.* Princeton NJ: Princeton University Press, 1983.

Mitchell, W. J. T., ed. *On Narrative.* Chicago: University of Chicago Press, 1980.

Moure, Nancy Wall. *American Narrative Painting.* New York: Praeger, 1974.

Shklovsky, Viktor. "Sterne's *Tristram Shandy:* Stylistic Commentary." *Russian Formalist Criticism: Four Essays.* Ed. and trans. Lee T. Lemon and Marion J. Reis. Lincoln: University of Nebraska Press, 1965. 25–57.

Perkins, Ann. "Narrative in Babylonian Art." *Narration in Ancient Art: A Symposium.* Ed. Carl H. Kraeling. Chicago: Oriental Institute, 1955.

Prince, Gerald. "Aspects of a Grammar of Narrative." *Poetics Today* 1.3 (1980): 49–50.

———. "Narrativity." *Axia: Davis Symposium on Literary Evaluation.* Ed. Karl Menges and Daniel Rancour-Laferrière. Stuttgart: Akademischer Verlag Hans-Dieter Heinz, 1981. 74–75.

Ricoeur, Paul. "Narrative Time." *Critical Inquiry* 7.1 (1980): 169–90.

Roskill, Mark V. *Dolce's "Aretino" and Venetian Art Theory of the Cinquecento.* New York: New York University Press, 1968.

Seymour, Charles, Jr. *Art Treasures for America.* London: Phaidon, 1961.

Shapley, Fern Rusk. "A Predella Panel by Benozzo Gozzoli." *Gazette des Beaux Arts* (February 1952).

Shklovsky, Viktor. "Sterne's *Tristram Shandy:* Stylistic Commentary." *Russian Formalist Criticism: Four Essays.* Ed. and trans. Lee T. Lemon and Marion J. Reis. Lincoln: University of Nebraska Press, 1965. 25–57.

Sitwell, Sacheverell. *Narrative Pictures: A Survey of English Genre and Its Painters.* New York: Schocken Books, 1969.

Smith, Barbara Herrnstein. "Narrative Versions, Narrative Theories." *On Narrative.* Ed. W. J. T. Mitchell. Chicago: University of Chicago Press, 1980. 209–32.

Smitten, Jeffrey R., and Ann Daghistany, eds. *Spatial Form in Narrative.* Ithaca NY: Cornell University Press, 1981.

Steiner, Peter. *Russian Formalism: A Metapoetics.* Ithaca NY: Cornell University Press, 1984.

Steiner, Wendy. *The Colours of Rhetoric: Problems in the Relations between Modern Literature and Painting.* Chicago: University of Chicago Press, 1982.

Turner, Victor. "Social Dramas and Stories about Them." *Critical Inquiry* 7.1 (1980): 141–68.

Weitzmann, Kurt. "Narration in Early Christian Art." *Narration in Ancient Art: A Symposium*. Ed. Carl H. Kraeling. Chicago: Oriental Institute, 1955.

White, Hayden. "The Value of Narrativity in the Representation of Reality." *On Narrative*. Ed. W. J. T. Mitchell. Chicago: University of Chicago Press, 1980. 1–24.

Witemeyer, Hugh. *George Eliot and the Visual Arts*. New Haven CT: Yale University Press, 1979.

Worth, Sol. "Pictures Can't Say Ain't." *Vs.* 12.3 (1975): 85–108.

Zagona, Helen Grace. *The Legend of Salome and the Principle of Art for Art's Sake*. Geneva: Librairie E. Droz, 1960.

5

Art Spiegelman's Maus *and the Graphic Narrative*

Jeanne Ewert

Graphic novels pose a unique challenge for the narratologist. As Gerald Prince notes in the preface to his *Dictionary of Narratology,* the privileging of verbal over nonverbal elements of narrative is one of the biases of narratology itself (vii). Robert Harvey, in his introduction to *The Art of the Comic Book,* reports a similar prejudice when literary critics talk about comics: "the emerging critical canon is consequently laced with discussions of plot, character development, and all the rest of the apparatus of literary criticism. But this approach ignores the narrative function of the pictures in comics" (3). [1] These observations suggest that a narratological method specific to the graphic novel must take into account the narrative forms that define it: both the content *and* the artwork contained in the panels. Using Art Spiegelman's acclaimed graphic narrative, *Maus,* as a case study, I will argue that the pictorial and graphic elements of *Maus,* rather than merely illustrating the story related in its verbal/textual content, serve important and distinct *narrative* functions. [2]

The visual grid of the classic comic book form and the enormous labor and time demanded by detailed drawings (Spiegelman worked for some thirteen years on *Maus*) sharply limit the number of scenes that can be illustrated. On the other hand, the presence of the illustrations in the panels limits the number of words that can be included in headings and speech balloons. In a rare negative review of *Maus* Hillel Halkin cites the multiplying effect of these constraints as the chief reason why the graphic novel form may be inappropriate to a story this complex: "language may be tyrannically word-bound, but the visual arts are no less tyrannically space-bound and yoking two tyrannies together in such a way that there is a minimum of room for maneuver within either is a poor strategy for overcoming them. All that happens in the comic strip is that one ends up more bound and chained than ever. The division into small boxes limits all utterances to the shortest and pithiest statements, ruling out nearly all verbal subtlety or complexity, while the need to fill each box with a drawing has a similar effect on the illustrations" (56). Stephen Tabachnik, responding to this review, recommends the study of the sonnet form, "which works precisely because of the tension between its constricted form and its content" (157).[3] The genius of Spiegelman lies both in his ability to condense without sacrificing the meaning of his father's oral narrative (listening to the tapes of Vladek's distinctive Yiddish-inflected English, one realizes how carefully that transcription is accomplished)[4] and in the sheer richness of the illustrations.

The images in *Maus* are replete with details that propel the story forward, saving (literal) page space that would otherwise be required for textual exposition. Transitional elements that move the narrative from one scene to the next, visual elements that condense or elide information that would otherwise appear in the verbal/textual narrative, and framing devices that negotiate between the temporalities of the verbal/textual narration all contribute to a complex narrative method requiring a comparatively small area of the page.

This economy of visual narration is evident in a passage from the first volume of *Maus*. Vladek Spiegelman and two of his relatives are standing on a street in the Jewish district discussing a Nazi officer who had nearly shot Vladek. Another character hurries up to them and says, "Hey, aren't you going over to Pesach's to buy some cake?" (1:119).[5] The surprise on the faces of those present (one of them holds his hand over his stomach, widens his eyes, and simply says, "Cake!") conveys the extent of their deprivation in the ghetto. The setting on a street corner—a few strokes outline walls, windows, and pavement—obviates the necessity for a motive for his appearance or a complex explanation of his relationship to the central characters; the transition from the topic of Nazi brutality to the shortage of luxury foods in the ghetto is smoothly made through visual rather than verbal elements. Economy of narration is obvious again in the next panel, when it turns out that the rare cake wasn't made with flour after all. Spiegelman draws a simple outline of the roofs of the ghetto at night. Issuing from each silhouetted building are groans of those attempting to digest laundry soap. The heading merely says, "We were, all of us, sick like dogs." The illustration, which occupies a mere sixth of the page, compactly conveys the extent of their suffering.[6]

A scene a few pages earlier in volume 1 further illustrates Spiegelman's use of transitional elements embedded in the visual narrative. Vladek is relating how he is caught out one day near the train station as the Nazis round up victims for transportation. Of the event itself he says only, "And it was going on there something terrible." The panel, however, illustrates the horror of the scene: people being beaten with truncheons, shot while running, a woman trying to protect her infant, bodies prostrate on the street, and the train with its boxcars standing ready to transport (1:80; fig. 5.1). In the next panel the reader sees the degree of Vladek's terror in his eyes and the drops of sweat on his face. His vulnerability is graphically registered as he stands in isolation poised for flight, in a panel that is entirely blank except for the deeply shaded Star of David that frames him and out of which his figure emerges. The contrast between the busy scene of slaughter, which fills the largest panel on this page, and the image of Vladek, visible and vulnerable, frozen in his star, is striking. The celebrated comic artist and theorist Will Eisner has pointed out that unframed panels open up the tightness of a narrative sequence and suggest an unlimited empty space (47). Here the star marking Vladek's space is unframed, indicating the enormity of the chasm in which he stands, alone.

Vladek is rescued on this occasion by his wealthy friend Ilzecki, who bustles him quickly into his own apartment building. From the windows of the apartment they watch the departing train. Another transition is neatly effected on the following page when, seated in front of these same windows, Vladek discusses with Ilzecki the possibility of hiding his small son Richieu along with Ilzecki's own son (1:81). Only the presence of the two children—playing with a train set (complete with boxcars) on the floor—indicates that this exchange occurs on a different and more peaceful day. The masterful use of the train motif, an icon of childhood games inside the apartment and fascist repression outside of it, demonstrates with remarkable efficiency the intersection of Nazi terror with the most mundane elements of private life.

The iconography of this scene, the dizzying *mise-en-abyme* by which the son on the floor at his father's feet innocently reenacts the father's peril, is a striking comment on the construction of *Maus* itself. One imagines Spiegelman, beside him on the floor the new tape recorder—another mechanical toy—purchased for just this reason, prompting his father through the memory of these events. Perhaps Spiegelman sees it himself; there is an eerie anticipation of this scene earlier in volume 1. Here Vladek has been recounting how he and other Jewish soldiers captured by German forces in Poland were singled out for persecution (1:52). They are given an impossible task, cleaning a stable in an hour's time, and punished for their failure. Vladek interrupts this narrative to chastise Art, who has been sitting on the floor at his feet, for dropping cigarette ash on the carpet.[7]

Figure 5.1. "And it was going on there something terrible." From *Maus I: A Survivor's Tale / My Father Bleeds History* by Art Spiegelman, copyright © 1973, 1980, 1981, 1982, 1984, 1985, 1986 by Art Spiegelman. Used by permission of Pantheon Books, a division of Random House, Inc.

"You want it should be like a stable here?" Vladek demands, making explicit the connection between his son's idle pleasures and the scene of his own torment.

The visual presentation of the graphic narrative may also condense information that would otherwise have to appear in the verbal/textual narrative. *Maus* is full of what could perhaps best be called "pictorial subnarratives," which subtly enrich the story told in the main narrative. One scene early in volume I illustrates this technique. Vladek's father has just come to seek his advice about whether or not he and his daughter Fela should report as ordered to the stadium for registration (1:89). He is worried that with her four children and no work papers, she will be selected for transportation to the camps. This is the main narrative movement in the scene. When he first arrives at Vladek's house, however, Vladek's father presents little Richieu with a cookie, saying only, "Aunt Fela baked it for you." For the next six panels Vladek and his father discuss the problem of registration, with Richieu hovering in the background but moving closer to the center of the conversation. Finally, in the last panel he tugs on his grandfather's sleeve and says, "Can I have another cookie?" Vladek's one-word reprimand ("Richieu!") is all that the reader gets in the textual register, but the visual narrative—the offer of the single cookie, the grandfather's haggard appearance, the child's hesitant movement into the scene, and the strength of the reprimand from a father who normally leaves discipline to his wife and mother-in-law—richly conveys the extent of hunger in the household and the degree of sacrifice represented by even a small gift of food.

An important subnarrative of this kind illustrates the tenuous relationship of the artist with his father, as it is played out in the illustration of Vladek's relationship with Richieu.[8] In this scene Vladek has just returned from POW camp and is enjoying a first meal with his wife's family. They are telling him about the strict rationing of food in the Jewish district. But another story runs parallel to the adults' conversation, in the images of the four panels. Vladek's young son misbehaves at the table, is reprimanded, bursts into tears, and, finally, is comforted by his mother, while his father ignores him completely (1:75). The panels include no text recounting Richieu's outburst, the reprimand, or his mother's comforting words. The reader deduces that Richieu craves his father's attention after Vladek's long absence in the POW camps but is unable to find an appropriate way to attract it. This tableau is crucial to an understanding of one of the book's principal themes: Spiegelman's anger over his parents' idolizing of the dead Richieu (who "never threw tantrums or got in any kind of trouble" [2:15]) and his own sense that his care was neglected by his traumatized parents. Thus, the sequence operates on several levels, inclusive of and supplementing the primary narrative it relates—and seems as much a comment on Spiegelman's problematic relations with his parents as a subtle attempt to depict Richieu's relations with his.

Visual narrative is used throughout *Maus* to convey information subtly to the reader that would otherwise require (literally) writing out descriptive details. Facial expressions and body language, for example, convey detail that would be impossible to include in the limited space of speech balloons. Anja's eloquent blush early in their courtship, when she discovers that Vladek understands English and knows what she and her friend have been saying about him, speaks volumes about her feelings (1:16). A series of panels showing her varied responses to a spiteful letter from Vladek's former lover, suggesting his infidelity and playboy nature, takes her from anger to sorrow to despair with a mere twenty-four words in the speech balloons

(1:22). The panels are small and succeed one another quickly, a technique suggesting limited duration and rapid timing (Eisner 33), illustrating the whirlwind of her emotional response. One panel, tilted askew, concretely emphasizes how her world has been turned upside down by the letter. The final panel in the series, larger and more detailed than the rest, breaks the rhythm. The reader is thus invited to slow down again and enjoy the lovers' reconciliation and celebrate their subsequent engagement.

A scene late in volume 1 shows Vladek yelling at his nephew Lolek, who has ventured out of their hiding place to search for food but returned with little to eat and several books (1:112). Lolek, who is never without a book—accessories also illustrate their owners' characters—hunches protectively over his find, his back to Vladek. Vladek's aggressive stance reinforces his constant emphasis on the practical, while Lolek's resentment of paternalistic attempts to control his behavior (his own parents were at the World's Fair in New York when war broke out, and so they survived) is evident in his posture and expression.

Two masterpieces of this technique merit special notice. Throughout *Maus* the German cats are drawn in such a way as to emphasize their ferociousness: eyes slitted, fangs drawn. In one scene in volume 2 one of Vladek's fellow prisoners pleads for his life, claiming that he is not Jewish but German and that his incarceration is a mistake. In Spiegelman's drawings he is transformed from mouse to cat as he makes his case—but not like the ferocious, scowling Nazi cats. His hunched posture, his wide eyes, his pathetic gestures, differentiate him from his tormenters and illustrate the futility of his protests (2:50). A few pages earlier Art explains to the reader the source of his depression since the publication of the first volume. Its critical success makes him feel guilty, and he is worried about the authenticity of his representation of the camps. As he describes his concerns, he becomes, before the reader's eyes, progressively infantilized. At the end of the speech a small child in the artist's clothes climbs off the artist's stool and toddles to his psychiatrist's office. During the therapy session he gradually inflates back to adult size (2:41–46). Without recourse to textual content (which surely would overstate this effect), Spiegelman conveys to the reader the devastating psychic effect of his commercial success.

In much of *Maus* Spiegelman doesn't need to depict these complex emotions in the speech balloons because of the eloquence of his illustrations of facial features. Conversely, he occasionally refuses to individuate the characters in *Maus,* mostly at moments when they are evading detection. For example, in a scene in the POW camp Vladek and his fellow prisoners are called out for inspection (1:58; fig. 5.2). Vladek observes briefly: "I

Figure 5.2. "I stood always in the second line." From *Maus I: A Survivor's Tale / My Father Bleeds History* by Art Spiegelman, copyright © 1973, 1980, 1981, 1982, 1984, 1985, 1986 by Art Spiegelman. Used by permission of Pantheon Books, a division of Random House, Inc.

stood always in the second line. I didn't want they should see me much." Spiegelman runs shading lines across all the prisoners standing in line, making their faces impossible to differentiate and suggesting powerfully and graphically their psychic need to blend into a crowd in moments of danger. On the next page the prisoners, their features still shaded in, are called out and released from the camp. At the moment that Vladek gives his name and rank, Spiegelman stops shading in his face. He becomes an individual before our eyes.

The shading that allows Vladek to hide in a crowd is carried to a logical extreme in the panels following. Vladek, trying desperately to reach his home in the German-controlled territory in Poland, "passes" as a Polish gentile to evade detection on the train (1:64). Spiegelman draws him, in a motif recurring throughout the rest of volume 1, with a pig mask tied to his face. This simple and elegant visual solution to a complex problem of characterization and essentialism evades a world of textual explanation: how does one pass from one group to another? What constitutes ethnicity? How are character traits that speak to ethnicity repressed?

On a practical level Spiegelman obsessively organizes the visual narrative to condense topographical, geopolitical, and chronological information critical to the historical background of the book. *Maus* is replete with maps of Poland, of the concentration camps, drawings of hideout bunkers and diagrams of the workings of crematoria, timelines, and charts. The carefully designed back covers of the volumes include full-color maps of occupied Poland and Auschwitz-Birkenau, with small maps of Rego Park and the Catskills superimposed over them. One of the most impressive of the many diagrams is one illustrating how to repair shoes, a skill Vladek learned in the ghetto and put to good use in the camps. Spiegelman's depiction of the process is so detailed and lucid as to give the reader confidence in her own ability to repair shoes, all in a drawing that requires a mere third of a page (2:60).

Using visual elements to provide smooth transitional moments and minimize verbal explanation is perhaps the most practical advantage of a rich visual style that exceeds the content of the speech balloons. In *Maus*, however, visual elements serve other, more highly symbolic functions. Iconic visual symbols are frequently deployed to foreground important material and to enrich the meaning of the narrative. Elsewhere I've discussed in detail the use of the mouse and cat metaphor,[9] which foregrounds Spiegelman's primary theme of the oppression of Jews by Nazi aggressors. I've also noted the metonymical value of his use of mouse tails in volume 1 and their disappearance in volume 2. But metonymic technique is used much more widely in *Maus*.[10] One powerful and chilling visual effect is that created by the use of the swastika to frame narratives of increasing Nazi brutality.

The German flag first appears in chapter 2 of *Maus*, a chapter ironically entitled "The Honeymoon." The chapter's frontispiece shows a group of Jews in silhouette against a bleak background of dark houses, almost huts. Only the luminous white of the men's collars and the woman's pearls reveal them to be dressed for revelry but frozen now, quietly gazing at the ominous black spider unfurled against a stark white moon (1:25; fig. 5.3). The starkness of the scene and the fearful quiet of the characters communicate to the reader the powerful emotional import of the scene,[11] which is carried over on successive pages, as tales filter into Poland of Nazi oppression of German Jews. In each case the German's brutality is represented in the harsh light of the Nazi emblem. The atrocities themselves are minimally verbalized ("The police came to his house and no one heard again from him") because the image of the swastika is so potent. Even the stark drawings—truncheon raised to strike a prostrate figure, a woman choked, arms pinned behind her back—are barely necessary because the events are so easily imagined as the swastika looms in the background. In the final pages of volume 1 Vladek and his wife, Anja, search in vain for a safe hiding place in their native city. Their path is drawn as a maze—a labyrinth composed of the many arms of the swastika and offering no way out (1:125).

In the second volume the iconography of the swastika is replaced by another symbol carrying the same metonymic freight—the black chimneys of the crematoria rising into the gray skies above Auschwitz. Again, Spiegelman needs minimal verbal content to make the sense of these images

Figure 5.3. "The Honeymoon." From *Maus I: A Survivor's Tale / My Father Bleeds History* by Art Spiegelman, copyright © 1973, 1980, 1981, 1982, 1984, 1985, 1986 by Art Spiegelman. Used by permission of Pantheon Books, a division of Random House, Inc.

clear. One panel consists of a panoramic view of trains arriving at the gates of Auschwitz, with a much smaller inset panel portraying only the smoking chimneys and Vladek's words ("Thousands—hundreds of thousands of Hungarians were arriving there at this time") suspended in front of them (2:55; fig. 5.4). The contrast between the larger scene of arrival, showing the boxcars presumably crammed with people, and the final, tiny image of the chimneys is a chilling example of iconic reduction. This visual shorthand is so powerful that Spiegelman recreates it three times in fourteen pages.

At the other end of the metonymic spectrum, the Star of David in volume 1 and the number tattoo on the arms of Jewish prisoners in volume

Figure 5.4. "Thousands—hundreds of thousands of Hungarians." From *Maus I: A Survivor's Tale / My Father Bleeds History* by Art Spiegelman, copyright © 1986, 1989, 1990, 1991 by Art Spiegelman. Used by permission of Pantheon Books, a division of Random House, Inc.

2 are equated with victimization and genocide. The Star of David is used visually to frame those at risk in the same way that the swastika is used to frame those who brutalize, as in the sequence showing Vladek caught out and vulnerable during a transport roundup. The tattoo, prominent on Vladek's own arm from the first pages of the frame story, appears in the embedded narrative at the beginning of volume 2, as Vladek explains that, while the number might mark him as a victim, the three two-digit sequences are themselves lucky in Jewish mystical thought, and this encourages him to believe in his own survival (2:28). Another lucky icon—that of the Red Cross—frames the story of the war's end and his return to Poland (2:88).

In addition to these visual instances of metaphor and metonymy, Spiegelman frames and emphasizes key moments with visual rather than verbal effects by putting foregrounded figures in silhouette against a lighted background and through the use of a "full moon effect"—drawing the characters against a circle of white to block out background distractions. The first technique is used in the opening sequence of volume 1, when Vladek tells Art about a lover he abandoned when he met the much wealthier Anja. Vladek admits that he and Lucia were lovers for several years and that he refused to marry her because she had no dowry. But he extracts from Art the promise not to put this unflattering material in the book, saying that it is irrelevant to his Holocaust story, that it is private, and that it "isn't so proper, so respectful" (1:23). The moment when Art raises his right hand

and promises is drawn with Art and his father starkly silhouetted in black against a white background. It is impossible to distinguish the features on either father or son—surely a symbolically appropriate visual style for a moment when the father's least flattering traits are exposed and the son who exposes them reveals the depth of his betrayal to the reader.[12]

The reverse of the silhouetted figure, the full moon framing technique is used twice to great effect, when Vladek is reunited with Anja after his return as a Polish prisoner of war and again, in an almost identical panel, when he is reunited with her after the end of the war (1:66, 2:136). The full moon device reveals fully the principal characters and blocks out background distractions. In each case Spiegelman creates a panel that has all the elements of comic book romance and happy endings—and in each case he ironically undercuts this effect. The full moon device is used in volume 1 to foreground the happiness of Vladek's reunion with Anja after his release from the POW camp. Two pages later Spiegelman uses it again, this time as Art walks away from his father's house, distraught over his father's efforts to control his behavior. Vladek has just thrown away his son's beloved old coat and forced him to take a Naugahyde windbreaker that Art considers a fashion embarrassment. Walking away from the house, framed by a full moon, Art's aloneness and distress force the reader to reevaluate the romance and togetherness represented by the same moon in the earlier panel (1:69). In the second scene, at the end of volume 2, Vladek and Anja's second, more miraculous reunion after Auschwitz is also framed by a full moon, and at the bottom Vladek's narrative voice says: "More I don't need to tell you. We were both very happy, and lived happy, happy ever after." The reader, of course, is familiar with the profound unhappiness of both Vladek and Anja's subsequent life—her survivor's guilt, depression, and suicide; his loneliness, ill health, and troubled relationships with his son and second wife. Vladek's claim, then, can only be read ironically.

Visual techniques are important in *Maus* not only to frame and foreground but also to negotiate between the temporalities of the verbal/textual narration. *Maus* uses a frame narrative in the present that contains Vladek's recounting of the Holocaust narrative. In an interview with Jonathan Rosen, Spiegelman noted that graphic narratives are uniquely suited to this function, since "a comic strip is made up of units of time placed next to each other so that one sees past and present simultaneously, before decoding the moments that are being depicted in any box" (Rosen 9). In *Maus* the movement between the present and the past is often guided by the use of visual transitional devices, most often the repetition of visual motifs between the two time frames. This technique is seen first in volume 1 as

Art and Vladek walk the streets with Art recording Vladek's narrative in a small notebook (1:105). In one panel their two figures are pictured against a background of front stoops of Rego Park row houses, and in the next they pace against a backdrop of guardhouse and barbed wire. The line drawings are the same texture and darkness in both panels, and the same patterns of vertical and horizontal lines are repeated from one to the next. Robert Storr borrows from poetry the elegant term *visual enjambment* to describe this effect (28).[13] In a similar series of panels in volume 2 the horizontal lines of the split rail fence as Art and Vladek walk through a resort in the Catskills become the horizontal lines of the wooden bunks in Auschwitz as Vladek describes his daily life there. Vladek in the Catskills demonstrates to his son how he had to parade in front of Mengele's desk during the selection process, and Art's figure holding a tape recorder in the present segues into the Commandant's figure holding a checklist in the past (2:58–59).

In both cases the horizontal lines of the drawings are used to pull the reader backward in time past the frame narrative into Vladek's story. A reverse movement happens when events from the past haunt Vladek and Art in the present. During Art's visit with his father in the Catskills, Vladek relates the fate of the four young girls who are hanged in Auschwitz for smuggling in ammunition to blow up a crematorium. Vladek, Art, and Françoise are driving through the forest, and the legs of the girls are shown hanging in the trees they drive among. Vladek's sigh at the end of the story needs no elaboration—he is still haunted by the traumas of the past (2:79). A similar effect is created when Art, struggling to find the emotional resources to finish his father's story, is shown in his studio with a guard tower visible beyond the window while a pile of corpses buzzing with flies lies on his floor (2:41).

In every case but one, the use of this technique of blending past with present pulls the reader into the horror of the past. The title page of chapter 4 in volume 2 juxtaposes Vladek's older, narrating self with his victimized younger self, and in the background an American flag replaces the swastika and crematoria pictures so often featured in previous chapter titles. The chapter is entitled simply "Saved" (2:101). In this case the reader understands that, rather than the past intruding into the present, it is the face of the present that represents hope to the prisoner in the past. Vladek will survive because he is there in the scene, telling the story.

Elements of the graphic narrative not only help the reader to negotiate between the temporal frames of the narrating, but they also allow her (even encourage her) to read against the grain of the verbal text. The visual elements, for example, help the reader to identify problematic moments of potentially unreliable narration in Vladek's account. The best example of this is a scene in volume 2 when Vladek, who has been telling Art about his Holocaust experience, describes how, as part of the work detail, he would march out of Auschwitz every morning (2:54).[14] Art mentions that he has read about the prison orchestra that played as the prisoners left the camp, and, in fact, Spiegelman's drawing of the scene includes the orchestra. But in the next panel Vladek says that he doesn't remember any orchestra. Art remarks that the orchestra's presence has been well documented and moves on to another subject. The panels, however, suggest that he questions the accuracy of his father's recollections. The image of prisoners marching to work is emended so that in the space where the orchestra was before there are only rows of workers, but a second look reveals that Spiegelman has refused to erase the orchestra completely. The conductor's ears and baton, and the top of the bass fiddle, are just visible over the heads of the marching mice. This is not to say that Spiegelman wholly rejects his father's account; the gesture toward redrawing the picture belies that. Yet it is entirely credible that Vladek, suffering all the trauma of the camp experience, simply didn't notice the orchestra or that his post-trauma recollection of the events is murky. And it is also clear from his refusal to erase the orchestra completely that Spiegelman is reluctant to disregard an event that is elsewhere well documented simply because his father cannot recall it.

In this respect the visual narrative created by Spiegelman does much more than illustrate his father's words: it also glosses them and provides editorial comments. The visual narrative also comments obliquely on father/son relationships, a theme that is conspicuously absent from Vladek's narrative but very much a part of Spiegelman's. Volume 1, for example, is organized around, and framed by, successive attempts by Art to exert more control over his own life and over the course of the book project. The first instance is that of the promise not to include the Lucia story, with which the volume opens. Spiegelman's violation of that promise signals to the reader issues of narrative control that will dominate this volume. In the precise center of the narrative, at the end of chapter 3, is the scene in which Vladek discards Art's coat, substituting his own windbreaker. Spiegelman's rage over his father's attempt to control his appearance, and the depiction of Art stalking away from the house muttering, "I can't believe it" (1:69), is visually structured precisely like the final scene in volume 1, when Art once again stalks away from the house in a rage. In this instance he has just learned that his father destroyed Anja's war diaries. Vladek, who is notorious for never getting rid of anything, claims to have suddenly remembered burning the diaries after Anja's funeral. Spiegelman has asked repeatedly for the diaries throughout the volume, while Vladek continually assures him that he has been looking for them (1:105). The sequence suggests subtly that the destruction might not have happened years before the book's writing began but perhaps in response to the competition from a narrative that would rival Vladek's own.

These three scenes, which both frame and bisect volume 1, achieve their effect largely through the visual forms and sequences of the narrative. As in the scenes with the two sons at their father's feet, they rely on a reader with an eye for detail who notices and recalls visual pictorial elements and page layouts in the narrative. For the narratologist learning to read for these purely visual devices must be the first step toward developing a poetics of the graphic narrative. Perhaps then, instead of seeing graphic novels the way Halkin sees *Maus*—as devoid of verbal or visual subtlety or complexity—critics will see them in the light suggested by Will Eisner, as "deploying images and words, each in exquisitely balanced proportion," and contributing to "the body of literature that concerns itself with the examination of the human experience" (142).

Notes

1. Several scholars of comics art have begun the task of theorizing and defining the ways in which comics are constructed, among them Scott McCloud in a landmark study (*Understanding Comics*) that was itself an example of graphic art.

2. Literary critics are latecomers to this thesis. Spiegelman himself argued as early as 1967 (in a college term paper focusing on Bernard Krigstein's short comic "Master Race") that graphic artists "have understood the importance of employing their artwork to illuminate and present other facets of the text—rather than as a repetitiously literal depiction of the word" ("Master Race" 86). This essay analyzes Krigstein's use of several techniques that Spiegelman will use later in *Maus,* including the metonymy of swastikas and trains, the imposition of images from the past onto the present, and the use of strong horizontal lines to pull the reader from one panel to the next and back and forth in time (88).

3. Writing within severe constraints is, of course, a well-established poetic and narrative practice. Other examples include the villanelle, the lipogram (a text that categorically excludes one or more letters of the alphabet, as in Georges Perec's novel *La Disparition,* written without the letter *E*), and pattern poetry.

4. The CD-ROM version of *Maus* published by the Voyager Company included several hours of tape from Spiegelman's interviews with Vladek.

5. The current permissions policy in place for *Maus* restricts reproduction of images to only four panels in a scholarly article—a stricture that ironically forces me to describe verbally a narrative in which I argue that the visual elements are of

crucial importance. I recommend that this article be read with a copy of *Maus* in hand.

6. Thomas Doherty points to "the exclamatory typography of the Sunday funnies" in this scene, which provides "an audacious interlude of true comic relief." I'm not sure how many readers will actually find the implication of starving people trying to digest soap humorous, but Doherty's discussion of Spiegelman's reliance on the tropes of the classic comic strip here and in the more sobering concentration camp diagrams is extremely useful for positioning Spiegelman's art (72–73).

7. I will refer throughout to the author of *Maus* as Spiegelman and to his cartoon avatar as Art.

8. I've discussed this scene in greater detail elsewhere: see Ewert, "Reading Visual Narrative" (82–88).

9. Ewert, "Reading Visual Narrative" (91–98).

10. Alison Landsberg points to the metonymical equation of Anja's diaries with Anja herself, when Vladek destroys them and Art calls him a "murderer" (70). This is, of course, a metonymical equation that exists in the textual rather than visual frames of the narrative.

11. Eisner provides several clear examples of the ways in which visual narratives elicit emotion in the reader (59).

12. See my longer discussion of the implications of this scene in "Reading Visual Narrative" (90).

13. Storr's term refers only to the visual field being carried over from one panel to the next; to describe the superimposition of the past on the present, Rick Iadonisi proposes *temporal seepage* (45), another useful concept for a poetics of graphic narration.

14. See my longer discussion of this scene in "Reading Visual Narrative" (88–90).

References

Doherty, Thomas. "Art Spiegelman's *Maus:* Graphic Art and the Holocaust." *American Literature* 68.1 (March 1996): 69–84.

Eisner, Will. *Comics and Sequential Art.* Exp. ed. Tamarac FL: Poorhouse Press, 1985.

Ewert, Jeanne C. "Reading Visual Narrative: Art Spiegelman's *Maus*." *Narrative* 8.1 (January 2000): 87–103.

Halkin, Hillel. "Inhuman Comedy." *Commentary* (February 1992): 55–56.

Harvey, Robert C. *The Art of the Comic Book: An Aesthetic History.* Jackson: University Press of Mississippi, 1996.

Iadonisi, Rick. "Bleeding History and Owning His [Father's] Story: *Maus* and Collaborative Autobiography." CEA *Critic* 57.1 (Fall 1994): 41–56.

Landsberg, Alison. "America, the Holocaust, and the Mass Culture of Memory: Toward a Radical Politics of Empathy." *New German Critique* 71 (1997): 63–86.

McCloud, Scott. *Understanding Comics: The Invisible Art.* New York: Harper Perennial, 1994.

Prince, Gerald. *A Dictionary of Narratology.* Lincoln: University of Nebraska Press, 1987.

Rosen, Jonathan. "Spiegelman: The Man behind *Maus.*" *Forward,* January 17, 1992, 1, 9, 11.

Spiegelman, Art. *Maus, A Survivor's Tale [I]: My Father Bleeds History.* New York: Pantheon, 1986.

———. "Master Race: The Graphic Story as an Art Form." *Comics, Essays, Graphics and Scraps.* Rome: Centrale dell'Arte, 1999.

———. *Maus, A Survivor's Tale [II]: And Here My Troubles Began.* New York: Pantheon, 1991.

Storr, Robert. "Art Spiegelman's Making of Maus." *Tampa Review* 5 (Fall 1992): 27–30.

Tabachnick, Stephen. "Of *Maus* and Memory: The Structure of Art Spiegelman's Graphic Novel of the Holocaust." *Word and Image* 9.2 (April–June 1993): 154–62.

3. Moving Pictures

Film theory was born as an academic discipline in the 1960s and 1970s, in the aftermath of the (re)discovery of Saussure's linguistics theory. Of all the domains that fall within the scope of media studies, it is still the most deeply indebted to a linguistic midwife. How does one appproach film narrative in a Saussurian-structuralist framework? In his book *Mythologies* (1957) Roland Barthes outlined a model that seemed at the time applicable to narrative in all types of media. This model was based on the idea of a hierarchy of signifying systems riding piggyback upon one another. According to Barthes, the signs (that is, combinations of signifiers and signifieds) of a primary system become the signifieds of a secondary system of representation. The primary system could be any medium: language, film, photographs, or music. As the secondary system, Barthes had in mind the cultural stereotypes that he calls "myth," but he envisioned his model as applicable to a wide variety of signifying practices: for instance, a Latin phrase with a narrowly defined lexical meaning can become the illustration of grammatical agreement in the secondary system of language teaching. The primary lexical meaning is not an end in itself but an instrument put into the service of the secondary meaning. If we regard "narrative" as a secondary system, the task of the narrative media theorist is easily defined: identify the units of the medium; identify the meanings that make up the medium-free system of narrative; and create a "lexicon" that maps the signs of the medium upon the meanings of the narrative system.

This program initially yielded intriguing results in the case of verbal narrative: for instance, Greimas proposed a taxomomy of actantial roles that mirrored a case system (agent = nominative, patient = accusative, beneficiary = dative, and so on); Todorov assimilated characters to nouns, actions to verbs, properties to adjectives, and the ontological status of events to the modalities of verbs (optative, conditional, and counterfactual, and so on); and the Genette school of narratology extracted three modes of narration from the conjugation of verbs: first, second, and third person.

(These modes actually correspond to the way of referring to the main character.) But these pairings of medium units and narrative units were often more analogies (*a* is to language what *b* is to narrative structure) than lexical definitions (language element *a* expresses narrative element *b*), and they could not be developed into a comprehensive system of relations. Barthes himself remained content with a global mapping of texts unto the whole of mythical meaning, without bothering to isolate discrete signifiers and signifieds in either the primary or the secondary system. The bi-leveled taxononic approach is even more questionable with those media, such as film, that resist analysis into discrete signs. How, then, should one conceive the relations between the medium and the narrative "system" of meaning?

David Bordwell's contribution to this volume outlines an alternative to the structuralist approach to film studies. His work has long militated for the liberation of his discipline from what he calls SLAB theory: Sausurian semiotics, Lacanian psyhoanalysis, Althusserian Marxism, and Barthesian textual theory (Quart 36). In "Neo-Structuralist Narratology and the Functions of Filmic Storytelling" he undermines the structuralist project of establishing systematic correspondences between film elements and narrative units by demonstrating the versatility of cinematic devices. The first structuralist school in film studies (represented by Christian Metz) claimed that the basic narrative unit of film had to be the equivalent of the sentence, or statement, in language. For Metz this unit was the image (26), but image is ambiguous in film: does it mean an individual frame or a whole sequence? The second structuralist generation answered this question by arguing that the basic unit is the camera shot. Bordwell deconstructs this claim by showing that several distinct narrative sequences, involving different characters, can be shown within a single shot. Or, conversely, a conversation between two characters—usually a strategic unit—may be presented through an alternation of shots focusing on the current speaker.

Bordwell's counterproposal to neo-structuralism is a "functionalist" or "cognitivist" approach in which media are regarded not as a code of signs with an intrinsic and fixed narrative meaning but as open-ended repertoires of resources and devices. In verbal narrative these resources would be discourse strategies; in painting, line, shape, shading, perspective, and color; in music, tones arranged according to scales, rhythm, harmony, and melody; in the cinema, camera angle and movements, transitions, montage, as well as the particular repertoires of the nonvisual tracks. Bypassing the ghostly figure of the cinematic narrator, postulated for purely formal reasons by most representatives of the structuralist school but usually lacking any imaginative reality for the spectator, the functionalist approach defines *film narration* as the "organization of a set of cues for the construction of a story" (*Narration in the Fiction Film* 62). The spectator is assumed to possess a narrative competence that determines certain basic expectations. To fulfill these expectations the text must solve a number of problems: initiate the appreciator into a world; create characters and give them distinct identities; give goals to the characters; suggest causal relations between events and states; monitor the flow of time and perform jumps across the chronological sequence; express or inspire value judgments; and so on. The narrative analysis of film consists of studying how the idiosyncratic resources of the medium are applied to such narrative goals.

For the functionalist approach there is no one-to-one relation between the goals to be achieved and the resources deployed; a given device can be put in the service of many effects, and a given effect can be achieved through many devices. Whereas the structuralist mapping of primary onto secondary signs systems ascribes meaning in top-down fashion, so that it can be predictably reconstrued, once we know what formal elements appear in the text, the functionalist approach involves a hermeneutic circle: the spectator interprets cinematic features bottom up, assessing their meaning for each particular text, but she does so by consulting the top-down schemata provided by narrative competence as well as by her experience of other films using similar devices.

The search for codes, units, signifiers, signifieds, and distinctive features in all media was not the only effect of the linguistic turn in the humanities. Another legacy of the influence of Saussurian linguistics was to regard semiotic codes as self-enclosed systems of signs. The members of such systems receive their identity not from positive relation to external referents but from differential relations to the other terms of the system. The absence of external referents makes different languages or sign systems incommensurable. Each language organizes human experience along its own lines, and a word of a language cannot have an exact equivalent in another, because its value is determined by different neighbors and by a different network of relations. This view provided support to the theory of linguistic relativism, according to which mental representations of reality, and consequently thought, are crucially determined by how language draws categories in what would be without it an undifferentiated sea of perceptions.

Relativism had a strong impact on contemporary literary theory, as, indeed, on all fields of cultural studies. New Criticism appropriated the idea of the incommensurability of sign systems and extended it to the case of translation within the same language by declaring the heresy of paraphrase and the ineffability of literary meaning ("a poem should not mean but be," as the poet Archibald MacLeish wrote in a poem). This attitude toward translation was reinforced by a second influence. Literary criticism, as we know it today, grew out of the nineteenth-century German tradition (and academic discipline) of biblical exegesis. It inherited from its theological forebearer a religious respect to the letter of the text that finds its expression in the dogma of the inseparability of form and content. Just as God is present in every word of the Scriptures, and only in those words, so literary meaning is uniquely incarnated in the whole of the text. To extract it from its textual body would amount to killing it. New Critics and poststructuralists hold on to the belief that changing only one word of the text would change the whole meaning, though they cannot say exactly how, since this would involve the translation of literary meaning into their own language.

Translation and transposition may be heretical to literary theologians, but this hasn't discouraged film directors from proposing movie versions of literary works and audiences from enjoying the fruit of their efforts. Confronted with the phenomenon of novel-to-film adaptation, what is the cultural, literary, and film critic to do? An easy solution would be to dismiss the idea of transmediation as theoretically naive: a novel and its screen adaptation have simply nothing to do with each other. But, while the partisans of radical semiotic autonomy bury their head in the sand, the parade of cross-medial adaptations rolls on and stamps their pronouncements with the seal of irrelevance.

For Kamilla Elliott film adaptation is not a semiotic aberration but a challenge to rethink the problem of form versus content. Her essay "Literary Film Adaptation and the Form/Content Dilemma" takes a sympathetic, yet not uncritically supportive, look at the theories, both implicit and explicit, that refuse to practice the politics of the ostrich. The originality of the article lies as much in its mode of presentation as in its questioning of literary-theoretical orthodoxy. Assimilating the issue of form versus content to the never-resolved mind-and-body problem of philosophy, Elliott presents various ways in which critics and adapters have constructed the relations between literature and film and illustrates these views with concrete readings of film versions of Emily Brontë's classical novel *Wuthering Heights*. Each theory is allegorized through an episode in either Brontë's text or one of the movies that highlights a particular conception of the relation between the corporeal and the spiritual. The "psychic model" tells, for instance, that a novel's spirit can migrate into a new body; it is therefore the film's mission to capture this wandering spirit. The "ventriloquist model" empties the body of the novel of its spiritual content and gives it a new voice. The "genetic model" postulates a common genetic code, or narrative deep structure, shared by the bodies of two siblings. The "merging model" has two spirits reuniting, as the bodies decompose, and the appreciator sees the adaptation as the sum of novel and film. The "incarnational model" regards the film as the visible body to which the novel's abstract language aspires. The "trumping model," finally, sees the film as performing the equivalent of a sex-change operation: the spirit of the novel grew in the wrong body, and the film restores it to its rightful material support.

Taken individually, each of these theories is as questionable as the dogma of the inseparability of form and content, yet at some time or another most of us have reacted to a film adaptation according to one of these schemes. There is no "true," definitive, all-encompassing theory of the relations of novel to film, no more than there is a definitive solution of the mind-body problem, but there is a choice of points of view that explain different types of spectator response. Points of view are by definition partial, since they can only reveal a side by hiding another. If we are going to have a theory of novel-to-film adaptation, this theory cannot be anything less than the sum of the possibilities outlined in Elliott's essay.

Film and television share the camera as their principal source of narrative material, but, technologically as well as culturally, they are quite distinct media. Spectators go to the movie theater; television comes to them in their own living rooms. Films run for a couple of hours; television runs all the time. Film plays to a captive audience; television shows must compete with countless distractions: eating dinner; doing homework in front of the tube; talking on the phone; surfing to other channels. Films are carefully constructed works long in the making; television runs on a short production schedule and offers the possibility, unknown to film, of broadcasting "in real time." All these differences explain why film and television narrative have taken diverging paths: film toward fantasy, television toward reality.

This trend is a telling illustration of the ripple effects of the introduction of a new species in the "media ecology." In the days before television, when cinema was the sole conveyor of moving pictures, feature films were preceded by newsreels, cartoons, and travelogues, and the ontological domain of the cinema stretched all the way from real life to imaginary worlds. TV has not only taken over the domain of the documentary; it has also introduced a new hybrid between the real and the fictional. If we define the real in the domain of moving pictures as the capture of events that take place independently of the camera and the fictional as the recording of a reality expressly staged to be filmed—namely, the simulation of events by impersonators—this hybrid is the production of real-world (that is, nonsimulated) events "made for television," such as sports competitions, games shows, or Oscar ceremonies. (A rare cinematic predecessor of this phenomenon is the staging of Nazi Party conventions for the camera of Leni Riefenstahl.)

The recent phenomenon of "reality TV" strives toward a much more literal form of narrativity, which means much more extensive shaping of its visual and audio materials, than we find in the previously mentioned brand of events made for TV. This shaping may affect the level of story as well as the level of discourse. The case of story manipulation is illustrated by the genre known as "voyeur TV," such as the TV shows "Survivor" and "Big Brother." These shows place a number of participants in a closed environment and let the drama of human relationships develop more or less spontaneously under the eye of a surveillance camera. The personalities of the contestants are carefully selected by the producers to maximize the chances of interpersonal conflict—the main source of narrative interest. The successful production of plot thus hinges on the design of a favorable environment for the hatching of behaviors that satisfy the norms of (re)tellability. When interesting action fails to develop, producers have been known to intrude into the show and to sow seeds of conflict, for instance, by replacing bland personalities with more aggressive ones.

The other form of manipulation in reality TV concerns the organization of the camera capture into proper narrative form through editing and framing techniques. In her essay "The Videodrome: Ordinary Horror in Reality TV" Cynthia Freeland examines this "narrative construction of reality" in an older brand of reality TV than the "Survivor" and "Big Brother" type, namely the genre illustrated by "Rescue 911," "When Animals Attack," and "Life in the ER." These shows consist either of real footage of catastrophic events interspersed with restrospective comments by the real-life participants or of dramatic reenactment of such events. As Freeland demonstrates, their narrative discourse fulfills a variety of rhetorical tasks, among them creating rises and falls in tension; highlighting narrative points; providing expositions and codas; and evaluating the represented events. Although Freeland does not invoke William Labov's work on oral storytelling, her analysis of the shows' narrative techniques presents startling similarities with his model of narrative discourse structure.

The main focus of Freeland's essay rests, however, on the nature of the spectator's fascination with graphic displays of everyday horror. The three interpretations of spectator response examined in the essay attribute increasing degrees of sophistication to the viewer. A familiar reaction of cultural critics assumes too easily that the spectator is hypnotized by the image. This assumption serves the critic's agenda, which is typically to blame the content of the shows for the spread of violence in contemporary society. A more subtle analysis holds the spectator to be sensitive to the ideological subtext of the shows, a subtext that promotes the reassuring image of a world of law and order in which brave white cops help distressed families fight against catastrophic natural events—events that cannot be blamed on problems inherent to American society. In this interpretation spectators are able to see beyond the immediate content, but they do not exercise critical faculties toward the underlying message, and they remain blind to the narrative techniques. Freeland does not dismiss this ideological interpretation, but she balances it with a third view that places far greater emphasis on the spectator's awareness of how the shows are made. She observes that these programs are so badly acted and so amateurishly produced that they have "gotten to the point of parodying themselves." Far from falling under the spell of the image, audiences watch these caricatures "in a subversive, ironic spirit," deriving their pleasure from the slightly cynical, metatextual, typically postmodern awareness that this is not reality but its made-for-TV version.

References

Barthes, Roland. *Mythologies*. Sel. and trans. Annette Lavers. New York: Hill and Wang, 1972.

Bordwell, David. *Narration in the Fiction Film*. Madison: University of Wisconsin Press, 1985.

Genette, Gérard. *Narrative Discourse: An Essay in Method*. Trans. Jane E. Lewin. Ithaca: Cornell University Press, 1980.

Greimas, Algirdas Julien. *Structural Semantics: Attempt at a Method*. Trans. Daniele McDowell, Ronald Schleifer, and Alan Velie. Intro. R. Schleifer. Lincoln: University of Nebraska Press, 1983.

Metz, Christian. *Film Language: A Semiotics of the Cinema*. Trans. Michael Taylor. New York: Oxford University Press, 1974.

Quart, Alissa. "The Insider: David Bordwell Blows the Whistle on Film Studies." *Lingua Franca* 10.2 (2000): 34–43.

Todorov, Tzvetan. *Grammaire du Décaméron*. The Hague: Mouton, 1969.

6

Neo-Structuralist Narratology and the

Functions of Filmic Storytelling

David Bordwell

In most humanities disciplines versions of structuralism have not weathered the 1980s well. It is therefore all the more surprising that recent theories of narrative within film studies have been quasi-structuralist ones. Christian Metz, Seymour Chatman, André Gaudreault, André Gardies, François Jost, and other theorists have over the last fifteen years produced a body of film-based narrative theory that can usefully, if awkwardly, be called "neo-structuralist."

A defining trait of this trend, I think, is its commitment to the belief that the characteristic principles of film narrative are best understood by identifying distinct narrative features and charting the internal relations among them. Neo-structuralist narratology is in this sense "feature centered." It thereby differs from a family of narrative theories I shall call "formal/functionalist."

Take a table fork. We can classify forks by shape, size, composition of the handle, or number of tines. Mounting such classifications might well prove useful, but, to explain why the features of the fork are as they are, we would also ask about the role they play in its overall design. Just as important, we would ask what purposes a fork serves. Once we understand that it serves to spear food and cut it into morsels, we understand certain design features better. We understand that tines are more efficient for spearing morsels than a single knife blade would be; we see how tines allow a thin blade to be inserted between them for fine slicing; we understand that the tines' curvature, through a sort of redundancy principle, helps the user cradle the speared morsels en route to mouth.

In trying to understand human artifacts, we often adopt such a "design stance." We ask: what purposes is the artifact meant to serve? How are those purposes manifested in the materials and structure of the whole? We offer, that is, a *functional explanation:* we analyze the artifact's overall form and explain it in light of the purposes we take it to be trying to fulfill.

By and large neo-structuralist narratology of film has avoided such explanations. The strategy has been to distinguish basic units or features of narrative and identify their presence in particular films. In this respect neo-structuralist narratology has continued the largely taxonomic enterprise of Propp, Todorov, and Genette. By contrast, a functionalist perspective links to a tradition that includes Aristotle, much work of the Russian formalist tradition, and recent studies by Meir Sternberg.[1] From this standpoint our effort to disclose principles governing narrative is guided by hypotheses about goal and effect.

This is the perspective I shall try to defend in this essay. I take it that narratives are like forks in that they are designed to fulfill certain purposes. These purposes can largely be conceived as aiming at certain effects— effects registered by a perceiver prepared to grasp a narrative. In inquiring into narrative structure and narration, we ought to presume that, as human cultural activities, making and consuming narratives may well obey functional principles not captured by feature-based taxonomies. More specifically, certain features of those narratives can be best explained if we adopt a design stance. The isolated figures we can discern in a narrative are not necessarily ends in themselves. They are most fruitfully considered as a byproduct of a holistic strategy, an effort after effect.

In order to focus the discussion, I shall concentrate on recent French works exemplifying the neo-structuralist trend, principally André Gaudreault and François Jost's *Le Récit cinématographique* (1990; hereafter cited as *RC*) and Christian Metz's *L'Énonciation impersonnelle; ou le site du film* (1991; hereafter cited as *EI*).[2] My critique explores what I take to be three problems with neo-structuralist narratology of film: an excessively atomistic conception of narrative devices; an assemblage-based approach to the films that manifest those devices; and an implausible conception of how spectators make sense of narrative. My criticisms also seek to highlight some ways in which the formal/functional perspective can avoid these problems.

I

Neo-structuralist narratologists of film largely avoid discussing function. They concentrate almost completely on classifying such narrative features as moments of overt narrational presence (often called "enunciation"), temporal manipulations (such as flashbacks), and point of view (or "focalization"). In accord with this taxonomic emphasis, the theorists tend to conceive of narrative structure and narration as assemblages of material units and isolable devices. I shall suggest by contrast that narrative structure and narration are better understood as *systemic*. They are organized around strategic functional principles, and they may manifest quite motley material divisions.

Take, as an example of the neo-structuralist tendency, the common assumption that the film shot is inherently a unit of narrative structure or narration. The assumption is explicit in Metz's *grande syntagmatique* of narrative cinema. All the segments he charts presuppose that durational continuity or ellipsis is manifested through relations among shots. [3] For instance, ellipsis can be rendered, according to Metz, only by eliminating intervals during shot changes.[4] Gaudreault is even more explicit: "There are two types of narrative in the cinema: the micro-narrative (the shot), a first level on which is generated the second narrative level" ("Film, Narrative, Narration" 71).

The view that the shot is a fundamental unit of narrative is theoretically untenable for the following reason. Any material unit we might pick out— a shot in a film, a sentence in a literary text—is not necessarily a pertinent functional unit of the system that includes it. A shot is a series of images; a narrative is a series of events and states of affairs. The two series have no common metric. That is, we can invoke no *theoretical* principle that would allow us to reduce narrative events and states of affairs to shots. To take a shot as a unit of narrative is like saying that the plot of *Parsifal* divides neatly into bars, notes, and chords.

Here is another way to see this point. In principle any manipulation of narrative action, time, or point of view can be presented within a shot. A single shot can, for instance, shift what Gerard Genette calls "focalization." The famous panning and tracking shot around the courtyard in Jean Renoir's *Crime of M. Lange* (1936) is at times optically subjective, at times independent of character knowledge. Even alternating simultaneous action, such as the last-minute rescue with the hero racing to catch the villain, can in principle be conveyed through the right amount of camera movements (maybe swooping helicopter movements over buildings and treetops) and clocks indicating the time passing.

The belief that the shot is inherently a unit of narrative has long-range theoretical consequences. On the basis of this assumption, for instance, Gaudreault and Jost claim that each shot necessarily presents a continuous duration. "It is of course the shot which, except in the case of fast or slow motion filming, always respects the durational integrity of the actions that it shows . . . This holds good for every shot (with the exceptions already noted [that is, slow and fast motion]) in all films in cinema history" (*RC* 118). Yet this statement is inaccurate exactly because a shot as a material unit carries no commitments to the sort of narrative relations it might represent. Many films in the history of cinema create temporal disjunctions within a single shot. Charles Musser informs us that Edwin S. Porter habitually conveyed an ellipsis by having a person leave the setting and immediately return. The audience would understand that several hours had been omitted, even though there was no change of shot.[5] Less outré possibilities come to mind as well. Panning across a room from one character to another, we can skip ahead centuries, repeat an action already shown, or flash back to an earlier scene (as in *Enchantment*). In Alf Sjöberg's *Miss Julie* (1951) the heroine is in the foreground and in the present, while in the background events take place in the past. Theo Angelopoulos's *Traveling Players* (1975) moves across years in the course of lengthy tracking shots.

Of course, in practice the shot does *tend* to function as a unit of narration; ellipses within a single shot *are* rare; disjunctions of time and space are often covered by cuts. But these are empirical goal-oriented choices, the result of the common practices that have grown up in the course of film history. It is an interesting and important fact about films that the shot has tended to *serve as* a narrational unit, but the theoretical point remains: any narrative relations can in principle be manifested in any configuration of shots, including a single shot.

A comparable difficulty arises in the neo-structuralist assumption that filmic narration is impossible without editing. Metz implies as much when he claims that only montage allows film to achieve anaphora, cataphora, consecutiveness, and causality (*EI* 182). Gaudreault and Jost suggest that the isolated shot is limited to mere *monstration,* showing; only with a series of shots (montage) does narration proper come into existence: "The film in a single shot . . . does not and cannot engage with problems of linearity and continuity of the action . . . It is only when the film presupposes more than one shot that it must resolve problems relative to the homogeneity of the plot" (*RC* 115).

As we've already seen, the authors have maintained that the single shot must adhere to the temporal integrity of the action it presents. They therefore believe that only editing can create those temporal variations intrinsic to narration. Expectably, the authors' application of Genette's taxonomy of durational reference refers almost completely to the articulation of shots. The summary, for instance, is handled in a sequence of shots (Metz's "episodic" and "ordinary" sequences).[6]

Again, however, it seems evident that the ways in which narrative principles mobilize material units is a contingent, norm-bound matter and not a theoretical entailment. One scene of Ozu Yasujiro's *Only Son* (1937) ends late at night, with a family sitting in muted despair and the mother, Sugiko, weeping softly. Cut to a shot of a corner of the room, the mother's sobbing still audible. Over nearly a minute of screen time the light changes, and the sobbing fades out. Morning arrives, and we hear the noises of a neighborhood waking up. The transition has not elided time, for there are no junctures. Ozu has *compressed* duration within a single shot. There is no theoretical reason that all films in the history of the cinema might not have used this sort of technique to manipulate time.

It is an error, then, to assume that a material unit (such as the shot) or a string of such units (such as the edited series of shots) ipso facto constitutes a narrative unit. This is to take contingent norms for logical necessities. Narrative structure and narration mobilize all sorts of material properties of the medium, in a wide variety of manners. This occurs because narrative structure and the process of narration are both function driven, and in varying historical circumstances different functions have come forward and have been fulfilled in distinct material ways. Some ways have been normalized, such as the tendency to articulate temporal ellipses by change of shot. but there always remains the possibility of fulfilling the same functions in other ways.

As function-driven processes, narrative and narration will often exhibit patterns and effects that are not decomposable into distinct material units. The *Only Son* shot is an integral physical unit, but we cannot say at what distinct points several hours got squeezed into fifty-six seconds. Moreover, the soundtrack presents its own continuum, which is impossible to segment exactly: Sugiko's offscreen sobbing fades out several seconds into the shot, followed by a gradually rising sound of morning activities, and these bleed over into the next shot.

A more extreme case is presented by the celebrated restaurant scene in Jacques Tati's *Play Time.* (1967). The sequence consumes about forty-five minutes of film, but it conveys an entire evening, from about eight o'clock, when the Royal Garden restaurant opens) until dawn, when its customers depart after having demolished large sections of it. What is interesting here is that there are no determinable ellipses between shots. Indeed, many shots are joined by matches on figure movement, thus indicating durational continuity. More significantly, the soundtrack consists almost wholly of diegetic music played by bands in the restaurant. Diegetic music is a standard cue for durational continuity, so, at the level of the soundtrack as well, we cannot identify any breaks that would demarcate an ellipsis. Without any temporal discontinuities among material units, several hours have been squeezed into forty-five minutes.

Such examples pose no problem for a functional theory. The *Play Time* sequence has as one purpose the condensing of time, and we can apply our knowledge of restaurants and the passing of time to make it comprehensible. Our world knowledge allows us to make sense of the sequence as a whole, just as we make sense of the *Only Son* shot.[7] These instances suggest that we do grasp a film's temporality not wholly through shots and sequences but also through relevant action schemas—the knowledge structures that enable us to recognize and categorize what we see on the screen. True, shots and sequences cue us to apply such schemas and help us carve up the action intelligibly. But that is an interesting fact about the history of film style, not an essential condition for cinematic narrativity. Furthermore, such examples suggest that viewers can make adequate sense of a narrative by means of a loose, rather approximate sense of temporality. Where, exactly, did night pass into dawn in the Ozu or Tati sequences? No viewer can say or probably even cares. A functionalist perspective, suitably informed by a sense of taxonomic options, is well equipped to identify and explain this sort of indeterminacy.

II

I've taken the idea that a shot is a basic unit of narration as an instance of what I've criticized as the "atomistic" conception of narrative features widespread in neo-structuralist narratology. A second major consequence of this program has been to treat the individual film as an assemblage of devices. It may sound odd to criticize structuralists for underplaying the importance of large-scale structure, but it does seem that within film studies this trend has led to fairly pointillistic conceptions of intratextual dynamics.[8] Conceiving narrative options as distinct "figures" has encouraged analysts to treat films as agglomerates of distinct moments in which those figures get instantiated.

Metz, for example, suggests that filmic enunciation (which he takes to be the process by which filmic discourse overtly addresses the spectator) is inherently reflexive: enunciation is "the semiological act by which *certain parts of a text* speak to us of this text as an act" (*EI* 20; emph. added). The reason, he maintains, is that there is no fixed set of deictic markers in cinema. True enough, but one might then go on to ask whether there are functional regularities that govern contexts in principled ways. Instead, Metz takes atomism as the best methodological option: "It is simpler to specify in each example what enunciative figures appear and what ones do not" (*EI* 180).

Like Metz, Gaudreault and Jost believe that cinema has no stable marks of subjectivity. They assert that enunciation is therefore a matter of context and the spectator's sensitivity (*RC* 44). Again, however, they do not consider the prospect of offering a theoretical account of those contextual regularities to which a spectator must *be* sensitive.[9]

By contrast, a formal/functionalist approach can usefully start from the premise that a film operates as a whole, its individual parts playing determinate roles in a larger pattern. Recognizing that pattern and its possible functions also presupposes relations to broader historical norms. That is, a functionalist theory encourages us to explore functions and holistic patterns recurring across a *body* of films. Within these contexts individual "figures" may fulfill conventional or unconventional purposes.

Consider as an example self-conscious enunciation, those moments when we feel that an overt narrational presence is shaping our relation to the story. These devices itemized by Metz and by Gaudreault and Jost do not pop up willy-nilly. In classical Hollywood films they tend to be reserved for certain moments. The beginning of the film, for instance, will characteristically insinuate us into the narrative world through a process of *moving inward* to explore an already developing chain of action. Think of the opening of D. W. Griffith's *Broken Blossoms* (1919), in which a series of shots takes us from the port into the neighborhood, or the opening of Ridley Scott's *Blade Runner* (1982), with its swooping camera movement into a Los Angeles of the future. This principle of large-scale form seeks to elicit certain effects. By gradually initiating us into its world, the classical film orients the spectator to the situation, exposing essential information and highlighting certain motifs that will become important. The gradual movement inward also arouses curiosity: what is the target of this narrowing field of view?

Whether these narrational gestures are performed within a single shot or several, by means of moving camera or moving characters, in a trembling handheld shot or not—such stylistic options differ significantly in effect, but they remain in an important sense functional equivalents. Like those stereotyped beginnings that we find in oral narratives ("Once upon a time," "Now let's tell lies!"), the movement inward serves to introduce us to the world of the narrative.

There are other transtextual regularities concerning self-conscious narration in the classical film. A scene may start with a sign on a door or a building to show the place of the action; this is for our benefit. A scene may end by concentrating on a detail that will be important in future action. Again, the purpose is to create a particular patterning of narrative information, and that purpose, along with canonical patterns, has become normalized within a particular filmmaking tradition. [10] So far as I know, no neo-structuralist has suggested that moving into a space or out of it, or concentrating on a detail, necessarily constitutes a marker of enunciation. Theorists would doubtless argue that it's all a matter of context. What I am arguing, however, is that an appeal to context tacitly depends on functionality. If the individual figure is not graspable in isolation, then only by assuming some sense of functionality can the spectator infer its meaning "from context." Furthermore, a local context is itself shaped by formal/functional principles, by its place in the developing whole, and by its canonical role in a particular filmmaking tradition. Classifying narrative techniques is necessary but insufficient; if we are to understand how films allocate and use their narrative resources, a taxonomy needs to be motivated by more regional functionality. Besides distinguishing among figures, the theorist needs to consider the possibility that some narrational functions are features of *entire* texts.

Particularly, entire texts in time. In the classical Hollywood film, for instance, a fading from more to less overt presentation is a pervasive principle of narrational coherence. All other things being equal, the beginning of any scene or sequence is likely to be more self-conscious in its narration than the middle portions of that unit. Thus, the spectator is guided to move from overt, self-conscious presentation to covert, character-centered presentation.

Although the fading principle is visible at the level of the individual scene, it also organizes narration across the film as a whole. The classical film's opening, when background information must be laid out, often presents the most overt, omniscient stretches of narration—as we've already seen in the tendency of classical films to open with a penetration into the fictional space. The same quality is particularly apparent in the use of nondialogue, or expository, intertitles.

According to Metz, expository titles in silent film resemble novelistic language in using the "epic preterite." He supplies some hypothetical examples ("All seemed well . . ."; "But suddenly she was seized by a suspicion" [*EI* 64]). Again, however, an examination of particular films would allow us to point out the contextual regularities that complicate such an apparently self-evident observation.

If we actually look, say, at American silent films after 1910 or so, we find that expository intertitles tend to dominate the opening portions of the film. In the course of the film they diminish. Soon most titles are dialogue titles, and in many features the last half-hour contains no expository titles at all. Now that the spectators possess the background information of the story, the character action takes over the film. We become less aware of being told something and more attentive to the fictional world.

As the expository titles wither away and the narrational burden passes to character speech and action, something else of interest happens. The verb tense of the expository titles shifts. Of course, some titles are mere phrases, lacking verbs and thus tenseless with respect to the time of the story action (for instance, "Sunset" or "On the trail of Trampas"). But in the film's opening portions the earliest titles that have tense typically use the past forms, whereas quite soon titles begin to use the present.

In *The Virginian* (1914), for example, the first expository title situates the action in the past: "In the heart of the West, where cattle pastured in every valley, and solitary horsemen rode the ranges, there reigned supreme that romantic figure—the cow-puncher." The next title tells us of the Virginian, who "*roped* steers more easily than the best." But the next expository title shifts to the present tense: "Back in Vermont, Molly Wood *struggles* for a living teaching music." And the following title confirms that the main story action has begun: "The Virginian, fearless and strong, *has* for his best friend the easily led, lovable Steve." Within the first three minutes of the film we are in the midst of an ongoing action. The shift from past to present tense contributes to the fading out of overt narration. As the narration becomes more covert, it distinguishes between the background exposition and the particular events that initiate the plot. The rest of the action will be taking place in the narrative now, as if before our eyes.

The patterning of expository titles is only one device serving classical narrational coherence, but it does sharply illustrate how the Hollywood film found diverse ways to guide the spectator's gradual "absorption" into the storyworld. To analyze such patterns we cannot stay at the level of this or that narrative device. What we want to track is a *process of narrative representation* in which individual devices, such as the camera movement inward or the past-tense intertitle, play canonized roles.

To date, none of the neo-structuralist theorists of film narrative have proposed a theory of such a process. Mounting such a theory requires *analyzing whole films* to disclose their patterns of narration, not simply isolating devices and arranging them taxonomically.[11] Such analyses will at least help us nuance our theories while also refining any taxonomies we may wish to mount.

III

I want to single out one more contrast between the neo-structuralist approach and the one I am sketching. This difference does not, I suppose, spring directly from the taxonomic impulse, but it may be related to it. This difference lies in the conception of spectatorial activity presumed by each perspective.

As I remarked at the outset, the neo-structuralist perspective is feature centered. It tends to look for isolable aspects of the film, treating it as a static array whose elements and relationships may be subsumed within a paradigm of differences. There is little explicit account of the sort of spectatorial activity required to make sense of the alternatives generated by the taxonomy.[12]

By contrast, a functionalist perspective of the kind I am outlining treats the film as designed to elicit certain sorts of effects. I would go farther and argue that, *as a methodological point of departure,* we ought to assume that the text is so made that it seeks certain intersubjective regularities of response.[13] When *The Only Son* or *Play Time* represents the passage from night to dawn, the spectator presumably grasps the action because she or he has the night-to-dawn concept stored as knowledge. Similarly, the narrational pattern of gradually slipping into the film's narrative world, manifested in a visible progress inward or in a shift in verb tense, probably aims to shape the spectator's assimilation of narrative information. Interestingly, devices that might seem anomalous from a feature-centered perspective may make sense from a design stance. In order to see how, let me return briefly to the problem of narrative temporality in film.

The neo-structuralist narratologists I am considering here are agreed that the film image is always "in the present tense." The chief argument they offer is that there are no univocal temporal markers in cinema. "Walk into a movie theatre after the film has started," suggest Gaudreault and Jost. "There is no way to determine whether the scene unrolling on the screen is a flashback or whether it belongs to the chronological series of told events. Contrary to language, which situates us immediately on the temporal axis, the film image knows only one time." That time, the authors claim, is Now. "Everything is always in the present in the cinema" (*RC* 101).

This notion, familiar as it is, ought to leave us puzzled. First, the relevant properties of "presentness" would seem to be manifested by any spectacle. Walk into a play or a ballet or a puppet show or an opera, and there will be nothing that tells you that the scene you are witnessing is a flashback or a chronologically sequential event. No medium of spectacle, so far as I know, has any unequivocal, universally accepted means of signaling that certain represented events come before or after others. In this sense, if film is always in the present, so too are all types of theater.

Perhaps, then, language is exceptional among representational media, insofar as verb tense specifies the pastness or presentness of an action? It doesn't seem so once verbs get taken up in a narrative context. For grammatical tense is no certain guide to a flashback in literary narrative.

Inspired by Gaudreault and Jost's just-walk-in-during-the-middle test, you open a novel, and your eye falls on this sentence: "The briefcase got as far as the x-ray scanner, and the next thing I knew airport security was squiring me away for what was nothing less than an interrogation." The verbs are all in the past tense, but that doesn't help me if I want to know where the actions lie in what Gaudreault and Jost call "the chronological series of told events." The browsing reader will have to look back to the previous sentence: "I never would forget flying to California carrying a large briefcase packed with sadomasochistic sexual paraphernalia" (Cornwell 106–7). Only in the light of this will the reader understand the next past-tense sentence as describing action in a flashback. Moreover, novels have been written, in whole or part, in the present tense. Yet in reading Dickens's *Bleak House* (1852–53) or Peter Høeg's *Smilla's Sense of Snow* (1993) we have no trouble understanding that some events happened before or after other ones. Our film *The Virginian* employs the past tense for its exposition and the present tense for the rest of the film, but surely the intelligibility of the successive events is not made problematic. Nor are they in this moment from Michael Crichton's *Sphere* (1987):

He stepped inside.
The sphere closed behind him.

There is darkness, and then, as his eyes adjust, something like fireflies. It is a dancing, luminous form, millions of points of light, swirling around him.
[and so on in the present tense for several pages]

His cheek rested on cold metal. He rolled onto his back and looked at the polished surface of the sphere, curving above him. (331–36)

Actions unfolding in chronological order are described in an alternation of past and present tense. The reader knows that the narration has not shuffled chronology because the action schema in place—the man enters the sphere and sees what's inside—is consistent across the variation in tense. Because of this, the reader can infer that the shift to the present tense functions expressively, to heighten our sense of the protagonist's awestruck state of mind.

In the right circumstances the present tense can also indicate an event *prior to* the narrative Now, which itself is treated in the past tense. Examples show up in colloquial Americanese: "I had a lot of troubles with my car last month. So I take it to the mechanic and I ask her, 'Will my car make it to Milwaukee?' and she says, 'If you don't mind walking back.'" Or a more up-to-date instance: "So he said, 'Take this exam for me,' and I'm, like, 'Why should I?'" (See *Clueless* [1995] for more examples.)

I have dwelled on the malleability of verbal narration because an idea of the inevitable pastness of the linguistic past tense forms the point of departure for many narratologists' claim that, in contrast to written narration, the cinema image is always in the present. Alternatively, a functionalist account of literary narrative could show that either past or present tense can, in the right circumstances, convey the same temporal relationships. The reader reads for pattern and function as well as for verb tense, and default values dictated by intrinsic norms of the whole text can justify disparities that arise on the verbal surface.

It seems likely, then, that the neo-structuralist program has once more succumbed to atomism. The search for isolable features (in this case, of grammatical tense) has blocked from consideration formal/functional principles that govern the context and which prompt the spectator to perform certain norm-bound operations.

I am inclined to think that the claim that a film is "always in the present" is vacuous. In any event, for the narratologist the issue is not what the image is intrinsically but how it is mobilized within the temporal scheme of the overall film and how spectators, armed with certain default values and norms, can make sense of it. A wide array of cinematic cues can indicate a flashback: changes in music, speed of motion, or tonality (color/black-and-white; high/low contrast); verbal information; more generally, an indefinitely large number of schema-based cues (an old man followed by images of the same character in his youth; or a dead man now living again, as in *Pulp Fiction* [1994]).

The neo-structuralists are right to suggest that there is no univocal set of temporal markers in cinema. But this is not because a film "is" inherently in the present and therefore needs special conventions to denote the past. Rather, it is because any isolated device functions in relation to norms established both inside and outside the text, and the spectator can construe a wide range of material cues in ways that conform, more or less approximately, to those norms.

If this is right, we ought not to expect that local devices can be taken at face value. The spectator's ongoing elaboration of the text can fill in gaps and overlook objective disparities. Texts are so designed as to encourage the spectator to pick up *partial* systems and still arrive at adequate inferences. Once more, consider the flashback.

A flashback in a classical Hollywood film is typically initiated by a character's remembering the past or recounting past events to a listener. This framing device has impelled many narratologists to conclude that the flashback actually represents the character's memory images or verbal report. Metz, for instance, asserts that a flashback rests on the assumption that a character's memory recreates the past with exactitude, down to the details of setting we see in the scenes of the past. Through a process he calls "transvisualization" the flashback replaces the character's words or thoughts with images, an exact representation of *"what she would have said"* (*EI* 121).

But how, on this account, do we explain a common inconsistency within Hollywood flashbacks? Very often the narrating or remembering characters who introduce a flashback *are not present to witness* events that they report or recall. In *Leave Her to Heaven* (1946) a minor character recounts virtually the entire plot to a casual listener, but the teller scarcely appears in the string of events he introduces; moreover, he could not have known many intimate details conveyed in "his" flashback. The limit case may be *Ten North Frederick* (1958). After a funeral the dead man's daughter begins to tell her brother about their father's life. In the course of this embedded flashback we learn that the father had a mistress. Yet the daughter does not know this. Indeed, only after the flashback is over and we have returned to the day of the funeral does the daughter learn of the mistress! Given the prevalence of this construction, we can hardly say, with Metz, that a flashback represents what the character would have said, since the character did not know the events that "her" flashback recounted.

From a functionalist standpoint this disparity becomes a pseudo-problem. Metz assumes that the flashback represents a character's memory or recounted story because a salient, isolated feature—the act of remembering or speaking—initiates the flashback. But suppose that a flashback represents the act of recalling or recounting only at the boundary points or at particularly stressed moments within the flashback itself (for example, when reinforced by voice-over commentary and action-based cues). Suppose, instead, that the chief purpose of a flashback in film is *to rearrange the order of events*. This rearrangement, in turn, serves to create specific effects—curiosity, suspense, surprise, or a mood of anxiety or nostalgia, a sense of irony or loss. In both *Leave Her to Heaven* and *Ten North Frederick* beginning late in the story sequence maximizes curiosity about what events led up to this state of affairs. The flashback provides the preconditions for understanding what we have already seen in the present. The move to the past is a means of sharpening curiosity or misleading the audience about a contemporaneous state of affairs.

But a "pure" flashback—say, starting at the father's funeral and then dissolving immediately back to his midlife crisis—is too brutally disorienting for the classical Hollywood tradition. The move into the past must be signaled and justified, and *this* is the purpose of the remembering/recounting frame. From a functional perspective presenting a flashback as a character memory or as a recitation of past events serves to motivate, via quasi-realistic means, temporal rearrangement of the action. But, once this motivation initiates the shift, the frame character has served her or his purpose, and fidelity to memory or verbal report or plausibility no longer matters.

This design stance explanation gains force when we reckon in the spectator. If we viewers realize the anomalies of flashback information only after we reflect on them, perhaps during normal viewing they simply don't register (at least in most of us). That may have to do with our pursuit of relevant narrative information, which is likely to involve causal/temporal relations rather than details of how knowledge may be restricted. And it is possible that, given the constraints of time-bound, mildly attentive viewing, recalling who's telling the story and what she or he could know at each instant has no payoff for comprehension. It would be worth a little time for students of filmic psychology to experiment with this question. We might find that here, as elsewhere, film directors are excellent practical psychologists, exploiting not only our abilities to perceive and comprehend and infer but also our deficiencies—all for the sake of guiding us to have the sort of experience they aim to generate.

I've tried to propose some ways in which the formal/functional perspective can offer more plausible analyses and explanations of narrational processes than have been forthcoming from the neo-structuralist tradition. I have concentrated on matters of narrative temporality, but I think that a functionalist critique could find comparable problems with neo-structuralist accounts of point of view and the "internal" narrator.[14] Above all, I have sought to show that, while taxonomies are useful, they help most when governed by a sense of the film's overall formal principles, the historical standards in place, and the purposes for which norm and form recruit specific narrative devices.

Notes

1. For Aristotle the relevant text is, of course, the *Poetics,* particularly chaps. 13–19. For the Russian formalists important examples of a functional perspective are offered by Tynianov and Eichenbaum. Sternberg has mounted eloquent defenses of a functionalist perspective in the pieces listed in the references.

2. Much of the following also pertains to some arguments set forth in Chatman; Stam, Burgoyne, and Flitterman-Lewis; and Gunning.

3. In passing, Metz suggests that, at least in the modern cinema, all of his syntagmatic types can to some extent be contained within the autonomous shot (*Essais sur la signification au cinéma* 134–35). He does not pursue the implications of this suggestion, which would, I think, lead him to abandon the distinction between single-shot and multiple-shot syntagms—the gesture that found the *grande syntagmatique* itself.

4. See his discussion of the "ordinary sequence," in which each shot "simply presents one of the unskipped moments in the action," and of the scene, in which screen duration and diegetic duration coincide (*Essais sur la signification au cinéma* 132).

5. See Musser's discussion of *Lost in the Alps* (1907), 359.

6. Gaudreault and Jost recognize Genette's "scene," with its durational equivalence of story time and screen time, as attainable both within a single shot and within an edited sequence. For reasons unclear to me, Gaudreault and Jost's examples suggest that they find Genette's pause principally manifested within the shot (*RC* 116–21).

7. Or the temporal compression within shots of Hitchcock's *Rope,* which in eighty continuous minutes of screen time presents a passage from late afternoon to night.

8. Much of what follows is inspired by points made by Meir Sternberg, particularly in "Telling in Time (2)" (485–98, 505). I am also grateful to Sternberg for private correspondence clarifying these issues.

9. For example, having reviewed types of focalization, Gaudreault and Jost say only that "focalization varies in the course of the filmic *récit* in relation to

the feelings and emotional states that are to be conveyed" (*RC* 143). The task, I suggest, is exactly to theorize the possible relationships between effects and narrative organization.

10. Several such scenes are discussed in chaps. 3–6 of Bordwell, Staiger, and Thompson.

11. This is what I seek to do in the third part of *Narration in the Fiction Film,* which is concerned with showing typical narrational patterns across films of various types (or "modes").

12. A noteworthy exception is chap. 1 of Chatman's *Story and Discourse,* which provides a suggestive account of the reader's inferential activity. Still, the bulk of the book remains taxonomic, and I do not see that any of the categories Chatman outlines depend upon his conception of "reading out" of a narrative.

13. Aside to Cultural Studiers: this does not entail that the design stance presupposes that *all* responses must be uniform. Many texts include zones of indeterminacy, allowing room for different interpretations and appropriations. Indeed, many producers of media texts build just such zones into them. My point is simply that the design stance presupposes *some* intersubjective regularities of response. Cf. Staiger.

14. For example, if a flashback is not substantively enframed by the memory or conversation that initiates it, this would seem to pose a problem for the communication model of narration proposed by Chatman in *Story and Discourse* (151). A functionalist account would also, I think, provide an alternative explanation for the "lying" flashback in *Stage Fright* to the one offered by Chatman in *Coming to Terms* (131–34).

References

Angelopoulos, Theo, dir. *Traveling Players.* 1975.

Aristotle. *Poetics.* Trans. and intro. Malcolm Heath. New York: Penguin, 1996.

Bordwell, David. *Narration in the Fiction Film.* Madison: University of Wisconsin Press, 1985.

Bordwell, David, Janet Staiger, and Kristin Thompson. *The Classical Hollywood Cinema: Film Style and Mode of Production to 1960.* New York: Columbia University Press, 1985.

Burgoyne, Robert. "Film-Narratology." *New Vocabularies in Film Semiotics.* Ed. Robert Stam, Robert Burgoyne, and Sandy Flitterman-Lewis. London: Routledge, 1992. 69–122.

Chatman, Seymour. *Story and Discourse: Narrative Structure in Fiction and Film.* Ithaca: Cornell University Press, 1978.

———. *Coming to Terms: The Rhetoric of Narrative Fiction and Film.* Ithaca: Cornell University Press, 1990.

Cornwell, Patricia B. *All That Remains.* New York: Avon, 1992.

Crichton, Michael. *Sphere.* New York: Ballantine, 1987.

De Mille, Cecil B., dir. *The Virginian.* 1914.

Dickens, Charles. *Bleak House.* London: J.M. Dent & Sons, ltd., 1932.

Dunne, Philip, dir. *Ten North Frederick.* 1958.

Eichenbaum, Boris. *O. Henry and the Theory of the Short Story.* Trans. I. R. Titunik. Ann Arbor: Michigan Slavic Contributions, 1968.

Gaudreault, André. "Film, Narrative, Narration: The Cinema of the Lumière Brothers." *Early Cinema: Space, Frame, Narrative.* Ed. Thomas Elsaesser. London: British Film Institute, 1990.

Gaudreault, André, and François Jost. *Le Récit cinématographique.* Paris: Nathan, 1990.

Gunning, Tom. *D. W. Griffith and the Origins of American Narrative Film: The Early Years at Biograph.* Urbana: University of Illinois Press, 1991.

Heckerling, Amy, dir. *Clueless.* 1995.

Høeg, Peter, dir. *Smilla's Sense of Snow.* Fox Searchlight Pictures, 1993.

Metz, Christian. *Essais sur la signification au cinema.* Vol. 1. Paris: Klincksieck, 1971.

——. *L'Énonciation impersonnelle; ou le site du film.* Paris: Klincksieck, 1991.

Musser, Charles. *Before the Nickelodeon: Edwin S. Porter and the Edison Manufacturing Company.* Berkeley: University of California Press, 1991.

Renoir, Jean, dir. *Crime of M. Lange.* 1936.

Sjöberg, Alf, dir. *Miss Julie.* 1951.

Staiger, Janet. *Perverse Spectators: The Practice of Film Reception.* New York: New York University Press, 2000.

Stahl, John, dir. *Leave Her to Heaven.* 1945.

Stam, Robert, Robert Burgoyne, and Sandy Flitterman-Lewis, eds. *New Vocabularies in Film Semiotics.* London: Routledge, 1992.

Sternberg, Meir. "Point of View and the Indirectons of Direct Speech." *Language and Style* 15.2 (1982): 67–117.

——. "Telling in Time (1): Chronology and Narrative Theory." *Poetics Today* 11.4 (1990): 901–48.

——. "How Indirect Discourse Means: Syntax, Semantics, Pragmatics." *Literary Pragmatics.* Ed. Roger D. Sell. London: Routledge, 1991. 62–93.

——. "Telling in Time (2): Chronology, Teleology, Narrativity." *Poetics Today* 13.3 (1992): 463–541.

Tarantino, Quentin, dir. *Pulp Fiction.* Bend Apart and Jersey Films, 1994.

Tati, Jaques, dir. *Play Time.* 1967.

Tynianov, Yuri. *The Problem of Verse Language.* Trans. Michael Sosa and Brent Harvey. Ann Arbor: Ardis, 1981.

Yasojiro, Ozu, dir. *Only Son.* 1937.

7

Literary Film Adaptation and the

Form/Content Dilemma

Kamilla Elliott

The official critical models of literary film adaptation are all formulated on the film's degree of fidelity to the literary text and have been used by critics both to foster fidelity maxims and to protest them. Geoffrey Wagner's three models of adaptation—so influential that they have formed the basis for all subsequent formal models—are valued and ranked according to their degree of *in*fidelity to the original. In the 1980s scholars such as Dudley Andrew argued more often for a balanced translation model, in which fidelity to the novel and to the conventions film are honored equally. In the 1990s into the 2000s the fidelity imperative emerges as the arch-villain of adaptation studies (Reynolds; McFarlane; Cartmell and others, *Pulping Fictions;* Cartmell and Whelehan; and Naremore). Peter Reynolds recommends that adaptations undertake a Marxist subversion of and dialectic with literature, rather than remaining deferent and subsequent to literature (3). Robert Stam advocates resistance to the "elitist prejudices" of fidelity imperatives through Michel Foucault's demystification of the author, Mikhail Bakhtin's notion of dialogic exchange, Jacques Derrida's blasting of the original/copy differential, and Roland Barthes's semiotic leveling of literature and film alike as "texts" (58). Some protest the fidelity imperative on formal grounds as well. Narratologist Brian McFarlane declares the fidelity preoccupation a "near-fixation," "unilluminating," and "a doomed enterprise" (8–9, 194).

Recent poststructuralist and cultural studies scholars argue that some literary critics gravitate toward adaptation studies because they support outmoded theories, such as New Criticism, and politically conservative theories, such as humanism, and foster a retrograde entrenchment of the literary canon and of classic literature against the rising tide of popular culture and cultural studies (J. O. Thompson 12). But surveying the criticism over the whole of the twentieth century, we find that adaptation critics have always been excoriated as outmoded and as lagging behind the critical times—by New Critics as well as by their high art humanist predecessors (Balázs 258–61; Bluestone 258; Babbitt 186 / ff.). There are many reasons for this ongoing excoriation. This essay addresses one century-long heresy: adaptation suggests that form is separable from content, after all. From Walter Pater to Ferdinand de Saussure to a host of New Critics and structuralists, critics have been adamant that form does not separate from content.[1] And, while poststructuralists have exploded form/content binarisms, they have debunked the notion of content so much that adaptation and adaptation studies appear more behind the times than ever. Adaptation affronts critical theories at every turn. It challenges New Criticism's denial of a paraphrasable core when screenwriting handbooks declare paraphrase the first stage of adaptation (Brady; Seger). It troubles the inviolable bond of structuralism's signifier and signified when words and images are decreed untranslatable as whole signs, leaving only some part, of a novel's signs available for transfer in adaptation. It raises for poststructuralism the untenable specter of an original signified, to say nothing of the more localized signifieds to which both novels and films claim to refer. Adaptation as it is popularly conceived is thus a theoretical impossibility. Adaptation is generally dismissed by the theoretically correct as a collective cultural illusion. Novelist and (significantly for this discussion) semiotician Umberto Eco insists that there is no relationship at all between his book, *The Name of the Rose,* and Jean-Jacques Annaud's film adaptation of it: they simply share the same name (qtd. in "Adaptations").

Yet the perception that something passes between book and film in adaptation holds firmly in filmmaker, popular, and critical accounts. This essay unfolds six concepts of adaptation gleaned from these accounts and from readings of aesthetic practice—concepts that attempt to explicate what passes between a book and a film in adaptation in terms of form and content. Because they have taken so many shapes in discourse, *form* and *content* must be defined loosely and variably in this discussion, ranging from whole art forms and their "themes" or ideologies to form and content splits within signs (signifier and signified). Under some concepts of adaptation one medium is the content of the other; under others, both gesture to some outer signified with different forms; under some others, novel, film, and audience response merge to form a composite sign. The concepts overlap as frequently as they differ and are by no means presented as theoretically viable or empirically proven. Rather, they are indicators of how relations between novels and films have been constructed and of what purposes these constructions have served. At times the novel is viewed as a monolithic signified to be faithfully represented by servile filmic signifiers; at others, it is seen as an incomplete mode of signification requiring incarnation by film; at still others, novel and film vie to represent an outer signified better than each other.

Semioticians and aestheticians have for centuries drawn on body and soul analogies to explicate theories of form and content. [2] Because of its preoccupation with relations between bodies and souls, *Wuthering Heights* provides an ideal case study for this discussion. From assertions regarding the shared soul of two bodies ("Whatever our souls are made of, [Heathcliff's] and mine are the same") to perplexities of how the dead inhere in the living (Heathcliff's "I *cannot* live without my soul!" leads to ghost chasing, alternating with necrophilia) to the perception that Cathy's spirit looks out through the embodied eyes of her relatives, a multiplicity of body and soul relations permeate *Wuthering Heights,* offering not only metaphoric reference points but also conceptual paradigms for the form/content issues of literary film adaptation (Brontë 80, 167).

The Psychic Concept of Adaptation

The persistent critical ghosting of content in the twentieth century is largely responsible for the prevalence of a psychic concept of adaptation, which figures what should ideally pass from book to film as "the spirit of the text." The psychic concept is everywhere in adaptation rhetoric—academic, practitioner, and lay. Academic critic Christopher Orr adduces: "A good adaptation must be faithful to the spirit of its literary source" (72). Filmmaker Luis Buñuel claims that his film of *Wuthering Heights, Abismos de Pasion* (1953), "Most importantly . . . tries to remain true to the *spirit* of Emily Brontë's novel (*Wuthering Heights* [1848])." Screenwriting handbook author Linda Seger replaces the form/content dichotomy with a form/spirit one: "The adapter looks for the balance between preserving the spirit of the original and creating a new form" (9). Author Irvine Welsh, whose novel *Trainspotting* was filmed in 1996, maintains that only the content/spirit can transfer from novel to film because of the difference in forms: "you can't have a faithful interpretation of something; you can maybe have it in spirit, but it's going to change as it moves into a different medium" (qtd. in Hodge 118).

But the psychic concept of adaptation does not simply advance an infusion of filmic form with literary spirit; it posits a process of psychic connection in which the spirit of a text passes from novel to reader (in adaptation the reader is a filmmaker) to film to viewer. The notion that a text has a spirit with which readers connect psychically finds its recent roots in the early nineteenth century, most prominently in the writings of Georg Wilhelm Friedrich Hegel: "art cannot merely work for sensuous perception. It must deliver itself to the inward life, which coalesces with its object simply as though this were none other than itself, in other words, to the intimacy of soul, to the heart, the emotional life, which as the medium of spirit itself essentially strives after freedom, and seeks and possesses its reconciliation only in the inner chamber of the spirit." In Hegel's account, although the spirit "needs an external vehicle of expression," ultimately, form is "unessential and transient" (525). Similarly, the psychic model figures what transfers from novel to film as an elusive spirit and the task of adaptation as capturing that spirit and conveying it through changing mediums and forms. Thus, the term *medium* functions in two senses of the word—of persons in touch with spirits and of communications media. Although the various mediums are indispensable to the operation of the psychic model, the essential point is that they can and must be dropped. The form can change; the spirit remains constant. The spirit of the text thus maintains a life beyond form that is not constrained by or dependent on form.

The psychic concept can be diagrammed as follows, the parentheses indicating the dispensable and dropped forms that allow for psychic connection:

THE NOVEL'S SPIRIT → (THE NOVEL'S FORM) → (FILMMAKER RESPONSE) → (FILM) → VIEWER RESPONSE

The spirit of a text originates and ends in formless consciousness as pretextual spirit (generally figured as authorial intent, personality, or imagination) and as posttextual response (something that lingers in the reader or viewer after the novel or film has been consumed). Orr astutely recognizes that a concept beginning with author intent and ending in reader response must elide the two, though they appear at opposite ends of a communications spectrum: "The spirit of a verbal or filmic text is a function of both its discourse (the manner in which the narrator communicates to the reader or viewer) and its narrativity (the processes through which the reader/viewer constructs the meaning of the text)" (73).

The spirit of a text, however, is most frequently equated with the spirit of the author rather than of the reader. Pater writes: "There are some to whom nothing has any real interest, or real meaning, except as operative in a given person; and it is they who best appreciate the quality of soul in literary art.

They seem to know a person, in a book, and make way by intuition" (24). Many twentieth-century critics render the spirit of a text synonymous with authorial intent. Reviewer Howard Thompson's assessment that a 1951 film of *A Christmas Carol* "may be exactly what Dickens had in mind" (47), for example, is figured by academic critic Lester J. Keyser as synonymous with being true to "the spirit of Dickens" (121–22). Others equate it with authorial imagination. Peter Kosminsky's 1992 film of *Wuthering Heights* opens with a preface that depicts Emily Brontë (played by an uncredited Sinéad O'Connor) wandering the moors and beginning to "imagine" her novel: "First I found the place. I wondered who had lived there; what their lives were like. Something whispered to my mind and I began to write. My pen creates stories of a world that might have been, a world of my imagining. And here is one I'm going to tell. But take care not to smile at any part of it." In this episode what comes last in the chain of literary film adaptation—the film—is figured as identical with pretextual authorial imagination.

Critics in search of more tangible manifestations of textual spirit find it in authorial style (for example, Battestin). Pater maintains, however, that, although this spirit may manifest itself in style, it can never be fully contained or expressed by style: "it is still a characteristic of soul, in this sense of the word, that it does but suggest what can never be uttered, not as being different from, or more obscure than, what actually gets said, but as containing that plenary substance of which there is only one phase or facet in what is there expressed" (24, 33).

Fidelity to the spirit of a text is almost always accompanied by an insistence on the necessity of *in*fidelity to its letter or form. The psychic concept of adaptation argues that to be true to the spirit of a text adaptation *has* to leave behind the literary corpse. A too-literal translation that dutifully substitutes novel signifier for film signifier, dead form for dead form, are less faithful than those that pursue the novel's spirit: "the supposedly literal transposition may falsify an original fiction far more than an intelligent analogy" (239; Wagner's preferred model, one that uses the text as a "seed of inspiration" for the film). Thus, the psychic concept's ghosting of what passes between novel and film in adaptation allows a host of personal, filmic, and cultural agendas to be projected onto the novel and identified as its own spirit. Little wonder that the concept is so popular with critics and filmmakers.

The authority of the literary author is essential to validating these imposed agendas and projections. The author has been slow to die in adaptation criticism and practice even as he lies moldering under other discourses, because he represents an author-ity on which both novel and film advocates call in an effort to assert their medium over the other. For most of the twentieth century the psychic concept placed adaptation criticism under the auspices of literary rather than film scholarship: literary scholars policed and judged whether a film had captured the authorial spirit. Brian McFarlane, for instance, summarizes an essay by Q. D. Leavis on *Great Expectations,* concluding: "This seems to me an accurate account of one of the novel's great strengths, and it offers a challenge to the would-be-faithful film-maker" (119). [3] In these and other accounts we see the subjection of authorial spirit to dominant literary critical schools.

In the 1990s, however, certain film and television makers appropriated the canonical literary author in a new titling trend that made the author's name part of the film title, as do *Bram Stoker's Dracula* (1992), *Mary Shelley's Frankenstein* (1994), *Emily Brontë's Wuthering Heights* (used for both 1992 film and 1998 television versions), *William Shakespeare's Hamlet* (1996), *William Shakespeare's Romeo + Juliet* (1996), and *William Shakespeare's A Midsummer Night's Dream* (1999). The expanded titles of promotions, reviews, and posters extended the possessive construction, making directors and production companies the authors' keepers rather than literary critics, as in "Francis Ford Coppola's *Bram Stoker's Dracula,*" "Kenneth Branagh's *Mary Shelley's Frankenstein,*" "Peter Kosminsky's *Emily Brontë's Wuthering Heights,*" or Baz Luhrmann's *William Shakespeare's Romeo + Juliet.*" These redoubled possessives assert not only the film's authentication by the literary author but also the director's or production company's ownership of that authorial authenticating power. The film *auteur* now authors the literary author at the same time that he is authorized by him.

Kenneth Branagh claims to understand the spirit of Mary Shelley's *Frankenstein*—in this instance formulated as author intent—in opposition not only to earlier filmic interpretations of the novel but also to its own textual manifestations: "We have all grown so accustomed to all those screen versions of 'Frankenstein' that we have forgotten that Mary Shelley had something entirely different in mind . . . Elizabeth is only talked about in the book, and I felt that had to be changed. It seemed ridiculous that she would not question what he was up to, and I felt we had to have her voice in our story. Considering how times have changed in attitudes toward women's roles in films, it would not seem right to have her in the story just as a love interest. Mary Shelley was a strong woman who I'm sure questioned Percy Shelley, and I'm convinced she intended Elizabeth to be a strong character" (qtd. in Koltnow 10). Here Branagh moves quickly from "times have changed" to "I'm convinced [Mary Shelley] intended," blatantly demonstrating the use of authorial intent to validate contemporary views and agendas. In so doing, he implies that Shelley failed her own authorial intent, an intent that his film restores and manifests on her behalf. The promotions thus prove truer than the title: this is "Kenneth Branagh's Mary Shelley" more than it is "Mary Shelley's Frankenstein."

Intriguingly, Branagh's film shares an identical title with Harold Bloom's 1987 volume of critical essays, *Mary Shelley's Frankenstein,* a volume in which feminist contributions feature prominently. Like these critics, Branagh reads modern feminism back into the text, reshaping the narrative. Here and in many other adaptations we see that authorial and literary spirit rendered inextricable from filmic projection (in both technological and psychological senses of the word).

The Ventriloquist Concept of Adaptation

The ventriloquist concept differs from the psychic concept of adaptation in that it pays no lip service to authorial spirit: rather, it blatantly empties out the novel's signs and fills them with filmic spirits. If Cathy and Heathcliff's idea of two bodies sharing a soul epitomizes the psychic concept, Heathcliff's necrophilia with Cathy's corpse epitomizes the ventriloquist concept of adaptation. Under the ventriloquist concept what passes from novel to film in adaptation is a dead corpse rather than a living spirit. The adaptation, like a ventriloquist, props up the dead novel, throwing its voice onto the silent corpse. As he digs up her coffin, Heathcliff knows that Cathy's corpse will be cold and unresponsive when he touches it. But he uses deliberate fantasy to offset this reality: "If she be cold, I'll think it is this north wind that chills *me;* and if she be motionless, it is sleep" (289). In this way the ventriloquist concept may dovetail with the psychic concept: when Heathcliff abandons Cathy's corpse to pursue her ghost, the ghost conveniently leads him to his own home—to his own domain, to his own territory and preoccupations.

The process of adaptation under the ventriloquist concept resembles Roland Barthes's theory of metalanguage, in which what passes between two signifying systems is figured as an empty form, subsequently filled with the content of the second system. According to Barthes, in metalanguage, "that which is a sign (namely the associative total of a concept and an image) in the first system, becomes a mere signifier in the second . . . When [the passing sign] becomes [pure] form, the meaning leaves its contingency behind; it empties itself, it becomes impoverished, history evaporates, only the letter remains" (114, 117). The ventriloquist concept can be diagrammed as two mathematical equations, adopting Barthes's typography for distinguishing the two systems (the top equation represents the first system, the novel, and the lower represents the second, the film adaptation):

The Novel's Signs – The Novel's Signifieds = The Novel's Signifiers
THE NOVEL'S SIGNIFIERS + THE FILM'S SIGNIFIEDS = THE ADAPTATION'S
SIGNS

These equations distinguish *film* from *adaptation:* the adaptation here is a composite of novel and film, rather than pure film.

This concept leads to readings that run contrary to most commentaries on adaptation, which lay the blame for an adaptation's semiotic impoverishment at the feet of film, focusing on those places where the novel's significations have been emptied out. Such criticism rarely attends to the significations that the film has added. While film adaptations typically do cut and condense the novel, they also add the semiotic richness of moving images, music, props, architecture, costumes, audible dialogue, and much more. All of these signs are laden with cultural and symbolic resonances. As in Barthes's account of metalanguage: "The meaning [of the second system] will be for the form [of the first] like an instantaneous reserve of history, a tamed richness" (118).

Equally, where films empty out content (in this model typically ideology, or "themes") from a novel, they replace it with new content. Critics complain, for example, that MGM's *Wuthering Heights* reduces Brontë's complex characterological passions to mawkish romantic movie sentiments. MGM unarguably omits most of the novel's more violent and transgressive words and actions, but it replaces them with a mercenary economic dynamic that preys on romantic desire—a scheme that resembles Heathcliff's preying on romantic illusions (Isabella's and the younger Cathy's) for financial gain. In MGM's *Wuthering Heights* the central love story becomes a metaphor for cinematic consumption, channeling viewers' vicarious erotic desire into a desire for cinematic fiction. Cathy's vacillation between Linton's pragmatic economic world and the dream world of romance with Heathcliff becomes a prescriptive template for the viewer's alternation between earning in the labor force and spending at the motion picture palace. Cathy (Merle Oberon) and Heathcliff (Laurence Olivier) run back and forth from the "real" world to their dream palace at Penistone Crag, where they play at princess and prince. In the same way film audiences are to earn in the workaday world then retreat to spend their earnings at the motion picture palaces, where they play vicariously at motion picture palace princess and prince, caught in an endless cycle of spending to dream and dreaming of spending. The happy ending of MGM's *Wuthering Heights* depicts the lovers' final and eternal return to Penistone Crag, forever filmic in a ghostly half-exposure. This is not the happily ever after of marriage but, rather, of eternal cinematic residence.

The Westinghouse live television dramatization of *Wuthering Heights* similarly aligns erotic, narrative, and material desire with Cathy's vacillation between Heathcliff and Edgar to urge consumption but of a different type of produce by a different audience in a different cultural context. Made in 1950s America, where movie palaces languished and consumer goods flourished, the Westinghouse adaptation of *Wuthering Heights* recasts the relationship between spending and entertainment, aligning the erotics of viewing and consuming fictional romance with the marketing of house-hold products: in some cases the very medium through which the fiction is consumed—the television set. The commercials interrupting the live dramatization to market Westinghouse products are themselves live performances by an actress who resembles the drama's heroine. The commercials are figured as consultations of a theater program ("And now, let's look at our Westinghouse program"), further eliding the television "program" with the marketing "program" through the dramatic analogy.

Wuthering Heights is adapted by Westinghouse to foster a tension between desire for what one does not have (Heathcliff, romantic fiction, Westinghouse goods) and the means of attaining it (Edgar, the 1950s husband and his income). Early in the film Cathy (Mary Sinclair) rejects the idea of marriage to Heathcliff (Charlton Heston) in original dialogue appearing nowhere in the novel: "It is not the bond to keep us together." In the novel the only obstacle to union with Heathcliff lies for her in his social degradation and poverty (80–82). This line suggests that marriage destroys romantic love. If marriage could satisfy all desire for romance, housewives would require no romantic fiction, and there would be one fewer vehicle through which to sell Westinghouse appliances. Therefore, in this adaptation Cathy enjoys extramarital romance with Heathcliff at Penistone Crag, but she returns to the duties of marriage and domesticity, to the family home, the space in which domestic appliances are consumed. The drama maintains a constant tension in which Cathy hovers on the brink of adultery but never commits it. Whereas the Cathy of 1939 flatly rejects adultery or any amatory foreplay, this Cathy ardently embraces Heathcliff at Penistone Crag. Ultimately, however, she resists the temptation of full-blown adultery, declaring: "Life is not lived on a point of rock. That green and pleasant valley is my home . . . I do love you, but I fear you as well.

If you were to have me, you'd crush me like a sparrow's egg." Heathcliff responds violently, cutting his wrist, demanding Cathy do the same in order to mingle blood with him, a clear metaphorical invitation to adultery. Frightened, Cathy runs back to the legitimate embrace of Edgar (Richard Waring). Quite strikingly, the dialogue of this scene derives from a passage in the novel concerning Isabella and Heathcliff, not Cathy and Heathcliff.[4] Westinghouse's Cathy elides with Brontë's Isabella, running from a mad and violent lover back to the safety of Thrushcross Grange. Additionally, this subliminally legitimates Cathy's liaison with Heathcliff by equating her with Heathcliff's lawful wife. In so doing, the adaptation transposes the literary Isabella's flight from her marriage to the television Cathy's flight back to hers. Thus, the adaptation arouses adulterous desire but ultimately sends wives back to their husbands, whose income is required for purchasing Westinghouse products.[5]

The commercials are themselves narratives: narratives of appliances that create desire, solve problems, and persuade consumption through echoing narrative threads in the adaptation. Westinghouse spokeswoman Daphne informs viewers that they can trade in their old refrigerator as credit toward a new Westinghouse model. The motif of trading old for new ties to the novel's temptation of trading in old love for new. In the novel Mr. Earnshaw's new love for Heathcliff displaces his old love for Hindley; Cathy abandons Heathcliff for Edgar then shifts her loyalties back to Heathcliff again; her daughter transfers her allegiance from Linton to Hareton. For Westinghouse, however, there is no dilemma: the old model can apply toward the purchase of the new so that the two become one, resolving the tension. That old husband is essential to financing new desires.

Westinghouse appliances are, therefore, heavily eroticized in the commercials. In touting the refrigerator, Daphne allures buyers with erotic talk of the appliance's "famous magic button," which does the work of defrosting at the same time that it keeps the freezer's contents desirably "firm" and the housewife labor free: "You never have to touch that button." A second commercial shows Daphne pulling a decidedly phallic component from a Westinghouse television set (so phallic that my students erupt in laughter without a word of commentary from me) to prove the technological prowess and dependability of the set. In these commercials size matters: Daphne urges viewers to purchase a larger screen in order to have a better view of Westinghouse television theater: "Have you a second balcony set?" she asks. "Why don't you get yourself a real front row set?" In this sales pitch viewers are aroused by the erotic elements of the fiction to desire a better means of watching that fiction.[6]

The Genetic Concept of Adaptation

If Cathy's corpse is inanimate and her spirit elusive, she finds a less ghoulish and intangible afterlife in her brother Hindley's genetic resemblance to her—one that evokes and recalls her ("Now that she's dead, I see her in Hindley" [180]). She finds a similar genetic afterlife in her resemblance to her daughter, Cathy ("a second edition of the mother" [154]), and to her nephew, Hareton ("his startling likeness to Catherine connected him fearfully with her" [324]).

The genetic concept of adaptation, though it has not hitherto been so named, is well established in narratological approaches to adaptation. Narratologists figure what "transfers" between literature and film as an underlying "deep" narrative structure akin to genetic structure, awaiting what Seymour Chatman has called a "manifesting substance" in much the same way that genetic material awaits manifesting substance in the cells and tissues of the body. The most recent book-length narratological study of literary film adaptation by Brian McFarlane defines *narrative* as "a series of events, causally linked, involving a continuing set of characters which influence and are influenced by the course of events." The "cardinal functions" of narrative constitute its deep structure, and these elements, according to McFarlane, can transfer directly from novel to film, although their specific manifestations require what he calls "adaptation proper"— the discovery of filmic signs equivalent to those of the novel. "Novel and film can share the same story, the same 'raw materials,'" McFarlane argues, "but are distinguished by means of different plot strategies," such as sequencing. The narratological approach thus attempts to circumvent the problem of form's separation from content. Yet, despite official adherence to form/content doctrine at the level of signs, the central terminologies of narratological theory nevertheless articulate a form and content divide at higher categorical levels, whether Seymour Chatman's *histoire* and *discours* or McFarlane's application of Benveniste's *l'énoncé* (statement) and *l'énonciation* (utterance) or David Bordwell's invocation of the Russian formalist terms *syuzhet* and *fabula*. In each case the first term represents a notion of content (what is told) and the second a concept of form (how it is told). The solution of the adaptation problem in light of form and content dogma is thus less a conceptual one than a categorical shift that allows the separation of form and content to take place in the larger category of narrative while averting heretical splits at the level of signs.

McFarlane rightly observes that even when signs transfer intact from novel to film (such as lines of dialogue from novel to actor performance), they are " 'deformed' by the catalysers that surround them," like embodied, costumed, photographed, audible actors (12, 23, 14). At times, however, changes at the level of manifesting signs go farther to deconstruct the deep narrative structure beneath. Paradoxically both for my own analogy for this concept of adaptation and for narratological theories of adaptation, genetic resemblances among characters in *Wuthering Heights* serve to dismantle aspects of narratological deep structure in adaptation to film. The novel's idea that Cathy and Heathcliff share a soul is most famously articulated in Cathy's ejaculation, "I am Heathcliff!" (82). It constitutes a cardinal thematic and ideological point, one that has been included in every film adaptation of the novel. Although the assertion emerges as a radical statement in any representational form, its expression in the manifesting structure of written words standing alone in an unillustrated novel is less systemically problematic and incongruous than its expression from the lips of an embodied actor in a sound film. The prose "I am Heathcliff!" engages in no grammatical travesties: the phrase conjugates the conjugal souls correctly; pronoun and proper name agree. *I* represents a pronoun in which many names and social identities can and do conjoin as it represents many users. No other semiotic form appears to contradict the words: there is no illustration of Heathcliff with Cathy manifesting. The novel may strip the bodies and their associated sociological identities for a fragment of grammatical space and time, but the films do not. The lightning, thunder, and violins accompanying the speech in the MGM and Westinghouse versions do not achieve such a dislocation, despite their invocation of the mythological. Uttered by an actress, the *I* emerges from a mouth in a female face and fails to equate with or encompass the male face and body representing Heathcliff. In the purely textual expression yoked pronoun and noun are separated by only the tiniest of bridges, the *am* that presses their identity even as it separates the referents. But in the narrative Heathcliff has already left Wuthering Heights when Cathy declares their synonymy, so that the visual representation of this speech belies their representational proximity. Under conventional Western models of proof—the word made flesh or the hypothesis proved by empirical evidence—the visualization of these adaptations appears as empirical evidence refuting Cathy's verbal hypothesis.

Because filmic attempts at visual synonymy between Heathcliff and Cathy prove either unconvincing or bizarre, a number of adaptations emphasize Cathy's biological resemblance to her relatives instead. Luis Buñuel's *Abismos de Pasion* extends physical resemblances to narrative resemblances in ways that deconstruct the deep narrative of the novel. In the final scenes of the film Catalina's (Cathy's) resemblance to her brother, Roberto (Hindley), is emphasized over any resemblance to Alejandro (Heathcliff), not only in terms of biological genetic structure but also of narrative structure. At Wuthering Heights, Roberto (Luis Aceves Castañeda) catches a fly and tosses it into a spider's web, smiling sadistically as the spider springs to the center of the web to feed on its trapped, live prey. José (Joseph, played by Francisco Reiguera) reads a nihilistic passage about the final terminus of death, the oblivion of the afterlife, the degradation of devils, and the shortness and tediousness of life. We hear that Alejandro (Jorge Mistral) has gone to Catalina's (Irasema Dilian's) grave. Roberto loads a rifle and goes out. The camera cuts to Alejandro as he approaches the cemetery in the darkness, accompanied by the impassioned strains of Richard Wagner's *Tristan and Isolde*. Finding the vault locked, he struggles unsuccessfully with the chain then penetrates the padlock with a pointed metal pole. As he throws back the vault's heavy double doors, the camera cuts to an unidentified arm pointing a rifle. A shot rings out. Alejandro clutches his heart. The gun lowers, and Alejandro enters the vault. The film cuts to the vault's interior, where Alejandro staggers down the steps toward Catalina's coffin. He throws off the lid, which falls with a loud clang. Catalina lies dressed in bridal white, an opaque veil covering her head and upper torso. Alejandro kneels and takes her hand, but, when he tries to pull it toward him, rigor mortis forbids. Dropping the unyielding arm, he turns his attention to her face, slowly lifting her veil and kissing her frozen lips. Catalina's echoing voice calls Alejandro's name from somewhere offscreen. Alejandro turns from the corpse toward the camera and the voice. A cut reveals Catalina standing on the vault steps, clad in her bridal-burial gown, smiling, one arm outstretched, beckoning to Alejandro. Suddenly—so suddenly that the viewer jumps—Catalina's shimmering image is replaced by the black-clad Roberto's, pointing a rifle from his similarly outstretched arm. In the superlative horror of Alejandro's necrophilia, the viewer has forgotten the mysterious gunman. A shot rings out, Alejandro falls forward across Catalina's corpse, Roberto slams the door to the vault, and the word *Fin* appears on the screen, enlarging as it moves toward the viewer.

As Catalina's image gives way to Roberto's, the novel-Catherine's "I *am* Heathcliff!" becomes the film-Catalina's "I *am* Roberto!" The manifesting substances of the film here alter the deep structure that identifies Cathy with Heathcliff in the novel, replacing it with an identification between Catalina and Roberto. From the beginning Buñuel has prepared us for this final identification of Catalina with Roberto, an identification based on narrative actions as well as on visual resemblances and positionings.

Roberto closes the film with a rifle shot, sending Alejandro to the death for which he longs; Catalina opens the film with a rifle shot, killing a buzzard to send it to "the liberty of death." In the final sequence, as Alejandro claws, buzzardlike, at Catalina's corpse, she is visually complicit with Roberto's gunshot, standing in the same pose and spot as her brother, calling him to the death that Roberto brings. Her corpse as well as her ghost colludes with Roberto's deed. Her body, with its gauze veil, resembles the spider in its gauzy web, which minutes before Roberto has fed with a live fly. As Roberto threw the live fly into the spider's web, so too, with his gunshot, he throws Alejandro onto Catalina's gauzy web. Her body thus becomes the bridal lure for the fatal trap, her ghost merging with Roberto's body to throw Alejandro onto hers.

McFarlane readily acknowledges "the inevitable degree of subjectivity" in even the most basic task of the narratologist: that of selecting what are a narrative's major cardinal functions (115). It is not so much the impossibility of removing subjectivity, however, that emerges troublingly from McFarlane's recommendations: it is the implication that this removal will provide a clearer understanding of adaptation. The next model, based in reader response theory, highlights and celebrates just such reader subjectivity in adaptation.

The De(re)composing Concept of Adaptation

The *Wuthering Heights* epitome of the de(re)composing concept of adaptation lies in Heathcliff's vision of his corpse buried next to Cathy's, decomposing and merging underground. There is no need here for a hovering spirit or a thrown voice to infuse life into the adaptation, for dead matter becomes organic life underground. Under the de(re)composing concept of adaptation, novel and film become a decomposed composite at "underground" levels of reading, often leading to confusion about which is novel and which is film. "By the time Linton gets to us," Heathcliff exults, "he'll not know which is which!" (288). The adaptation is a (de)composite of textual and filmic signs merging in audience consciousness together with other cultural narratives.

Keith Cohen insists that an "adaptation must subvert its original, perform a double and paradoxical job of masking and unveiling its source . . . redistribute the formative materials of the original and . . . set them askew" (255). This deconstructive recommendation suggests one type of decompositional merger: a deconstructive one. Umberto Eco suggests another in his discussion of cult objects: "In order to transform a work into a cult object one must be able to break, dislocate, unhinge it so that one can remember only parts of it, irrespective of their original relationship with the whole" (447). Adaptations of canonical novels frequently truncate high culture into "cult" object by detaching parts of the novel and representing them as the whole in defiance of the novel's whole. A filmmaker-reader's response to one part of the novel may distort or override the adaptation of the whole. For instance, a reader's affection for or identification with a particular character may cause her or him to retain only certain aspects of that character in adaptation. J. Hillis Miller has written: "each [critic of *Wuthering Heights*] takes some one element in the novel and extrapolates it toward a total explanation" (50). Readers who make film adaptations have done likewise: a subtext may become the main text of a reading at the expense of the whole.

Consequently, many so-called unfaithful adaptations are operating under a de(re)composing concept of adaptation. They are deemed unfaithful because critics read only one way, from novel to film, and find that the film has made changes. But, if one reads in both directions—from novel to film and from film back to novel—one often finds that many supposed infidelities appear clearly in the text. Some apparently total departures from the novel by an adaptation serve to fulfill the disappointed hopes and desires of its characters. A 1966 Bombay adaptation, *Dil Diya Dard Liya* (Give Your Heart and Receive Anguish), allows Heathcliff (Shankar) to return in time to prevent Cathy's (Roopa's) marriage to Edgar (Mala). Even Buñuel's apparently original ending, celebrated for its surrealistic shock value and clever betrayal of the canonical reader, realizes a wish expressed by Heathcliff in the novel. As Brontë's Heathcliff stands with the unconscious Cathy in his arms, ready to confront Edgar, he exclaims, "If he shot me so, I'd die with a blessing on my lips" (162). Buñuel's ending spares Heathcliff eighteen years of suffering, uniting him body and soul with Cathy immediately after her death. It fulfills other character wishes as well: it allows Hindley's attempt to shoot Heathcliff, frustrated in the novel, to succeed and realizes Isabella's unheeded invective to Heathcliff, "if I were you, I'd go stretch myself over her grave, and die like a faithful dog" (176). In this way fragments of character desire overtake and displace narrator and authorial authority in reader identification.

The Incarnational Concept of Adaptation

The incarnational concept of adaptation is, like the psychic concept, a familiar if not a didactically identified one in the rhetoric of adaptation.

Predicated on the Christian theology of the word made flesh, wherein the word is only a partial expression of a more total representation that requires incarnation for its fulfillment, it makes adaptation a process of incarnation from more abstract to less abstract signs. The words, which merely hint at sight, sound, touch, taste, and smell, tantalize readers into longing for their incarnation in signs offering more direct access to these phenomenological experiences. Anthony Burgess notes: "Every best-selling novel has to be turned into a film, the assumption being that the book itself whets an appetite for the true fulfillment—the verbal shadow turned into light, the word made flesh" (15).[7]

A rhetoric of incarnation, materialization, and realization permeates adaptation criticism throughout the twentieth century. The producers of the 1922 *Vanity Fair* adduced that "those who are intimate with the books . . . will be gratified to see the characters so reverently brought to life" ("Vanity Fair" 59). Sergei Eisenstein wrote in the 1940s: "For litera-ture—cinema is an expansion of the strict diction achieved by poetry and prose into a new realm where the desired image is directly materialized in audio-visual perceptions" (182). Lester D. Friedman concluded his 1981 essay on James Whale's adaptation of Mary Shelley's novel, *Frankenstein:* "As this analysis of the film demonstrates, Whale viewed the Frankenstein story much in the same way as did Mary Shelley . . . if Mary Shelley wrote the word, James Whale made it flesh" (66).

The incarnational concept differs from the psychic concept in that it posits the novel not as a transcendental signified to which the film must attach appropriate signifiers but, rather, as a transcendental signif*ier.* The incarnational concept of adaptation represents the novel's signs as tran-scendental signifiers, wandering ghosts located neither in the heaven of the transcendental signified of the psychic model nor in the dead corpse of the empty signifier of the ventriloquist model. In the context of adaptation the transcendental signifier seeks not a signified but another signifier that can incarnate it. This model heightens the abstraction of the more abstract form and emphasizes the concreteness of the less abstract one, effecting a concomitant perceptual dematerialization of the novel's signs as the film's signs incarnate them. MGM's *Wuthering Heights* opens with a shot over-cast with thick white letters obscuring Lockwood's shadowy figure as he struggles through a storm: "On the barren Yorkshire moors in England, a hundred years ago, stood a house as bleak and desolate as the wastes around it. Only a stranger lost in a storm would have dared to knock at the door of Wuthering Heights." The thick white letters block the viewers' view, making them impatient for the removal of the words, eager to see the film without textual obstruction. As the letters dissolve, the incarnation occurs, the word *stranger* giving way to a shot of a stranger, the words *Wuthering Heights* dissolving into the film set of Wuthering Heights.

As psychic and ventriloquist concepts of adaptation represent two sides of the same coin, so, too, do genetic and incarnational concepts. The embodied ghost is also more fearsome than the intangible ghost of the psychic concept. Under the psychic concept readers eagerly seek the authorial spirit. Under the incarnational concept, however, they fear and resist it. Many readers long for a novel's characters and scenes to be made visible, audible, and tangible in adaptation. As film historian Jim Hitt attests: "we long to see the physical reality of a cherished novel or short story, to see the ethereal become solid, touchable" (2). Others, like Charles Lamb, recoil in horror from such manifestations. Reacting to theatrical adaptations of literature early in the nineteenth century, Lamb exclaims: "Never let me be so ungrateful as to forget the very high degree of satisfaction which I received some years back from seeing for the first time a tragedy of Shakespeare performed . . . It seemed to embody and realize conceptions which had hitherto assumed no distinct shape." Yet he notes a greater loss than gain in the incarnation:

> But dearly do we pay all our life afterwards for this juvenile pleasure, this sense of distinctness. When the novelty is past, we find to our cost that, instead of realising an idea, we have only materialised and brought down a fine vision to the standard of flesh and blood. We have let go a dream, in quest of an unattainable substance.
>
> How cruelly this operates upon the mind, to have its free conceptions thus cramped and pressed down to the measure of a strait-lacing actuality . . . characters in Shakespeare which are within the precincts of nature, have yet something in them which appeals too exclusively to the imagination, to admit of their being made objects to the senses without suffering a change and a diminution. ("Tragedies" 166–67, 189)

The word made flesh is also the word brought down to the level of flesh. As such, adaptation often appears as sacrilege against the word. Christian texts narrate that for centuries the Jewish people longed for the incarnation of their Messiah, for their God to be made flesh. But, when he was thus incarnated, they recoiled, condemning and crucifying him. Condemning paintings of Shakespeare's plays, Lamb writes: "I am jealous of the combination of the sister arts. Let them sparkle apart. What injury (short of the theaters) did not Boydell's Shakespeare do me with Shakespeare? . . . instead of my, and everybody's Shakespeare [t]o be tied down to an authentic face of Juliet! To have Imogen's portrait! To confine the illimitable! . . .'out upon this half-faced fellowship'" (*Letters* 394). From the full-faced "authentic" Juliet of the paintings, to the "half-faced" association of theater and painting in adaptation, something has been effaced for Lamb. That something is the loss of language's lack, a lack that promised illimitability and universality, which the specificities of incarnation have exposed as illusive and empty.

Protests that incarnation reduces language mask the real threat that incarnation and visualization present to the word. Incarnation reveals the limitations of language. Incarnational adaptation may appear too real because it exposes language as less real. As Lamb attests, "Contrary to the old saying, that 'seeing is believing,' the sight actually destroys the faith." Incarnation disrupts the partly revealing, partly concealing limbo of language—what Lamb has called "all that beautiful compromise which we make in reading," which "the actual sight of the thing [outweighs]" ("Tragedies" 188, 190). Lamb does not pursue the possibility that the lost faith in language was a misplaced one to begin with. Incarnation's exposure of the lack and emptiness of language gains support in that Lamb and others find it impossible to return to the illusions of the word after seeing an incarnation of it. Lamb records: "I confess myself utterly unable to appreciate that celebrated soliloquy in 'Hamlet,' beginning, 'to be or not to be,' or to tell whether it be good, bad, or indifferent, it has been so handled and pawed about by declamatory boys and men" (167–68). Once one sees that the emperor has no clothes, one cannot reconstruct the clothing.

Rather than pursue the disruptions and critique that the incarnational concept presents to language, however, most critics prefer to castigate realization as carnalization, a sordid, morally reprehensible corruption of spiritual and transcendental signification and of a romanticized "divine" imagination.

The Trumping Concept of Adaptation

The trumping concept of adaptation is concerned with which medium represents better. Although it can take either side, since the majority of adaptation criticism favors the novel over the film, my discussion emphasizes instances in which the film claims to trump the novel in adaptation. Instead of asking, "What's wrong with the adaptation?" as so much of adaptation criticism does, this side of the trumping concept asks, "What's wrong with the original?" Like Cathy's scrawled marginalia in printed texts, deemed by Lockwood "not altogether legitimate" (18), the trumping concept tests the novel's representations against other texts deemed more authoritative—against written and artifactual history, psychoanalytic theories, and contemporary politics—and finds them not altogether legitimate.

Under the trumping concept of adaptation the novel's signs lose representational authority in the name of a signified that the novel "meant to" or "tried to" or "should have" represented when the adapting film is perceived to have represented it better. The trumping concept of adaptation splits the novel's form from its content to assert that the one has betrayed the other: that the novel's signifiers have been false to and have betrayed their own signifieds.

An especially common form of filmic trumping grows out of the incarnational concept. As the adaptation seeks to realize material culture represented only in words by the novel, its historical research often finds fault with the novel's representations and "corrects" them. An interview with Hugo Ballin, director of a now lost 1923 film of *Vanity Fair,* illustrates the process. The title of the interview, "Hugo Ballin Edits 'Vanity Fair,' Cutting the Anachronisms," refers not to the film's editing of its own footage but to its editing of the novel: to its re-edition of the novel's visual representations as well as to its correction of verbal descriptions of material culture. Ballin explains: "the costumes in the picture are more correct than those described in the book . . . [Thackeray] had whiskers on his soldiers [when] there was at that time a rule in the British army against any growth of hair on the face . . . The novelist also describes men smoking cigars in the presence of ladies. This was decidedly 'not done' at the time of the Battle of Waterloo . . . He speaks of the use of envelopes for letters; the historical fact is that envelopes were not used until 1839 . . . in the picture we strove to get all these details as nearly right as humanly possible, as a matter of course" ("Hugo Ballin" 6:3). These representations are "unfaithful" to Thackeray's drawings in the name of a higher fidelity to history. In the process they correct, rather than incarnate, the novel's signs. Ballin represents such changes "as a matter of course," much as textual editors might correct an author's spelling and punctuation. He assumes that both novel and film signs point to an authoritative outer signified—in this case, material history—which the film must above all represent correctly and faithfully, even if it means being unfaithful to the novel. Hyperfidelity to the text's context here mandates infidelity to the text itself.

The line between correcting a novel's material historical inaccuracies and its ideological ones has proven a fine one. Peter Bogdanovich's *Daisy Miller* (1974) includes a scene of mixed nude bathing. Defending criticisms of this scene, he asserts: "The mixed bathing is authentically of the period." McFarlane astutely counters: "Authentically of the period, perhaps, but not so of Henry James" (9). Implicit in this historical embellishment is a criticism of James's heterosexual reticence, one that participates in post-1960s perceptions of Victorian sexual repression more than of historical material culture. Twentieth-century adaptations of Victorian novels have been obsessed with correcting Victorian psychology, particularly Victorian sexuality. In 1974 Bogdanovich expressed a wider cultural consensus regarding Victorian novels and novelists in general when he quipped, "What James meant to say with the story [*Daisy Miller*] doesn't really concern me . . . I think all that stuff is based on some other kind of repression anyway" (qtd. in Hitt 50). Bogdanovich represents his film as an outing of Victorian repression, as saying what James "really" felt and thought underneath his overt representation. Thus, the adaptation is presented as doing the work of psychoanalysis for the novel. Similarly, Patricia Rozema's *Mansfield Park* (1999) contains a superadded feminist postcolonial critique of slavery that adapts late-twentieth-century literary criticism of the novel more than it does the novel itself. In these ways insertions or amplifications of contextual historical "facts" run into ahistorical corrections of authorial values and viewpoints.

Film adapters build on a hyper-correct historical material realism to usher in a host of anachronistic ideological "corrections" of the novel. Even as these adaptations pursue a hyperfidelity to nineteenth-century material history, they ardently and inconsistently reject Victorian psychology, ethics, and politics. When filmmakers set modern politically correct views against historically correct backdrops, the effect is to authorize modern ideologies as historically authentic.

Conclusion

Clearly, to dismiss the idea that something passes between novel and film in adaptation as theoretically incorrect, as a naive popular illusion harking back to outmoded semiotic theories and as, therefore, unworthy of serious scholarly attention, is to miss a great deal about the perceived interaction between literature and film in adaptation. Indeed, it is in the heresies committed by the practice and criticism of adaptation that we learn most about literature and film in relation to each other. And it may be that in time the heresies of adaptation and of adaptation criticism may challenge dominant theories to such an extent that the theories themselves will come under renewed scrutiny.

Notes

1. "As it is impossible to extract from a physical body the qualities which really constitute it—colour, extension, and the like—without reducing it to a hollow abstraction, in a word, without destroying it; just so it is impossible to detach the form from the idea, for the idea only exists by virtue of the form" (Pater 28). "Language can be compared with a sheet of paper: thought is the front and the sound the back; one cannot cut the front without cutting the back at the same time; likewise in language, one can neither divide sound from thought nor thought from sound" (de Saussure 649).

2. For example, Georg Wilhelm Friedrich Hegel uses the body/soul analogy throughout his discussion of form and content in *The Philosophy of Fine Art,* and Jacques Derrida's rejection of the original signified is predicated on a rejection of the Christian theology of incarnation.

3. See also Beja, Bluestone, and Wagner, to cite only a few of many more such examples.

4. In the novel Cathy tells the love-struck Isabella, "He'd crush you like a sparrow's egg, Isabella, if he found you a troublesome charge. I know he couldn't love a Linton, and yet he'd be quite capable of marrying your fortunes and expectations" (102).

5. The excision of outdoor scenes is partly a result of the theatrical format, but it also serves to prioritize domestic spaces.

6. Since the video has excised the commercials from the *Wuthering Heights* Westinghouse production and John Maslansky, Video Yesteryear director of licensing and sales, affirms that the CBS stock footage has also removed the commercials, these examples are taken from the Westinghouse adaptation of *Jane Eyre* (aired August 4, 1952), which targeted a similar audience. The intertextuality of *Jane Eyre* and *Wuthering Heights* (trading in old love for new is a central theme in both) and their shared twentieth-century cultural currency, advanced most notably by Patsy Stoneman, seemed to justify the liberty. Moreover, my extensive research into Westinghouse adaptations reveals that every commercial plays either on resemblances between spokesmodels and leading actresses or on affinities between the text's plot and the sales pitch, so that my broader arguments hold firmly here.

7. I am indebted to McFarlane for this reference.

References

Books and Articles

Adaptations: Novel to Film (online). Urbancinefile, April 2000. Available from World Wide Web at <*http://www.urbancinefile.com.au/home/view.asp?Article_ID=3463*>. "Hugo Ballin Edits 'Vanity Fair,' Cutting the Anachronisms." *New York Tribune,* May 6, 1923, 6:3.

"Vanity Fair." *Bioscope,* January 26, 1922, 59.

Andrew, Dudley. "The Well-Worn Muse: Adaptation in Film History and Theory." *Narrative Strategies: Original Essays in Film and Prose Fiction.* Ed. Syndy M. Conger and Janice R. Welsch. Macomb: Western Illinois University Press, 1980.

Babbitt, Irving. *The New Laocoön: An Essay on the Confusion of the Arts.* Boston: Houghton Mifflin, 1910.

Balázs, Béla. *Theory of Film: Character and Growth of a New Art.* Trans. Edith Bone. 1952. Reprint. New York: Dover, 1970.

Barthes, Roland. *Mythologies.* Trans. Annette Lavers. New York: Hill and Wang, 1984.

Battestin, Martin C. "*Tom Jones* on the Telly: Fielding, the BBC, and the Sister Arts." *Eighteenth-Century Fiction* 10.4 (July 1998): 501–5.

Beja, Morris. *Film and Literature.* New York: Longman, 1976.

Bloom, Harold. *Mary Shelley's Frankenstein.* New York: Chelsea House Publishers, 1987.

Bluestone, George. *Novels into Film.* Berkeley: University of California Press, 1957.

Bordwell, David. *Narration in the Fiction Film.* Madison: University of Wisconsin Press, 1985.

Brady, Ben. *Principles of Adaptation for Film and Television.* Austin: University of Texas Press, 1994.

Brontë, Emily. *Wuthering Heights.* Oxford: Oxford University Press, World's Classics, 1995.

Burgess, Anthony. "On the Hopelessness of Turning Good Books into Films." *New York Times,* April 20, 1975, S2:1.

Cartmell, Deborah, I. Q. Hunter, Heidi Kaye, and Imelda Whelehan, eds. *Pulping Fictions: Consuming Culture across the Literature/Media Divide.* London: Pluto Press, 1996.

Cartmell, Deborah, and Imelda Whelehan, eds. *Adaptation: From Text to Screen, Screen to Text.* New York: Routledge, 1999.

Chatman, Seymour. *Story and Discourse: Narrative Structure in Fiction and Film.* Ithaca: Cornell University Press, 1978.

Cohen, Keith. "Eisenstein's Subversive Adaptation." *The Classic American Novel and the Movies.* Ed. G. Peary and R. Shatzkin. New York: Ungar, 1977. 245–55.

De Saussure, Ferdinand. "The Nature of the Linguistic Sign." *Critical Theory since 1965.* Ed. Hazard Adams and Leroy Searle. Tallahassee: Florida State University Press, 1986. 546–657.

Eco, Umberto. "Casablanca: Cult Movies and Intertextual Collage." *Modern Criticism and Theory: A Reader.* Ed. David Lodge. New York: Longman, 1988.

Eisenstein, Sergei. *Film Form: Essays in Film Theory.* Trans. Jay Leyda. New York: Harcourt, Brace and World, 1949.

Friedman, Lester D. "The Blasted Tree." *The English Novel and the Movies.* Ed. Michael Klein and Gillian Parker. New York: Ungar, 1981. 52–66.

Harold Bloom. *Mary Shelley's Frankenstein.* New York: Chelsea House, 1987.

Hegel, Georg Wilhelm Friedrich. *The Philosophy of Fine Art: Critical Theory since Plato.* Ed. Hazard Adams. New York: Harcourt Brace Jovanovich, 1971. 518–31.

Hitt, Jim. *Words and Shadows: Literature on the Screen.* New York: Citadel, 1992.

Hodge, John. *Trainspotting and the Shallow Grave.* London: Faber and Faber, 1996.

Keyser, Lester J. "A Scrooge for All Seasons." *The English Novel and the Movies.* Ed. Michael Klein and Gillian Parker. New York: Ungar, 1981.

Koltnow, Barry. "Kenneth Branagh Picks Up the Pieces in Mary Shelley's Monster Classic." *Buffalo News,* November 5, 1994, 10.

Lamb, Charles. "On the Tragedies of Shakespeare. Considered with Reference to the Fitness for Stage Representation." *The Collected Essays of Charles Lamb.* Intro. Robert Lynd; notes by William MacDonald. New York: Dutton, 1929. 163–96.

———. Letter to Samuel Rogers, n.d. (December 1833?) *The Letters of Charles Lamb.* Ed. E. V. Lucas. New York: Dutton, 1945. 394.

McFarlane, Brian. *Novel to Film: An Introduction to the Theory of Adaptation.* Oxford: Clarendon Press, 1996.

Miller, J. Hillis. "*Wuthering Heights:* Repetition and the Uncanny." *Fiction and Repetition: Seven English Novels.* Cambridge: Harvard University Press, 1982. 42–72.

Naremore, James. *Film Adaptation.* New Brunswick NJ: Rutgers University Press, 2000.

Orr, Christopher. "The Discourse on Adaptation." *Wide Angle* 6.2 (1984): 72–76.

Pater, Walter. "Style." *Appreciations.* London: Macmillan, 1890. 1–36.

Reynolds, Peter, ed. *Novel Images: Literature in Performance.* New York: Routledge, 1993.

Seger, Linda. *The Art of Adaptation: Turning Fact and Fiction into Film.* New York: Henry Holt, 1992.

Stam, Robert. "Beyond Fidelity: The Dialogics of Adaptation." *Film Adaptation.* Ed. James Naremore. New Brunswick NJ: Rutgers University Press, 2000.

Thompson, Howard. *The New York Guide to Movies on Television.* Chicago: Quadrangle Press, 1970.

Thompson, John O. "Film Adaptation and the Mystery of the Original." *Pulping Fictions: Consuming Culture across the Literature/Media Divide.* Ed. Deborah Cartmell, I. Q. Hunter, Heidi Kaye, and Imelda Whelehan. London: Pluto Press, 1996.

Wagner, Geoffrey. *The Novel and the Cinema.* Rutherford NJ: Farleigh Dickinson University Press, 1975.

Films and Television Productions

Dil Diya Dard Liya. Dir. A. R. Kardar. Kary Productions, Bombay, 1966.

Abismos de Pasion. Dir. Luis Buñuel. Plexus Films, Mexico, 1953.

Emily Brontë's Wuthering Heights. Dir. Peter Kosminsky. Paramount, Hollywood, 1992.

Bram Stoker's Dracula. Dir. Francis Ford Coppola. Columbia, Culver City, 1992.

Mary Shelley's Frankenstein. Dir. Kenneth Branagh. Columbia, Culver City, 1994.

Emily Brontë's Wuthering Heights. Dir. David Skynner. LWT and WGBH/Boston, 1998.

William Shakespeare's Hamlet. Dir. Kenneth Branagh. Columbia, Culver City, 1996.

William Shakespeare's Romeo + Juliet. Dir. Baz Luhrmann. Fox, Los Angeles, 1996.

William Shakespeare's A Midsummer Night's Dream. Dir. Michael Hoffmann. Fox, Los Angeles, 1999.

Wuthering Heights. Dir. William Wyler. MGM, Los Angeles, 1939.

Wuthering Heights. Dir. Paul Nickell. Westinghouse Television Theater, CBS, New York, 1950.

8

Ordinary Horror on Reality TV

Cynthia Freeland

In this essay I will consider reality-based television shows featuring what I call "ordinary horror."[1] My focus is primarily on programs that appeared or had series runs in the 1990s and thus were precursors to today's game-contestant reality shows such as "Survivor." I have in mind programs such as "Cops," "Rescue 911," "When Animals Attack," and "America's Most Wanted" that present crimes, accidents, natural disasters, and other scenes of everyday horror as entertainment.[2] I will explore how reality TV shows employ various narrative strategies to produce certain effects—both moral and aesthetic. Many of these shows both presume and cultivate the audience's interest in spectacles of violence. They seem to promote conservative aims by sustaining racist fears about criminals, desires for more police intervention, faith in medical expertise, and the worship of (typically male) authority figures. They thus invite the criticism that they are ideologies produced by the culture industry. I contend, however, that the sheer proliferation of these programs invites a variety of responses, including irony, cynicism, and subversive humor. Of course, there may be a gap between such responses and thoughtful moral critique. Even so, I believe that the prevalence of ordinary horror on reality TV is less disturbing than some media critics have claimed.

The Videodrome

Since the horror on reality TV programs is formatted for entertainment and earns high ratings, we seem to have entered the realm of *Videodrome,* a 1982 science fiction/horror film directed by David Cronenberg that offered a prescient forecast of today's many reality TV shows. The movie demonstrates how a basic human interest in spectacles of horror leads to violent and ultimately self-destructive behavior. *Videodrome* was about a television network that broadcasts real scenes of murders, rapes, tortures, and deaths. In the film this "Videodrome" channel is captured through satellite pirating by television executive Max Renn (James Woods), whose own network already specializes in "everything from soft core pornography to hard core violence." [3] Max becomes hooked and begins to hallucinate at the same time as he becomes entangled in s/m adventures with "radio personality" Nicki Brand (Deborah Harry). Nicki says that she is aroused by pain and was "born to be on Videodrome." As frightened by his interactions with Nicky as by his hallucinations, Max turns for help to "media prophet" Brian O'Blivion. O'Blivion is a professor who agrees only to be interviewed on TV if he is shown via a monitor on the set—he will only appear "on TV, on TV." [4] He intones dire statements such as "The television screen has become the retina of the mind's eye" and "Television is reality, and reality is less than television."

In the movie's most graphic and famous images, human flesh merges with the television, fulfilling O'Blivion's prophecies about the birth of a "new flesh." Video disks throb, the television's hard surfaces become pliant and sensuous, and Max embraces Nicki as her luscious lips pulse out from the TV screen's surface. The professor explains: "The television screen is part of the physical structure of the brain. Therefore whatever appears on the television screen emerges as raw experience for those who watch it." Max also develops a vagina-like gash in his abdomen through which his Videodrome controllers insert tapes that direct his increasing tendency toward violence. O'Blivion eventually confides to Max that Videodrome's transmissions made him sick: "I had a brain tumor, and I had visions. I believe the visions caused the tumor, and not the reverse." The network's transmissions are literally cancerous: they cause tumors, and people who watch them begin to hallucinate and go mad, killing others or themselves. As the story concludes, we learn that the Videodrome network was developed and used by a conservative vigilante group to purify their nation of the "scum" who would watch such shows. Eventually, Max foresees, then enacts, his own suicide on the monitor during a Videodrome broadcast.

Some might say that *Videodrome* anticipated various developments of the last twenty years. Groups such as the Coalition on Television Violence have denounced the proliferation of violence on TV by insisting upon the dangers and harmful effects of media images of aggression. For example, Daniel Gerbner, former head of the Annenberg School of Communication at the University of Pennsylvania, comments that "television . . . presents a coherent vision of the world . . . [which] is violent, mean, repressive, dangerous—and inaccurate. Television programming is the toxic by-product of market forces run amok. Television has the capacity to be a culturally enriching force, but . . . today it breeds what fear and resentment mixed with economic frustration can lead to—the undermining of democracy." [5] Professor Gerbner considers television violence dangerous because it is indifferent and formulaic, meaningless and inconsequential "happy violence." He sounds much like Professor O'Blivion, who equated the Videodrome transmissions with a cancer. Is there another possible conclusion besides these laments that reality has become mean as it becomes "less than television"? I think so; both O'Blivion and Gerbner have failed to notice the *contradictory* messages and effects of images of horror on reality TV. Such programs are both arousing and deadening, frightening and reassuring, serious and comical, "real" and "unreal." And audiences need not simply consume them passively.

Categories of Reality TV

Reality TV shows that center on ordinary horror are quite varied. The clearest cases of what I have in mind are regular weekly (or sometimes even nightly) shows such as "Trauma: Life in the ER," "Cops," "Rescue 911," "Code 3," "Emergency Call," and "I Witness Video." [6] Instead of developed plots, TV horror stories unfold in compressed time and usually feature the aftermath of horror. Ordinary TV horror is not, like film horror, about monsters and evil but about destruction, damage, fear, and weeping. Film horror often uses well-developed plot structures that elicit an audience interest in problem solving. The feature film's length permits it to show some elaborate stage setting with a slow onset of horror and gradual discovery of a monster behind it. But in contrast to the relevant audience response to film, an empathetic search for *causes* and *solutions,* television's ordinary horror is usually much more simplistic, using very sketchy narratives and tending to focus on *effects.* [7] Despite this general pattern, reality TV horror takes on a number of guises that can be conveniently sorted into two broad categories. First, there are many shows that highlight horrors of *nature;* second are those featuring *people* affected by either crimes or accidents.

In many ways, I find the nature programs the worst and most disturbing—in contrast to Gerbner, who has denounced the shows about human violence and crime. [8] The human-focused shows offer more traditional resolutions and more reassuring messages than the nature-based shows. The human horrors on TV are usually dealt with by competent professionals, whether cops or doctors. By comparison, horrors of nature are completely unpredictable and irrational; no real response is available other than coping with the aftermath. Often the scenes shown in programs about nature's horrors have been recorded by amateurs during their encounters with floods, fires, or storms, as with "Twister: Rage on the Plains." The Discovery Channel's "Raging Planet" series featured millennially spectacular fires and floods, plus stupendous volcano footage. Shows about wildlife have become dismayingly gory, with predator and prey of every stripe, skin, sphere, and size spilling a lot of blood—not all of it red. Often such programs zoom in on faces of hapless baby animals being swallowed by a predator, whether lion or alligator.

The strongest such fare is found in Fox Network's programs such as "When Disasters Strike" and "When Animals Attack" (which evolved into a series of specials).[9] The former program was divided into categories such as water, fire, and wind. On one such program I saw a man filming the oncoming storm, while his wife screamed at him to come inside; a piece of the roof fell off and hit him, whereupon the camera first fell then went dark. On the animal attack programs we could watch real footage of humans being attacked by elk, alligators, elephants, lions, bees, snakes, gorillas, grizzly bears, pit bulls, you name it. These programs broke existing canons of bad taste on American television and were extremely controversial (though they won consistently high ratings). Toyota, the sponsor of "When Disasters Strike," asked that it not be repeated, and these programs were blasted by an NBC executive as nothing but "snuff television."[10]

Of course, shows with horror involving humans and those involving nature may be blended in various ways. Some nature-horror program tilt toward human interest; on these we typically see that the humans are resilient, strong, and capable of coping. And not all the programs in each of these categories are alike. To focus more closely on reality TV's narrative strategies, I will set aside the nature-horror programs and look next in more detail at variations within the second category, ordinary horror about people. I want to explore how these programs' narratives are structured so as to elicit certain thoughts and emotions, considering how they analyze the horrors on which they dwell.

Horror in Reality TV about People

Programs of reality TV featuring people are varied and include cop shows, doctor shows, and disaster stories. These programs offer a dizzyingly wide range of variations on "reality." They utilize both real and re-created footage of human criminals: a nanny abuses the toddler in her care by slamming her into the kitchen cabinet; police raid a drug dealer's home; there is a fracas at a bar; a drunk driver kills someone. Accidents are featured on "Rescue 911" and programs on the Learning Channel's "Adrenaline Rush Hour," such as "Trauma: Life in the ER." These shows, too, use a combination of real footage and re-creations of emergencies as medical teams are called to the scenes of car accidents, shootings, and stabbings. The recordings of such accidents have been significantly increased by home videos. "Rescue 911" often depicts emergency situations involving children: a boy gets a toothbrush impaled in his throat; a child is trapped under a heavy overturned tool shelf; a boy at school gets his tongue stuck in a metal canteen. The standards of horrific depiction on the medical shows permit them to be much more gruesome than the police shows—again, a fact overlooked by Gerbner. Once "Trauma" showed in close-up someone's amputated fingers and thumb laid out for reattachment.

It is helpful to describe these programs as falling along a continuum from what I shall dub "verism" to "reenactment." "Veristic," or mimetic, shows are ones like "Cops" and "I Witness Video" that use all or mostly actual video footage. "Cops" is a paradigm of this type of reality TV show; it is made up entirely of "real" video footage of cops at work. It uses voice-overs by the cops at the start and end of each short sequence, but it does not include any host narratives or on-camera interviews. There is rarely any reference to the inclusion of the camera. "Cops"'s catchy reggae-style theme music, "Bad Boys," is used only at the outset and close of the show, not during the segments. [11] Realism is also constructed through use of a handheld camera, unscripted dialogue, and random sounds punctuated by the scratch of police radios. The police officers on "Cops" usually deal with very mundane crimes: they intervene in a domestic argument or chase a man for petty theft. But occasionally the program gets more gruesome: in one episode (which aired on September 3, 1993) police in a rural area responded to a murder call and entered a home where two strangled bodies were found. As family members wailed outside, the camera showed surprisingly graphic images of the dead, even nude, bodies.

The dramatic structures of these shows are hidden because the programs purport to present a rough, raw "immediacy." Despite such seeming randomness, they do have structures. Although shows such as "Cops" are in fact highly edited, they present themselves as unmediated and random scraps of reality. [12] The "Cops" creator has described three fundamental variations employed on the program: action sequences, lyrical ones, and "thought" pieces. [13] Probably the best-known sequences of "Cops," however, and ones that attract a core audience mimic the action film formula.

Here moments of boredom and everyday duty lead first to exciting interventions, with some suspense, and then afford a brief resolution.

In the medical veristic shows, by comparison, the dominant mode is melodrama. The focus is on the intense emotions of both professionals and victims in response to the emergency situation and its horror. We often see children crying or adults screaming, as sirens wail. There is blood on screen and death hovers close by. Programs such as "Trauma: Life in the ER" employ longer segments than the short ones on "Cops," and these facilitate a more sustained character portrayal of both victims and professionals. The narrative structure tracks certain individuals at one hospital throughout a full hour, typically showing several emergencies that occur in one evening, together with their aftermath and resolution. Such shows present a far more structured story with a clearly demarcated beginning, middle, and end. They also afford greater emotional closure. "Trauma" follows several cases to their end result, which takes one of two forms: a hospital release (happy ending) or a death as the doctor tells the family there is no hope (sad ending). Since one episode of the program generally narrates two or three accident stories, the show as a whole will typically offer samples of each type of ending.

At the other end of the spectrum are *reenactment* shows. Although they, too, adopt a realistic format, they use actors to recreate dramatic scenes, while the real participants narrate them on camera. "Top Cops," "America's Most Wanted," and "Real Stories of the Highway Patrol" are examples. (Reenactments are also often incorporated into programs about crimesolving such as the Discovery Channel's show "The New Detectives: Case Studies Forensic Science.") In the reenactment shows the narrative structures follow the formulas of melodrama. There is less focus on suspense, plot, actions, and outcomes and more on basic situations that involve emotions such as pity and fear. Sorrow, weeping, and empathy are prominent. On some reenactment programs, such as "Top Cops," it is easy to differentiate between the actors and the real cops, and no attempt is made to blur the distinctions. This show switches from on-screen interviews with actual policemen recounting and reliving their major success stories to reenactments of the drama of arrest—in which the real people are inevitably portrayed by more handsome and younger actors using stereotypical "brave cop" mannerisms. In one horrifying episode of "Top Cops" (which aired on August 27, 1993) the "good cops" chased a black suspect for no apparent reason and engaged in brutal punching and name-calling.

The reenactment programs use music, staging, acting, lighting, on-camera interviews, and framing to heighten audience emotions. They also employ TV or cinematic strategies that emphasize suspense by highlighting an impending disaster, the participants' resulting fear and distress, and their ultimate relief at an escape or resolution. For example, an episode of "Rescue 911" told about a fire that burned down someone's new home. When the Christmas tree catches fire in the reenactment, the camera focuses on the dog, who was first to notice the fire. In classic "Lassie" style he begins whimpering as he tries to warn the humans, but the family blithely goes about its business. Suspense builds as we worry about when this family will notice that their house is burning down.

These programs often switch their video technique from the development, or onset, phase of the situation, which is shown in reenactment, to the emotional reaction, cued for the audience in on-camera interviews of the real people who were involved in the disaster. People often cry as they retell the incident; even men weep as they think about the potential (but averted) loss of a house or a child. Their voices break, and then the camera zooms in to show their tears.

When the programs move on to the inevitable resolution, their narrative technique switches back to use reenactment. The disasters in "Rescue 911" all have happy endings—even endings that are shown to be miraculous, as is indicated by showing a scene of the family praying together before the rescue. Thus, the narrative structure suggests that some divine power has heeded their prayers and intervened. Every sequence on this program also has a coda. This shows a bright and happy scene of the family reunited and at play, swimming, having a lobster picnic by a pristine lake, swinging, or walking with their dog through the park. These bucolic and sunny scenes on "Rescue 911" are the antithesis of the grainy nighttime sequences on "Cops," yet the resolutions often carry the same message—that problems can be taken care of by heroic individuals or professionals, so that people "like us" in the presumed viewing audience (middle class, mostly white) are safe and secure.

"Rescue 911" was an especially odd blend of realism and reenactment. Although sometimes this show used the format of "Top Cops," switching between actors and on-screen, real-people narrators, more typically on "Rescue 911" the *actual people* who were involved in an emergency *played themselves* in the reenactment (with credit to an acting coach listed at the end). These people may include not only the victims themselves and their family members but also the heroic rescuers: doctors, nurses, telephone switchboard operators, and ambulance crews. The various participants were interviewed on camera at a later date commenting on how they felt at the time, and then these *very same people* appear in the reenactment segments driving ambulances, performing surgery, crying, calling 911, or being wheeled into the ER. Most dramas on "Rescue 911" were rather mundane, but they could be quite horrific: a woman was smothered in mud under an overturned truck; a boatload of people were trapped in a flooding river; a man accidentally shot himself in the heart with a nail gun at a remote construction site. The on-camera interviews are interspersed among the unfolding narrative of the emergency in a formulaic way, with close-up monologue describing and heightening the emotions as the action is momentarily halted. These interviews contribute to the melodramatic effect, since, as I have said, they emphasize intense emotions of either weeping or thankfulness.

"I Witness Video" was one of the most interesting and disturbing reality TV shows. It did not fit the action formula of "Cops" or the melodrama formula of "Trauma" and "Rescue 911." It was more like the ordinary TV shows featuring horrors of nature, with disasters that were more genuinely random and often left unresolved. The show was based on video footage of disasters submitted by viewers, making it the sober-sided counterpart of "America's Funniest Home Videos." Like the latter show, it played at an early prime-time family hour. Typical fare included home movies made during fires or floods, with occasional alternatives such as a blimp crash or an abusive nanny. This show combined host narratives with the submitted videos and on-camera interviews with participants. Some episodes at the start of the series run were quite horrific: the first show that aired used a segment from a police car's camera that recorded the officer being shot and killed as he made a traffic arrest. Another segment showed a man in a flood who was swept away to obvious death. These gruesome scenes prompted such adverse reactions that later episodes were toned down so as not to show an obvious death. But, even so, the later episodes could be fairly horrific, such as the show featuring the abusive nanny. In this episode a couple who had suspected their nanny of harming their child set up a secret video camera to film her while they were away. They "succeeded" in the sense that they captured on videotape a fairly extended segment in which the nanny repeatedly slammed the screeching baby onto the kitchen floor. The horror of this spectacle was enhanced in the show's format by the simple expedient of being replayed at least three times. This film segment acquired new resonance after the well-publicized Louise Woodward "au pair" trial in Boston convicting the young English nanny of the murder (later reduced by the judge to manslaughter) of the toddler in her charge. Of course, the episode also offered reassurance by narrating the resolution—that the nanny had been deported.

Methods of Assessing Reality TV

Reality TV programs with apparent snuff content such as "When Animals Attack" as well as the shows on "Trauma" and "I Witness Video" have reached levels of depicted violence that appeared feasible twenty years ago only within a science fiction world like that of *Videodrome*. The programs offer themselves as seeming samples of reality rather than as aesthetic objects. What does this indicate? One approach to the study of television violence is demonstrated by a variety of professional social scientists. [14] Their studies conclude that violence on TV desensitizes audiences and encourages more cycles of violence. Social science studies of violent TV often lead researchers to draw moral, as well as factual, conclusions.

Gerbner, for example, argues not just that the messages of reality TV are false but that they serve the interests of a dominant class: watching TV violence inculcates attitudes that foster fascism. The shows' overemphasis upon, and decontextualization of, violence invite paranoia and fears, especially of the underclasses. Gerbner's research led directly to efforts at censorship: he helped found the Cultural Environment Movement (CEM). Groups such as this one and the National Coalition on Television Violence, lobbied for legislation in the 1996 Telecommunications Act requiring all U.S.-produced televisions to be equipped with the "v-chip" by February 1998.

While empirical analyses of the effects of various kinds of representations can be informative, most social science studies of violence (like similar studies of pornography) overlook certain important issues about the aesthetics of representation. I think this leads to an overemphasis on audience passivity and an underemphasis on audience's critical potentials. [15] The complexity of audience activities of reading mass media texts is also emphasized in Noël Carroll's 1998 book, *A Philosophy of Mass Art*. [16] Carroll argues that there is significant audience activity in the reception and interpretation of mass art. On the other hand, both sociological studies and ideology critique practiced by humanities scholars often implicates "the masses" in a kind of dumb victimization; this patronizingly suggests they require professorial liberation and enlightenment. A number of rhetorical functions are played by diverse types of mass art, not all of them very savory—but, still, audiences are not merely passive victims of such rhetoric. Carroll's analysis of the controversial and overused concept of ideology underlines two aspects at its core: an *epistemological* one (an ideology presents false information) and a *dominance* one (the false information serves the ends of a dominant class or group). To show how a given form of mass art (such as reality TV) is ideological in this sense would require a combination of content analysis along with different kinds of empirical studies. As a cognitivist, Carroll believes we must explore how various genres of the mass media function by presupposing a range of audience capacities for both feelings and thoughts.

If we apply this point to reality TV shows, we will acknowledge that such programs are structured and employ specific narrative strategies so as to produce particular effects. Advocates of a cognitive approach to film and television studies, such as Carroll and myself, argue that people's emotional responses to stimuli in movies and TV programs depend upon the exercise of complex, well-developed cognitive, perceptual, and emotional abilities. In order to read the representations of violent TV, a viewer must formulate thoughts and opinions, not all of which need be dictated by the programs being viewed. The cognitivist strategy provides a new framework for ideology critique that acknowledges both the structures of texts and the psychological abilities of audiences—including *critical* abilities. By looking both at the aesthetic features of representations and at the audience's cognitive and emotional responses to them, we can recognize greater complexity than allowed for in most social science studies. [17] Such readings will locate the audience's interest in a cognitive or narrative context provided by the programs, but the results may be less straightforward than some of the points claimed by critics such as Gerbner.

What is missing, in short, from many studies of television violence is attention to details of how those representations are structured and presented so as to invite particular readings. Further, we need more close attention to how people actually interpret the representations that they see.

Reality TV Shows: Features and Functions

Earlier I showed that reality TV programs with a focus on the everyday horrors that can befall ordinary people have a distinct structure. Drama is produced both by the careful editing of real video footage and by carefully constructed reenactments. Melodrama typically involves the calculated use of on-camera interviews after the event. The dramatic programs involve more plot development, though within narrow parameters (happy or unhappy endings).

Various types of reality TV shows share certain aims and effects. One obvious shared function is to provide entertainment. Like classic horror, mystery, and melodrama, reality TV entertains by being scary, suspenseful, or emotional. But the shows typically lack the deeper structures of their related fictional genres, because their "plots" are so reduced, formulaic, and thin.

The melodramatic programs do not sustain a deep sense of tragedy, since even in the more elaborate stories we become so little acquainted with the victims. Not only are these typically people whose lives are quite ordinary and not remarkable like an ancient tragic hero, but they are people who have done little to contribute to any tragic downfall. The resulting empathy, even in the shows that employ melodrama, is very forced and shallow.

On the other hand, for programs that seem based less on character than on spectacle, the horror is often diffused: "snuff TV" is simply not shown on most reality TV programs about people. Instead, these programs afford a very safe voyeuristic thrill because they are usually packaged with neat resolutions. The worry on behalf of the people during the emergency is accompanied with relief that this disaster has not happened to the viewer. Even in the worst-case scenarios there is an acceptance of the inevitable— as with deaths on "Trauma," in which we know that the doctors have done their best.

A second and related structural feature shared by many of the reality TV shows about people, then, is that they offer reassurance. The horror that is shown is typically denied or downgraded because it can be dealt with by competent professionals or everyday heroes, including even children— those who remember to dial 911. These programs present the message that all is really well in this country: they showcase frightening spectacles precisely in order to invoke images of safety. Reality TV shows typically champion the nuclear family and the traditional forces of law, criminal justice, religion, and medicine. They revel in horrific spectacles for some minutes but then offer up an explanation and a sweet, happy resolution. The nanny whose abuse of the baby is secretly videotaped gets caught; the man who put a nail into his heart with a nail gun is saved by the hospital team; the radio broadcaster covering the hurricane on Kauai gets married over the air to provide everyone a reason to celebrate after the disaster; the "Top Cops" arrest the cop-killing drug dealers, and so on.

The vanilla reassurance of ordinary horror programs suggests to me that these programs do not actually foster the sort of paranoia that Gerbner worries about as an inducement to fascism. Of course, it still seems justi-fied to call them ideologies, in that they present false messages that pre-serve the social class hierarchies of the status quo.[18] Despite poor national statistics on domestic violence, marriage is redeemed as salvational; despite our nation's extraordinary health care inequities, the emergency teams are celebrated; despite the existence of notorious racial discrimination by cops, we see that it is really always the black offenders (in the reenactments) who are scary and violent "scum."

A third structural feature of such programs is that they represent and defend the values of traditional religion and middle-class people. "Cops" suggests that the only criminals the police deal with are low-life scumbag alcoholics and drug addicts who clearly deserve to be locked up—and who *will be* locked up. [19] "Rescue 911" thrives on, but simultaneously assuages, typical middle-class worries: can you be sure that your nanny won't abuse your infant, that your child won't accidentally impale his throat with a toothbrush, that a rapist won't break into your bathroom, or that a Christmas tree fire won't burn down your new house? For one thing, you can try prayer: after the child with a brain injury is miraculously saved by the surgical team, which in the show's discourse is represented as occurring after his father's prayers, he and his family go to church together. On these shows the evil nanny is convicted and deported, the injured child is saved, the rapist is caught, and the house is rebuilt. These programs hint at how you can control your life to avert harm. Above all, watch more of these shows, so if your child gets a toothbrush stuck in his throat, you will know what to do—and then you, too, might get to put in an appearance on "Rescue 911."

By this combination of worry and vanilla reassurance, reality TV blocks understanding of social conditions behind crime and efforts at genuine social change. But so, too, I think, do the studies and movements that condemn represented violence. Ending TV violence will not end child abuse, poverty, illiteracy, and racism. [20] Ordinary horror obscures the truth about how current social arrangements work to produce a climate of violence: racism; inequities in education, health care, social and economic status, and political power; unemployment; urban blight and flight; drug use; and gun laws. Why is there never any white-collar crime on "Cops"? Why should women avoid showers or rapists, rather than men having to change their attitudes about sexual violence? Why should cops have to step in and solve domestic violence situations, rather than social attitudes changing to stop men from battering and to offer women in such situations viable alternatives?

A fourth structural feature shared by reality TV shows is that they perpetuate the values of patriarchy and the traditional nuclear family. In "Cops" there are frequent episodes about domestic violence. An "episode" of "Cops" occurs between commercials and runs for at most seven minutes. Each episode must be resolved in this time. In one episode the cops removed the offending man and told his wife or partner she had better go stay somewhere else. In another episode a cop told the couple they needed to learn how to communicate better. I was astonished to hear the wife rail at the cop not to condescend to her, that their problems were deeper than his little message recognized. Nevertheless, in the narrative logic of the program the cop was "right" and the woman was "wrong," and the husband was shown at the end hugging her, saying he loved her, and embracing his children, who all the while had been looking on, crying and upset. When a horde of male cops carry out a sting and catch a hooker, she is shown as morally corrupt, while the men are pure strong heroes—and the johns are altogether ignored, often with faces blurred out on-screen. Very few female cops are featured on the program.

It is also typical in reality TV programs, especially "Rescue 911," "Real Stories of the Highway Patrol," and "Code 3," to showcase efforts of ordinary people—almost always men—who emerge as "heroes" by rescuing the children from the swamped raft, overturning the wrecked car to free its occupants, and so on. Their skill with tools or sheer strength win the day. These men are then featured at the show's conclusion in "Aw shucks, I ain't no hero" types of interviews, accompanied by mushy music. The ideological message here is that the forces of patriarchy/authority know best, that men are strong and virtuous, that fathers are appropriate heads of households, and that, once the cops intervene and model appropriate male behavior, the problems will go away—a false and dangerously reductive message.

My claims about the gender messages of these programs can be reinforced by looking at their hosts. Not a single one of the reality TV shows I have mentioned has a female host. And, furthermore, each host is a superannuated hero: "Rescue 911" has "Star Trek" 's Captain Kirk (William Shatner), "Code 3" had Buck Rogers (Gil Gerard), "When Animals Attack" had PI Robert Spenser (Robert Urich), and "Unsolved Mysteries" has Elliott Ness (Robert Stack). Surely, it is significant that these are all men with an iconographic involvement in our cultural mythology about heroism, good cops, adventurous admirals, and honest detectives. This is like having people who've played doctors on TV hawk products such as Tylenol; their screen presence provides an air of spurious expertise and authority. The presence of familiar icons on the disaster programs helps to reinforce the message that heroism is, after all, alive and well.

So far I have described four basic structural features of reality TV programs that foreground ordinary horror in situations of crimes or emergencies. Such programs use variations of basic narrative structures to entertain, reassure, uphold, existing social class structures and reinforce values of patriarchy. I think another feature of the content of such programs is more complex and one that most likely also figures into the popularity of the newer breed of "Survivor"-type reality TV programs. This is to offer fifteen-minute fame to ordinary people. The various types of reality TV blur the lines between reality and representation, enabling ordinary people to become protagonists in the interesting realm of the television. (And in the reenactments you might be played by someone far better-looking than you are!)

Ironically, as the represented world on reality TV has come to possess more of the ordinary character of everyday reality, what is real is not itself experienced (deletion was made here) "nakedly" and immediately. It is instead experienced, as it were, vicariously or in a way that is superior if it is itself mediated. To witness a tornado or to establish the reality of child abuse, one must record the experience through the camcorder. We even experience real disasters as mediated. This is often remarked upon by survivors of horrific incidents such as the Oklahoma City bombing who described the scene as looking "like a disaster movie." (This comment was, of course, also often made in the wake of the World Trade Center attack.) An advertisement for an Acura car took this kind of attitude to absurd lengths. This car "lets you live your life like a movie" in which "you have front row seats" and you "choose your own soundtrack"!

Critical Readings of Reality TV

In describing specific features of the content of reality TV programs, it will probably seem as if my assessments of reality TV turn out to be quite negative; perhaps I, too, sound much like the media critics such as (the real) Gerbner or (the fictitious) O'Blivion. But in this section I want to turn from features of content onto more features of audience response, suggesting that there are actually a variety of ways to envisage more critical audience readings of reality TV programs. Gerbner, like Brian O'Blivion of *Videodrome,* feels that our familiarity with such horror will incite violence and increase paranoia. I am not sure that this view recognizes how the narratives of such programs actually work. I have, instead, described a deadening or flattening effect. This, too, of course, might seem to indicate desensitization. But let's think about it further.

I would like to suggest that the sorts of television shows considered here create a postmodern reversal: although television may have acquired some sort of status that puts it at a level above reality, at the same time it appears to present an indifferent reality, one that is mindless, formulaic, and boring, despite its graphic scenes of spectacle. If the narratives and spectacles of violence on TV are equated with the flat, unreal experiences of reality, this may be so because people are actually seeking a more rich and meaningful narrative of violence and evil—one, say, more like the ideal for classical tragedy described by Aristotle in his *Poetics*. The on-screen depiction of gore might not be so immoral if it accompanies the yearning for a more genuinely moral message in a meaningful plot. Perhaps, then, it is not surprising that people find more depth and meaning in fictions, even fictions about current events, which create more comprehensible narratives. When television narration is lost, reduced, flattened, and subordinated to spectacle as affectless and commercial visual display, then the meaning of horror as evil is also lost. Comparing the "real" images of the Gulf War to the "fictive" images of *Die Hard, Terminator II,* or *True Lies* or of the Afghan war to *Saving Private Ryan* and *Black Hawk Down,* it is obvious which ones are more real and powerful—the ones with more standard heroes, villains, developed narrative, and clearer cues to emotional response.

Many media critics deride the audience's search for "significance" in fictionalized stories of World War II or of events such as the Holocaust, enjoying films like *Saving Private Ryan* and Spielberg's *Schindler's List.* But a critic such as Gerbner should not be able to have it both ways. People in mass audiences are caught in an inescapable dilemma by this logic, which shows nothing but scorn for their abilities. If they turn to fictive spectacle, they are escapist, whereas, if they watch real ones, they are voyeurs. Perhaps the desire for a deeper narrative delineating good from evil is not so despicable, after all.

A second reason for ascribing more potential to audiences for critical readings of reality TV is that the ordinary horror on TV has become so inherently repetitive and flattening that people perhaps really do just enjoy it from a stance that is ironic, participatory, humorous, and parodistic. [21] If so, this, too, would mean that audience's response to reality TV is not uniformly the kind of dangerous addiction or cancer that led to Max Renn's murders and suicide in *Videodrome.* Yes, the programs are formulaic and shallow, and, yes, they do convey troubling messages. Yet their attempts to up the ante of prurience are so visible that they function to make the programs funny. The redundant multiplication of such images, their easy availability, their familiar packaging, involves an inherent possibility for humor, irony, and self-parody.

On the most obvious level the fact that there is humor in audience's experience of reality TV programs shows up in the frequency of satires and parodies concerning them. Just as disaster movies such as *Airplane* gave rise to a Leslie Nielson cottage industry of slapstick comedic put-downs of the disaster film genre, so also have there been some wonderful parodies of reality TV. The recent movie *Series 7: The Contenders* took the formula to ridiculous lengths by staging an alleged reality TV game show that required contestants to murder one another in order to win. [22] There have been numerous parodies of reality television on TV itself, such as the superbly titled "World's Dumbest Criminals in Scariest Police Chases." Another program, "When Cars Attack," was one of the most hilarious things I have ever watched. The program used a deadpan but worried style of narration to describe incidents of cars running amok and acting strangely. It showed very cleverly staged sequences of cars that were apparently driving themselves, whirling about to elude capture, for example, while being tackled by wary policemen.

In fact, many programs of reality TV have gotten to the point of parodying themselves. It is implausibly condescending to mass audiences to suppose that they are unable to recognize how many bad, weird, and strange programs have proliferated under the guise of reality TV. Reality TV can prove amusing by its ramified self-referentiality. Sometimes programs rely upon the audience's sophisticated knowledge and understanding of the genre itself. An anniversary episode of "Rescue 911" showcased over one hundred lives that had allegedly been saved by people who watched prior episodes of the program. "America's Most Wanted" had its own TV movie in which actors portrayed a "real" family originally featured on the program. In a crucial but metaphysically confusing scene the TV actors watched themselves playing the real family on a TV episode of "America's Most Wanted"! On a more local level reality TV also can have similarly comical, if macabre, aspects. In a Houston newspaper John Makeig reported that a local actor had been arrested four times after portraying crooks for eight and a half years on the local TV show "Crimestoppers": "Carrying a police identification card has made it easier to get released, but it has not kept him from looking down gun barrels at arresting officers" (29A).

Some examples of reality TV reduce the genre so drastically to rudiments that they, too, become self-parodying. One episode of "Code 3" highlighted three scenes of disaster. All three of these were veristic in my sense: they were not reenactments but used actual footage. The first featured dry humor as an elderly man and woman were rescued from a flash flood in Phoenix. In voice-over narration the man intoned flatly: "When they got me to dry land, my first thought was thank God I'm out of there. I didn't think, 'Now how are they going to get the wife out of there, because she can't swim.'" The second segment segued to Bambi-like sweetness with scenes of a dolphin being rescued. This involved some clever transitional narrative along these lines: "It's not only human lives that can need salvaging."

Suddenly, after this somewhat light and happy episode, without much warning, the third segment switched to show footage of the aftermath of a horrific natural gas explosion in Guadalajara, Mexico. There were scenes of the disaster, a few shots of people trapped in the wreckage, and an interview (translated) with a man who was rescued from the rubble and said tearfully that he now had found a new relationship with God. Again, the program undermined the horror through its saccharine message and superficiality. In closing, Gil Gerard intoned the inane commentary: "This disaster caused $300 million in property damage. But there can be no price put on human life. Every life is precious. Join us next week . . . ." A program like this needs no parodying![23]

A similarly inane program, "Emergency Call," reduces the genre to its elements in such a ritualized, formulaic way that it, too, ends up as a form of weird caricature. Instead of the strongly masculine host such as the handsome Robert Stack, "Captain Kirk," or "Buck Rogers," this program features a short pudgy man we've never heard of before with an incongruously deep radio voice. The show uses siren sounds, heartbeats, and other devices, such as flashing statistics, to build up incredible hype before each segment, but all these devices seem to enter in randomly with no effect. Unlike other reality TV shows, this program often cuts away from the scene of disaster without offering any resolution. One program started out with some sequences from car accidents. First, there was an accident in which parents were injured by not wearing seat belts, but the children were fine, buckled in their car seats. A comparison scene shows an accident in which children had been injured and had not worn seat belts. The moral of the story was very clear, but the narrator reinforced it with solemnity. In the next sequence we see touching scenes of ambulance workers with tears on their face as they collect the shoes of a small accident victim. The little boy is loaded onto a stretcher and into the ambulance. It drives off. Then the narrator intones grimly: "The race is on. Doctors are standing ready to buy the little four-year old . . . the chance to see five." But there's a commercial, and that's that! Does the four-year-old child car accident victim die or not? Who knows? Who cares? After the break we are on to a new scene of disaster with a stabbing on the street in Philadelphia. It implies that those kinds of happy endings are just pasted on anyway.

How do audiences read the programs of reality TV? I have met a number of people who confess to being hooked on "Real Stories of the Highway Patrol," but in every case they all say it is because it is so fascinatingly bad. The abysmal camerawork, bad acting, and overhyped drama are simply too funny for anyone to take seriously. No wonder the program perfectly fits into the parody format of "Saturday Night Live" (which featured parodies in both 1993 and 1998). [24] This leads me to hypothesize that the program and audiences have a kind of pact or understanding. Everyone recognizes the formulaic, prosaic nature of the genre, and we participate in watching such parodies in a subversive, ironic spirit.

Coda: Speaking of Being Plugged In

A third and final phenomenon that deserves mentioning and supports my hypothesis about possibilities of critical responses to reality TV involves an important media development that was not forecast by *Videodrome's* Professor O'Blivion. I refer here, of course, to the Internet. This medium has provided many common people with the means to express their own views and become participants in a global creation of new media versions of reality, versions also not discussed by experts such as Gerbner. Homemade Internet sites can be created by many ordinary people without impressive wealth, institutional status, or even computer coding expertise. "Web logs," or "blogs," are proliferating and enable people to express their opinions on any subject whatsoever, sometimes attracting thousands of hits. [25] Numerous fan sites and chatrooms permit even broader participation and interaction between fans and stars (as on the Web site *www.williamshatner.com*). The variety of points of view expressed at such sites is hugely varied and not subject to particular corporate blandishments, even if the sites themselves are commercial ones. Web sites range from the sophisticated and well designed to the charmingly amateurish. They provide avenues for both mundane discussion and developed critical assessment and make a range of opinions available from witless enthusiasm to rude and vulgar ridicule.

The Internet has opened up space for a kind of democratic participation and self-expression (or self-seduction?) not possible in previous commercial media such as radio, television, and film studio production (not to mention refereed journal articles). The world of the Web—by its very nature instantaneous, ephemeral, and flexible—permits both speedy and multiple ongoing dialogues, along with high levels of detailed interaction and exchange. The Web thus facilitates what I have referred to as audience's potentials for critical response by way of viewer participation, criticism, and parody. Searching for audience reactions to reality TV on the Web takes one very quickly into a realm where fan sites proliferate and many critical reactions are available.

For example, I found an excellent online article with a sharply critical review of Fox's "When Animals Attack II" on a university-based Web site that published student TV reviews. Cleverly titled "When Reality Attacks," the article made it clear that an average viewer can bypass the prurient content[26] to discern the economic interests behind studio offerings of shows such as Fox's popular series on animal attacks. More amusing and very common are parody fan sites—for example, "Big Fins," which uses Flash technology to present numerous short videos on-screen with often hilarious parodies, such as "Survivor 4: Infection Ward" and "Pig Killer."[27]

The ordinary horror of reality TV is a phenomenon that has become prevalent and disturbing enough to merit philosophical consideration. Key features of ordinary horror on reality TV cry out for some assessment: the everydayness of the horror, plotlessness, the foregrounding of spectacle, and the confusion between reality and representation. Unlike some media critics whose views I have mentioned here, both real and fictional, my own assessment finds in reality TV a paradoxical field with dual effects, including some that are quite conservative but also others that recognize the audience's nihilism, skepticism, and cynical ability to produce subversive interpretations, perhaps even moral critique.

Notes

1. My essay takes programs such as "Cops" (which debuted in 1989) as the paradigm. I do not discuss the more recent generation of these programs, such as "Real World," "Survivor," and "Big Brother." See also Web sites such as Reality

2. I am grateful to Deckard Hodge and Marie-Laure Ryan for reading a draft of this article and suggesting many improvements and additional references.

2. Reality TV Links, <*http://www.realitytvlinks.com*>, which lists literally dozens of such programs in the United States, not to mention many more worldwide. I also do not include "newsmagazine" programs such as "Dateline" and "Hard Copy." Other programs that could be counted as reality TV include "America's Funniest Home Videos" (90 percent of the humor there is cruel and involves, for example, someone falling off a log or into a mud puddle). For a brief history of reality TV, see Rowen. Rowen traces the origins of the genre back as far as "Candid Camera" in 1948 and even before that to "reality radio": "Allen Funt originally taped and broadcast the complaints of fellow servicemen on Armed Forces Radio and took his idea to network radio in 1947 as *Candid Microphone*."

3. The movie first presents the programs as originating from somewhere outside the country and then specifies that they are being sent from Pittsburgh—probably a sly allusion to director George Romero, who made *Night of the Living Dead* and its sequels there.

4. In fact, we later learn that he is dead and that the tapes are constantly being updated and circulated from a vast library maintained by his daughter, Bianca O'Blivion.

5. See Stossel 86–104; my references are to the online version.

6. Other examples include "Yearbook," "Verdict," "True Detectives," "On Scene," "Inside Edition," "Unsolved Mysteries," "Top Cops," "America's Most Wanted," "Hard Copy," and "A Current Affair." For further references and discussion, see Carter; and Stewart.

7. For more on the role of plot, narrative, and thoughts or ideas in horror films, see Carroll, *Philosophy of Horror;* and Freeland.

8. The following passage is particularly representative of Gerbner's position: "Violence on U.S. television has declined for the third consecutive year, but a new source of violent programming—'Shockumentaries'—has increased, a University of California at Los Angeles study reports. The study found that the number of violent television series shown on the four networks declined during the 1996/97 season compared to the two previous seasons. Violence was also down in made-for-TV movies and on-air promotions. But the report said there were serious new issues of concern in reality-based action specials, or 'Shockumentaries,' on such topics as 'World's Most Dangerous Animals,' 'When Animals Attack,' 'Video Justice: Crime Caught on Tape' and 'World's Scariest Police Shootouts.' " Jeffrey Cole, the director of the UCLA Center for Communications Policy Study and author of the report, said: "While the majority of programming deals responsibly with violence issues, reality-based specials do not. The number of these violence-filled specials continued to grow during the 1996/97 season."

9. There was an even a television commercial for 1–800-COLLECT, featuring Peter McPheeley, the hunter attacked by the deer on this show. (I am grateful to Deckard Hodge for this information.)

10. "A top NBC executive ripped Fox on Tuesday for the growing use of so-called reality TV shows, saying a program showing animal attacks was 'one step short of a snuff film.' Fox officials suggested that Don Ohlmeyer, president of NBC West Coast, should worry about his own network. Fox's broadcast of 'When Animals Attack 2' on Nov. 18 was the network's sixth highest-rated program for the week, according to Nielsen Media Research. Fox ran the special about angry animals twice during November—a 'sweeps' month, when local television use ratings to set ad rates. Ohlmeyer said Fox 'feels no shame' in presenting such programming. He compared the animal broadcast to a snuff film, a form of pornography that features killings. During the past month, Fox has also shown 'When Disaster Strikes,' a program with footage about earthquakes, floods, tornados [*sic*] and other natural calamaties [*sic*], and 'Close Call: Cheating Death,' with depictions of near-death experiences. Fox officials say they're not alone in broadcasting these types of shows, noting that NBC has recently promoted a 'Dateline NBC' segment that featured someone who was gored by a bull" (Associated Press).

11. On rare segments of "Cops" there is musical accompaniment. For instance, I saw an episode featuring various drug sweeps with a soundtrack overlay of exciting percussion music.

12. "Cops" creator John Langley explains his strategy: "I had always loved the

idea of following cops around, without a host, without narration, and without reenactments. All the material comes back to Los Angeles, with the field staff tagging what looks like potential stories. Then our editorial staff cuts together the most interesting material, whereupon I determine what goes in the shows after recutting or refinessing if needed." For a more cynical assessment, by a journalist who helped work to do the editing, see Seagal.

13. "Basically we try to put together interesting combinations. For example, an action piece (which hooks the audience), a lyrical piece (which develops more emotion), and a think piece (which provokes thought on the part of the audience)" (Langley).

14. There are many publications in this field; some of the major ones are Hamilton; Weaver and Tamborini; and two online resources: "The National Television Violence Study" <*http://www.ccsp.ucsb.edu/ntvs.htm*>; and "Violence on Television" from the American Psychological Association <*http://www.apa.org/pubinfo/violence.html*> (March 25, 2002).

15. I believe that criticism of research studies on media violence can benefit from critiques of the simplistic nature of research about pornography. See, for example, Vance. For criticisms of the Gerbner studies, see Gitlin, who writes: "However morally and aesthetically reprehensible today's screen violence, the crusades of Senator Paul Simon and Attorney General Janet Reno against television violence, as well as Catharine MacKinnon's war against pornography, are cheap shots. There are indeed reasons to attribute violence to the media, but the links are weaker than recent headlines would have one believe. The attempt to demonize the media distracts attention from the real causes of—and the serious remedies for—the epidemic of violence" (000).

16. See Carroll, *Philosophy of Mass Art*, esp. 360–412.

17. One example of this more complex sort of analysis, of the important horror genre of the slasher film, may be found in Ryan and Kellner, 192–93.

18. See Fiske, esp. chap. 15.

19. Kathleen Curry reports: "The majority of the respondents said that the program did not affect either their fear of crime or their trust level of others. On the contrary, most respondents resounded a concern corresponding to the following quote: 'I think that's a problem with the show . . . it distances you. Because I think, oh, this is there but I am here, and I live in this neighborhood, so it's not going to happen to me . . . It makes me not fear crime like I probably should, like anybody should . . . unless I go in those neighborhoods' (Marty, 23 year old, Caucasian female)" (180).

20. Similar points are made very strongly, and well, by Gitlin.

21. In another article I would link the nature of reality TV programs about ordinary horror to talk shows, many of which also showcase spectacles of the horror of intimate family dramas in which sexuality and aggression run amok ("She slept with her stepson" or "Mom stole daughter's fiancé").

22. Tim Kreider writes: "Director David Minahan wants to have his cake and

let us eat it too. Although he savagely parodies the reality-TV genre, mocking its transparently manipulative techniques, scripted suspense, and cheap human interest, he also uses those same techniques for his own dramatic ends."

23. On this topic, see Postman.

24. See *<http://snltranscripts.jt.org/scripts/98dpatrol.phtml>*. See also a critical Web site: "If you want to see something really low, check out *Real Stories of the Highway Patrol.* It's exactly like *Cops,* but less classy. I'm not kidding. The crimes are 10 times less dramatic and just slightly more exciting than watching people get speeding tickets" (Cop Clones, by "Fries Mister," *Hotwired <http://hotwired.lycos.com/teevee/ 96/38/b.html>* [March 29, 2002; April 26, 2002]).

25. On the "blog" phenomenon, see Howard Kurtz, "Who Cares What You Think? Blog, and Find Out," *Washington Post,* April 22, 2002, C01; online at *<http://www.washingtonpost.com/wp-dyn/articles/A25512–2002Apr21.html>* (April 26, 2002).

26. The author was Chris Brown (November 24, 1996); I have not saved a copy of the original article, and the site is no longer active.

27. See "Survivor 4" and other parodies with both art and music (including "Bush and Cheney sing Convoy") at *<http://bigfins.com/survivor.html>*. See also Reality TV Fans, *<http://www.realitytvfans.com>*.

References

Associated Press. "NBC Exec Rips Fox for Reality TV." *New York Telegraph Herald,* November 11, 1996.

Carroll, Noël. *The Philosophy of Horror.* New York: Routledge, 1990.

———. *A Philosophy of Mass Art.* Oxford: Clarendon Press, 1998.

Carter, Bill. "NBC News Decides to Stop Using Dramatizations." *New York Times,* November 21, 1989, 13Y.

Curry, Kathleen. "Mediating *Cops:* An Analysis of Viewer Reaction to Reality TV." *Journal of Criminal Justice and Popular Culture* 8.3 (2001): 169–185.

Fiske, John. *Television Culture.* London: Methuen, 1987.

Freeland, Cynthia. *The Naked and the Undead: Evil and the Appeal of Horror.* Boulder: Westview, 1999.

Gerbner, Daniel. "Study Finds U.S. TV Violence Declining." Reuters News Service, January 14, 1998.

Gitlin, Todd. "Imagebusters." *American Prospect* 5.16, December 1, 1994. Online at *<http://www.prospect.org/print/V5/16/gitlin-t.html>* (March 25, 2002).

Hamilton, James T., ed. *Television Violence and Public Policy: Duke Conference on Media Violence and Public Policy.* Ann Arbor: University of Michigan Press, 1999.

Kreider, Tim. "Review of *Series 7: The Contenders.*" *<http://www.lipmagazine.org/ articles/revikreider_108.htm>* (April 12, 2002).

Kurtz Howard. "Who Cares What You Think? Blog, and Find Out." *Washing-*

ton Post, April 22, 2002, C01; online at <*http://www.washingtonpost.com/wp-dyn/articles/A25512–2002Apr21.html*> (April 30, 2002).

Langley, John. "Interview." <*http://www.tvcops.com/pages/exclusive_langley_crime.html*> (August 17, 2001).

Makeig, John. "Actor as Crook has Pulled 82 Robberies, Carjackings, Rapes." *Houston Chronicle,* February 18, 1994, 29A.

Postman, Neil. *Amusing Ourselves to Death: Public Discourse in the Age of Show Business.* New York: Viking, 1986.

Rodley, Chris, ed. *Cronenberg on Cronenberg.* London: Faber and Faber, 1992.

Rowen, Beth. "Reality TV Takes Hold." Infoplease.com, (c) 2002 Learning Network, March 29, 2002. <*http://www.infoplease.com/spot/realitytv1.html*> (April 12, 2002).

Ryan, Michael, and Douglas Kellner. *Camera Politica: The Politics and Ideology of Contemporary Hollywood Film.* Bloomington: Indiana University Press, 1988.

Stewart, Susan. "Re-enactment Shows Blur the Lines on Everything but Shock." *Detroit Free Press,* July 14, 1991, G1.

Stossel, Scott. "The Man Who Counts the Killings." *Atlantic Monthly* 279.5 (May 1997): 86–104.

Vance, Carole S. "The Pleasures of Looking: The Attorney General's Commission on Pornography and Visual Images." *The Critical Image.* Ed. Carol Squiers. Seattle: Bay Press, 1990. 38–58.

Weaver, James B., III, and Ron Tamborini, eds. *Horror Films: Current Research on Audience Preferences and Reactions.* Mahwah NJ: Lawrence Erlbaum, 1996.

4. Music

Music is perhaps the most easily accessible of all arts; the one that touches, in one form or another, the widest segment of the world's population; the most vital to the human mind and soul. Yet it is also the most technically complex and, on the theoretical level, the most esoteric. A conversation between music scholars will lose the layman in a way that a conversation between literature specialists will not, unless the speakers are narratologists. As an art made of signifiers without signifieds, music eludes verbal description. The composer Aaron Copeland was reportedly once asked: "Does music have meaning?" "Absolutely," he replied. "Can it be put into words?" "Absolutely not."[1] In recent years critical music studies have been swept by the phenomenon widely known as the "narrative turn" in the humanities. To find the words that Copeland thought impossible and to overcome the isolation of their discipline in its technical vocabulary, musicologists have increasingly turned toward narrative theory. For the French musicologist Jean-Jacques Nattiez (paraphrased here by Carolyn Abbate), "music analysis is itself born of a narrative impulse . . . we create fictions about music to explain where no other form of explanation works" (224). Narrative metaphors may sometimes be the only way to talk about music.

The relations between music and narrative are multiple and too familiar to require more than a quick enumeration: dramatic scripts or narrative texts set to music (opera, lieder, cantatas); instrumental compositions illustrating well-known narratives (*The Sorcerer's Apprentice,* by Paul Dukas) or sketching new ones (*Night on Bald Mountain,* by Moussorgsky); verbally narrated music (*Peter and the Wolf,* by Prokofiev); and the use of extradiegetic music (that is, music that does not originate in the fictional world) to set or undermine the mood in film and drama. All of these examples involve specific musical compositions. But there is also a pervasive sense among scholars that music partakes of a deeper, essential narrativity. (Or it could be narrative that partakes of a deep, essential musicality, as Nietzsche argued in *The Birth of Tragedy Out of the Spirit of Music.*)[2] The kinship of the two forms of expression stems from a common dependency on temporality as a source of meaning. The philosopher Paul Ricoeur regards the narrative emplotment of experience as a way to come to terms with the "being-in-time" of human existence. Another philosopher, Susanne Langer, defines music as a virtualization of time: "The direct experience of passage, as it occurs in each individual life, is, of course, something actual, just as actual as the progress of the clock or the speedometer . . . Yet it is the model for the virtual time created in music. There we have its image, completely articulated and pure . . . The primary illusion of music is the sonorous image of passage, abstracted from actuality to become free and plastic and entirely perceptible" (113).

In verbal narrative the invisible passage of time is made perceptible through the transformations undergone by concrete objects (mostly characters), just as in nature the invisible force of the wind is made visible through the shaking of trees or the waving of flags. This is another way of saying that the apprehension of narrative time is inseparable from a representation of space, as David Herman argues in *Story Logic*. In music, too, time is experienced as transformation, but the events that succeed one another on the timeline do not affect spatial objects. Whereas content-based narrative creates a time-space continuum, the abstract narrative of music captures time in its pure form. This is not to say that music cannot evoke a sense of space; compositions such as Antonin Dvořák's symphony *From the New World* and Alexander Borodine's *In the Steppes of Central Asia* undoubtedly do so for many listeners. But, unless it is conveyed by all music and without the help of a title, this sense of space cannot be regarded as constitutive of a deep narrativity.

In the absence of specific semantic content and spatial dimension, the deep narrativity of music is an essentially metaphorical phenomenon. It eliminates characters and setting, retaining only the forward movement, the desire-for-something-to-come, the false or fulfilled expectations, the rise and falls of tension, the sense of an ending, and the memories of something past that modulate the narrative experience. Aristotle would describe the causality that links its chain of events as formal rather than material. To use the concepts developed in the introduction, we can say that it possesses narrativity without being a narrative. This narrativity can be either illustrative or autonomous, but in the second case it represents the indeterminate mode, since (as Tarasti points out in his contribution) it does not tell a specific story.

According to John Neubauer, narrative is not something that goes into, but something that comes out of, the musical text. It is the listener who emplots the text by filling its empty signifiers with personal representations. Neubauer conceives the narrative study of music as the collection and analysis of the images and scenarios that listeners spontaneously associate with music, such as this description in E. M. Forster's novel *Howard's End* of a young girl's experience of the third movement of Beethoven's Fifth: "The music started with a goblin walking quietly over the universe, from end to end. Others followed him. They were not aggressive creatures; it was that that made them so terrible to Helen. They merely observed in passing that there was no such thing as splendour or heroism in the world. After the interlude of elephants dancing, they [the goblins] returned and made the observation for the second time." (The stories continue for several lines [46–47; qtd. by Neubauer 117].) Locating the narrativity of music in the mind of the listener, just as locating the meaning of literature in the mind of the reader, can be either the end or the beginning of inquiry. It will be the end if one regards interpretation as an entirely free activity. It will be a beginning if one assumes that interpretation is the reader's or listener's response to precise textual features.

For the Finnish musicologist Eero Tarasti the verdict that musical narrativity lies in the ear (and imagination) of the listener is, indeed, a challenge to pursue inquiry into the features that inspire narrative interpretation. His work of the past twenty-five years has been a continuous effort to isolate and describe the formal properties that elicit the response "How narrative" to a piece of music. The essay presented here is a survey of the many approaches attempted by Tarasti to justify his intuition that music possesses an "existential" narrativity similar to that of life itself. It also offers a historical overview of narrativity in music history. The essay is meant to give the reader a quick taste of how a musicologist working in the tradition of the French school of semiotics (represented by A.-J. Greimas, Claude Lévi-Strauss, Claude Bremond, and the early Roland Barthes) approaches the issue of musical narrativity. Most of the examples and diagrams presented in the essay are the subject matter of detailed discussions in Tarasti's other publications, to which interested readers should turn, but a detailed coverage of each topic would exceed the technical level of the present volume.

Tarasti defines the minimal condition of narrativity as the "transformation of an object or state of affairs into something else through a process that requires a certain amount of time." To model this process of transformation, Tarasti borrows several concepts from classical structuralism. One of them is the Proppian notion of function. Looking for a musical unit equivalent to the function, he rejects the concept of theme: whereas a standard fairy tale uses more than a dozen different functions, each occurring only once, musical themes are limited in number, occur multiple times, and undergo transformations. If musical structure can be mapped upon narrative structure, themes will not represent events but individual agents, and their variations will stand for the tribulations in the lives of characters. A diagram inspired by Lévi-Strauss's analysis of the Oedipus myth enables Tarasti to show simultaneously the diachronic development and the synchronic organization of the symphonic poem *Tasso* by Liszt.

The Lévi-Strauss model captures narrativity on the level of the thematic structure of a particular work. To describe the narrative dynamics inherent to all musical discourse, Tarasti resorts to the Greimassian method of analysis. The premise of this method is that the diachronic unfolding of the work actualizes an achronic structure represented by the so-called semiotic square. The musical work is the product of tensions hidden in its "syntactic structure." The listener's sense of the accomplishment of a narrative program is the result of the resolutions of these tensions, as the musical discourse visits the elements situated at the four corners of the semiotic square and mediates their oppositions. Tarasti invokes another Greimassian concept, "modality," to divide the musical piece into units and describe what he calls its "generative course." To Tarasti the use of the concept of modality in music is a way to talk about meaning in a purely abstract sense, without pinning it down to specific contents. We could perhaps say, with the Danish linguist Louis Hjelmslev (another leading figure of classical structuralism), that modalities describe the form rather than the substance of musical meaning. The analysis of music in terms of modalities is an attempt to give a precise semiotic expression to Schopenhauer's intuition that music captures in its pure form the principle of Will, a principle regarded by the German philosopher as the basis of reality and as the most elementary life-giving force. In Tarasti's system music is not simply Will but the interplay of all modalities: Be, Can, Do, Must, Believe, and Know.

One of the issues that preoccupies "narratological musicologists" is the status of music with respect to the diegetic/mimetic dichotomy. The prominent musicologist Carolyn Abbate has, for instance, pronounced herself in favor of the mimetic analysis: "music is fundamentally different [from told stories], not diegetic but mimetic; like any form of theater, any temporal art, it traps the listener in present experience and the beat of passing time, from which he cannot escape. Mimetic genres perform the story, in the present tense. They cannot disarm the story, or comfort us, by insisting upon its pastness" (228). Yet, as David Bordwell argues in *Narration in the*

Fiction Film, "you can hold a mimetic theory of the novel if you believe the narrational methods of fiction to resemble those of drama, and you can hold a diegetic theory of painting if you posit visual spectacle to be analogous to linguistic transmission" (3). Since the narrativity of music is metaphorical anyway, each approach may provide insights that cannot be reached from the other.

In "If We Put Our Thoughts in Practice: Music, Genre, and Narrative Theory" Peter Rabinowitz takes the diegetic approach. In contrast to Tarasti, Rabinowitz does not focus on the abstract narrativity of instrumental music but on the role of the score in the complex semiotic medium of texted music. His object text is the Broadway musical *Show Boat.* While the essay presents an intriguing analysis of the plot—one in which the final reconciliation of Magnolia and Gaylord Ravenal is interpreted not as the triumph of true love but as the repression of Gay's homosexual identity—its main point is to develop and put into practice a rhetorical approach to musical discourse. (By *rhetorical approach* Rabinowitz means attention to the interplay of the various voices and audiences involved in narrative communication.) Rabinowitz attributes the subversion of the official, stereotyped happy ending of the staged action to a narrative discourse embodied in the score. For Rabinowitz the score is a discourse that originates outside the fictional world: the spectator hears it, but the characters do not; when Magnolia sings to Ravenal, for instance, he interprets her utterance as speech. The voice of the *orchestral* score (as opposed to the tunes of the songs) adds another layer to the narrative onion, the layer of an (implied) authorial/narratorial comment. The opera thus presents the complex situation of a mimetic action reflected upon by a diegetic narration. The extradiegetic nature of the music enables it to perform a wide variety of rhetorical functions, including an ironic relativization of the feelings and values expressed in the plot.

The boldest move in Rabinowitz's analysis of the subversive role of the score with respect to the staged action is the postulation of a fictional use of music. The distinction fiction/nonfiction is a well-established one in verbal narrative. It is also widely used and easily definable in movies and drama. In both cases fictionality is the result of a splitting up of persona: author (or implied author, for those who regard the concept as necessary) versus narrator in diegetic narration; and actor versus character in performance. In nonfiction, by contrast, author and narrator are the same person, and people in real life are expected to perform their own identity.

There have been some attempts to apply the concept of fictionality to the visual arts, with mixed results, but Rabinowitz is the first to propose a musical interpretation of the contrast between fiction and nonfiction. There are, of course, obvious cases of fictional music: for instance, Magnolia performing a song for an audition in the plot of *Show Boat*. Here the music is an intradiegetic phenomenon that can be heard by the members of the fictional world. (The performance should actually be regarded as an embedded fiction, since a singer impersonates Magnolia, who impersonates a character, who is speaking, not singing, in the second-order fictional world.) But Rabinowitz argues that fictionality can occur even in purely instrumental music, whenever musical performance involves the pretense of another performance: for instance, a piece of music in which a "professional concert violinist performing Rimsky-Korsakov" is made by the score to pretend "to be an old blind violinist scratching out Mozart." In either case the fictionality creates a split in the audience. When Magnolia performs an audition song, as Rabinowitz argues, the audience in the theater and the audience in the fictional world do not hear the same song: "For the authorial audience what we have is a good parody of 'bad' music; but from the perspective of the narrative audience, the ragged-up version is an aesthetic sellout." It is the impressive achievement of narratological models and rhetorical approaches to reveal and be able to analyze meaning processes of this degree of subtlety.

§

Because music theory is a relatively esoteric field rarely visited by outsiders, this introduction is followed by an overview, written by Emma Kafalenos, of recent work on the relations between music and narrative.

Notes

I am indebted to Emma Kafalenos for attracting to my attention the musicological articles quoted in the introduction.

1. Anecdote told during a membership drive at the Denver-based public radio station KVOD, 90.1 FM, May 2002.

2. This is the full original title of *The Birth of Tragedy*.

References

Abbate, Carolyn. "What the Sorcerer Said." *19th-Century Music* 12.3 (Spring 1989): 221–30.

Forster, E. M. *Howards End*. Harmondsworth: Penguin, 1989.

Herman, David. *Story Logic: Problems and Possibilities of Narrative*. Lincoln: University of Nebraska Press, 2002.

Langer, Susanne K. *Feeling and Form: A Theory of Art.* New York: Scribner's, 1953.

Nattiez, Jean-Jacques. "The Concepts of Plot and Seriation Process in Music Analysis." Trans. Catherine Dale. *Music Analysis* 4 (1985): 107–18.

Neubauer, John. "Tales of Hoffmann and Others: On Narrativizations of Instrumental Music." *Interart Poetics: Essays on the Interrelations of the Arts and Media.* Ed. Ulla-Britta Lagerroth, Hans Lund, and Erik Hedling. Amsterdam: Rodopi, 1997. 117–36.

Nietzsche, Friedrich. *The Birth of Tragedy and the Case of Wagner.* Trans. Walter Kaufmann. New York: Random House, 1967.

Ricoeur, Paul. *Temps et récit.* Vol. 1. Paris: Seuil, 1983.

9

Overview of the Music and Narrative Field

Emma Kafalenos

The puzzle of what and how music communicates has been the focus of a number of interdisciplinary approaches in the two decades since the publication by the Modern Language Association of a collection of essays surveying relations between literature and other disciplines. That volume, *Interrelations of Literature* (1982), both heralded and encouraged the flourishing of interdisciplinary studies. In an influential essay in that volume Steven Paul Scher divided the field of "musico-literary study" into three categories: "literature in music" (program music: music for which paratextual elements—a title or epigraph, for instance—suggest extramusical connotations); "music and literature" (text settings, ranging from songs by individual performers to full-scale opera), and "music in literature" (literature that emulates musical sounds or strategies or re-presents in words a real or imagined musical passage). Writing in 1989, Lawrence Kramer coined the term *melopoetics,* which Scher approves and uses ("Preface" xiv). As defined by Kramer, *melopoetics* is "a musical/literary criticism" that might "offer [music criticism] greater explicitness, resources of enrichment, wider interpretive adventure" (159, 167).

With this definition Kramer expands the field of interdisciplinary studies in music and literature to include, on the one hand, literary theory and, on the other hand, the object of a potentially enriched criticism: music. Thus, in addition to the three categories of combined forms that Scher envisions as objects of study, Kramer's definition opens the field to instrumental music—sometimes called "untexted music" or "abstract music"— and to methodologies including narrative theory. Instrumental music offers the limit-case example in relation to which to examine whether the lens of literature and literary theories can reveal information about music. For this reason I focus primarily in what follows on relations between narrative theory and instrumental music. Like Kramer, I gauge the value of interdisciplinary studies by how much they contribute to our understanding not only of the borders between disciplines but also the disciplines on each side of the border. According to this criterion, interdisciplinary studies in music and narrative are successful if they reveal something new about how either music or narratives communicate.

Even before Kramer's introduction of the term *melopoetics,* several studies appeared that explored ways of considering instrumental music and narratives or narrative theory in relation to each other. I draw attention to two books by Robert K. Wallace and three articles in *19th-Century Music.* Wallace, whose degrees are in literature but whose background includes broad experience with music, undertook in *Jane Austen and Mozart: Classical Equilibrium in Fiction and Music* (1983) three comparative studies, each analyzing one of Austen's novels in relation to one of Mozart's piano concerti. Demonstrating similarities between the novels and the concerti in form (both large-scale and local-level) and in spirit, he develops for the correspondences he discerns an added value as illustrative of the historical period in which the paired works were written and composed. Both in this book and his later book on Emily Brontë and Beethoven, Wallace reports his findings in a degree of detail that I find informative and satisfying and in language in which he successfully limits the technical terminologies of both music theory and literary studies.

In an article in *19th-Century Music* the musicologist Anthony Newcomb begins by positing that for Schumann instrumental music "was an expressive enterprise and a form of communication, reflecting in some ways the experience of its creator" and then explores possible means through which such communication may occur (233): thematic metamorphosis, the implications of form and genre, intertextual allusions through formal elements to other pieces, and an idea of "plot archetypes" that he develops in a later article (and to which I will return later). In another article in the journal the musicologist Carolyn Abbate uses narrative theory, including the Aristotelian distinction between the diegetic and the mimetic (both of which are forms of narrative according to the definitions used in the present volume), to explore the powerful effects available to music. "Mimetic genres," including music, she notes, "perform the story, in the present tense. They cannot disarm the story, or comfort us, by insisting upon its pastness" (228). Moreover, she points out, instrumental music's inability "to posit a narrating survivor of the tale who speaks of it in the past tense . . . cannot be said to impoverish music; rather it lends music a terrible force to move us by catching us in played-out time. When music ends, it ends absolutely, in the cessation of passing time and movement, in death" (230). In the same journal the composer and music theorist Roland Jordan and I (primarily a literary theorist) describe what we see as a similar structural ambiguity in works from 1892 by Brahms (his Intermezzo, op. 119, no. 1) and Henry James (his story "Owen Wingrave"). [1] The experience of listening to the Intermezzo and of reading the story is colored throughout in both cases, we argue, by contradictory signals that create ambiguity—about the mode and tonality of the Intermezzo (B minor or D major) and about the genre of "Owen Wingrave" (ghost story or realist narrative). Only with the last chord of the Intermezzo can the listener be sure that the tonal center of the piece is B minor; only at the very end of James's story can a reader finally be sure that she is reading a ghost story.

Among the questions elicited by these and other attempts to analyze instrumental music in relation to narratives or narrative theory, I draw attention to three: (1) Do the perceived sounds of instrumental music provide information that permits listeners to (re)construct any form of meaningful sequential pattern, however abstract? (2) If so, are such patterns more akin to narrative or to lyric patterns? (3) In either case, how free is the listener's process of interpreting such patterns as representations of events and agents?

To consider the first of these questions, I want to look at Newcomb's description of "plot archetypes," which he describes as: "various standard configurations of actions or intentions, configurations that are a fundamental part of our vocabulary for interpreting the design and intention of human action and its simulacrum, narrative. These archetypes . . . inform our understanding of liturgies, of paintings, (nowadays) of films—indeed, of all human actions, symbolic or other, wherever we confront them . . . Mastery of this (culture-specific) typology of plots is part of any narrative understanding" ("Narrative Archetypes" 119). Specifying further that the interaction of plot archetype with "formal paradigm, thematic character and recurrence [is not] something external to the musical happenings [but] *produced* by these musical happenings" (120), Newcomb admits that the difficulty of verbalizing the listening process he conceives leaves him naming and describing it "gropingly" (119); talking about how instrumental music means is never easy. I cite Newcomb's comments at some length, both because his description (as I understand it) seems valid and to draw attention to the correlation he sees between plot archetypes in music and the patterns by which we understand events in our lives and in verbally represented narratives. Instrumental music may be most closely related to narratives told in words in that both art forms offer us a repertoire of patterns we can use to shape events in our world while giving us the comfort of experiencing patterns that are more elegantly and more permanently shaped than those we can construct in our lives.

Undoubtedly, our means of specifying how music communicates patterns of events is not yet developed to the degree one may hope it reaches. In my own work on functions (interpretations of an event's causal position in relation to the other elements in a sequential set, according to the definition I use), I assume that readers respond to verbal narratives by constantly interpreting and reinterpreting the causal relations among reported events ("Not [Yet] Knowing"). Listeners, I suggest, may similarly (re)construct a causal sequence of events—events that except for their causal relations remain otherwise unspecified. Other recently developed approaches to understanding how narratives communicate may also prove useful in explaining how listeners interpret meaning in instrumental music. Cognitive theory offers, for instance, the idea of "scripts": grouped pre-interpreted actions (previously experienced actions that are stored in memory along with interpretations of their chronological and causal relations) (see Schank and Abelson; Herman).

The second question pertains to genre: if instrumental music communicates patterns of events, are these patterns more closely related, or more clearly elucidated, with reference to narrative or lyric forms? Lawrence Kramer, responding specifically to Jordan's and my "Double Trajectory" but more generally to all of the early studies that looked at music through the lens of narratives or narrative theory, graciously agrees that considering music (some music) as or in relation to narrative can lead to new understandings about music. But in this article (163–64), as well as throughout his work, Kramer's analyses convincingly demonstrate that music (some music) shares local and global rhythms of lyric forms. Twentieth-century literary texts that elude generic classification, in tandem with recent work in narratology that takes examples of the lyric as objects of study, make any definitive generic distinction unnecessary. But narrative theorists should probably remember that (much) music is often thought to be more closely related to the lyric than to narrative.

To consider the third question—to what degree the listener, if she hears patterns of events in instrumental music, is free to interpret them as representations of specific events and agents—I cite the position John Neubauer expresses in his recent survey of ideas about and examples of narrativizing instrumental music from E. T. A. Hoffmann's famous analysis of Beethoven's Fifth Symphony through the mid-1990s. Neubauer quotes the philosopher Peter Kivy, who proposes that, with the exception of music that imitates sounds in our world, "musical narrative comes down to musical illustration of a narrative text" (Kivy 195). Responding, Neubauer makes two strategic moves. First, he shifts the focus of analysis from the composer's activity to the listener's activity: "[Kivy] may be right if we restrict emplotment to those intended by the composer. Without Berlioz' verbal account we would not know what he encoded in the *Symphonie fantastique*. But this limitation on the composer is precisely the source of freedom for listeners, who may tailor plots to music" (119). Second, Neubauer historicizes the plots that listeners tailor: "Our ability to respond to music from other ages and cultures may [in part] be due to its openness to reemplotment" (126). Whatever one's individual preference (an issue to which I will return), I think that Neubauer is correct in recognizing the variety—and the value of the variety—in whether or not, and with what degree of variation, listeners tailor specific events and agents to fit patterns they hear in music.

In sum, if we refer to the three minimal conditions of narrativity that Marie-Laure Ryan lists in her introduction to this volume, we can argue that instrumental music fulfills the second and third conditions more or less successfully. Most music moves in ways nearly everyone hears as changes of state (condition 2): from one rhythmic pattern to another, theme to theme, fast to slow, major to minor, tonality to tonality. Moreover, listeners need not ascribe these changes of state (or the "events" that introduce the changes) to anthropomorphic agents to (re)construct patterns of goals and successes, networks of causal relations (condition 3); these are patterns that trained listeners will agree (in broadest terms and, of course, with variation) that they hear. For Ryan's first condition, however—that a narrative text create a world and populate it with characters and objects—instrumental music clearly falls short. Instrumental music creates and populates a world only through the imaginative acts of listeners who create, for example, from music that indicates a way of moving, an anthropomorphic character who moves—and who may bear no resemblance to characters that other listeners create in response to the same music.

For some listeners, perhaps many listeners, the power of instrumental music to represent changes of state and causal relations *without* specifying events or agents is a positive rather than a negative quality. The visual arts offer a comparison. When I look at a painting that I see as nonrepresentational, my pleasure is diminished if someone guides me to identify a vertical column as a smokestack or to interpret a pattern of subtly shading bluish reds as a product of infrared photography. Similarly, in my experience of instrumental music there is motion and change and as complex a network of causal interrelations as in a deeply satisfying novel, but no anthropomorphic beings and no specific actions in which such beings could engage. From the more limited cultural perspective of an earlier era, one perceiver's preference for abstraction and another perceiver's preference for peopling a world defined contrasting positions on an elite-popular cultural axis. In the poststructuralist era ushered in by the publication of *S/Z* in 1970, evaluation is aligned, Roland Barthes announces, with the "writerly"; the reader is to be "no longer a consumer, but a producer of the text" (4). The composer Benjamin Boretz accords to the listener (not the composer or the performer) "the ultimate act of musical creation": "Listening is do-it-yourself composing. Composing is speculative listening. Potentially, the realm of musical experience can be the creative-intellectual responsibility of each music-experiencing (hence, music-making) person" (107–8). Neubauer from a post-elitist cultural perspective, Barthes from a poststructuralist aesthetics, and Boretz from a phenomenological position all concede authority to the perceiver's creative act. Barthes, moreover, specifically links the aesthetic (and perhaps ethical) value he claims for the writerly to its polysemy: "The more plural the text, the less it is written before I read it" (10). Instrumental music, because it is unburdened by the semantic meanings (however polysemous) attached to verbal signifiers, is more writerly than even the most plural constructs made from words.

In any comparative enterprise it is as important to pay attention to differences as to similarities. When unaccompanied by text or paratext, instrumental music shares narrative features but should probably not be thought of *as* narrative. [2] Because music, like narratives told in words, offers a formally patterned experiencing of time and instrumental music does this without the world building and populating that so readily absorb readers' attention, music offers to music theorists and narrative theorists a laboratory to explore the puzzle of how (and what, in addition to worlds) narratives communicate. In complementary fashion narrative theory offers strategies that can unlock pieces of the puzzle of what and how music communicates.

Notes

1. When this article was published, I had not yet read Shlomith Rimmon-Kenan's important book on James, in which she locates in certain of his late stories and novels "structural ambiguity": the coexistence of two mutually exclusive *fabulas* (stories) in one *sjuzhet* (discourse) (41, 50). Our findings repeat hers.

2. The music theorist Fred Maus ends his entry on "Narratology, Narrativity" in

The New Grove Dictionary of Music on a similarly provisory note: "The exploration of instrumental music as narrative remains a tantalizing, confusing, problematic area of inquiry" (May 5, 2002).

References

Abbate, Carolyn. "What the Sorcerer Said." *19th-Century Music* 12.3 (Spring 1989): 221–30.

Barthes, Roland. *S/Z: An Essay* (1970). Trans. Richard Miller. New York: Hill and Wang, 1974.

Boretz, Benjamin A. "The Logic of What?" *Journal of Music Theory* 33 (1989): 107–16.

Herman, David. "Scripts, Sequences, and Stories: Elements of a Postclassical Narratology." *PMLA* 112.5 (October 1997): 1046–59.

Jordan, Roland, and Emma Kafalenos. "The Double Trajectory: Ambiguity in Brahms and Henry James." *19th-Century Music* 13.2 (Fall 1989): 129–44.

Kafalenos, Emma. "Not (Yet) Knowing: Epistemological Effects of Deferred and Suppressed Information in Narrative." *Narratologies: New Perspectives on Narrative Analysis.* Ed. David Herman. Columbus: Ohio State University Press, 1999. 33–65.

Kivy, Peter. *Sound and Semblance: Reflections on Musical Representation.* 2d ed. Ithaca: Cornell University Press, 1991.

Kramer, Lawrence. "Dangerous Liaisons: The Literary Text in Musical Criticism." *19th-Century Music* 13.2 (1989): 159–67.

Maus, Fred Everett. "Narratology, Narrativity." *The New Grove Dictionary of Music Online.* Ed. L. Macy. <http://www.grovemusic.com> (May 5, 2002).

Neubauer, John. "Tales of Hoffmann and Others: On Narrativizations of Instrumental Music." *Interart Poetics: Essays on the Interrelations of the Arts and Media.* Ed. Ulla-Britta Lagerroth, Hans Lund, and Erik Hedling. Amsterdam: Rodopi, 1997. 117–36.

Newcomb, Anthony. "Once More 'Between Absolute and Program Music': Schumann's Second Symphony." *19th-Century Music* 7.3 (April 1984): 233–50.

———. "Narrative Archetypes and Mahler's Ninth Symphony." *Music and Text: Critical Inquiries.* Ed. Steven Paul Scher. Cambridge: Cambridge University Press, 1992. 118–36.

Rimmon-Kenan, Shlomith. *The Concept of Ambiguity—The Example of James.* Chicago: University of Chicago Press, 1977.

Schank, Roger C., and Robert P. Abelson. *Scripts, Plans, Goals, and Understanding: An Inquiry into Human Knowledge Structures.* Hillsdale NJ: Lawrence Erlbaum, 1977.

Scher, Steven Paul. "Literature and Music." *Interrelations of Literature.* Ed. Jean-Pierre Barricelli and Joseph Gibaldi. New York: Modern Language Association, 1982. 225–50.

————. "Preface." *Music and Text: Critical Inquiries.* Ed. S. P. Scher. Cambridge: Cambridge University Press, 1992. xiii–xvi.

Wallace, Robert K. *Jane Austen and Mozart: Classical Equilibrium in Fiction and Music.* Athens: University of Georgia Press, 1983.

————. *Emily Brontë and Beethoven: Romantic Equilibrium in Fiction and Music.* Athens: University of Georgia Press, 1986.

10

Music as a Narrative Art

Eero Tarasti

As a general rule, the minimal condition of narrativity is the transformation of an object or state of affairs into something else through a process that requires a certain amount of time. It is true that narrativity may emerge in nonlinear (and consequently nontemporal) texts, such as painting. But in this case the movement of the mind leads vertically toward what lies under the text rather horizontally with the flow of the text: a picture is narrative if it is iconographically related to some mythological event or if it represents a decisive turning point in a story. On the basis of these hypotheses we may argue that music constitutes a fundamentally narrative art. It unfolds in time, and very often we feel that something happens in a musical piece— even if we are completely unable to verbalize our experience. In the case of the purest form of music—the "absolute" music of the Western erudite tonal art—we may think of the meaning that the composition tries to convey as an abstract plot. There are admittedly scholars who believe that music as such does not tell us any story; it is only we, music listeners, who put our personal associations and meanings into the musical text. It is in this spirit that Claude Lévi-Strauss characterized music as "le langage moins le sens" (language minus meaning) (*Mythologiques* 579). The semiotic approach to music that I will expose in this essay does not claim to be able to show that music is able to *tell* particular stories. I will try, instead, to show which structures in music enable us to *associate* it with stories. The issue of narrativity in music is a complex matter that varies according to styles, periods, and cultural contexts. In what follows I shall deal with many facets of this problem, drawing inspiration from some of the most sophisticated models of narrative grammars developed in the history of semiotics and applying them to a wide variety of musical discourse and musical styles.

Music Narrating Myths: The Proppian Model

In archaic societies—or, as we may say, "ethnosemiotic societies"—myths are transmitted through tales that are often performed with music. It is therefore understandable that Western music began its narrative development by applying its storytelling capacity to mythical content. The cultural manifestation of myth includes a variety of sign systems and discourses besides music. Throughout cultural history we see certain myths occupy over and over again the imagination of authors, painters, and composers. Referring to Claude Bremond, one may say that myth can be transposed from one technique to another without losing any of its essential qualities. We are reading words, looking at pictures, and perceiving gestures—but through them we follow a common story. We can thus distinguish two interacting levels of narrativity: "the related" (*le raconté*), or the story which is told; and "the relator" (*le racontant*), the special manner in which it is told (*Logique* 12). This opposition is known as *fabula* versus *sjuzhet* in Russian formalism and as story versus discourse in American narratology (see, for example, Chatman).

The story to be narrated does not consist of words, pictures, or tunes but of events, situations, and behaviors. How, then, can we examine the mythical narrative lurking behind the signs? The Russian school of folklore, more particularly Vladimir Propp in his analysis of Russian folktales, undertook the development of a model that reveals the articulation of mythical stories. Propp calls the minimal unit of such a narration a "function." *Function* is to be conceived as an act of some protagonist in the narration, an act whose meaning is defined in relation to the story as a whole. Propp hypothesized that the number of functions in folktales is limited and that they always follow the same successive order. On the basis of the functions represented in his corpus, Propp was able to categorize folktales with different content as belonging to the same type. He listed thirty-one functions, among them "the hero's absence," "interdiction," "violation," "departure," "struggle," "return," and "pursuit," and "recognition." Each story picks its own functions from this repertory and composes its own sequence. Propp condensed these individual sequences and compiled them into a prototypical chain. This chain, which constitutes a paradigm for all the narratives of the same type, is only incompletely manifested in individual texts. Consequently, where at the outset there are several parallel and defective chains of functions (Tarasti, *Myth and Music* 56–60),

A . . . . C . . . . G

```
. . . . . B . . . . . . . . . D . . . E . . . . . G
A . . B . . . . . . . . . . . . . . E . . F . . . .
```

Propp reconstructs the master sequence:

$$A \ldots B \ldots C \ldots D \ldots E \ldots F \ldots G$$

This model can be transposed to various domains of Western erudite music, such as opera, ballets, symphonic poems, and symphonies that try to narrate a mythical story. The functions of the mythical story, "the related" (*le raconté*), are distributed on two narrative levels, mythical text and music:

```
Myth as text    A . . . B . . . C . . . D . . . E . . . F . . . G
Music                   A' . B' . . C' . D' . . E' . . F' . . G'
```

In this example the story is told through two simultaneous channels, verbal text and music. This situation describes the opera. But music can also take over the narrative function in those spots where the text keeps silent:

```
Myth as a text    A . . . B . . . . . . . . . . . . E . . . . . . . . . G
Music                   . . . . . . . . . . C . . . D . . . . . . . . F . . . .
```

In the extreme case we have the situation of an abstract symphony or almost abstract symphonic poem carrying the narration without any textual support.

We must keep in mind that Propp originally developed his model to deal with folkloric texts and not with artistic texts such as operas or symphonies. The psychology of the protagonists of a mythical story in the authentic sense may be no longer valid for the conduct of heroes in other sociosemiotic contexts. I have nevertheless attempted to apply Proppian, as well as Levi-Straussian, [1] models to analyze the narrative techniques of the symphonic poems of Franz Liszt. (Lévi-Strauss's study of the myth of Oedipus is found in *Mythologiques* [235–42].) These poems illustrate the case of the complete disappearance of the mythical text. It therefore falls to the music alone to manifest an immanent mythical structure. "Functions" in such a narration are closely related to the concept of musical theme. Yet the musical themes of these compositions could not provide viable counterparts for mythical functions because their number is too limited: the symphonic poems typically contain only one to five different themes. It is, rather, the transformations of these few and distinctly discernible themes in the course of the composition, as well as their appearance in always new orchestral colors and harmonic modulations, that depict musically the mythical functions.

It was Liszt's idea—or actually Berlioz's—to identify individual themes with a mythical hero. In this approach the variations on a given theme in the various sections of the composition reflected the vicissitudes of the life of the hero and his variable moods. In his essay on Berlioz's *Harold Symphony,* written in 1855, Liszt exposes his theoretical conception of the musical form of a programmatic, symphonic poem. Liszt's themes can be classified according to their isotopies and semes, as the research of Marta Grabócz, and my own, have shown (Grabócz, *Morphologie* 116–23). But what interests me the most in Liszt's music is the processual aspect of its narrativity: how the story launches, unfolds, and closes. Claude Bremond has suggested that every narrative passes through three phases: (1) eventuality (virtualité), defined as the situation that opens the possibility for an event or action; (2) passage to either action or nonaction; and (3) outcome of the action (that is, its success or failure). These phases correspond to the three moments in the unfolding of musical form identified by the Russian musicologist Boris Asafiev: *initium, motus,* and *terminus.* For instance, the symphonic poem *Tasso* by Liszt is based on four themes: Lamento, Strepitoso, Tasso, and Pastorale. Basing the analysis on the occurrences of these themes, the whole piece can be projected into the chart of figure 10.1, which can be read in the same two ways as the "orchestral" scores used by Lévi-Strauss in his analysis of myths—either by following the vertical columns and observing the different variants and occurrences of a single theme or by following the succession of themes horizontally, the musical structure then being observed in its temporal order, that is, in the same order as we hear it.

In *Tasso* the tonal relations between various occurrences of the same theme have an important structural and narrative function. The most effective point is the transition from the C minor at the beginning of the work to such a distant tonality as F sharp major in the pastoral section in the middle of the work. This produces a tritonic tension. Then the musical narration returns (or is "engaged" [*embrayé*], if we follow Greimas's terminology) to the tonic starting point.

Narrativity in Music History

Musical narration can be approached as a musico-historical problem, especially if one places the issue in the context of the global cognitive models that organize both musical discourse and discourse about music in different periods. (The Classical and Romantic period had a particularly strong discourse model.) To address the issue of the evolving conception of narrative

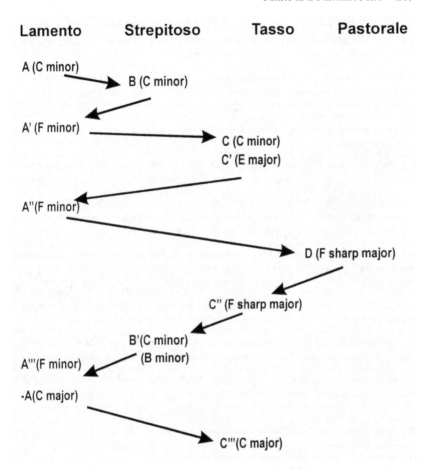

Lamento	Strepitoso	Tasso	Pastorale
A (C minor)	B (C minor)		
A' (F minor)		C (C minor)	
		C' (E major)	
A'' (F minor)			D (F sharp major)
		C'' (F sharp major)	
	B' (C minor)		
A''' (F minor)	(B minor)		
-A (C major)			
		C''' (C major)	

Figure 10.1. Analysis of the symphonic poem *Tasso* by Liszt, according to Lévi-Strauss's structural model of myth.

in music history, it will be useful to distinguish two kinds of narrativity: one is inherent to musical structure, and the other corresponds to a particular gesture, a given narrative style. For the proponents of the second viewpoint not every musico-syntactic structure is a narrative structure; otherwise, all music would be narrative. An undeniable fact of musical experience is that, when we listen to, say, the first measures of Scriabin's First Symphony, we might sigh and say, "How narrative!" On the other hand, there is a lot of music that does not try to tell a story. Our first task is consequently to determine the distinctive features of narrativity in music.

One way to approach the problem is to view musical narrativity as a latent trait that only emerges through certain modalizations, that is, through certain ways of interpreting and performing a musical work. It seems that some artists have a special ability to perform music in a narrative way. Some pianists or violinists are said to possess a narrative touch or sound. This possibility seems quite believable, since we generally have to distinguish between two conceptions of musical semantics. In the first a musical utterance possesses an invariant semantic content; in the second a musical utterance can be pronounced in a way that imbues it with semantic significance. French semioticians—or, rather, the so-called Paris school of semiotics—would say that narrativity should be investigated on the level of musical utterance (*énoncé musical*) as well as that of musical performance (*énonciation musicale*). There is consequently a type of narrativity that only emerges when the performer or listener connects an element from what Boris Asafiev calls the "intonational store" (that is, the collection of musical motifs held in a collective memory) to a musical structure. This type of narrativity cannot be analyzed without accounting for the interaction between musical subject and object in the process of musical communication.

Let us consider some cases in music history that show how narrativity emerges through specific processes of signification. As we investigate these processes, it is important to remember that semiotics involves two phenomena: communication *and* signification (Sebeok, *A Sign* 22–35). We may thus speak in music of structures of communication and of structures of signification. The term *communication* describes the entire process through which messages are transmitted from a sender, or destinator, to a receiver, or addressee. In a musical work a structure of communication is one of those forms that a composer needs to master in order to convey a certain idea or meaning to a listener (Tarasti, *Theory* 16–17). Such structures vary according to periods: if you were a Baroque composer, you would certainly master general bass and fugue techniques; if you were a Viennese classicist, you would resort to forms such as sonata or symphony, and, if you were a contemporary avant-garde composer, you would need to learn techniques ranging from spectral music to serialism and aleatorics. These structures are needed to transmit ideas that possess their own internal structure. This is what I would call "a structure of signification." It consists of a particular combination of signifier and signified, and it can be described through semiotic concepts such as semes and isotopies.

Both of these types of structure need to be taken into account in the study of musical narrativity. Which one is the more fundamental?

Let me discuss some historical examples. The first is the subject of J. S. Bach's Fugue in C sharp minor, from book 1 of the *Well-Tempered Clavier* (fig. 10.2).

Figure 10.2. Musical motive in J. S. Bach's Fugue in C sharp minor.

What does this musical motive mean? An entire five-voice fugue is constructed upon it, and in this sense it represents "absolute" music—the piece involves no semantics, only the syntactic rules of the fugal technique. For music listeners of the Baroque period, however, this fugue subject functioned as a meaningful musical sign: it represented the Cross and thus the death of Christ, as shown in figure 10.3.

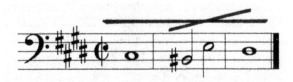

Figure 10.3. Musical motive in J. S. Bach's Fugue in C sharp minor interpreted as symbol of the Cross.

Competent listeners of the time were familiar with this meaning and would have recognized it in Bach's fugue subject. The same religious meaning is preserved when that subject is quoted, for instance, in the prelude to César Franck's Prélude, chorale et fugue, even though nineteenth-century listeners might no longer have been aware of the original symbolism. Some later interpreters have taken the religious quality of this theme and of the entire fugue so seriously that they play it as a deeply mystic, almost silent music. This is how Sviatoslav Richter plays it. Others do not "modalize" the music in the same way as Richter did. The Viennese professor Bruno Seidlhofer writes, for instance, that if "Bach writes a five-part fugue it is certainly not a silent music."

As another example, let us consider the opening motive of Beethoven's Piano Sonata in E flat major (Op. 81a), "Les Adieux," shown in figure 10.4.

Figure 10.4. Opening motive of Beethoven's Piano Sonata in E flat major (Op. 81a), "Les Adieux."

What is it that makes this motive sound both pastoral and melancholic at the same time? The interval sequence of major third–perfect fifth–minor sixth appeared in many works by eighteenth-century composers such as Mozart and Haydn. This particular sequence of intervals referred to courtly "hunting calls" and, by extension, to the outdoor life of nobles. Beethoven knew this, but he added to the standard signification the intimacy of romantic thought. Normally, the "horn fifths" ascend; here, by having them descend and close on a false cadence, Beethoven makes the horn call a symbol of "farewell." This is one of the ways musical signs function: they can be shifted from one context to another in such a way that they change from signals into symbols. When many such musical signs are linked together in a piece, according to a certain plan, or "plot," music becomes a narrative art. Mozart also knew this technique—see, for instance, his Fantasy in C minor K. 396, which offers us as a series the topos of "Storm and stress," "French Ouverture," "Empfindsamkeit," "Galant," and "Learned style" (see Ratner; see also Tarasti, *Theory* 26).

We have thus imperceptibly moved from music as the conveyor of isolated meanings to music as a narrative art. Any music lover of the time could follow the plot of a piece, if the plot were constructed on the surface level of easily recognizable topics. But only the specialist knew about the deeper tonal-harmonic implications. The success of the so-called classical style was based on a multilayered organization that offered something to all types of music listeners.

Continuing in this tradition, Romantic composers often associated their music with literary and poetic programs, which were indicated either by the title of the piece or by a direct quotation printed in the score. A good example is Robert Schumann's Fantasy in C major, a three-movement piano work of almost symphonic dimensions. The score quotes as its motto the following lines from a poem by Friedrich Schlegel:

Durch alle Töne tönet
im bunten Erdentraum
ein leiser Ton gezogen
für den der heimlich lauschet.

(Through all the tones sounds in a bright dream of the earth, a silent tone to the one who listens secretly.)

Schumann thus clearly indicates that the piece should be played and understood in the light of this enigmatic poem. What is that "silent" tone that can be heard only secretly? Some say it is the descending fifth as a sign evoking the composer's famous spouse, the pianist and composer Clara Wieck. This interval is indeed prominent in the piece. The problem, of course, is that it also appears in countless other works by Schumann and by other composers as well. The Schumann example suggests that musical meanings are not strictly lexicographic but always depend on the context in which they appear.

Literary association must be invoked for other passages in the piece—for instance, in the third movement with its timelessly floating upper-register melody over the arpeggiation: this has always evoked, at least to me, the final scene of Goethe's *Faust II,* the choir of the spirits in the mountains. This is almost the only music in German romanticism sufficiently immaterial and spiritual to activate this literary interpretant.

In the late nineteenth century the investigation of literary texts as a source of musical meaning became the province of musical hermeneutics. Writing in 1936, the musical hermeneuticist Arnold Schering argued that every Beethoven composition had a "secret" program that referred to some literary work by Goethe or Schiller. For instance, the funeral march theme of the Allegretto of Beethoven's Seventh Symphony evoked the funeral of Mignon in Goethe's *Wilhelm Meister;* Beethoven's Piano Sonata in A flat major (Op. 110) referred to Schiller's tragedy, *Maria Stuart;* the Waldstein Sonata to Goethe's poem *Hermann und Dorothea;* and so on. Schering was criticized for these proposals (see, for example, Ringbom), but he defended himself by saying that he had not claimed that narrative programs would necessarily be associated with these compositions by the listener. They had only served as tools and support when the "building" was being constructed, but they could be left out after it was completed.

It cannot be denied that composers of the Romantic period drew inspiration from the interrelations of the arts. For instance, when Beethoven composed overtures to Shakespeare's *Coriolanus* and Goethe's *Egmont,* he spontaneously assumed that the music he was writing would be understood as "narrative" in nature. But musical narratives do not necessarily follow the same routes as literary ones do. For instance, in *Egmont* the sinister Spanish court is portrayed at the very beginning by ominous, heavy chords. It is difficult to pinpoint the musical sign of the character Egmont, but the music's dramatic conflicts forcefully portray his struggles for the freedom of the Flemish people. Yet the ending of Beethoven's music is significantly different from the last scene of Goethe's play. At the end of the drama Egmont is in prison, where in a dreamlike vision he sees himself celebrated as a hero. After this uplifting scene, however, the play closes on the dark note of his execution. Beethoven's composition reinterprets the narrative by inverting these two moments: first we hear the execution, followed by a chorale, and then the music celebrates the triumph of the hero, suggesting that he has not died but continues to live, at least symbolically, in a transcendental form.

In the overture to *Coriolan* the music highlights the gender issues that the narrative puts into play. Coriolanus, an extremely stubborn, proud, and capricious character, has his iconic theme appear very early in the composition. The continuously flickering eighth-note texture of the main section seems to depict and develop the intrigues of the Roman people against him. Coriolanus' spouse, mother, children—all the characters who represent softness, peacefulness, feminine qualities, in the play—are depicted with a beautifully singing side theme. As we know from the drama, Coriolanus leaves Rome, joins the army of its enemies, and returns to Rome as their leader. In a desperate move the Romans send Coriolanus' wife, mother, and children to persuade him not to attack his hometown. Giving in to the tender emotions aroused by the sight of his loved ones, Coriolanus then decides to act against his basic character. His change of heart causes him to be killed. This process is portrayed in Beethoven's music by the victory of the feminine side theme over the masculine Coriolanus theme. This example could be invoked in support of the well-known theory of the musicologist A. B. Marx, who analyzed the sonata form in terms of a masculine main theme and a feminine side theme.

As Arnold Schering observed, literary programs sometimes disappear in the course of the composition process. According to what we know about the life of the composer, Ernst Chausson's famous violin piece "Poème" is based upon Turgenev's story "L'Hymne de l'amour triumphant" ("The

Song of Triumphant Love"). The narrative program is designated as such in the first draft of the piece but not in the final draft. Knowing these facts, we hear and experience the piece quite differently from the way we would respond to it if we did not know about the program.

Musical pieces are like decks of cards: they may consist of the same cards as the literary work that provides their narrative program, but the games we play with each deck are quite different. The cases discussed here should make the point that music is not just one simple sign among other signs; it is a logically ordered sequence of signs—that is to say, a narrative.

Let us now scrutinize the other theory of musical narrativity: namely, the view that narrative is a structure inherent to music. This theory derives from a broader conception of narrative, according to which narrative is a basic category of the human mind, a specialized competence that manifests itself in the temporal ordering of events into a syntagmatic continuum. This continuum has a beginning, development, and end. Yet, according to some analytic systems, such as the semiotic theory of A. G. Greimas and the music theory of Heinrich Schenker (see also Littlefield), the linear unfolding of a work is supported in the background by some totally achronic structure. For Greimas this structure is the so-called semiotic square, with its network of logical relations among semes s1 and s2 and their "negations" non-s1 and non-s2; for Schenker it is a tonic triad. According to these theorists, the narrative-generative process unfolds as a gradual expansion, or "composing out," of this achronic fundamental structure. Schenkerian analysis, which is the dominant method on the American musicological scene, is admittedly concerned with musical space (registral and tonal organization or the so-called pitch structure) and *not* with temporal organization per se. Schenker said, for instance, that there is no rhythm in the *Hintergrund* (that is, in its deep structure). Yet Schenker's method could easily be developed into a method of narrative analysis for musical compositions. Its basic premise—that a musical work is a totality created by a structure in which all events relate to a basic model and to the tension provided by this model—offers a close equivalent to the syntagmatic demand of narrativity. (There have been some efforts to combine Schenker and Greimas by John Ellis in the United States and by Tom Pankhurst from Manchester, England, but there is still a lot of work to be done in this promising avenue.) We may postulate that narrativity in music is based on an immanent process of signification, that is, on modal structures that are tensions hidden in the syntactical structures. How these tensions can be analyzed is our next question.

The Greimasian Model in the Analysis of Musical Narration

The most fundamental problem in the narrative analysis of music is the segmentation of the musical text into units suitable for a closer examination. If we conceive the essence of music as processual and dynamic, it is difficult to discuss and analyze a piece as a whole with all its subtleties: we simply need to divide the piece into smaller "narrative programs." For instance, in the Polonaise Fantasy by Chopin, I have distinguished ten programs and in his G minor Ballade thirteen. The main purpose of my dissection of the former piece was to define which terms of the semiotic square are given first and which ones remain hidden, "hanging in the air" and given only at the end of the piece as a "solution" to the initial problem (see fig. 10.8). In this case the terms given first were the opening chords representing "plunging" and the opening arpeggio, which portrayed the principle of rising. These two terms are situated at s2 and non-s1, respectively. Many have asked why they are not taken as s1 and non-s2. The opening cannot be anything like a "positive" statement—and hence s1—since what is involved is in many senses a "distanciated" polonaise, both rhythmically and harmonically. The arpeggio cannot be seen as something positive either; it is, rather, a negation of something not yet heard as a particularly firm statement. One may, of course, question altogether the relevance of the semiotic square for music, as David Lidov has done (*Elements* 136). I propose it here tentatively as a tool that may help us distinguish logical possibilities in the semantic field of a given piece, as it articulates its inherent tensions (Tarasti, *Myth and Music* 138–54).

The basic purpose of my analysis of Chopin G-minor Ballade was to propose the concept of a "generative course" (Tarasti, *Myth and Music* 154–80). This concept is my own free adaptation of Greimas's model to musical texts. A generative course consists of four levels: (1) Isotopies; (2) Spatial, Temporal, and Actorial articulations; (3) Modalities; and (4) Phemes/Semes. Through this structuration it is already a narrative model. My approach postulates that isotopies form the deep level from which all signification emanates. Isotopy is consciously left as an intuitive, somewhat vaguely defined idea of a "level of meaning" from which a text or its parts derive their coherence. In the process known as "discursivization" isotopies manifest themselves in space and time or through actors. In musical space one may distinguish between external, or outer, and internal, or inner, space, the former meaning the different registers (high/low) that music occupies and the latter the inner movement from tonic to dominant—in atonal music, for instance. In the time dimension, again, two paradigms come into play: the paradigm of memory, which means the accumulation of musical events in the memory of a listener, and the paradigm of expectations, which of course reach their high point at the beginning of the piece. These principles correspond to the information-theoretical principles of redundancy and entropy. At the beginning, when anything can still happen in a musical piece, the entropy and information are at a maximum. As the piece progresses, the content of memory increases, and so does the redundancy that grows along with it. The concept of "actoriality" represents the anthropomorphic side of music. In the European classical-romantic style, it is normally identified with a theme and with thematicism, but in a broader sense it represents all that by which a listener projects him- or herself into the music. Even the slightest reference to the musical practices of previous centuries in an avant-garde piece serves as a glimpse of actoriality in music. It is hard to imagine any music without a hint of it.

From the articulations of these categories, which can be objectively measured and observed, emerge what is perhaps the most important aspect of musical narrativity, namely the play of modalities. Greimas himself described the elaboration of a system of modalities as a "third semiotic revolution." (According to Greimas ["Vers une troisième révolution"], the first revolution in semiotics was the development of semantics as an independent discipline, thanks to the French linguist Michel Bréal, and the second was the invention of structural linguistics by Ferdinand de Saussure.) The concept of "modality" is ambiguous. In logic it means ideas such as "must" or "know," and it forms the basis of the so-called deontic and alethic systems. (For an application of these systems, see the work of George Henrik v. Wright on the logic of action.) In linguistics it means the way by which we animate our speech and provide it with human content. Examples of such modalities are expectation, certainty, and the expression of various emotions. In music theory we speak of the so-called Church modes, which correspond to special types of musical scales, such as Ionian, Phrygian, and Lydian. These meanings are not entirely separate from one another. According to the theory of "ethos" in the antiquity, a musical mode can, for instance, have a modal content in a logical or linguistic sense.

The most important aspect of the concept of modality is that it provides music and other sign systems with a meaning that cannot be fixed into any lexicographic unit or verbal concept. It represents semanticism without any particular semantic content. The presence of modalities in the musical utterance—that is, in the score itself—means the existence of a kind of structural logic that is embedded in the musical message. One can also speak of modalities—that is to say, of a process of modalization—in the performance of or listening to music. This means practically the same thing as what we normally understand by musical interpretation: we can "modalize" the same piece in different ways. For instance, I have studied twenty-one different interpretations, or modalizations, of the same melody by Gabriel Fauré, "Après un rêve." Each enunciator can adopt a different approach to the modalities of the piece. We can thus regard modalities as the source of musical narrativity, without implying that a particular story is being told (Tarasti, *Myth and Music* 193–208, 293–301).

The prevalent modalities of music are "being" and "doing," in addition to the normal temporal process of music, which I call "becoming." *Being* means a state of rest, stability, and consonance; *doing* is synonymous with musical action: event, dynamism, and dissonance. The alternation between tension, doing, and de-tension, being, forms a tiny "narrative" program, or, to speak metaphorically, a kind of "organic narrativity." A number of theories, from Wilhelm Furtwängler to Ivanka Stoïanova, elaborate on this alternation. Stoïanova speaks about architectonic and immobilizing forces that try to stop the musical flow, whose normal course is the forward movement of doing, and reduce it into being (*Manuel* 9). Some music theorists, among them Asafiev and Schenker, regard the two forces as a kind of "biological" necessity inherent to tonal music. Bu this type of metaphysics has generally fallen into discredit.

The basic modalities of being and doing are sur-modalized by several others: *will,* the so-called kinetic energy of music, its general direction, its tendency to move toward a goal;[2] *know,* the information conveyed by music, its cognitive moment; *can,* the power and efficiency of music, what is displayed in performance: techniques, idiomatic writing, virtuosity; *must,* the control exercised by the rules of genres and formal types, such as sonata, fugue, rondo, chaconne—more generally, the pressure for a musical composition to follows aesthetic or technical norms and prescriptions specific to its time—and, finally *believe,* the epistemic values of music, its persuasiveness in reception, the distribution of epistemic values such as truth/untruth, lie/secret, in short the music felt as a "true speech," to quote the formula of Boris Asafiev (*Musical Form* 710).

Musical modalities manifest themselves in various degrees. We can have either too much or too little of each of them. They are, of course, continuous and processual in nature, but we can for analytical purposes "digitalize" their presence into five distinct degrees: *excessive,* indicated by the sign ++; *rather much* (+); *sufficient* (0); *too little* (-); and *insufficient* (= ———). Despite the apparent arbitrariness of these divisions, the values and degrees of modalities are not subjective properties, although it takes a competent

Table 10.1. *Analysis of narrative semes in Chopin's G minor Ballade*

	Be/Do	Will	Know	Can	Must	Believe
I	not to-do	+	+	0	0	mãb
II	to be	0	+	0→+	+	mab̄
III	to do	++	-	+→++	+→0	mab→m̃ab̄
IV	not-to-do	0	+	0	+	m̃ab
V	not-to-be, trans-	-	0	0	0	m̃ab+
VI	not-to-be, trans+	+→++	-	0	-	m̃ab→m+ab
VII	to appear to do	++	+→-	+→++	0	m+ab̄
VIII	not-to-be	+	+→-	++	0	m+āb→m̃ab
IX	to appear to be	-→0	0	++	-	mab̄
X	to be	0→+	-	-	++	m̃+ab
XI	not-to-be, trans+	+→++	-	-	+	m̃+ab̄→m̃ab
XII	to do	++	+→0	-→++	-	m+ab
XIII	to do = to be	++→0	+→++	++	0	mab

music listener to notice their distribution all over the piece. Leo Treitler recently told me that he believes that modalities are something that the analyst brings into music. I do believe, on the contrary, that they exist immanently in the structure of the musical text, but they can also be introduced in the musical performance. It is clear, however, that the interpreter cannot modalize music arbitrarily: the modalities of the performance and those inherent to the score must be compatible with each other. It could be objected that the modalities defined here are not universal, that is, independent of the style and culture. Modalities have not yet been studied in ethnomusicology, but, if a semiotic theory is to be valid, it should be so in the broadest anthropological sense.

The last phase of musical generation produces the level of phemes and semes, that is, the surface structure of music, the music actually heard. The analysis of this level focuses on the smallest units of signifiers and signifieds, namely the phemes and semes. Thus, narrativity can be analyzed as a very complex, multilayered process. It leads ultimately into a formalized model that appears in the aforementioned case of Chopin G minor Ballade as follows (Tarasti, *Myth and Music* 177):

One may ask about the utility of such a rigorous procedure. I believe that we need such a technical metalanguage in order to take the problem of narrativity to a higher conceptual level. The model enables us to analyze narrativity in music with methods similar to those that have already proved fruitful in other fields, especially in literary studies. One of the tasks of the musicologist is to make explicit the implicit structures of music in such a way that they will be understandable even for those who belong to a different culture. We live in a multicultural world in which everybody, in principle, has access to any musical style. But not everybody has the competence necessary to understand musical narrativity. In order to build this competence we need to analyze music into parameters and entities, so as to explain on what elements musical narrative is based.

The Subjects of Musical Narrative

The role of the subject in musical narration forms its own problem. In the so-called musical hermeneutics of the Romantic age the subject of the enounced (*énoncé*) was naively confused with the subject of the enunciation. Listeners identified the sufferings and glorifications of the Fantastic Symphony by Hector Berlioz with those of the real composer. Biographical studies still easily fall into this trap. In some cases the biography of the composer is the only evidence for the claim that a certain theme was indeed a portrayal of a certain real person in a composer's life. The alto theme in Alban Berg's violin concerto or certain themes in the Symphonie Pathétique by Tchaikovsky have, for instance, been interpreted as representations of the composer's real-life lover. I rather endorse the view of Carl Dahlhaus, who insisted as a matter of principle that the hero of a Mahlerian symphony cannot be the composer himself.

We cannot apply directly to music the simple model of communication, according to which a message encoded as an acoustic stream of sounds goes from a sender (composer) to a listener via a performer working with or without instruments. The simple model should be replaced by a model of narrative action because a narrative model takes a step toward the universe of signification. A musical situation lies at the crossroads of signification and communication, the place where physical/implied author and physical/implied listener meet (cf. Chatman; Booth).

The whole world of a narrative musical text unfolds between the implied composer and the implied listener. This means that Beethoven as a physical person and Beethoven as an "implied composer" are two different entities. By the same reasoning the Duke Razumovsky as a physical listener and the implied listeners postulated by the implied composer "Beethoven," the master of the classical style, are two different entities. Moreover, in the work itself there is a (musical) narrator, who organizes musical events according to an inner logic while taking into account a possible audience. For instance, a narrator in the song "An die ferne Geliebte" presumes a distant beloved to whom the musical story is addressed. In the sonata "Les Adieux" a narrator arranges the events into a plot and assumes that his audience will be able to "decode" it correctly. One can go a step farther: a composition may produce a theme actor, who acts musically in such a way that it influences another theme actor, who functions as recipient of this action. Music thus instantiates a relationship between agent and patient. For instance, in the first movement of "Les Adieux" the horn motive that opens the introduction influences the motive in the attacca beginning of the Allegro.

To represent this analysis graphically, the narrativity of music—and in this case all music is theoretically narrative—has the type of structure shown in figure 10.5 (Tarasti, "Signs as Acts" 47).

C   iC(N/iN1,iN2 . . iNn ——————— iA1,iA2 . . . . iAn/A)iL   L

in which:

> C=physical composer
> iC=implied composer
> N=narrator
> iN=implied narrator, or theme-actors as agents
> L=physical listener
> iL=implied listener
> A=audience
> iA=implied audience, or theme-actors as patients

Figure 10.5. The communicative structure of music, version 1.

In music as well as in verbal texts there exist consequently many embedded levels of narration, that is, chains of composer-narrator-listener-audience or agent-patient. When speaking about situations, it is important to separate them carefully from one another.

Narrative situations—and the concept of situation is crucial in my new existential semiotics (see Tarasti, *Existential Semiotics* 8)—can also be observed in the real world. Composers and listeners are subject to historical and organic processes: they get ill, they enjoy themselves, they make political and other decisions, they struggle to survive, they consume music as a part of a certain way of life, and so on. The investigation of this physico-cultural level is important to studies of musical communication. By simplifying the aforementioned model, emphasis goes to the "boxes" of the chain (see fig. 10.6).

> composer → implied → message ← implied ← listener
>   composer   listener

Figure 10.6. The communicative structure of music, version 2.

But a semiotic, narrative analysis cannot stop there. In the next scenario the focus shifts one step, toward the inner core of musical signification. It is in this movement from composer to implied composer, and from listener to implied listener, that representation is launched in music: elements of outer reality are internalized so as to form factors that wield influence inside the musical discourse. For instance, the implied composer is someone with a certain competence, who provides his musical message with signs that the implied listener can presumably receive and decode correctly (fig. 10.7).

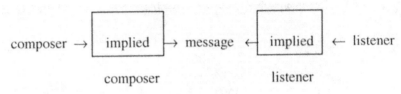

Figure 10.7. The communicative structure of music, version 3.

Finally, the musical narrative or message itself can be interpreted as a model, that is to say, as a micro universe whose elements stand in various relationships to one another. In some cases this involves a kind of reflection from the two outer circles upon the inner one. But just as often the transformation takes place on the level of implied composer-listener and does not therefore communicate anything directly from the social, historical, or physical situation (from so-called reality). The "model" represented by the message, with its purely musical communications and actions, can even be deliberately antithetical to the presuppositions of the implied composer and listener. In any case the distinction between these three degrees of agents-patients forms the first step toward the clearing up of the conceptual confusion that reigns in the analysis of musical narrativity.

Glossary of Semiotic Terms

The author who proposed the term is given in brackets. The definitions are derived from Prince and Colapietro.

Enounced and enunciation	[Benveniste] [French *énoncé* and *énonciation*] Terms used to draw a distinction between what is uttered (the enounced) and the process or act of utterance (enunciation). The enounced is a stretch of text linked by a principle of coherence and perceived as constituting a whole. *Enunciation* is often

used to refer to the act by which the utterer assumes a position within language through the use of pronouns, deictics, tense, modalizers, and evaluative terms. The two concepts have been adapted to the investigation of semiotic systems other than language, in particular to the cinema.

Function
: [Propp] An act of a character in a narrative defined in terms of its significance to the plot as a whole.

Isotopy
: [Greimas] The repetition of semiotic features that constitutes the coherence of the text. In its more restricted adaptation the term is taken to designate the repetition of semantic units in a text; in its broadest sense it designates the repetition of units on the level of the signifier (that is, syntactic, phonetic, prosodic features) as well as on the level of the signified.

Narrative program
: [Greimas] A syntagm at the level of narrative surface structure representing a change of state effected by an actor and affecting another (or the same) actor.

Pheme
: The equivalent of seme on the side of the signifier. In language these would be the features that distinguish the phonemes (minimal unit of sound) from one another. The phonemes /b/ and /p/ are, for instance, distinguished by the feature + voiced / - voiced, while they share the features + bilabial, + stop.

Seme, sememe
: [Greimas] The smallest unit of meaning. A semantic feature. In the word *tomcat* the semes are feline, male, adult, neutered; and their respective values are +, +, +, -.

Semiotic square
: [Greimas] The visual representation of the logical articulation of the semantic structure of a text; the constitutive model describing the elementary structure of signification. Given a unit of sense s_1 (for example, rich), the square defines signification in terms of its relation with its contrary s_2 (poor), its contradictory —s_1 (not rich), and the contradictory of its contrary —s_2 (not poor). According

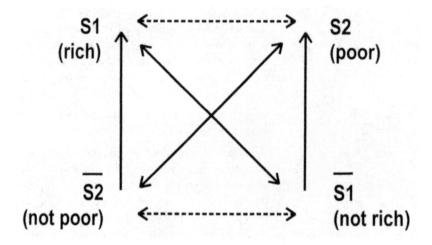

Figure 10.8. Semiotic square.

| | to Greimas, the semantic course of a narrative is a movement along the terms of the semiotic square. |
| Syntagm | Any combination of units that makes sense. |

Notes

1. More specifically, Lévi-Strauss's analysis of the Oedipus myth.

2. Along this line L. B. Meyer and Eugene Armour have proposed their "implication" model—but, of course, talk about "will" goes back as early as Schopenhauer in his metaphysics.

References

Asafiev, Boris. "Musical Form as a Process." 3 vols. Trans. and comm. J. R.Tull. Ph.D. diss., Ohio State University, 1977.

Booth, Wayne. *The Rhetoric of Fiction.* 2d ed. Chicago: University of Chicago Press, 1983.

Bremond, Claude. *Logique du récit.* Paris: Seuil, 1973.

Chatman, Seymour. *Story and Discourse: Narrative Structure in Fiction and Film.* Ithaca: Cornell University Press, 1978.

Colapietro, Vincent M. *Glossary of Semiotics.* New York: Paragon House, 1993.

Grabócz, Márta. *Morphologie des oeuvres pour piano de Liszt. Influence du programme sur l'évolution des formes instrumentales.* Paris: Editions Kimé, 1996.

———, ed. *Méthodes nouvelles, musiques nouvells. Musicologie et création.* Strasbourg: Presses Universitaires de Strasbourg, 1999.

Greimas, Algirdas Julien. "Vers une troisième révolution sémiotique." Lecture at the second annual meeting of the Semiotic Society of Finland, University of Jyväskylä, 1983.

Greimas, Algirdas Julien, and Joseph Courtés. *Sémiotique. Dictionnaire raisonné de la théorie du langage*. Paris: Hachette, 1979.

Charles, Daniel. *Musiques nomades*. Ed. and intro. Christian Hauer. Paris: Editions Kimé, 1998.

———. *La Fiction de la postmodernité selon l'esprit de la musique*. Paris: Presses Universitaires de France, 2001.

Hatten, Robert S. *Musical Meaning in Beethoven: Markedness, Correlation, and Interpretation*. Bloomington: Indiana University Press, 1994

Lévi-Strauss, Claude. *Anthropologie structurale*. Paris: Plon, 1958.

———. *Mythologiques IV: L'homme nu*. Paris: Plon, 1971.

Lidov, David. *Elements of Semiotics*. New York: St. Martin's Press, 1999.

Littlefield, Richard. *The Margins of Music Analysis*. Acta Semiotica Fennica XII. Approaches to Musical Semiotics 2. Helsinki: International Semiotics Institute at Imatra, Semiotic Society of Finland, 2001.

Meyer, Leonard B. *Explaining Music*. Chicago: University of Chicago Press, 1973.

Monelle, Raymond. *Linguistics and Semiotics in Music*. New York: Harwood Academic Publishers, 1992.

———. *The Sense of Music: Semiotic Essays*. Princeton: Princeton University Press, 2000.

Narmour, Eugene. *Beyond Schenkerism: The Need for Alternatives in Music Analysis*. Chicago: University of Chicago Press, 1977.

Nattiez, Jean-Jacques. *Fondements d'une sémiologie de la musique*. Paris: Union Générale d'Edition, 1975.

Prince, Gerald. *Dictionary of Narratology*. Lincoln: University of Nebraska Press, 1987.

Propp, Vladimir. *Morphology of the Folktale*. Trans. L. Scott. Bloomington: Indiana University Press, 1958.

Ratner, Leonard C. *Classic Music: Expression, Form, and Style*. New York: Schirmer, 1980.

Ringbom, Nils-Erik. *Über die Deutbarkeit der Tonkunst*. Helsinki: Edition Fazer, 1955.

Schenker, Heinrich. *Neue musikalische Theorien und Phantasien 3: Der freie Satz*. Vienna: Universal, 1956.

Schering, Arnold. *Beethoven und die Dichtung*. Berlin: Junker und Dünnhaupt, 1936.

Sebeok, Thomas A. *A Sign Is Just a Sign*. Bloomington: Indiana University Press, 1991.

———. *Global Semiotics*. Bloomington: Indiana University Press, 2001.

Stefani, Gino, Eero Tarasti, and Luca Marconi, eds. *Musical Signification between*

Rhetoric and Pragmatics: Proceedings of the 5th International Congress on Musical Signification. Bologna: CLUEB, 1998.

Stoïanova, Ivanka. *Manuel d'analyse musicale. Les formes classiques simples et complexes*. Paris: Minerve, 1996.

Tarasti, Eero. *Myth and Music: A Semiotic Approach to the Aesthetics of Myth in Music, Especially That of Wagner, Sibelius and Stravinsky*. Approaches to Semiotics 51. Berlin: Mouton de Gruyter, 1979.

———. *A Theory of Musical Semiotics*. Bloomington: Indiana University Press, 1994.

———. "Signs as Acts and Events: An Essay on Musical Situations." *Musical Signification between Rhetoric and Pragmatics: Proceedings of the 5th International Congress on Musical Signification*. Ed. Gino Stefani, Eero Tarasti, and Luca Marconi. Bologna: CLUEB 1998. 39–62.

———. *Existential Semiotics*. Bloomington: Indiana University Press, 2001.

Von Wright, Georg Henrik. *Norm and Action: A Logical Enquiry*. London: Routledge and Kegan Paul, 1963.

11

Music, Genre, and Narrative Theory

Peter J. Rabinowitz

Rarin' to Go

Over the past decade or two the rise of the so-called New Musicology—including the work of such critics as Fred Maus, Susan McClary, and Anthony Newcomb—has fostered renewed attention to the relationship between music and narrative.[1] Working against the extreme formalism that dominated their field for many years—a formalism crystallized in Milton Babbitt's assertion that a work of music can be "completely and accurately" understood as "events occurring at time points" (14)—these theorists have reinserted important questions about musical meaning into musicological discussions. Yet in one crucial way their narrative analyses have been partial: they've been Proppian rather than Boothian, stressing the level of story rather than the level of discourse.[2]

That, of course, is a fairly schematic way of putting it. But it does, I think, point to a real limitation. Broadly speaking, the narrative theorizing by the New Musicologists (as well as the critiques of their work by others who see narrative theory as a false step for music) has viewed narrative primarily as a "sequence of events" (see Dell'Antonio et al. 42) and has consequently focused on issues of "plot"—both on the ways in which musical events fit together as wholes unfolding over time (including the ways in which expectations are aroused, satisfied, and thwarted) and on the ways in which music can represent actors and agents. But for the most part they've ignored the act of narration itself:[3] in particular, there has been insufficient attention paid to the ways in which music might parallel the rhetorical functions that are performed by such narrative elements as irony or focalization. Thus, when Roland Jordan and Emma Kafalenos argue convincingly for the ways that "listening to music can be enriched by . . . narratological concepts," they put their stress on "those concerned with syntagmatic relations," relations that open up music's temporality, rather than on issues of point of view (111). Similarly, when McClary discusses the last movement of Mozart's Symphony No. 38, she talks in detail about the stories that involve "the playful tune that serves as protagonist" (65)—including issues of class and gender—but not about who is narrating those events or what perspective that narrator (as opposed to composer or protagonist) is taking.

Those are not exceptional cases: generally speaking, musicologists have been unconvincing when it comes to explaining music's *position* on what it narrates. When literary critics want to know what perspective *1984* is asking us to take when Winston is superficially triumphant on the final page, we have a number of analytic tools that allow us to discuss it. But what would seem to be similar questions about the ending of the Shostakovich Fifth leave critics baffled, ultimately forced to work through their disagreements with biographical rather than musical/narratological analysis.[4]

Given all this, it is no surprise that some writers have questioned whether narrative theory provides anything more than a cachet of trendiness to musicological concerns. Even Maus, one of the most distinguished musical narrativists, has suggested that "instrumental music may often be closer to drama than to prose narrative" ("Narratology" 642).[5] The naysayers may well be right, but I do not want to give up so easily. Rather, in this essay I will begin to show how what I'll call "rhetorical narrative theory" can help address this weakness.

Rhetorical narrative theory? These days, the word *rhetoric* has so may different academic uses, ranging from deconstructive theory all the way to what used to be call "public speaking," that it's possible, even common, for two critics who agree on nothing whatsoever to both claim allegiance to "rhetorical" criticism. A brief definition is therefore necessary: in this essay I'll be using the term *rhetorical narrative theory* to refer to the particular branches of narrative theory stemming from the work of such diverse theorists as J. L. Austin and Wayne Booth. These branches, whatever their differences, conceive of narrative not primarily as a formal object but as a rhetorical act within a conventional framework, that is, a purposive communication of a certain kind from one person (or group of persons) to one or more others according to some preexisting rules. More specifically, for traditional structural narratologists, a minimal definition of narrative might be "something happened." For rhetorical narrative critics a minimal definition might be "someone, using conventionally agreed-upon techniques, told someone else for some purpose that something happened"—a definition that places greater emphasis on the act (and the motivations) of telling itself.[6]

I have argued elsewhere, in somewhat different terms, that this kind of narrative theory can be helpful even when dealing with untexted music such as the Mahler Sixth or the Shostakovich symphonies.[7] Here I would like to turn instead to the way rhetorical narrative theory can help us understand the function of music in opera. This may at first seem counterintuitive: after all, opera is usually considered closer to drama than to fiction, and its "narrative" dimension is therefore usually seen in its story (or its mimesis) rather than its telling (or its diegesis). Rhetorical narrative theory, with its stress on the act of telling, would thus seem beside the point. I will argue, however, that canonical nineteenth- and early-twentieth-century opera can more usefully be seen as a form of diegetic narrative, with a narrator as well as a story. And, in exploring the rhetorical function of music in opera, I'll elaborate in particular on what I call "fictional music"—music that can open up a special kind of split between composer and character. Central to my argument will be my demonstration of how fictional music can invite the listener to occupy several different listening positions simultaneously. This multiplicity, analogous to certain techniques central to purely verbal narrative (especially fiction) allows the music not merely to "represent" various states but also to manipulate the listener into taking a position with respect to them.

The application of rhetorical narrative theory has a second benefit as well, although one tied less explicitly to narrative per se than to more the general interpretive questions: it can heighten our understanding of the importance of starting points—in particular the importance of audience preconceptions of genre—in generating musical meaning. For, despite their antiformalist assumptions, the New Musicologists have in certain ways nonetheless treated the work as a more or less fixed object. This may seem, at first, an odd criticism to level at critics who have so steadfastly dismantled the "positivist" musicology of their predecessors and who have been so sensitive to the ways in which music is inflected by its context of production: McClary's analysis of Mozart, for instance, starts out with a recognition of Mozart's "wrestling" with the "tensions" of "eighteenth-century bourgeois culture" (69). Even so, they do underestimate the ways in which listener's perception actually influences what the music "is" to begin with, thus ignoring a whole series of questions surrounding the nature of musical meaning that I hope my methodology can help clarify.

A Harbor Meant for Me

It's commonplace to claim that all interpretation needs to be docked to theory, but it's equally true (although less readily accepted) that theory needs to
be moored in interpretation. Narrative theory, for instance, can easily flood
literary discussions by multiplying distinctions without a difference—offering schemas, for instance, that aren't actualized in any literary texts. To
my mind, any theory needs to be able to answer the question "What's at
stake?"—and the routes charted out by the best narrative theory, whether
it be Wayne Booth's *Rhetoric of Fiction* or Gérard Genette's *Narrative Discourse* or James Phelan's *Narrative as Rhetoric,* are always guided by preexisting interpretive questions. Before turning to theory, therefore, I'd like
to start by exploring some of the questions raised by a particular literary-
musical text: the Jerome Kern / Oscar Hammerstein II *Show Boat.*

Show Boat may seem an odd choice. Certainly, whenever I've mentioned
that I was working on it, I've gotten puzzled responses, even from colleagues who accept my pop culture work on Sue Grafton or the nearly
forgotten nineteenth-century novelist Mrs. E. D. E. N. Southworth. There
are, I think, three reasons for their surprise. First, many of them know the
work through the 1951 MGM film—a Cold War travesty that systematically
scrubs away nearly everything of interest in the 1927 original. Second,
many responses are anchored in the accusations of racism inspired by
the Toronto staging that later moved to New York—accusations leading
to a debate that, unfortunately, barely touched on the complexity of the
racial politics of the novel and opera (and out of respect for the academic
setting of this essay, I'll call it an "opera" rather than a "musical"). [8] Most
important, however, they are responding to a real problem in the work.
Show Boat's creators had made a dangerous gamble: they had attempted
to resist the ideological complacency—especially in the area of sexuality—
that marked musical productions on Broadway. But, because of audience
predispositions, genres have more tenacity than we often recognize, and
they often take their revenge on authors who are unfaithful to them. That's
what happened to *Show Boat:* the opera was ultimately caught in what I
call "generic grip."

I'd like to take this opportunity to show how a rhetorical narrative analysis of the music can help explain how this happened. But, in order to do
so, I'll have to set out my own interpretation of *Show Boat,* with particular
attention to the sexual ideology of the ending. At first glance the opera
seems to have a traditional, if unusually deferred, happy-reunion ending.
The complex story centers around Magnolia (Nola) Hawks, daughter of

"Cap'n" Andy and Parthy Hawks, who run the show boat *Cotton Blossom.* After a denunciation by a jealous coworker, Pete, the troupe's romantic leads, Julie and Steve, are accused of miscegenation by a Mississippi sheriff (Julie is part black) and quit the show boat—and, against Parthy's wishes, their places are taken by Nola and Gaylord Ravenal, a good-looking gambler who happens to show up at the right place at the right time. Nola and Gay soon fall in love and, in a ceremony cannily mined by Cap'n Andy for its potential publicity value, they get married. The relationship flounders for several years, and Magnolia is eventually abandoned; only after she and their daughter, Kim, through hard struggle, attain independent success on the stage does Ravenal realize what he has lost and return before the final curtain.

This might seem yet another variant of the "love conquers all" formula familiar from the melodramas, such as the adaptation of Mary Jane Holmes's *Tempest and Sunshine,* that were the bread and butter of the *Cotton Blossom* itself. Yet there are striking incongruities. First, it's quite different from the ending of the Edna Ferber novel on which the opera is based, a 1926 best-seller that many members of the original audience are likely to have read. Ferber explicitly rejected the melodramatic endings in which "love triumphed, right conquered, virtue was rewarded, evil punished" and in which "onrushing engines were cheated of their victims" (65, 102). And in her novel Ravenal (unlike Julia in *Tempest and Sunshine*) does not return for last-minute redemption. Second, the opera's ending needs to be read in the context of the antiromantic irony that has eaten away at the entire work, not only in its details (for instance, the rhyme of *romantic* and *frantic* in the act 1 finale or the sardonic reference to Hamlet and Ophelia as model lovers in "I Would Like to Play a Lover's Part")[9] but in its larger moments, too. Thus, for instance, one of the most popular numbers— and superficially one of the sweetest—is "Why Do I Love You?" But it's sung by Nola and Ravenal just before he's trading her in for an evening of gambling—and, although the chorus cheerfully consoles her with the line "Hours are not like years," those hours *do* turn to years in the very next scene (Hammerstein, *Show Boat* 65).[10] More poisonous still, the song is doubled by Andy and Parthy, whose relationship is anything but loving.[11] And, more broadly, the final reunion has to be seen in the context of all the other sexual relationships, which—at least, those involving white characters—are seriously flawed. This hardly seems a nourishing context for a reaffirmation of marriage vows.

But the question of how we read the ending goes beyond the question of marital stability. For the plot resolution is intimately tied to the issue—

studiously ignored in discussions of this work—of Ravenal's ambiguous sexuality. Granted, sexuality is not a simple matter here. Ferber was not one to make a neat hetero-homosexual distinction, and she was careful not to map any simple congruence between male sexual preference and the masculine-effeminate grid. If you've read *Giant,* for instance, you may remember the antagonism between Bick and his son over appropriately manly behavior. Still, it can't be accidental that the main character is named Gay[12] or that in the novel Parthy, whose antipathy toward him is almost palpable, describes him as follows: " 'He's got hands white's a woman's and fusses with his nails. I'll wager if you ask around in New Orleans you'll find something queer,' " adding, " 'It isn't just clean fingernails . . . It's everything' " (113).

It's also worth attending to Gay's reluctance to follow through on his apparent seductions. As Ferber puts it: "He was not a villain. He was, in fact, rather gentle, and more than a little weak. His method, coupled with strong personal attractiveness, was simple in the extreme. He made love to all women and demanded nothing of them. Swept off their feet, they waited, trembling deliciously, for the final attack. At its failure to materialize they looked up, wondering, to see his handsome face made more handsome by a certain wistful sadness"(111). This image is amplified by Ferber's descriptions of Ravenal painting scenery (122–23), by her reference to his "neat, delicate" handwriting (212), and by the way that he always accompanies Magnolia when she goes shopping—for, unlike Magnolia, who "knew little enough about chic attire," Ravenal "knew what was what" (160). And, although we cannot coalesce Ravenal with Kenneth Cameron, the son-in-law he never meets, the recurring parallels between Kim and her mother (indeed, in the opera they're traditionally played by the same actress) might lead us to draw some parallels between their husbands. And Ferber clearly codes Kenneth as gay:

Her marriage with Kenneth Cameron was successful and happy and very nice. Separate bedrooms and those lovely negligées—velvet with Venetian sleeves and square neck-line. Excellent friends. Nothing sordid . . . Ken's manner toward Kim was polite, tender, thoughtful. Kim's manner toward Ken was polite, tender, thoughtful . . . Ken's voice. Soft, light. It was the—well, Magnolia never acknowledged this, even to herself, but it was what she called the male interior decorator's voice. You heard it a good deal at teas, and at the Algonquin, and in the lobby between the acts on first nights and in those fascinating shops on Madison Avenue where furniture and old glass and brasses and pictures were shown you by slim young men with delicate hands. I *mean*—! It's just one of those things. (229)

I am not suggesting here that Gaylord, this "slight and dandified figure" (Ferber 128), "is" gay in any unproblematic sense—only that his sexual relationship to Magnolia seems to be vexed in part by unanswered (even unasked) questions about his own sexual identity and that his desertion of her gains in psychological resonance when it's seen in this context, rather than interpreted simply as a preference for gambling. I'm suggesting, too, that the more alert members of the original audience could reasonably have been expected to pick this up. These were, after all, people who had read the novel; they knew the gossip that Alexander Woollcott had been the go-between Ferber and Kern; they were watching the opera just a few months after the arrest of Mae West for her play *Sex,* as part of a police crackdown on gay-affirming theater, which led shortly thereafter to the New York state legislature's banning of any play " 'depicting or dealing with the subject of sex degeneracy, or sex perversion' " (Chauncey 313). And I'm suggesting that our reading of (and listening to) the ending in this context takes on a psychological resonance as well: it will largely determine what position we believe the work is taking on sexual possibilities.

Let me elaborate on the way those sexual possibilities are set out in the opera. *Show Boat* pivots around a central dichotomy. In many ways it prefigures today's distinction between *essentialism* and *constructionism.* But those terms dehistoricize the work by bringing aboard the baggage of current debates, so, instead, I'd like to use terms suggested in the opera by the two central songs that set out the opposing stances. On the one hand, we have what we might call the *biological* position, presented in "Can't Help Lovin' Dat Man," which suggests that sexuality is a force of nature parallel to the one that forces fish to swim or birds to fly. Alternatively, there's the position articulated by "Make Believe," which argues that through pretense, acting, or sheer *declarative* force one can create the sexual world one inhabits.[13]

Ferber herself does not appear to have seen this as an easy either/or distinction, for she smudged the lines between these two ways of looking at the world. Thus, many of her novels are novels of female declarative self-construction: as Clio, in *Saratoga Trunk,* puts it: "Then remember that no matter what I say I am—that I am. I shall be what it suits me to be." But there's often a biological complication: in that early novel, for instance, Kakaracou suggests that Clio's "play-acting" is a genetic inheritance from her great-grandmother (45).[14]

Still, Ferber's balance is generally toward the declarative, rather than the biological alternative, and the opera lists even further in the same direction. Not coincidentally, as we shall see, "Can't Help Lovin' Dat Man," the very song that most explicitly expresses the biological side, the very song that most vigorously argues for the power and permanence of love, is the one that's itself most unstable, the one that is most radically transformed by context at each reprise, in ways that belie its own philosophical position.

I'm not arguing that the opera is *endorsing* declarative self-construction as a good way to live: the opera is making an ontological, rather than an ethical, claim, and its moral consequences vary considerably.[15] But there's no doubt that its ontological reach is represented as covering a wide variety of relationships besides the sexual. Thus, for instance, the whole notion of "family" is reduced to acts of declaration: Magnolia's father, Cap'n Andy, the spirit behind the *Cotton Blossom,* insists that he can create a family simply by announcing that the members of his troupe are "just one big happy family" (Hammerstein 10). It's Andy, in fact, who stages the romance of Magnolia and Ravenal, who plans their marriage, and who transforms it into a theatrical event. And Ravenal uses the song "Make Believe" not only to construct his relationship to Magnolia but, later on, to define his relationship to his daughter, Kim, as well.[16]

More interesting still, race is treated as a declarative, rather than a bio-logical, category. The most dramatic scene in the opera occurs when Julie and Steve are accused of miscegenation. Significantly, Julie has already "revealed" her race to the black cook Queenie—not by any genetic qualities she may or may not have (she doesn't look black) but by the verbal acts she performs, specifically the songs she sings. And Steve redefines the racial component of their relationship by quibbling with words—he makes him-self black by drinking some of Julie's blood and then declaring that there's "nigger blood in me." His use of the word *nigger*—over which he hesitates, in both the opera (34) and in the novel (88)—is a choice made with his audience, a Mississippi sheriff, in mind, and his blackness is clinched not by any physical evidence but by the declarations of the others on the show boat.[17] In the opera ethnicity is a matter of declaration in a similar way—the "exotic" Dahomey dancers at the Chicago World's Fair are, in fact, black New Yorkers who "make believe" that they are natives of an African village. In Ferber's novel, in fact, even arithmetic is undermined by declarative acts: the "Cotton Blossom Floating Palace Theatre Ten Piece Band" has six players; the "One Thousand Seats!" in the auditorium hold only six hundred people (14).

But there are two poles of the declarative position (and, of course, a number of gradations between them): what we might call the "existential" (you are what you choose to be) and what we might call the "conventional" (you are what social forces declare you to be). Thus, even within the declarative framework there are at least two opposing ways of reading the ending. Either Gay has personal control over his sexuality and he heroically chooses at the end to return to the heterosexual love that he personally has forged, or Gay is ultimately defeated by social conventions that force him to submit to the heterosexual norm by coming back to the "one big happy family."

What might make a person choose one reading over the other? My argument is that Hammerstein and Kern structured their opera—both the text *and* the music—in such a way as to encourage their audience to read the ending negatively, as Gay's defeat at the hands of convention, rather than positively, as the victory of true love. One key, in my reading, is the second-act Trocadero audition. In this scene Magnolia, abandoned by her husband, seeks a nightclub job—and she convinces a producer to hire her only when she agrees to sing "Can't Help Lovin' Dat Man" as a then up-to-date rag number. But, in order to see how that scene works in terms of my total interpretation, it is necessary to look more generally at the way in which music works rhetorically in opera. And that involves returning to the theoretical issues I raised at the beginning of the essay.

Convention's P's and Q's

I've argued elsewhere (in particular, in *Before Reading*) that literary and musical conventions lie as much in readers and listeners as in texts; that is, they can be seen not only as patterns made up of textual elements but also as shared strategies for making sense of the artworks we consider. And genres can thus be seen not only as sets of formal features but also, from the audience's perspective, as menus of interpretive procedures for unlocking literary meaning. These strategies include what I've called "rules of notice" (which tell us where to direct our attention), "rules of signification" (which allow us to draw the meaning from the details we notice—for instance, to draw conclusions about Ravenal's character from what is said about his fingernails), "rules of configuration" (which permit readers to put elements into an emerging formal pattern and, hence, develop expectations and a sense of closure), and "rules of coherence" (which allow us to ascribe generalized meaning to the completed experience of the work). From this perspective, reading (and I'm using that term broadly to include listening and viewing) is always "reading as": reading Chandler's *The Long Goodbye* "as" a detective story is a significantly different experience from reading it as a political text or a psychological novel, each of which calls a different set of reading strategies into play.

I do not mean to suggest that interpretation is a linear process. In fact, as we'll see, the rules interact in complex and often unpredictable ways. Furthermore, one of the central sets of rules of signification in fictional texts—the ones that allow us to determine what is "true" within the world of the text—requires readers to take on several simultaneous roles whose interpenetration provides a major ingredient in the aesthetic impact of the reading experience. The two most important of these roles are what I call the "authorial" and "narrative" audiences.

First, no author can know who, in fact, will actually read his or her book—but, at the same time, no author can even begin to write without making assumptions about his or her readers' knowledge and beliefs. Authors meet this need by writing for a hypothetical audience, the authorical audience. But reading fiction requires another step. Like all works of representational art, fictional narratives are imitations, in the specific sense that they appear to be something that they are not: Nella Larsen's *Passing*, for instance, appears to be an account of the vexed relationship between two women in Harlem in the 1920s. One way of conceptualizing this extra dimension in fiction is to recognize that, since a novel is usually an imitation of some nonfictional form (often history), so the narrator (whether dramatized or not) is an imitation of an author; and, just as an actual author always writes for a hypothetical authorial audience, so a narrator always writes for an imitation audience, the narrative audience. The audience's experience of such works is thus always at least double: we can treat the work neither purely as what it is nor purely as what it appears to be but must hold these competing (and mutually incompatible) perspectives simultaneously in our consciousness. We are not reading *Passing* intelligently if we treat the story as "real" and try to hunt down the particular apartment window from which Clare falls in the climactic scene, but, at the same time, readers should not close off sympathy for the pain Clare suffers under heterosexism and racism simply because she's not a real person. More generally, to read something as fiction, we must not only join the authorial audience (which recognizes what it reads as an invented artifact and, hence, treats the characters as constructs) but also *pretend* to be members of the narrative audience (which takes what it reads as history and treats the characters as real).[18]

Any fictional text engages both the authorial and narrative audience, but different texts ask us to balance them in different ways. Some (for example, *In Search of Lost Time, Gone with the Wind*) create such a seductive narrative level that readers often forget they're reading fiction at all; others (for example, Calvino's *If on a Winter's Night a Traveler* . . .) make such a consistent pitch to the authorial audience that it is difficult, if not impossible, to engage seriously as narrative audience. (Brecht's alienation effect, although not couched in these terms, was an attempt to encourage critical thinking by attacking the narrative level.) Some, such as John Fowles's *The French Lieutenant's Woman,* depend crucially on the tension between these two levels.

The authorial/narrative distinction is itself thematized in Ferber's novel. And that's one of the themes most aggressively taken up by the Kern/Hammerstein opera, which consistently plays off the roles of the characters as "people" and as "actors" in the internal dramas performed on the *Cotton Blossom.* Magnolia and Ravenal kiss for the first time when they are rehearsing a scene for *The Parson's Bride,* one of the show boat's repertory items, and the chorus points out that it is both pleasurable and easy to play "a lover's part" with someone you really love, since rehearsing the "kissing scene" is a delight and showing one's "ardent fire" does not demand any "dramatic art." [19]

The split is most explicitly dramatized, however, by the scene in which the backwoodsman, failing to recognize the difference between authorial and narrative levels, interferes with a performance of *The Parson's Bride* in order to save the heroine onstage from the villain.

Are there musical analogues to this split? Yes—but in order to see how they work, we need to look more carefully at the structural role of music in opera. As I said earlier, the narrative dimension in opera is generally considered to lie in its story, rather than in the way that story is told. But I would argue (and I realize this is a controversial claim) that in its zero-degree form, nineteenth- and early-twentieth-century opera can more productively be seen the other way around. Certainly, the libretto viewed on its own has the outward appearance of drama, but, in terms of the full score, the text is more profitably seen as inserted dialogue—direct reported speech—within a musical fabric that serves as narrator's commentary. I liken it to a narrator's commentary, rather than to authorial commentary, because if it were put into words—for instance, "Mimi and Rodolfo are getting increasingly interested in each other"—they'd be the equivalent of the narrator's, not the author's, words in a literary text. In this regard the music is structurally similar to a voice-over in film. [20]

That commentary may be externalized, in the same way that Flaubert's narrator's commentary is externalized when he describes his first glimpse of Charles Bovary: "His hair was cut square on his forehead like a village choir boy; he looked reliable, but very ill at ease" (1). Although, on the surface, he is discussing Charles's mental state, he is not really offering an internal perspective; he is telling us what Charles looks like, not what he is thinking. We have the musical equivalent when Richard Strauss chooses oafish, pretentious music with a faux-noble cast to accompany the entrance of Ochs in *Der Rosenkavalier:* although the music reveals the baron's character, it's from the outside, not the inside.

But musical commentary may also be internal. In fact, there is even a musical equivalent of the *style indirect libre. Style indirect libre,* or free indirect discourse, is a technique by which the narrator represents a character's thoughts without some introductory tag such as "he thought." "She was only half to blame" ("Elle n'était qu'à demi coupable"): so Proust's narrator describes one of Swann's many conflicting reactions to Odette's confession of her repeated and recent lesbian activities (*Swann's Way* 522; *À la recherche* 367). The sentence represents Swann's thoughts, not the narrator's—but, although *style indirect libre* traditionally retains certain idiosyncracies of a character's speech and thought patterns, there is always some ambiguity about the precise location of the line between the character and the narrator. In this case, for instance, it would be difficult to be sure whether or not Swann was thinking of the specific word *coupable,* with all its ramifications, or whether his thoughts were more inchoate. [21] We can hear the musical equivalent near the end of Prokofiev's *War and Peace* when, at the final meeting of Natasha and Andrei, the orchestra plays a reminiscence of the waltz they danced at the ball in scene 2. Neither character speaks of that particular event, but, as listeners, we can tell that they are thinking of it because the narrator tells us so. There's no reason, however, to believe that they are thinking of the waltz itself: the decision to use the waltz as a metonymy for the whole event is the narrator's decision, not the characters'.

A more complicated instance is the famous wrenching chord in the final scene of Strauss's *Salome*. Salome has just kissed the bloody lips of John the Baptist's severed head—and the orchestra triumphantly begins one of Salome's familiar motifs in a triumphant response. But it passes through an unexpected dissonance (just before rehearsal number 361)—and, since the dissonance is blared out fortissimo, with an added sforzando, by the full orchestra, you don't have to be a trained musician to recognize the disruption of expectations. You don't have to be a trained musician to recognize it as a commentary on Salome's state of mind, either: I've found, when teaching the opera to nonmusicians, that they were able to talk extensively about the psychological implications of that single chord. But, just as Proust's narrator using *style indirect libre* has taken the responsibility for transforming Swann's perhaps inchoate thoughts into precise verbal form, so here Strauss's narrator has taken responsibility for transforming Salome's thoughts into a musical image, which is presented to us, so to speak, behind the character's back. [22]

We see both external and internal commentary working in *Show Boat*, too. The most obvious kind of external commentary is found, for instance, in the return of the ominous, tritone-ridden music from the opening of the first act—the sort of music one might expect to describe a silent movie villain—when the sheriff Vallon first comes onstage. Something more subtle, but no less external, occurs when the "narrator" fortifies the theme of "declaration" in the opera. Religion is another of those areas, like race and family, that is treated as a matter of declaration, but in this case it's expressed in the music, not the text: if you listen carefully to the pious music in the second act convent scene, you realize that it's a variant of the "Captain Andy" theme, associated throughout the opera with showmanship and spectacular pretense.

But there is internal commentary as well. We see it, for instance, in the way Robert Russell Bennett, the opera's orchestrator, tried to communicate to the audience (behind the back of the characters) something of Gay's sexual ambiguity in "Make Believe." As Gerald Bordman describes it, "Bennett's orchestration of the lovers' first song, 'Make Believe,' had strings under the hero and woodwinds supporting the heroine. Kern insisted the opposite should prevail. His argument was that strings were warm and feminine while the cooler woodwinds were more masculine. Bennett challenged the composer, seeing Ravenal as the more immediately impassioned of the two, and Magnolia as more reserved, even teasing" (284).

In all of these cases there is a split between narrator and characters. But in none of them do we find a musical equivalent of the authorial/narrative split. The music may be equivalent to the narrator's, rather than the author's, commentary—but in these cases we have an omniscient narrator who is not part of the story, one who, in Boothian terms, is so close to the implied author that there's little point in making the distinction. Something more complicated happens, however, when we have fictional music. Fictional music is music that imitates other music—in particular, some other performance of some other music. [23] Thus, when in Rimsky-Korsakov's *Mozart and Salieri* the solo violinist performs the beginning of "Batti, batti" from *Don Giovanni,* we have fictional music: he or she is simultaneously a professional concert violinist performing Rimsky-Korsakov and pretending to be an old, blind violinist, somewhere else at some other time, scratching out Mozart.

In this particular case the "other music" is some real, preexisting work—but not all fictional music is citation. The march in Berg's opera *Wozzeck* is fictional, too, even though it is entirely original with Berg. What's key here is not the act of quotation but, rather, the pretense of another performance. Music that quotes other music (say, Shostakovich's Fifteenth Symphony, with its pivotal quotations from Wagner and Rossini) without this kind of pretense is not fictional in my sense, nor, of course, is music that imitates some familiar style without imitating some other performance. Chavez's Sixth Piano Sonata, which "imitates" Mozart's style without evoking another performance, is not fictional, but the "Pianists" section of Saint-Saëns's *Carnival of the Animals* is fictional, because it not only imitates the style of Hanon and Czerny exercises but also parodies a *performance* of that music.

Two points bear stressing. First, like fictional narrative, musical fictionality is not a quality found in the text itself but is, rather, a *perspective brought to bear on the music* by the listener. That is, in literature there are no formal markers that define fictionality in the way that certain formal markers define a poem as a sonnet; rather, fictionality, with its characteristic split between authorial and narrative audience, is a *way of reading*. Likewise, what makes this appearance of "Batti, batti" (in contrast to its appearance in *Don Giovanni*) fictional—that is, music existing on a different level from the music around it—is not a quality of the notes themselves, which are essentially the same notes we hear in Mozart's original; rather, the passage becomes fictional when we listen to it in a particular way. Second, hearing music as fictional, like reading narrative as fictional, requires the listener to take multiple simultaneous roles.

Fictional music occurs whenever a character chooses to sing *within the world of the opera*. In a sense this puts the music in quotation marks—and it changes its status in very much the way that quoted speech does in a novel. [24] But the phrase "putting the music in quotation marks" is misleading: it's certainly possible (and Prokofiev's use of the earlier waltz music in Andrei's death scene is a clear example) to "quote" music, even in an opera, without creating the musical equivalent of quoted speech. What matters is not repetition but whether the music exists on the same narrative level as the words in the libretto—that is, whether the characters have access to it on the level of the narrative audience. Generally speaking, the characters do not have access to the music coming from the orchestra pit. At the end of *Der Rosenkavalier* there's discussion of Ochs's character and conduct, but there can't be any discussion of whether Ochs's ponderous music really has the right touch, because no one in the opera can hear it.

But, when Nola sings "Can't Help Lovin' Dat Man" during her audition, the music and the performance are available to the characters for discussion. And, indeed, they make use of that availability, commenting on the music's quality and encouraging her to change the style. This music thus inhabits a different narrative plane than the music of, say, the Overture.

More significant to my argument here, in the audition scene, Magnolia's ragging of "Can't Help Lovin' Dat Man of Mine" makes us conscious of the gap between what is heard by the audience listening to the opera *Show Boat* (analogous to the authorial audience) and what is heard by the narrative audience we *pretend to be* as we imagine that we are listening not to Kern's opera but to the audition.

It's worth noting that the split here centers on a question of aesthetic judgment. It is not simply that the song is altered by the context in which Magnolia finds herself. More important, the song—a song that Magnolia insists is "the most beautiful song I know" (78) and that Joe, the opera's closest thing to an authorial spokesperson, has earlier called his "favourite" (23)—is *impoverished* by the alterations brought about by this new context. From the perspective of the authorial audience what we have is a good parody of "bad" music, but from the perspective of the narrative audience the ragged-up version is an aesthetic sellout. Furthermore, that aesthetic sellout is a not consequence of Magnolia's free choice but, rather, a consequence of her economic difficulties and the pressures of the show-biz industry.

The narrative structure of the audition scene summons up several rules of signification. First, most fiction involves a difference in knowledge or belief between the authorial and narrative audiences: for instance, the narrative audience of C. S. Lewis's *The Lion, the Witch, and the Wardrobe* believes in the existence of Narnia, although the authorial audience does not.[25] Any time a work evokes a difference in aesthetic judgment, we're thrown off balance—thrown off balance in a way that heightens our awareness of the authorial/narrative split and reminds us that we are engaging in a fiction. This in turn engages what I call the "Rule of Ironic Distance": when a work of art distances itself from its readers by calling attention to its authorial level, we are encouraged to actualize the work's potential for irony.

Second, there's a general rule of signification that might be called the "Rule of Intertextual Parallel": works of art within works of art can often be taken as guides (either positive or negative models) for our interpretation of the work at hand. It's reasonable to assume that Tolstoy's discussions of Mikhailov's portrait of Anna Karenina bears some relationship to the way we are to read the novel in which they appear.[26] And in *Show Boat* it is reasonable to assume that the social pressures on Magnolia's music making are intended to illuminate our experience of the opera more generally—more specifically, to heighten our consciousness of the ways in which personal freedom is checked.

By calling up these two rules of signification, the audition scene has a major bearing on how we read the ending. Rules of coherence encourage us to read endings in such a way as to make them congruent with what has come before. This requires that we somehow come to terms with the disjunction between the "oppositional" stance generated by the audition scene and the rather conventional stance generated by the fact that the ending so neatly fulfills generic melodrama expectations. How are we to navigate this difference? There are, I think, two reasons to give priority to the disruptive elements. First, as a general rule, in serious works of modern Western art, signification is more important than configuration—symbolism, for instance, is more important than plot. Second, there's a rule of coherence that I call the "Rule of Disruptive Priority": given alternative readings authorized by a text, the one that's more ironic, challenging, provocative of the reader is the one to be accepted, unless there is strong reason to believe otherwise. These two principles work together to encourage us to read the ending *through* the disruptions earlier in the text, specifically in the light of the ways in which commercial forces have reshaped artistic objects. Read in that way, the music seems to be making the authorial audience aware of the conventionality of the ending. More specifically, the rules of signification launched by the audition scene encourage us to see that artistic conventionality as a figure for the social conventionality of Ravenal's distinctly nontriumphant return on the narrative level. The happiness of the happy ending is thrown into doubt—as is the whole ideology that equates happiness with heterosexual marriage.

Though the Cold and Brutal Fact Is . . .

Unfortunately, no one else I've encountered has ever read *Show Boat* the way I have, as a critique of Ravenal's submission to sexual norms, rather than as a tribute to true love. Why not? It would be pleasant to be able to claim superior vision, but I think it's more productive to see if we can figure out what has served to block this particular reading—for that may, in turn, give some insight into generic grip, the ways, as I've suggested, that genres take their revenge on authors who would bend them to new purposes.

At the heart of the problem is a question of interpretive hierarchy. As I suggested earlier, interpretive rules intersect in often unpredictable ways. Thus, my analysis gives priority to signification over configuration and to disruption over stability. But one could just as reasonably give priority to the work's configuration over its signification, putting it together by using fulfillment of the expectations generated by the conventional romance configuration—girl meets boy, girl loses boy, girl regains boy—as a shelter from the more disturbing sexual/political issues of signification that the opera has raised. On what grounds can we choose one interpretive stance over the other?

If, as I've suggested, reading is always "reading as"—if genre is a cluster of previously learned interpretive strategies that the reader or listener applies to the work at hand—then the interpretation of a work of art will, to a large extent, turn on the reader's initial decisions about how to approach it. And thus, while my decision to privilege signification and disruption is not a random, idiosyncratic choice, it *is* less a consequence of my experience with *Show Boat* than a result of certain decisions I had made before even listening to it. That is, I had decided from the outset to consider *Show Boat* a "serious modern work," and I consequently applied to it the kinds of interpretive procedures I would apply, say, to *Threepenny Opera.* (In this regard my decision to call *Show Boat* an opera is more than an innocent issue of nomenclature.) That's a legitimate choice—even, I would argue, the authorially intended choice. But it's not forced on us by the work itself.

And what happens if we initially decide *not* to treat it as a serious modern work but to treat it, instead, as if it were a member of a more popular genre—what Robert Brustein called a "leaky old scow" (36)? Suppose, for instance, we choose to associate Allan Jones, the Ravenal of the 1936 film, not with the *Saint Matthew Passion* (which he had recorded in 1932) but with *Night at the Opera,* in which he also starred? I've argued elsewhere that the difference between "popular" and "high" art is really a generic distinction in the way I've defined *genre:* that it stems less from differences in the textual features than in the interpretive rules that the reader or listener decides to apply. In particular, reading a novel as a popular rather than as a potentially canonical text tends to give priority to rules of configuration, rather than to rules of signification (plot rather than symbolism in this case).[27] There's plenty of historical evidence to conclude that reading something as a popular text has often been construed to involve giving priority to its stabilities rather than its disruptions—and it's probably true that treating a work as popular tends to privilege the narrative rather than the authorial audience, which in this case would diminish the gap caused by the audition scene and consequently diminish the ironic pull. Thus, while my interpretation of *Show Boat* makes sense for someone who is, from the initial chords, willing to grant it the status of a serious opera rather than a musical comedy, the listener who goes in expecting a musical will find no serious blockages to interpreting it in a way consistent with that initial mind-set.

I think that explains one of the ways in which popular genres are resilient: interpreting them according to conventional rules often produces conventional results, and it's not easy for an author or composer to force an audience that is not prepared to try alternative ways of intepreting to strike out on a new path. That's particularly true when one tries to undermine its signification as a way of unmooring the implications of its configuration, rather than vice versa. [28] For readers or listeners, once they are comforted by a familiar plot pattern that fulfills their expectations, are apt to accept the comfort of familiarity and be done with it. [29]

The 1951 film—which figured *Show Boat* as a sumptuous classic of the romantic musical genre, rather than as a radical show that broke all the rules—only served to encourage the most conventional kind of popular reading. Indeed, the generic placement encouraged by the critics not only put priority on configuration over signification; it also put priority on the pleasures of abstract music over both. As Philip Hartung put it in his *Commonweal* review of the film, "The plot is just an excuse for another hearing of the wonderful Kern-Hammerstein songs" (286). Or, as John McCarten insisted even more strongly in the *New Yorker:* "The book of this show need not trouble us here . . . What I think we should all remember is that the music by Jerome Kern and the lyrics by Oscar Hammerstein II are as good as any you're going to get in a very long, long time" (49).

Significantly, the 1951 film simply removes the crucial second half of the audition scene. This not only closes the authorial/narrative split opened up by the original musical at this point; it simultaneously turns "Can't Help Loving Dat Man" into an enduring sentimental ballad, one we have to take nonironically as the key to the whole show. Even someone who managed to resist the interpretive strategies encouraged by the context in which the film was presented, then, simply would not have the antiromantic reading of the ending available as an option.

In the end, then, it is ironically appropriate that *Show Boat* ends with a reprise of "Ol' Man River." In the serious opera reading "Man River" is a song of protest, and it comes across as another criticism of the slick reunion scene. But in the pop musical reading it's a return of the familiar. And, for all the subversion that's potential in the opera, most listeners seem to hear it the second way, as an invitation for them, too, to keep on rolling along between their familiar banks. Rhetorical narrative theory, unfortunately, probably can't change the direction of the audience's response, but it can at least help us understand why it follows the course it does.

Notes

Earlier versions of this essay have been delivered at several venues, and I am indebted to the commentary of numerous listeners—especially Elizabeth Hudson and Mary Ann Smart, who, as organizers of the Conference on Representations of Gender and Sexuality in Opera at SUNY Stony Brook in 1995, first encouraged me to work on this subject. In addition, the suggestions of Lydia Hamessley, Emma Kafalenos, Nancy Rabinowitz, Jay Reise, and Marie-Laure Ryan, as well as the research assistance of Jessica Kent and Kara Stanek, have been invaluable.

1. For a sampling of influential work in this area, see, for instance, Maus, "Music as Narrative," "Narratology," and "Narrative, Drama, and Emotion"; McClary, "Narratives"; Newcomb, "Narrative" and "Narrative Archetypes."

2. It is thus emblematic of the field that Fred Maus begins "Music as Narrative" with references to *Morphology of the Folk Tale*.

3. For exceptions, see, for instance, Abbate's *Unsung Voices* and Kramer's *Music as Cultural Practice* (esp. chap. 6), which have more in common with literary deconstruction than with either structural narratology or Boothian criticism. For further discussion, see McClatchie.

4. For a further discussion of Shostakovich's Fifth, see my essay "Circumstantial Evidence."

5. He also raises the issue in "Narrative, Drama, and Emotion." See, in this regard, the slippage between narrative and programmatic in Novak (25); it is significant, too, that, when Novak employs Roland Barthes's narrative codes, he eliminates the symbolic.

6. See, for instance, Phelan, *Narrative as Rhetoric,* 4.

7. See, for instance, "Pleasure in Conflict" and "Circumstantial Evidence."

8. See, for instance, Philip, Henry, and Breon; see also Duberman's discussion of the black reaction to the first production (Duberman 114–15, 203). For a different perspective, see Robeson's claim, in 1935, that " 'Show Boat' is the most interesting thing I have done" (qtd. in Foner 103). See also defenses in the popular press by Simon ("One of the worst things about reverse racism is that it prevents an understanding of the past such as art combining with history can most enlighteningly offer us" [89]); and Kroll.

9. This number was dropped before opening night but was later restored for the EMI recording.

10. Even more than most operas and musicals, *Show Boat* exists in multiple editions. Page references in the text, except as otherwise noted, are to the Chappell edition.

11. In this regard it's interesting that Hammerstein used the song as a way to spoof Kern. During the Pittsburgh pre-Broadway run, Kern was trying to write this song. He finally got it and gave a copy to Hammerstein: "Oscar came back with a set of lyrics filled with all the words and expressions, notably 'Cupid,' that he knew Jerry detested. Jerry grew angrier and angrier as he played, until he suddenly

realized Oscar's game. He laughed so hard tears ran down his cheeks. Oscar then handed him a second set of lyrics, one whose chorus asked, 'Why do I love you?' " (Bordman 285).

12. For a discussion of the history of the word back to the 1920s, see Chauncey 14–23.

13. I am tempted to use the word *rhetorical* rather than *declaratory* here, except that I would like to keep that word in reserve for its somewhat different meaning in the phrase "rhetorical narrative theory." And, of course, the word *performative*, which would also fit the bill, has too many specialized meanings in the work coming out of J. L. Austin and Judith Butler.

14. For a different view of self-construction in Ferber, see Ellen Uffen's claim that "the enormous popularity of Edna Ferber's novels lay in her ability to create a consistent fictional universe based in popularly known and accepted American mythology: plucky, self-reliant boys and girls gain success and fame in colorful settings ranging from the old Wild West to the new wilds of Alaska . . . Edna Ferber, in the guise of implied author, differs [from Fitzgerald and Faulkner] in that she believes in mythology as reality, or more precisely, as paradigmatic real possibility" (82). Uffen simplifies when she insists that Ferber's women are, for all their courage, not really central: "In the novels of another author, perhaps these women would be heroines. Here, however, they are overwhelmed by the sheer magnificence of the men, and this is because Ferber is a bit in love with her own heroes" (85). This certainly does not apply to *Show Boat* or *Giant*.

15. See Kreuger: "When one considers how seriously both Gay and Magnolia have been hurt by the song's philosophy of fantasying as a way to obtain life's goals, it is grimly ironic that Ravenal is now offering the same advice to his own daughter" (*Show Boat* 45).

16. "The second half of *Show Boat* would seem to be about the breakup of families" (Brustein 37).

17. The dramatic situation is apparently based on a real event: "The miscegenation scene is based on a story Charles Hunter told Edna Ferber. Hunter once worked as a musician in a band with a 'rag front' carnival. One of the attractions was an all-Negro minstrel show. The owner of the show, a Mr. Henry, was living with a mulatto woman named Bessie. Henry fired one of his employees. The man in anger informed the authorities of Henry's living arrangements. Warned that he was going to be arrested, Henry pricked Bessie's thumb with a needle and sucked her blood. He swore on the witness stand he had Negro blood in him, so the judge allowed him to go free. Hunter claimed the incident took place in Charlotte, North Carolina" (Francis 142).

18. For a fuller discussion, see my book *Before Reading*. See also Phelan's useful distinction between the synthetic and the mimetic in *Reading People*.

19. As noted earlier, this number has only recently been restored and is hence not found in most versions of the text. It can, however, be found in the EMI libretto (86).

20. It would be impossible in a short essay to do justice to the variety of positions taken by theorists with regard to this question, although any discussion of the matter would certainly have to address the influential work of Edward Cone, whose work on musical and narrative discourse has been especially valuable. Among the recent theorists who have tackled the issue, one of the most provocative is Michael Halliwell. Halliwell agrees with me that opera is fundamentally narrative, rather than dramatic: "the narratorial role," he claims, "is . . . embodied in the orchestra." Halliwell, however, is not sufficiently sensitive to the different ontological levels inhabited by author and narrator. He argues that "the characters in fiction are the direct result of a narrative act performed by a narrator" and that, consequently, "operatic characters [are] the result of an act of narration by the orchestra-narrator," that the "characters are 'thought' into existence by the orchestra-narrator" (142). Because it minimizes the distinction between author and narrator, his schema does not allow one to analyze the kinds of effects, such as those I discuss here, produced by the complex interplay of authorial and narrative audiences.

21. Literary interpretation of passages such as these often depends heavily on matters of tense, and music, of course, has no clear markers of tense. For discussion, see Abbate, *Unsung,* esp. 52–56. For further discussion of music and *style indirect libre,* see my essay "Singing"; for a different way of conceptualizing the relation between fictional and operatic discourse, see Halliwell, esp. 143–44.

22. Whether it's possible for the music to take the role of an unreliable narrator is an issue that would require an essay for itself. One can certainly find examples (say, the handling of "The Man I Love" in Gershwin's *Strike Up the Band*) in which the words spoken by the characters serve to undermine superficially "serious" music. But it is not easy to tell in such cases whether we have irony by the narrator or irony by the implied author at the expense of the narrator.

23. "Fictional" music has a certain connection to what Abbate has called "phenomenal" music, but I prefer the term *fictional* because it highlights the narrative dimension of the phenomenon. Film theorists often use the words *source music* and *diegetic music* to refer to related phenomena; see, for instance, Brown. For a more elaborate analysis of fictional music and its distinction from other types of musical imitation and quotation, see my essay "Fictional Music."

24. Zoppelli, too, sees operatic music in a way that raises issues of diegesis, although his analysis, which does not account for the authorial/narrative distinction, turns out to be significantly different from mine.

25. There is also an actual audience, however, which may respond in quite a different way. One of my students describes sitting for hours on end in a wardrobe as a child, waiting for the back wall to dissolve so she, too, could go to Narnia.

26. For a fuller discussion, see, for instance, Mandelker, esp. chap. 5.

27. See *Before Reading,* chap. 6. Even when viewed as a genre distinction, of course, the demarcation between popular and serious art (as well as the use of the terms *popular* and *serious* to describe the categories) varies with the audience (academics are apt to chart the territory differently from nonacademic readers)

and with history. Still, I would argue that the distinction I'm making here has been roughly held by most American readers and listeners from the time of *Show Boat* to the present—even though there have been dramatic shifts in what works have been placed into which category.

28. As Chandler's experience in *The Big Sleep* suggests, even undermining configuration can backfire.

29. That may help explain Hammerstein's later regret over his decision to have Ravenal return (Kreuger, "Some" 17).

References

Abbate, Carolyn. *Unsung Voices: Opera and Musical Narrative in the Nineteenth Century.* Princeton: Princeton University Press, 1991.

Babbitt, Milton. "The Structure and Function of Musical Theory." *Perspectives on Contemporary Music Theory.* Ed. Benjamin Boretz and Edward T. Cone. New York: Norton, 1972. 10–21.

Booth, Wayne C. *The Rhetoric of Fiction.* Chicago: University of Chicago Press, 1961.

Bordman, Gerald. *Jerome Kern: His Life and Music.* New York: Oxford University Press, 1980.

Breon, Robin. "*Show Boat:* The Revival, the Racism." *The Drama Review* 39.2 2 (Summer 1995): 86–105.

Brown, Royal. *Overtones and Undertones: Reading Film Music.* Berkeley: University of California Press, 1994.

Brustein, Robert. "Robert Brustein on Theater: Boat Show." *New Republic,* November 7, 1994, 36–37.

Chauncey, George. *Gay New York: Gender, Urban Culture, and the Making of the Gay Male World, 1890–1940.* New York: Basic Books, 1994.

Cone, Edward T. "The World of Opera and Its Inhabitants." *Music: A View from Delft.* Chicago: University of Chicago Press, 1989. 125–38.

———. "Poet's Love or Composer's Love?" *Music and Text: Critical Inquiries.* Ed. Steven Paul Scher. Cambridge: Cambridge University Press, 1992. 177–92.

Dell'Antonio, Andrew, Richard Hill, and Mitchell Morris. "Report from the University of California at Berkeley: Classic and Romantic Instrumental Music and Narrative." *Current Musicology* 48 (1991): 42–50.

Duberman, Martin Bauml. *Paul Robeson.* New York: Knopf, 1988.

Ferber, Edna. *Saratoga Trunk.* Garden City NY: Doubleday, Doran, 1941.

———. *Show Boat.* In *Show Boat, So Big, Cimarron: Three Living Novels of American Life.* Garden City NY: Doubleday, n.d.

Flaubert, Gustave. *Madame Bovary.* Ed. and trans. Paul de Man. New York: Norton, 1965.

Foner, Philip S., ed. *Paul Robeson Speaks: Writings, Speeches, Interviews, 1918–1974.* New York: Brunner/Mazel, 1978.

Francis, Michelle. "The James Adams Floating Theatre: Edna Ferber's Showboat." *Carolina Comments* 28.5 (1980): 135–42.

Genette, Gérard. *Narrative Discourse: An Essay in Method.* Trans. Jane E. Lewin. Ithaca: Cornell University Press, 1980.

Halliwell, Michael. "Narrative Elements in Opera." *Word and Music Studies: Defining the Field. Proceedings of the First International Conference on Word and Music Studies at Graz, 1997.* Ed. Walter Bernhart, Steven Paul Scher, and Werner Wolf. Rodopi: Amsterdam, 1999. 135–53.

Hammerstein, Oscar, II. Libretto. *Show Boat.* Music by Jerome Kern. London Sinfonietta. Cond. John McGlinn. EMI CDS 7 49108 2, 1988.

———. *Show Boat: A Musical Play in Two Acts.* London: Chappell, n.d.

Hartung, Philip T. "The Screen." *Commonweal* 54, June 29, 1951, 286.

Henry, William A., III. "Rough Sailing for a New Show Boat." *Time,* November 1, 1993, 84–85.

Jordan, Roland, and Emma Kafalenos. "Listening to Music: Semiotic and Narratological Models." *Musikometrika* 6 (1994): 87–115.

Kramer, Lawrence. *Music as Cultural Practice, 1800–1900.* Berkeley: University of California Press, 1990.

Kreuger, Miles. *Show Boat: The Story of a Classical American Music.* New York: Oxford University Press, 1977.

———. "Some Words about *Show Boat.*" Liner Notes. *Show Boat.* By Jerome Kern. EMI CDS 7 49108 2, 1988.

Kroll, Jack. "Stormy Trip for 'Show Boat.'" *Newsweek,* November 1, 1993, 76–77.

Mandelker, Amy. *Framing Anna Karenina: Tolstoy, the Woman Question, and the Victorian Novel.* Columbus: Ohio State University Press, 1993.

Maus, Fred Everett. "Music as Narrative." *Indiana Theory Review* 12 (1991): 1–34.

———. "Narrative, Drama, and Emotion in Instrumental Music." *Journal of Aesthetics and Art Criticism* 55.3 (Summer 1997): 293–303.

———. "Narratology, Narrativity." *The New Grove Dictionary of Music and Musicians.* 2d ed. London: Macmillan, 2001.

McCarten, John. "The Current Cinema: Old Perdurable." *New Yorker,* July 28, 1951, 49.

McClary, Susan. "Narratives of Bourgeois Subjectivity in Mozart's *Prague* Symphony." *Understanding Narrative.* Ed. James Phelan and Peter J. Rabinowitz. Columbus: Ohio State University Press, 1994. 65–98.

McClatchie, Stephen. "Narrative Theory and Music; or, The Tale of Kundry's Tale." *Canadian University Music Review* 18 (Winter 1997): 1–18.

Newcomb, Anthony. "Once More between Absolute and Program Music: Schumann's Second Symphony." *19th-Century Music* 7 (1984): 233–50.

———. "Narrative Archetypes and Mahler's Ninth Symphony." *Music and Text: Critical Inquiries.* Ed. Steven Paul Scher. Cambridge: Cambridge University Press, 1992. 118–36.

Novak, John K. "Barthes's Narrative Codes as a Technique for the Analysis of

Programmatic Music: An Analysis of Janáček's *The Fiddler's Child.*" *Indiana Theory Review* 18.1 (Spring 1997): 25–64.

Phelan, James. *Reading People, Reading Plots: Character, Progression, and the Interpretation of Narrative.* Chicago: University of Chicago Press, 1989.

———. *Narrative as Rhetoric: Technique, Audiences, Ethics, Ideology.* Columbus: Ohio State University Press, 1996.

Philip, M. Nourbese. *Showing Grit: Showboating North of the 44th Parallel.* Toronto: Poui, 1993.

Proust, Marcel. ———. À *la recherche du temps perdu.* Vol. 1. Paris: Bibliothèque de la Pléiade, 1954.

———. *In Search of Lost Time.* Vol. 1: *Swann's Way.* Trans. C. K. Scott Moncrieff and Terence Kilmartin, rev. D. J. Enright. New York: Modern Library, 1992.

Rabinowitz, Peter J. "Fictional Music: Toward a Theory of Listening." *Bucknell Review* 26.1 (1981): 193–208.

———. "Pleasure in Conflict: Mahler's Sixth, Tragedy, and Musical Form." *Comparative Literature Studies* 18.3 (September 1981): 306–13.

———. "Circumstantial Evidence: Musical Analysis and Theories of Reading." *Mosaic* 18.4 (Fall 1985): 159–73.

———. *Before Reading: Narrative Conventions and the Politics of Interpretation.* Ithaca: Cornell University Press, 1987.

———. " 'Singing for Myself': *Carmen* and the Rhetoric of Musical Resistance." *Audible Traces: Gender, Indentity, and Music.* Ed. Elain Barkin and Lydia Hamessley. Zurich: Carcifioli Verlagshaus, 1999. 133–51.

Simon, John. "Theater: Show of Shows." *New York,* November 1, 1993, 89–90.

Strauss, Richard. *Salome.* New York: Dover, 1981.

Uffen, Ellen Serlen. "Edna Ferber and the 'Theatricalization' of American Mythology." *Midwestern Miscellany* 8 (1980): 82–93.

Zoppelli, Luca. "Narrative Elements in Donizetti's Operas." Trans. William Ashbrook. *Opera Quarterly* 10.1 (August 1993): 23–32.

5. Digital Media

The computer has infiltrated so many domains of human activity that, if we used the term *digital* to select those media that use electronic technology for their production or operation, we would obtain a set that includes virtually all transmissive media and a sizable portion of the artistic ones. Nowadays the writing of novels is done with word processors, graphic art is produced through the digital manipulation of images, movie frames are constructed on computers, and music is composed with software that directly translates the notes played on an electronic keyboard into a written score. Yet the output of these programs are compositions, images, and texts that do not depend on the computer for their display, performance, or distribution. The computer can also act as a transmissive medium for a variety of artifacts that did not necessarily involve digital technology in the production stage: we can view Jackson Pollock's paintings on the Internet, read Jane Austen's *Pride and Prejudice* on our eBook Machine; play a CD of Beethoven's Ninth Symphony, or watch a DVD version of *Casablanca* on our PC. To qualify as an application of a digital medium, a text (here I use the term in its largest possible sense) must not merely use but necessitate the computer for both its production and display. Genuinely digital texts cannot be taken away from the computer, because digital technology is their life support.

What makes a text dependent on a digital environment is its exploitation of what I regard as the most distinctive feature of computer systems: their responsiveness to a changing environment. When the changes are due to user input, we call this property interactivity.[1] The interactive character of digital texts manifests itself as a feedback loop that sends information from the user's body and its extensions (mouse, keyboard, joystick, magic wand, data glove, or headset) to the processor, often through the mediation of a virtual user body; from the processor to the display, which is modified by the execution of the command issued by the user; from the modified display to the mind of the user; and back to the acting body. Digital media do not simply place us in front of a static text; they situate us inside a system that continually produces a dynamic object. In the words of N. Katherine Hayles, "We are the medium and the medium is us" (37).

Judging by the number of computer-supported narrative forms that have appeared since 1980, the technological innovations of the last two decades have been a pivotal event in the history of narrative. These forms include: hypertext fiction, the "nonlinear," forking-path version of the postmodern novel; interactive drama, a plot-driven, Aristotelian script in which the user interacts with AI-generated characters; "narrative worlds," designed environments in which users create their own character and dialogue with other users in real time; and computer games, which can hybridize with any of the other categories. Yet, despite this blossoming of new genres, the question of the narrative benefits of interactive environments is far from settled. Interactive narratives obviously exist. But is the most distinctive property of digital media a boost, or is it an obstacle, to the creation of narrative meaning? When an interactive text achieves narrative coherence, does it do so by working with or against its medium?

Let me approach this question through the claims of hypertext theory, not because hypertext exhausts the narrative possibilities of digital media but because its advocates have been the most vocal on the narrative benefits of the computer. The first generation of hypertext theorists not only believed that narrative would thrive in an interactive environment; they also claimed that interactivity would thoroughly rewrite the rules of narrativity. In his groundbreaking book on hypertext George Landow titles a chapter "Reconfiguring Narrative." This reconfiguration begins with the role of the reader: "In hypertext the reader is a reader-author . . . The active author-reader fabricates text and meaning from 'another's' text in the same way that each speaker constructs individual sentences and entire discourses from 'another's' grammar, vocabulary and syntax" (Landow 196). Reconfiguration continues with traditional narrative structures: "Hypertext calls into question ideas of plot and story current since Aristotle" (181). Why is it that hypertext challenges Aristotelian notions of plot? "In electronic hypertext fiction, narrative takes shape as a network of possibilities rather than as a preset sequence of events" (Hayles 210). "There is no single story of which each reading is a version because each reading determines the story as it goes. We could say that there is no story at all; there are only readings" (Bolter 124). One may, of course, wonder whether these critics are not using the concepts of narrative and of story in such a loose way that they becomes synonymous with *literary fiction.* It is obvious that hypertext, based as it is on a different medium, provides a different textual experience than traditional print novels. Denying this would amount to rejecting the basic premise of the present volume. Are we, however, entitled to conclude that the novelty of the textual experience affects the basic constituents of narrativity—namely, plot, character, events, temporality, and causality? Or is the output of the hypertext machine not a new kind of plot but, rather, multiple or incomplete drafts of plot? According to some scholars who do not mind practicing a blend of theory and futurology, digital technology will enhance the human mind with the added power of the memory and speed of computers. If the much-hyped hybridization of human and machine intelligence is ever to happen, "we" (as human machines) should be able to process infinitely more complex structures than linear sequences of events. This raises the question: can narrative be radically different from what it was in previous ages and still be called narrative?

Prophets of the posthuman may view the hypertextual subversion of traditional narrative structures as a cultural gain. Those who like to be immersed in a story count it as a loss. The most vocal of the defenders of "book form" narrative is the literary critic Sven Birkerts, who argues that, if readers are really caught in narrative suspense, eager to find what happens next or emotionally bonded to the characters, they would rather turn pages under the guidance of the author than freely explore a textual network.

Much of the debate between traditional narrativity and interactive textuality has been conducted on the level of propaganda. One of the few critics who have been willing to look at the roots of the problem is Lev Manovich. According to Manovich, the distinctive properties of digital media include: (1) their vast storage resources; and (2) their random-access capabilities. The informational structure that takes the best advantage of these features is the database. Manovich defines *database* as "a structured collection of data. The data stored in the database is organized for fast search and retrieval by a computer and therefore, it is anything but a simple collection of items" (218). Databases consist of two components: a collection of individual objects, arranged according to a certain structure; and a search algorithm with flexible parameters that enables users to retrieve objects according to their personal needs. Insofar as the content of the database is made of individual, autonomous objects, the order of retrieval is not significant. Nor do users need to explore the entire database to make proper use of its objects: databases are open structures, to which new elements can always be added. The typical digital work, or "new media object," is thus "a collection of items on which the user performs various operations—view, navigate, search" (219). Narrative, by contrast, is a way of organizing experience that follows a rigorous internal logic, makes sequence supremely significant, and strives toward closure. Narrative cannot be interrupted in midstream: once a character has decided to take action to solve a problem, the story must follow the course of actions to its conclusion, either in success or failure. Moreover, as Vladimir Propp has shown, the actions of characters are "functions" that receive their meaning from their role in the story as a whole. This means that narrative cannot be consummated piecemeal. These differences lead Manovich to the conclusion that "database and narrative are natural enemies" (225). "If the user simply accesses different elements, one after another, in a usually random order, there is no reason to assume that these elements will form a narrative at all" (228).

But even natural enemies can sometimes be summoned to the negotiation table. To say that digital media, as randomly accessible data banks, have no built-in affinities for narrative does not mean that they cannot support a narrative experience. Between the extreme cases of a totally fixed reading protocol, which ignores the main property of the medium, and of random access to all elements from any given point, which offers too much choice with too few reasons to choose, there is room for a variety of compromises. It will take proper design—that is, proper limitations of users' fields of options, proper selection of plot structure, and proper choice of themes— to coax narrative meaning out of an interactive database. Art has always been about overcoming constraints, but to merit adoption constraints must yield some dividends. The restriction of users' options will pay off only if digital narrative is able to channel these options toward a goal that gives meaning to users' actions or to capitalize on the other properties of the medium. The task of the writer, in the digital age, is to design a narrative experience that grants agency to users; the task of the critic is to elucidate what is to be gained by meeting this challenge.

§

The first two essays in this section work from starkly different agendas with respect to the concept of narrative. My essay represents the attempt by a narrative theorist to examine in what form, under which conditions, and in which mode narrative manifests itself in digital media. Espen Aarseth's contribution expresses the position of a cybertext and computer game theorist who asks: to what extent is the concept of narrative useful for the researcher who wants to capture the essence of computer games?

In "Will New Media Produce New Narratives" I rely on the definition of *narrative* presented in the introduction. Through its distinction between "being a narrative" and "having narrativity" as well as through the postulation of latent or virtual modes of narrativity, my definition recuperates, at least as borderline cases, phenomena we do not normally think of as narrative. This includes computer games, which are generally not played for the sake of their plot but frequently rely on concrete narrative elements—characters, setting, action—to lure players into the game world. The richness of this narrative background is indeed one of the main differences between computer games and classic board games such as Chess or Go. In this approach games may be read narratively without being narratives in either a diegetic or a strict mimetic sense (though they come closer to the mimetic than to the diegetic mode). The essay argues that, if digital media can be said to create new forms of narrativity, this novelty does not concern semantics but, rather, presentational strategies (that is, discourse) and, above all, pragmatic factors: new modes of user involvement; new types of interface; and new relations between the author (or, rather, system designer), the plot (or plots), and users.

In "Beyond the Frontier: Quest Games as Post-Narrative Discourse" Espen Aarseth rejects any attempt by classical narratology or literary theory to colonize the territory of computer games. Aarseth has been a tireless advocate of a discipline of "ludology," which studies computer games not as a brand of literary discourse but in the context of game theory. His dismissal of literary and narratological models has nothing to do with lack of aesthetics value: on the contrary, he has long insisted that computer games are "unique aesthetic fields of possibilities" (*Cybertexts* 17). But the pleasure of games does not rely on the criteria that normally apply to literary narrative: believable characters, well-constructed plot, or high-flying metaphysics. The enjoyment of players is, rather, a matter of feeling empowered, of engaging in competition, of finding clever new ways to beat the system (pleasure is particularly intense when the solutions were not foreseen by the game designer), and of experiencing through the avatar's movements the spatiality of the gameworld. The fact that computer games, like narratives, involve characters, settings, and events does not erase the profound difference between the narrative and the gaming experience: a game is a game; it is not a story. Aarseth ascribes the similarities between games and narratives not to a common nature but to a common inspiration from life. But, whereas narrative relates to life as representation, games relate to it as simulation. What is the difference? Narrative representation looks backward—it presents again—and it ascribes meaning to events from the perspective of their outcome. As Aarseth observes (quoting work by Ragnild Tronstad), its illocutionary mode is the constative, since its purpose is to tell us what happened. Simulation, on the other hand, is oriented forward, and its illocutionary mode is the performative. Users resort to action in order to achieve a goal, as they would in real life. To players who are caught in the fire of the action (an expression that the preferred thematics of games make particularly appropriate), meaning is suspended: it will only become available when the quest is achieved—that is to say, when players look retrospectively at their performance. In my own view a retrospective availability of meaning is sufficient to ascribe narrativity to games. Aarseth would reply that when the game is over it is over, and its fall into narrativity means its death as simulation. If we want to catch the essence of gaming—not just of computer games but of games in general— we must look not at what happens after the game but at the live, real-time experience.

The last essay in this section, "The Myths of Interactive Cinema" by Peter Lunenfeld, takes an honest, hard look at the future of digital art. As his essay shows, the theoretical hype that greeted the development of hypertext in the early 1990s is still being lavished upon the idea of interactive cinema and television. The rhetoric is eerily similar, as if the advocates of interactive movies had directly lifted their arguments from the book on hypertext theory: interactivity will free the audience from the passivity of the watching experience and will turn users into an "active partner in the presentation and shaping of story" (Davenport, qtd. by Lunenfeld). Just as literary theorists thought that one could take a narrative literary form, the novel, and make it infinitely better by giving the reader a choice between many developments, the proponents of interactive cinema thought that one could take the narrative type of movie cultivated by Hollywood and improve it by allowing the spectator to customize the plot. The marriage of Hollywood-style dramaturgy (with its strictly Aristotelian development) and interactive design has so far resulted in such unforgettable productions as the fifteen-minute "B" movie *I'm Your Man,* in which spectators are granted the incredibly empowering freedom to decide which character to follow to a party; whether the female protagonist should behave like a "good girl" (work with the police) or a "bad girl" (use her seductive power to solve her problems); and whether the male character should act like a coward or a hero. Hypertext, meanwhile, has been a darling of academic critics, but it has failed to make a dent in the fiction market. Its most memorable specimens have captured the reader's interest for the novelty of the medium and its kaleidoscopic effects, as Janet Murray calls the rearrangement of the same units in ever new configurations, but hardly anybody reads hypertext for the sake of the plots or other narrative qualities. What does this tell us? Are we still waiting for the interactive masterpiece that will raise the novel and the narrative movie to a higher level? Or should we give up the idea of improving on what we already have and look for radically different ways to place the power of computers in the service of artistic expression? Lunenfeld argues that our culture is already so saturated with narratives that it becomes enough to reference story arcs. He describes a system not of hypertexts but, rather, of hypercontexts, interactive layers that support and enfold linear narratives, and claims that this explosion of reference itself refers to networked culture's "accessible archive of everything." He concludes by sidestepping the failures of interactive cinema as it exists and looking instead at the rich fulfillment offered by the pulsating world of video art installations.

Notes

1. While all truly digital texts have the ability to modify themselves, at least if by *text* one understands what users experience, not all of them do so under user input. Espen Aarseth mentions some cases of cyberpoetry (for example, "The Speaking Clock" by John Cayley) in which the text reacts to the computer clock.

References

Aarseth, Espen. *Cybertexts: Perspectives on Ergodic Literature.* Baltimore: Johns Hopkins University Press, 1997.

Birkerts, Sven. *The Gutenberg Elegies: The Fate of Reading in an Electronic Age.* New York: Fawcett-Columbine, 1994.

Bolter, Jay David. *Writing Space: The Computer, Hypertext, and the History of Writing.* Hillsdale NJ: Lawrence Erlbaum, 1991.

Hayles, N. Katherine. "The Transformation of Narrative and the Materiality of Hypertext." *Narrative* 9.1 (2001): 21–39.

Landow, George P. *Hypertext 2.0: The Convergence of Contemporary Critical Theory and Technology.* 1992. Reprint. Baltimore: Johns Hopkins University Press, 1997.

Manovich, Lev. *The Language of New Media.* Cambridge: MIT Press, 2001.

Murray, Janet. *Hamlet on the Holodeck: The Future of Narrative in Cyberspace.* New York: Free Press, 1997.

12

Will New Media Produce New Narratives?

Marie-Laure Ryan

From the very beginning of the revolution that turned computers from business machines into poetry engines, the relation between narrative and digital media has been the object of contradictory opinions. Who should we follow: George Landow, who claims that hypertext will reconfigure the narrative experience by turning readers into coauthors; Janet Murray, who regards digital media as a new stage on which old narratives will be replayed in new dimensions (as the title of her book, *Hamlet on the Holodeck,* suggests); Espen Aarseth, who thinks that the future of cybertexts lies not in storytelling but in computer games; or Katherine Hayles, who equates digital meaning with complexity, fragmentation, fluidity, resistance to totalization, aporia, paradox, emergence, or self-organizing capabilities— features more likely to bring in a post-narrative, post-human literature than to transform the basic conditions of narrativity?

To start this discussion of the narrative potential of digital media on solid ground, three issues must be covered. First, we need to define *narrative.* Here I will work from the definition outlined in the introduction to this volume: a narrative text is one that brings a world to the mind (setting) and populates it with intelligent agents (characters). These agents participate in actions and happenings (events, plot), which cause global changes in the narrative world. Narrative is thus a mental representation of causally connected states and events that captures a segment in the history of a world and of its members. This logico-semantic characterization of narrative is sufficiently abstract to be regarded as a cognitive universal but flexible enough to tolerate a wide range of variations: simple plots, complex plots, parallel plots, epic plots, Russian doll plots (that is, recursively embedded stories), dramatic plots, and so on. It is on the level of these variations, as well as on the level of thematic content, that narrative is affected by historical, cultural, and medial factors.

The second preliminary issue concerns the distinctive properties of digital media. To make a list of these properties does not mean that digital media form a unified field and that each of their idiosyncratic features is available to every application. On the contrary, there are several genres within digital textuality, and different genres exploit different properties. I would like to single out the following five properties of digital media as the most fundamental. [1] These properties affect narrativity in either a positive or a negative way.

1. Reactive and interactive nature. By this I mean the ability of digital media to respond to changing conditions. *Reactivity* refers to responses to changes in the environment or to nonintentional user actions; *interactivity* is a response to a deliberate user action.

2. Multiple sensory and semiotic channels, or what we may call "multimedia capabilities," if we are not afraid of the apparent paradox of talking about multimedia media.

3. Networking capabilities. Digital media connect machines and people across space and bring them together in virtual environments. This opens the possibility of multi-user systems and live ("real-time") as well as delayed communication.

4. Volatile signs. Computer memory is made of bits whose value can switch back and forth between positive and negative. Unlike books or paintings, digital texts can be refreshed and rewritten, without having to throw away the material support. This property explains the unparalleled fluidity and dynamic nature of digital images.

5. Modularity. Because the computer makes it so easy to reproduce data, digital works tend to be composed of many autonomous objects. These objects can be used in many different contexts and combinations, and undergo various transformations, during the run of the work.

While the full expressive power of digital media cannot be described without mentioning all of these properties, I believe that the first one, interactivity, is the truly distinctive, and consequently fundamental, one. A novel can be digitized, made available on the Internet (property 3), and even daily updated (property 4) while remaining a traditional novel, as the recent publishing experiment by Stephen King has shown. Similarly, cinema offers multiple channels (property 2) and fluid images that replace one another easily on the screen (property 4); [2] moreover, a movie can be shown on the Internet (property 3) without significant consequence for its narrative potential. But, when interactivity is added to the text or the movie, its ability to tell stories, and the stories it can tell, are deeply affected.

The third issue to be addressed before we can begin our discussion is the refinement of the concept of interactivity. This essay will be based on a typology of user participation in digital media that involves two dichotomies, internal versus external involvement and exploratory versus ontological involvement.[3]

Internal/External involvement

In the internal mode users project themselves as members of a virtual (or fictional) world, either by identifying with an avatar or by apprehending the virtual world from a first-person perspective. In the external mode readers situate themselves outside the virtual world. They either play the role of a god who controls the fictional world from above, or they conceptualize their activity as navigating a database. This opposition is not strictly binary: the position of the user may be more or less internal or external, or the same text may give rise to different imaginative acts. Some users will spontaneously situate themselves inside the textual world; others prefer a distanced point of view.

Exploratory/Ontological involvement

In the exploratory mode users are free to move around the database, but this activity does not make history, nor does it alter the plot; users have no impact on the destiny of the virtual world. In the ontological mode, by contrast, the decisions of the user send the history of the virtual world on different forking paths. These decisions are ontological in the sense that they determine which possible world, and consequently which story, will develop from the situation in which the choice presents itself. This opposition is much more binary than the preceding one, though a hybrid case will also be discussed here.

The cross-classification of these two dichotomies yields four types of user participation in the text: internal/exploratory, internal/ontological, external/exploratory, and external/ontological. I do not claim that my typology exhausts the field of possibilities; for instance, interactivity can be described as either selective (clicking on a link) or productive (participating in a narrative action through dialogue and gestures). Nor do I wish to say that every text fits neatly into one of these classes: sometimes the user's role changes in the run of the program; sometimes the user's mode of participation can be viewed in two different ways. I have chosen these four categories because they provide a convenient frame for the presentation of the various modes of interactive narrativity. Here I will discuss five digital genres: hypertext, text-based virtual environments, interactive drama, computer games, and live Internet image transmission through Webcams.

Hypertext

By now the idea of hypertext should be quite familiar to students of literature: hypertexts are networks of textual fragments, called "lexia" or "textrons," connected by links. Readers move through the text by clicking on buttons, and, since most fragments contain many buttons, readers have a choice of many different itineraries. The significance of this multiplicity has been an object of endless theorizing. Of special relevance to our topic is the claim that, since every reading follows a different path, hypertext is capable of endless self-regeneration. I call this interpretation the Alephic conception of hypertext, by analogy with "The Aleph," the short story by Jorge Luis Borges in which the scrutiny of a cabalistic symbol enables the experiencer to contemplate the whole of history and of reality, down to its most minute details. The Aleph is a small, bound object that expands into an infinity of spectacles, and the experiencer could therefore devote a lifetime to its contemplation. Similarly, hypertext has been conceived as a matrix that expands into a multitude of texts, as readers unravel new strings of signs from its finite database of discrete lexia.

If we equate these strings of signs with "narrative," hypertext becomes a machine for the production of stories, just as the grammar of a language is a machine for the production of sentences. It is in these terms that Michael Joyce envisions the novelty of hypertext with respect to print narrative: "Reordering requires a new text; every reading thus becomes a new text . . . Hypertext narratives become virtual storytellers" (193). Joyce's now classic hypertext novel *afternoon* allegorizes this idea of hypertext as a matrix of different stories by proposing several different versions of the fictional world. The common theme of all these variations is the narrator's witnessing of a car accident. In one version the accident is fatal, and the narrator's ex-wife and son are the victims. In another version the victims are strangers. In a third the accident is not serious. In a fourth the narrator himself causes the accident. Or everything could have been dreamed or hallucinated. For those who endorse the Alephic interpretation of hypertext, every reading session leads to different lexia, creates different semantic connections between them, and consequently constructs a different story around the theme of the accident.

As seductive as this conception appears—aren't we all enamoured with the idea of an open, constantly self-transforming work?—it cannot be taken literally. First, it is not so much because of the interactive nature of hypertext that *afternoon* proposes different versions of the same event but because Michael Joyce deliberately chose to include lexia with contradictory content in his database. He could have done the same thing in a print environment. There are indeed many postmodern novels that refuse to construct a solid actual world based on an authoritative version of facts. Second, the conception of hypertext as a story-generating machine puts questionable emphasis on linear sequence and the narrative significance of the link. If we take literally the claim that every traversal of the database determines a different story, readers who encounter three segments in the order A then B then C will construct a different story than readers who encounter the same segments in the order B then A then C. If readers could place the information given by each lexia wherever they wanted in a developing narrative pattern, it would not matter in which order they visit the lexia themselves, and the sequences A B C would yield the same story as B C A. Take the case of readers who first encounter a lexia telling them that a certain character is dead and later discover another lexia in which the same character is still alive. Readers have two choices. If linking and sequencing are narratively significant, they will assume that the character has been resurrected—an interpretation that presupposes a supernatural world that may clash with the semantics of the text as a whole. (There is nothing supernatural about the world of *afternoon,* for instance.) Alternatively, they may decide that the sequence established by the links does not represent causal and temporal order. They will then treat the lexia telling of the death as a prolepsis (flash-forward), and they will reconstruct the same story as readers who encounter the two fragments in the opposite order.

If narrativity is a mental representation constrained by logical principles, it is simply not possible to construct a coherent story out of every permutation of a set of textual fragments, because fragments are implicitly ordered by relations of presupposition, material causality, psychological motivation, and temporal sequence. It is only in hypertexts with a very simple map, such as the tree-shaped diagram that underlies the children's stories known as Choose Your Own Adventures, that narrative continuity can be maintained for every traversal. On a tree diagram different readings follow different branches, but on a given branch a lexia is always preceded and followed by the same lexia. This makes it easy for the author to control the progression of the reader and consequently to guarantee proper logical sequence. But the vast majority of literary hypertexts are based on more complex networks that make it possible for a given lexia to appear in different contexts. The author may control the path of the reader out of a certain node, but after a few transitions the path becomes unpredictable.

In keeping with his well-known theory of readers as coauthors, George Landow puts the burden of filling in the logical gaps between fragments on readers' imaginations: "In a hypertext environment a lack of linearity does not destroy narrative. In fact, since readers always, but particularly in this environment, fabricate their own structures, sequences or meanings, they have surprisingly little trouble reading a story or reading for a story" (197). But it would take a mind with angelic—or, rather, post-human—powers to fit lexia in a narratively coherent pattern for every order of appearance. For merely human minds what hypertext offers is not a story-generating machine but something much closer to the narrative equivalent of a jigsaw puzzle: readers try to construct a narrative image from fragments that come to them in a more or less random order, by fitting each lexia into a global pattern that slowly takes shape in the mind. Just as we can work for a time on a puzzle, leave it, and come back to it later, readers of hypertext do not start a new story from scratch every time they open the program but, rather, construe a mental representation over many sessions, completing or amending the picture put together so far. It is by creating what Espen Aarseth has called a "game of narration" (94), a scrambled picture that readers try to put back together, that hypertext narrative takes advantage of the interactive properties of its medium. Out of new syntactic features—fragmentation and linking—hypertext thus creates a new type of discourse.

The role of readers in this game of narration can be described by the parameters of external and exploratory interactivity. Involvement is external, because readers are not cast as members of the textual world and because it takes a perspective akin to a god's-eye view to appreciate the design of the textual network. Readers regard the text more as a database to be searched than as a world in which to be immersed.[4] And, in spite of George Landow's theory of readers as coauthors, involvement is exploratory, rather than ontological, because readers' paths of navigation affect not the narrative events themselves but only the way in which the global narrative pattern (if there is one at all) emerges in the mind. Similarly, with a jigsaw puzzle the dynamics of the discovery differ for every player, but they do not affect the structure that is put together. Just as the jigsaw puzzle subordinates the image to the construction process, external/exploratory interactivity de-emphasizes the narrative itself in favor of the game of its discovery. Many scholars (for example, Davenport and Sloane) have indeed observed that hypertext is not a good medium for the creation of compelling plots that live from suspense and emotional participation in the fate of characters.

Thematically speaking, the external/exploratory interactivity of classical hypertext is better suited for self-referential fiction than for narrative worlds that hold the reader under their spell for the sake of what happens in them. It promotes a metafictional stance, at the expense of immersion in the fictional world. This explains in part why so many literary hypertexts offer a collage of literary theory and narrative fragments.[5]

In recent years, however, hypertext has taken a new direction that shifts its conceptualization from the model of the scrambled narrative to what Raine Koskimaa has called the model of the searchable archive. This new direction is tied to the improving multimedia capabilities of digital systems.[6] In the multimedia phase hypertext can return to more solid narrative structures, and to a more linear presentation, without reverting to the mode of signification of the standard novel, because interactivity can now take the form of moving from one medium to another, rather than jumping around a text. Here I must fundamentally disagree with Robert Coover, who thinks that the golden age of digital literature came to an end when hypertext ceased to be purely verbal. Hypertext can learn from the artist's book, pop-up children's books, activity books, advent's calendar, and art CD-ROMs to spread many surprises along the visitor's way. Visible or hidden links can be used to give the tactile pleasure of mousing over hot spots and of making something happen—the expansion of the textual world into a diversified sensory experience. Readers of these texts will be cast into the role of an investigator who digs into the history of the textual world by freely exploring a collection of documents. The type of topic and structure best suited to this idea of searching an archive will be collections of little stories, such as family sagas, narratives of cultural memory, local history (for instance, the communal story of a village) or biography. These subjects lend themselves particularly well to the relatively free browsing of hypertext because the story of a life or a community is not a dramatic narrative aimed at a climax but an episodic narrative made of many self-sufficient units that can be read in many orders.

Text-Based Virtual Environments (MOOs and MUDs)

A text-based virtual environment is a social meeting place accessible through a network. Users log on to the system and interact with one another under the mask of a fictional character. This character, known in the jargon as "avatar," is created by posting its description, just as a novelist creates characters through the performative value of fictional discourse. The same method is used by the builders of the system to create a permanent setting, typically a large building with many rooms furnished with textually described objects. In both the building of the setting and the performance of identities, MOOs are largely dominated by fantastic themes.[7] When they are not used as platforms for serious business, they provide a forum for free flights of fancy, black humor, and surrealist incongruities. Most of the interaction that takes place on the MOOs consists of small talk and gestures, hardly the stuff of narrative, but this small talk easily develops into conversational storytelling:

> Carrot grins
> Carrot waves
> Turnip waves to Carrot
> Carrot says Hi
> Turnip says What's up
> Carrot says Want to hear a good joke :-;
> Turnip says
> Carrot tells joke

The joke told by Carrot to Turnip is a standard example of diegetic storytelling. It is told in writing but according to the real-time pressures and stylistic conventions of oral interaction: you have to be a fast typist as well as a fast mind to be a good performer on the MOOs. Even the gestures that traditionally accompany storytelling can be textually simulated. From a discourse point of view, this hybrid status between oral and written communication is the truly distinctive feature of MOO storytelling. When the users are sufficiently imaginative, however, MOO interaction rises to the level of a dramatically enacted narrative. For instance:

> Bek throws Panther a box, wrapped prettily. "Open it! I bought it just for you."
> Lilypad gets the box open and takes out a puppy.
> Lilypad (*to* Bek): She's a wonderful puppy . . . Where did you get her?
> Bek (*to* Lilypad): I found her in an old warehouse. I took her home and cleaned her up. I hope you like her. Here, I have a toy for her. (Adapted from Kolko 115)

MOO participants have been known to construct imaginary objects—here the puppy—and to build elaborate scenarios around these props. When this creative role playing actually takes place, MOOs become the stage of a collaboratively created narrative performance. Since the participants improvise this script for their own gratification, they are at the same time authors and spectators, actors and characters. On the pragmatic level the singularity of the MOO experience can be described as an alternation between three different forms of interactivity:

- Ontological-external: creating a character or building a room by posting its description. (Out-of-character behavior)
- Ontological-internal: interacting with other users by performing actions or posting dialogue. (In-character behavior)
- Exploratory-internal: wandering around the MOO, visiting rooms, and looking at objects. (Neutral behavior)

Can we call MOOs a new form of narrative? The problem does not reside with the very obvious novelty of the platform but with the narrativity of the performance. MOOs readily offer two of the three basic elements of narrative: setting and characters. The question mark concerns the plot: as Elizabeth Reid has suggested, MOOs create a stage but not a script. [8] Most of the time MOO visitors are satisfied with small talk. It is up to the improvisational skills, willingness to pay roles, and cooperativeness of the participants to produce a dramatic trajectory retellable as a story.

Interactive Drama in VR Environments

While text-based virtual environments are multi-users platforms, virtual reality installations can only accommodate a limited number of participants. If the technology is ever perfected, VR will enable users to take their body into three-dimensional simulated worlds and to experience these worlds through most of their senses. In the wildest dreams of developers these simulated environments will support an interactive form of drama. According to Brenda Laurel, "The user of such systems [will be] like audience members who can march up onto a stage and become various characters by what they say and do in their roles" (16). Janet Murray conceives the future drama form on the model of the Holodeck of the popular TV show "Star Trek." The Holodeck is a kind of VR cave, in which the crew members of the starship *Enterprise* retreat for relaxation and entertainment. In this cave a computer runs a three-dimensional simulation of a fictional world, and visitors—let's call them "interactors"—become a character in a digital novel. The plot of this novel is generated live, through the interaction between human participants and computer-created, AI-operated virtual characters. In the example discussed by Murray, Kathryn Janeway, the female commander of the starship *Voyager*, sneaks into the Holodeck and becomes Lucy, the governess of the children in an aristocratic Victorian household. Lucy falls in love with the father of the children, Lord Burley, and they exchange passionate kisses, but the very responsible Kathryn realizes that this love for a virtual human is detrimental to the fulfillment of her duties in the real world, and she eventually orders the computer to delete the character. Murray interprets this action as evidence that vr-based interactive drama can match both the entertainment and the educational value of literary narrative: "The Holodeck, like any literary experience, is potentially valuable in exactly this way. It provides a safe place in which to confront disturbing feelings we would otherwise suppress; it allows us to recognize our most threatening fantasies without becoming paralyzed by them" (25).

The viability of the concept of the Holodeck as a model of a digital narrative is questionable for both technological and algorithmic reasons: we don't have the hardware to produce truly lifelike three-dimensional virtual worlds, and we don't have the AI to produce complex characters.[9] The closest attempts so far to implement the Holodeck experience are the projects in interactive drama currently developed at Carnegie Mellon University, under the direction of Joseph Bates (until 1999) and Michael Mateas. These projects use a strongly Aristotelian script (following the curve prescribed by the Feytag triangle), and they are meant for a fifteen-minute visit of intense emotional involvement by a single human player (as Mateas calls the visitor). Anything longer would strain the system as much as the participant. Players impersonate a character and interact, mostly through dialogue, with AI-animated characters. The system allows a half-dozen plot variations, all triggered by the behavior of the player. After that many visits, the player will consequently feel that all the narrative possibilities are exhausted. Although the ultimate goal of developers is to stage the projects in three-dimensional VR environments with full-body immersion, at the present time the interface is a computer screen, a keyboard, and a mouse. (See Mateas and Stern for a technical description; and Ryan, chap. 10, for a narratological discussion.) Here is the plot of Mateas's current project.

> Grace and Trip are apparently a model couple, socially and financially successful, well-liked by all. Grace and Trip both know the player from work. Trip and the player are friends; Grace and the player have gotten to know each other only fairly recently. Shortly after arriving at their house for dinner, Grace confesses to the player that she has fallen in love with him. Throughout the rest of the evening, the player discovers that Grace and Trip's marriage is actually falling apart. Their marriage has been sour for years; deep differences, buried frustrations, and unspoken infidelities have killed their love for each other. How the veneer of their marriage

cracks, what is revealed, and the final disposition of Grace and Trip's marriage, and Grace and Trip's relationship, depends on the actions of the player. (Mateas and Stern 2)

This plot evidently strives toward high emotional drama, but its feasibility is questionable: how could a lifelong relationship be resolved in the fifteen minutes allowed for the project? In *Who's Afraid of Virginia Woolf* Edward Albee needed no less than two hours to break down a marriage. It is admittedly the essence of dramatic art to make long-simmering problems reach a crisis and resolution in the limited time frame of the stage action. But it would be an extraordinary achievement to bring the marital problems of Grace and Trip to an outcome, and to do so in a believable manner, in a fraction of Albee's time.

The predominantly affective nature of the plots suggested by Murray and Mateas presents a serious emotional problem: what kind of gratification will experiencers receive from becoming a character in a drama or a story? The entertainment value of the experience depends on how interactors relate to their avatar: will they be like an actor playing a role, internally distanciated from their character and simulating emotions they do not really have, or will they experience their character in the first-person mode, actually feeling the love, hate, fears, and hopes that motivate the character's behavior? The destiny of most literary characters is so unpleasant that interactors would have to be out of their mind—literally and figuratively—to voluntarily experience it in the first person mode. If we derive aesthetic pleasure from the tragic fate of Anna Karenina, Hamlet, or Madame Bovary, if we cry for them and fully enjoy our tears (as well as theirs), it is because our participation in the plot is a compromise between the first-person and the third-person perspective. We simulate mentally the inner life of these characters, we transport ourselves in imagination into their mind, but we remain at the same time conscious of being external observers. Any attempt to turn empathy, which relies on self-conscious mental simulation, into first-person, genuinely felt emotion would in the vast majority of cases trespass the fragile boundary that separates pleasure from pain. I suspect, therefore, that the aesthetic gratification of players of Mateas's project will be less a matter of emotional involvement than a matter of curiosity about the cleverness of the system. It will take the full six or seven visits for players to appreciate the dramatic architecture of the project.

An even more serious problem with the idea of becoming a character in a novel or drama is the reconciliation of users' freedom of action with the creation of an aesthetically enjoyable plot. A plot is a global design, imposed top down on the fictional world by a godlike author, while the actions of characters write the story of the fictional world from within this world itself. Characters live their life looking forward, while the author arranges their destinies with an eye on the global trajectory of the plot. How can interactors be coaxed into maintaining the plot on a proper aesthetic course while acting in the name of a fictional persona whose concern is survival in a material world, rather than living their life according to the demands of aesthetic teleology? Joseph Bates and his colleagues (Kelso and others) have argued that interactive drama is meant to be played, not to be spectated, and that we judge a plot in which we participate by different standards than a plot that we watch. This could mean that the criteria applying to interactive drama may not be as strict as those through which we judge literature and traditional drama. But the problem of how to script users' actions in VR environments and gently guide participants onto the path of aesthetic gratifications is far from being resolved.

I believe that both the emotional and the design problem of interactive drama can be minimized by abandoning the idea of building a full-fledged dramatic (that is, Aristotelian) plot around the persona of the interactor. Most dramatic plots feature the mind of their characters as the theater of uncontrollable passions, and their fate as a struggle against the blind forces of destiny. But, if we are going to enter a virtual world, it is to be agents and not patients. This means that only selected types of emotional experiences, and consequently selected types of participation, will lend themselves to the first-person perspective of interactive drama. Rather than becoming a character in a novel or a drama—and thereby losing their identity—interactors could play a counterpart of themselves in a foreign environment. If we consider the whole gamut of fictional characters, which ones would we rather emulate: (1) Hamlet, Emma Bovary, Gregor Samsa in *The Metamorphosis,* Oedipus, Anna Karenina, the betrayer Brutus in *Julius Ceasar;* or (2) the dragon-slaying hero of Russian fairy tales, Alice in Wonderland, Harry Potter, or Sherlock Holmes? As far as I am concerned, I would pick a character from list (b), which means a rather flat character whose contribution to the plot is not a matter of rich inner life and intense affective experience but, rather, a matter of exploring a world, performing actions, solving problems, competing against enemies, and, above all, dealing with interesting objects in a visually stimulating environment. This kind of involvement is much closer to playing a computer game than to living a Victorian novel or a Shakespearean drama. On the other hand, if the authors of the future insist on staging the equivalent of high literary plots in VR environments, interactors will be better off playing the marginal role of observer. They will exercise their agency by navigating the virtual world and by selecting their point of view on the events that unfold in it, rather than by being existentially entangled in these events. I see, therefore, two possibilities for interactive drama in VR environments: ontological/internal involvement when the plot focuses on adventure and problem solving; or exploratory/internal participation when the plot focuses on interpersonal relations and deeply affective experiences.

Computer Games

The third genre, computer games, may be the least adventurous in the domain of narrative theme and structure, but, as millions of game addicts have proven, it is the most successful in terms of turning users into characters. The secret to the narrative success of games lies in their ability to exploit the most fundamental of the forces that move a plot forward: the solving of problems. The player pursues the goal specified by the game by performing a series of moves that determine the destiny of the gameworld. This destiny is created dramatically, by being enacted, rather than diegetically, by being narrated. But, in contrast to standard drama, the enactment is autotelic, rather than being directed at an observer: performing actions is the point of the game and the main source of the player's pleasure. Players are usually too deeply absorbed in their task to reflect on the plot that they write through her actions, but, when people describe their sessions with computer games, their reports typically take the form of a story. Consider, for instance, this review by Peter Olafson of the game Combat Mission, which simulates the German campaign in Russia during World War II: "My two panzer IVG tanks got lucky. Approaching the crossroads, they cleared a rise and caught two Sherman tanks out of position, one obstructing the aim of the other. Concentrating their fire, they quickly took out the Allied units and the surviving crews abandoned the flaming hulks and retreated into the woods nearby" (*New York Times*, October 5, 2000). Many people will rightly argue that computer games are played for the sake of solving problems and defeating opponents, of refining strategic skills and of participating in online communities, and not for the purpose of creating a trace that reads like a story. In contrast to the genres discussed so far (with the possible exception of social MOOs), the narrativity of games is not an end in itself but a means toward a goal.[10] The most sophisticated games do not need to dress up in narrative garb to attract players onto their field. In classic games such as Go, Tetris, Chess, and Pac-Man users manipulate wholly or partly abstract objects, and the game lives from the strategic cleverness of its design, rather than from the imaginative impact of its world. The purpose of narrative scenarios is to make up for the absence of an original, truly superior design by providing what Kendall Walton has called "a prop in a game of make-believe." Scenarios create diversity on the level of the imaginative experience, when rules fail to create sufficient diversity or novelty on the level of strategy.

The importance of the narrative background varies with the genre of the game. There is in principle no reason why a complex fictional plot could not be presented in game form and constitute the focus of player/readers' interest. Players would be solving problems or accomplishing certain tasks to be allowed to get to the next episode. Experience has shown, however, that the formula is not very successful. When readers are really interested in "what happens next," they do not want to find unnecessary obstacles thrown in their way. The narrative element of computer games is therefore typically subordinated to the playing action. Plot is the most visible, and elaborate, in the so-called RPG (role-playing) games to which I allude in the MOO section. In these games participants spend a lot of time creating and customizing their own character, they encounter many "NPGs" (nonplaying characters) during their wandering in the fictional world, and the games present many "cut-scenes," that is, lengthy movie clips. But the development of an elaborate plot cuts into the player action time, since movie clips and the dialogue of nonplaying characters can only be spectated. In the pure action games plot is merely a pretext for fast-paced action (having something to do all the time seems to be a prerequisite for success), and players quickly forget, in the fire of combat, the narrative purpose of their moves. Since the narrative scenario of action games is dictated by strategic design and since design types are limited, action games offer thematic variations of the same master plots: rescue the princess from the dragon; save the earth from evil aliens; disarm terrorists or be a terrorist yourself. It is indeed an urgent problem in the game industry to gain larger audiences by developing new narrative schemes.

Computer games represent several distinct genres, and the issue of narrative configuration and mode of participation must be treated separately for each of them. Let me briefly discuss the three principal types.

Adventure Games

The best-known representatives of adventure games are the so-called first-person shooters, such as Doom, Quake, and Half-Life. Adventure games illustrate the case of internal and ontological participation. Players operate a character in the fictional world, and their playing skills determine the fate of their avatar. The interaction between users and the fictional world produces a new life for the character, and consequently a new life story, for every run of the system. The preferred narrative structure of the adventure game is the archetypal plot of the quest of the hero, as described by Vladimir Propp and Joseph Campbell. As Torben Grodal has observed, these games stretch their plot endlessly in time through the piling up of levels, episodes, and action cycles with similar structures. Because of their repetitive nature, the narrative scripts of typical adventure games would never sustain interest in a nonparticipatory environment, but in this case repetitiveness is an asset, since it is by performing the same actions over and over again that players acquire the physical skills necessary to excel at the game.

Repetition, in its modular form, is also the adventure game's solution to the conflict between user freedom and narrative design. It is because users' choices are quite limited in every situation and because every opportunity for action forms a relatively self-contained episode that games maintain the plot on the proper trajectory. In a shooting game, for instance, the choices of players consist of the directions in which to move, of deciding whether to shoot or to flee when an enemy appears, and, in the former case, of selecting and aiming weapons. The only memory needed by the system in computing these choices is keeping track of the resources available to players: how many weapons, how many soldiers, are left? In the complex plots of novels, by contrast, the options of characters at every decision point are both much richer and much more tightly constrained—richer because their range is that of life itself but also more constrained because the future is produced by the past and because every life intersects with, and is influenced by, multiple other destiny lines.

Simulation Games

The classics of simulation games are Simcity, Civilization, Caesar, Babyz, and The Sims. Here participation is ontological and external. Users are cast as a powerful but not quite omnipotent god who holds the strings of the members of a complex and dynamic system, such as a city, an empire, or a human group. The elements of the system react to players' decisions according to built-in behaviors specified by artificial intelligence algorithms. Through the manipulation of individual objects players write the history of a collective entity. The true hero of the story has no consciousness of its own: it is just the sum of multiple microprocesses. The purpose of players' actions is to maintain the system in a state of relative equilibrium and to avoid steering the fictional world toward disaster, but the number of variables is too large for players to anticipate all possibilities. The computer complicates matters by throwing in random events. Players cannot win, since the fictional world is in perpetual evolution, but they derive satisfaction from competent management and from observing the relatively unpredictable behavior of the system.

While the operation of a simulation system requires a godlike position of power, many of the games mentioned here try to increase dramatic interest by casting users as a member of the fictional world. In Caesar, for instance, users are the ruler of the Roman Empire; in Simcity, the mayor of the city. The emperor or the mayor do not exist in the same space and time as their subjects. They rule the system from above, as the god's-eye perspective of the graphic display indicates, and they do not operate in a simulacrum of real time, since they have all the time in the world to make their decisions. All these features categorize them as external interactors. But, insofar as the personal fate of these characters is at stake in the way they govern, they are also internal participants. The mayor will be voted out of office if his administration of the city does not please his constituents, and Caesar will be dethroned if the Barbarians invade his empire. This combination of features places the games in question halfway between external and internal participation.

Mystery Games

Mystery games foreground what Roland Barthes has called the "hermeneutic code": the goal of the player is to solve an enigma. This genre allows greater narrative sophistication than the others because it connects two narrative levels: one constituted by actions of users, as they wander through the fictional world in search for clues, and the other by the story to be reconstructed. Since the story of this second level is independent of the actions of users, it can be as fully controlled by the author/designer as the plot of a novel. This genre illustrates the case of internal/exploratory participation. But the game architecture may occasionally blur the distinction between ontological and exploratory involvement. Imagine a game in which users receive the mission of investigating the past. Imagine further that, depending on the actions users take, one of two possible pasts is implemented, while the other branch is relegated to the realm of the counterfactual. Unbeknownst to them, users have written the past history of the fictional world. Something of that order happens in the classic game Myst. Players must decipher the events that led to the imprisonment of two evil brothers and their father, the good wizard Atrus (Murray 140–

41). They do so by retrieving the pages of a book that tells the story of the fictional world. Depending on how they play the game, one of two endings takes place: in one ending players free Atrus; in another they free one of the evil brothers, who quickly imprisons the player. The narrative of the past thus extends into a player's present, and players determine the destiny of the fictional world without being aware of the ontological consequences of their actions.

Webcams

A narrative phenomenon that takes unique advantage of properties 3 (networking) and 4 (volatile signs) is the live recording of the evolution of a miniature world through a Web camera. Aimed at a particular setting, Webcams capture images at regular intervals and post them on the Internet for everybody to see. The most successful of these shows, needless to say, are those that focus on potential sites of sexual activities, such as the Webcams associated with Reality TV ("Big Brother," "Loft Story"), but truly dedicated digital voyeurs seem to find rewards in much less exotic subject matters, such as the utterly ordinary daily life of the family of a California hacker displayed on *www.nerdman.com.* There are even Webcams that show corn growing in Iowa.

No matter how banal their capture, however, Webcams provide a brand new twist on the idea of narrativity—if we loosen the concept to mean an episodic series of events featuring a specific group of individuals. Webcams do not tell stories, since all they do is place a location under surveillance, but they provide a constant stream of potentially narrative material. Their capture is the visual equivalent of what Hayden White calls a chronicle: a chronological list of events that presents neither the closure nor the causality nor the formal organization of a plot. It is up to the viewer to construct a story out of this material. The output of Webcams is not meant for lengthy viewings but for quick visits, known in the jargon as "grabs."[11] By studying the habits of the creatures under surveillance, clever cyber-voyeurs will quickly learn when to check the Web site to catch the most interesting action. In the Nerdman game, for instance, players "score," in their own mind, by spotting the ghosts that occasionally traverse the screen. The biggest reward is to meet a human being, but in this dramatically impoverished environment—as in minimal art—the smallest change of state becomes a narrative event: a shadow stroking a linoleum floor, a car leaving the office parking lot, or a change of pattern in the sand of the cat box. Just as novelists cull the dramatic highlights from the continuous fabric of their characters' lives, viewers sample the steady output of Webcams in the hope of catching the truly exciting episodes—the moments when memorable events "walk," so to speak, into the camera's field of vision. While checking is spotty, the lives we imagine from our peeks into the system are continuous and full; the members of the world facing the camera may not always be visible, but they are always, in some sense, available, since we can always visit their living space and look at the traces of their presence. The Webcam narrative experience can be pragmatically described as running in real time and customized by users grabbing images from an archive of transitory materials. Its interactivity is exploratory and external, since users look in from the outside and do not control the fate of the denizens of the fishbowl.

Conclusion

If we opt for a universalist conception of narrative and if we think of narrative in terms of semantic requirements, the answer to the question that forms the title of this essay is purely rhetorical: digital media have no more impact on the cognitive model through which we filter texts and make sense of human action than the experiments of postmodern fiction. The texts supported by digital media may satisfy to various degrees the universal cognitive model, or they may produce creative alternatives to a narrative experience, but they do not and cannot change the basic conditions of narrativity.

But there is more to narrative theory than the formulation of basic conditions. A complete grammar of language comprises three elements: semantics, syntax, and pragmatics. In narrative theory semantics becomes the study of plot, or story; syntax becomes the study of discourse, or narrative techniques; and pragmatics becomes the study of the uses of storytelling and of the mode of participation of human agents in the narrative performance. Digital media affect narrative in three ways. (See table 12.1 for a summary.)

On the pragmatic level they offer new modes of user involvement and new things to do with narrative: exchange stories in real time; impersonate a character; participate in the collective creation of a story; and explore a world in the pursuit of a story. (See the columns labeled "type of interactivity" and "user role" in table 12.1.) They also attribute various degrees of prominence to narrative in the total communicative event (see the last column in the table).

On the discourse level they produce new ways to present stories, which

Exploited*	Mode	Techniques	Structures	Involvement	User Role	Design Problem	Narrative
Hypertext 1 (2) 4 5	Diegetic narration (telling)	Fragmented display; chunking and linking	Metafictional narrative Archival narrative	External Exploratory	1. Putting scrambled story back together 2. Searching archive	Maintaining logical coherence in multilinear environment	Central, but can be linked to nonnarrative texts as part of a collage
Text-based virtual reality (MOOs) 1 3 4 5	Enactment through performative statements Dialogue Diegetic storytelling	Objects with internal behaviors Navigable space Written orality	Personal relationships Fantastic themes	Internal or external Exploratory or ontological	Playing roles Exploring world and interacting with its members	Creating guiding script	Intermittent (dramatic action and storytelling alternate with small talk)
Interactive Drama 1 2 4 5	Enactment through relatively free dialogue and gestures	3D panoramic display Presence of body in virtual world Navigable space	*Attempted:* Aristotelian plots *Recommended:* Fantastic themes Exploration Episodic narrative	Internal Ontological or exploratory	User as coauthor, character, actor, and beneficiary of performance	Creating guiding script that allows user participation while maintaining narrative logic and form	Central
Computer Games 1 2 (3) 4 5	Enactment through actions defined by the system	Navigable space Objects with internal behavior	Quest Evolution of complex entity Mystery stories	All combinations except for external/ exploratory	Performing specific task	Lack of variety of plots Providing alternatives to violent themes	Instrumental
Webcams 1 3 4	Showing	Live, chronological presentation	Everyday life Sexual activities	External Exploratory	Reader as voyeur "Grabbing" highlights	Too little narrative action	Intermittent (Many dead moments)

*Numbers given to properties refer to the list in the text (page 338).

necessitate new interpretive strategies on the part of users. For instance, the "chunking-linking" technique of hypertext, as Hayles calls it, leads to the jigsaw puzzle mode of reading. (See the column labeled "discourse/techniques.")

On the semantic level, finally, the impact of digitality on narrative is not a matter of developing a new logic but, rather, a matter of finding the right fit between the medium and the form and substance of the narrative content. Each medium has particular affinities for certain themes and certain types of plot: you cannot tell the same type of story on the stage and in writing, during conversation and in a thousand-page novel, in a two-hour movie and in a TV serial that runs for many years. The most urgent of the issues that faces developers of new media narrative is to find what themes and what kinds of plots take proper advantage of the built-in properties of the medium. The fourth column of the table, themes and structures, proposes the beginning of an answer to this question. As my survey has shown, combining the inherent linearity of narrative structures with interactive protocols is not an easy thing to do, but the task will be much less daunting if we remember that there is no need for digital narrative to emulate Victorian novels or Shakespearian drama.

If we look back at the history of narrative, we can see it has survived the transition from orality to writing, from manuscript to print, from book to multimedia, and from the stage to moving pictures. Each of these technological innovations has liberated new narrative energies and exploited new possibilities. Given its well-demonstrated resiliency, narrative should easily weather the digital revolution. But I may be asking the wrong question. The survival of narrative does not depend on its ability to adapt itself to new media; narrative has been around so long that it has little to fear from computers. Rather, it is the future of new media as a form of entertainment that depends on their ability to develop their own forms of narrativity.

Notes

1. Many theorists of digital media have proposed lists of distinctive properties, and each of them comes up with a different list. But the different labels often cover related ideas. Janet Murray lists, for instance, the "four essential properties of digital environments" as being (1) procedural (that is, being operated by computer code); (2) participatory (my "interactive"); (3) spatial (but why single out spatiality and omit temporality?); and (4) encyclopedic (71–90). Lev Manovich lists: (1) numerical representation; (2) modularity (a category I borrow directly from him); (3) automation (Murray's "procedural"); (4) variability (my "volatility"); and (5) transcoding (the technical property responsible for my "multiplicity of channels")

(27–48). Which properties are considered essential depends on the purpose of the writer as well as on the criteria used in the selection: should these lists be restricted to properties unique to digital media, or should they include features that these media implement particularly efficiently but share with other media (for example, Murray's spatiality and encyclopedic scope); should they be concerned with aspects of technological implementation hidden from the user (for example, numerical representation); or should they limit themselves to openly displayed features? In my own list I favor features that have an impact on narrativity; that are either unique to digital media or taken by them to a new level; and that the user can perceive directly.

2. This holds of the screen image; the film from which the image is projected cannot be easily updated, unless it is a computer file.

3. These two pairs are adapted from Espen Aarseth's typology of user functions and perspectives in cybertexts, which is itself part of a broader cybertext typology (*Cybertexts* 62–65). But I use different labels that shift the emphasis toward the user's relation to the virtual world.

4. See Lev Manovich's definition of a database in the introduction to this section.

5. For instance, Michael Joyce, *afternoon;* or Mark Amerika, *Grammatron.*

6. The best examples of this type of work are two hypertexts by M. D. Coverley, *Califia* (Eastgate, 2000), and the work in progress *The Book of Going Forth By Day.*

7. MUD stands for Multi-User Dungeon and MOO for Multi-User Dungeon, Object Oriented. *Object Oriented* refers to the programming technique.

8. The earliest MUDs were textual game environments with a built-in plot. (The acronym refers indeed to the role-playing game Dungeons and Dragons.) In the 1980s and 1990s MOOs developed into chatrooms and social meeting places, and the system-defined plot was lost. But the idea of a combination of goal-driven, emplotted game action and free talk was resurrected in the late 1990s with enormously popular games, the so-called massively multi-player role-playing games, such as Ultima Online and EverQuest. In contrast to the earliest MUDs, these environments offer textual communication in a graphically represented world. Players, who number in the hundred thousands, no longer need to create their characters through verbal description; they can construct the appearance of their avatar from a menu of visual elements.

9. Selmer Bringsjord, a computer scientist who has developed a state-of-the-art story-generating program called Brutus, has argued, with the support of logical proofs, that AI will never produce characters approaching the complexity of human-generated literary characters. His argument offers a sobering rebuttal to the prophecies of cyber gurus such as Ray Kurzweil, who claims that by 2029 many of the leading artists, including novelists, will be machines (223). For Kurzweil, however, the machines take a shortcut that renders the development of AI algorithms unnecessary: they are able to write novels because nanotechnology allows the downloading of the human brain into digital circuits. The mind of Proust

preserved in silicon will be able to create literary masterpieces forever. But will this silicon Proust qualify as a machine?

10. Not all game developers would agree with this statement. For Brenda Laurel, whose now defunct company Purple Moon developed games for girls that tried to address issues specific to the experience of growing up female, narrative content is not instrumental but central to the gaming experience. The ultimate purpose of the Purple Moon games was to provide "cultural content" through stories, as did myth in ancient societies (*Utopian Entrepreneur* 61).

11. Theresa Senft's term (qtd. by McLemee 7).

References

Aarseth, Espen. *Cybertext. Perspectives on Ergodic Literature.* Baltimore: Johns Hopkins University Press, 1997.

Amerika, Mark. *Grammatron.* <*http://www.grammatron.com*> (April 28, 2002).

Barthes, Roland. *S/Z.* Trans. Richard Miller. New York: Hill and Wang, 1974.

Bringsjord, Selmer. "Is It Possible to Build Dramatically Compelling Digital Entertainment (in the form, e.g., of computer games)?" *Gamestudies* 1 (2001). <*http://www.gamestudies.org/0101/bringsjord/index.html*> (April 30, 2002).

Coover, Robert. "Literary Hypertext: The Passing of the Golden Age." <*http://www.feedmag.com/document/do291lofi.html*> (March 24, 2000; no longer available).

Coverley, M. D. *Califia.* Watertown MA: Eastgate Systems, 2000. (Hypertext software.)

———. *The Book of Going Forth by Day.* <*http://califia.hispeed.com/Egypt*> (April 28, 2002).

Davenport, Glorianna. "Your Own Virtual Storyworld." *Scientific American* (November 2000): 79–82.

Grodal, Torben. "Stories for Eye, Ear, and Muscles: Computer Games, Media, and Embodied Experiences." *The Video Game Theory Reader.* Ed. Mark J. P. Wolf and Bernard Perron. London: Routledge, 2003. 129–55.

Hayles, N. Katherine. "The Transformation of Narrative and the Materiality of Hypertext." *Narrative* 9.1 (2001): 21–39.

Joyce, Michael. *Afternoon, a Story.* Watertown MA: Eastgate Systems, 1987. (Hypertext software.)

———. *Of Two Minds: Hypertext, Pedagogy, and Poetics.* Ann Arbor: University of Michigan Press, 1995.

Kelso, Margaret Thomas, Peter Weyhrauch, and Joseph Bates. "Dramatic Presence." *Presence: Teleoperators and Virtual Environments* 2.1 (1993): 1–15.

Kolko, Beth. "Building a World with Words: The Narrative Reality of Virtual Communities." *Works and Days* 13.1–2 (1995): 105–26.

Koskimaa, Raine. Digital Literature. "From Text to Hypertext and Beyond." Ph.D. diss., University of Jyväskylä (Finland), 2000.

Kurzweil, Ray. *The Age of Spiritual Machines.* New York: Viking, 1999.

Landow, George P. *Hypertext 2.0: The Convergence of Contemporary Critical Theory and Technology.* 1992. Reprint. Baltimore: Johns Hopkins University Press, 1997.

Laurel, Brenda. *Computers as Theatre.* Menlo Park CA: Addison-Wesley, 1991.

———. *Utopian Entrepreneur.* Cambridge: MIT Press, 2001.

Mateas, Michael, and Andrew Stern. "Towards Integrating Plot and Character for Interactive Drama." Working Notes of the Social Intelligence Agents: The Human in the Loop Symposium. AAAI Fall Symposium Series. Menlo Park CA: AAAI Press, 2000. Version used here online at: <*http://www-2.cs.cmu.edu/~michaelm/publications/SIA2000.pdf*> (April 24, 2002).

McLemee, Scott. "I Am a Camera." *Lingua Franca* (February 2001): 6–8.

Murray, Janet E. *Hamlet on the Holodeck: The Future of Narrative in Cyberspace.* New York: Free Press, 1997.

The Nerdman Show. <*http://www.nerdman.com*> (April 28, 2002).

Olafson, Peter. "Game Theory." *New York Times,* October 5, 2000.

Ryan, Marie-Laure. *Narrative as Virtual Reality: Immersion and Interactivity in Literature and Electronic Media.* Baltimore: Johns Hopkins University Press, 2001.

Sloane, Sarah. *Digital Fictions: Storytelling in a Material World.* Stamford CT: Ablex, 2000.

Walton, Kendall. *Mimesis as Make-Believe: On the Foundations of the Representational Arts.* Cambridge: Harvard University Press, 1990.

White, Hayden. "The Value of Narrativity in the Representation of Reality." *On Narrative.* Ed. W. J. T. Mitchell. Chicago: University of Chicago Press, 1980. 1–24.

13

Quest Games as Post-Narrative Discourse

Espen Aarseth

Recently, a new country was added to the national economies of the world. This country, called Norrath, has no geophysical existence, no borders with other countries, no diplomatic ties with anyone, and no representation in supernational agencies such as the UN. Still, its gross national product per capita places it seventy-seventh among the world's nations (just below Russia), and its coin, the platinum, has an exchange rate valued close to the yen and the lire.[1]

Norrath is imaginary but not fictional. It exists in the "massively multiplayer" role-playing game EverQuest, developed by Verant and owned by Sony. There are 300,000 to 400,000 people who play (and work) in Norrath on a regular basis; some spend more than half their current lives there. The economy is driven by the production and trade of useful items, such as spells, weapons, armor, and entire avatars, bought and sold for real money at places such as *playerauctions.com*. Since you also can buy the Norrath currency at these places, it becomes a real currency, and the Norrath economy becomes a place in which real people can make a real living. EverQuest may be a game (some would say a primitive form of entertainment), but the complexities and real-world ramifications of these massive games are far larger than those of any other entertainment genre, perhaps sports excepted. The thought that these complex media can be understood by any existing media theory, such as narratology, which was developed for a totally different genre, grows more unlikely with every stage of the ongoing computer evolution.

Few, if any, cultural genres have evolved and expanded more rapidly than the computer game over the last three decades. From humble beginnings in the 1950s and 1960s (automated chess and checkers opponents such as Arthur Samuel's self-learned Checkersplayer, which reached grandmaster status in the early 1960s) to the modern 3D games of the 1990s, an amazing cultural evolution is still very much taking place. Or perhaps this is not one but several evolutions toward several specific cultural practices. To simply talk about "games," or even "digital games," seems irresponsible: there are large and widening differences between game genres, gaming situations, and game technologies. In this essay the focus will be on a certain type of game, the digital quest game.

The prevalent view among academic commentators of computer games seems to be that the games are ("interactive") stories, a new kind of storytelling that can nonetheless be analyzed and even constructed using traditional narratology. This article will argue against that view, based on the following observations:

- There are essential discursive differences between stories and computer games, much more crucial than those between novels and film (cf. Juul).
- Narrative theory (often the most basic and archaic kind, for example, Aristotle's poetics) seems to be used because there is nothing better to use, not because it fits particularly well (and, yes, games do have beginnings, middles, and ends).
- When games are analyzed as stories, both their differences from stories and their intrinsic qualities become all but impossible to understand.
- The narrativistic approach is also unfortunate because it imposes an external aesthetic on the games, treating them as inferior narrative art, which may be redeemed only when their quality reaches a higher "literary" or artistic level.[2]
- Computer games studies needs to be liberated from narrativism, and an alternative theory that is native to the field of study must be constructed.
- Only then can we begin to see clearly how games relate to stories, how stories sometimes are used in games and integrate or conflict with the games' action in a simulated world, and maybe learn something new about both discursive modes.

This essay will analyze three different digital quest games and show how the analysis breaks down if conducted with traditional narratological means and models. The games are the first-person multiplayer shooter Return to Castle Wolfenstein (ID/Raven, 2001), the space combat/exploration/trade game x—Beyond the Frontier (Egosoft, 1999), and the real-time fantasy battle simulator Myth II: Soulblighter (Bungie, 1997), with special emphasis on their openness: how it is possible and sometimes necessary for the players to construct their own discursive strategy and use the games' building blocks in their own, idiosyncratic ways.

Games in Virtual Environments

But, first, let us discuss the larger game genre that digital quest games belong to, starting with the problems of game genre definitions. There are many ways to partition the game field into genres. Most of them seem to originate with the popular press and the games industry, as marketing categories. There is nothing wrong with that, but the ideological pressure of the market is usually not the best environment for scholarly, analytical practice. What works well as a sales term might not work at all as a theoretical perspective, although there is every reason to take these ad hoc terms and categories seriously and give them a thorough evaluation. In the case of games, however, the categories are clearly problematic and overlapping.

A typical list of game types might be: action, adventure, driving, puzzle, role playing, simulation, sports, and strategy.[3] The problem with this classification should be obvious if we apply it to a recent game such as Jason Jones and others' Halo (Bungie, 2001), a science fiction combat game set on a ring world in a universe where humankind are threatened by extinction from various alien races. Halo is a first-person shooter but also, occasionally, a "third-person driver," since there are vehicles to drive around in (and squish your adversaries with), and the perspective changes from first to third as one enters the driver's seat. Halo is definitely an *action* game but also a *puzzle* game, since there are problems to solve, such as labyrinths. *Strategic* thinking, rather than brute force and reflexes, is required to get past many of the obstacles. In the role of the cybernetically enhanced, nameless "Master Chief" there is not a lot of *role playing* for the player, but the linear progression of the game, from one level to the next, makes it a typical *adventure* game, interspersed with cut scenes of prerecorded dialogue. Since practically all computer games are *simulations* of some sort of physical environment, this category is a particularly unhelpful one, if taken literally. And what about *sports?* Well, in Halo's multiplayer repertoire there are several definitively sportslike game types, such as Oddball, King of the Hill, Capture the Flag, and Rally. In short, with the exception of role playing, Halo fits every one of the categories. And it would not be hard to imagine a role-playing layer added to the game.

Halo's multimodality is hardly exceptional. Most modern computer games are equally characterized by several of the types on our list. In fact, the list is a heuristic remnant from the days when games were less complex and multifaceted than today, but even then it would not have stood up to this kind of scrutiny. Today what we call games (Quake Arena, Starcraft, Age of Empires, to name a few of them) are technical infrastructures that are better described as game *platforms*, like a deck of cards that can house so many different games: Solitaire, Poker, Bridge, Blackjack, and so on.

Clearly, if we want to study game genres we need a better typology than lists like the one I offered earlier, but this is not the place for a detailed effort. Instead, let it suffice to partition the field of digital game genres in two main categories: (1) *digitized* versions of traditional games (card games, board games, dice games, mechanical arcade games such as Pinball); and (2) *games in virtual environments.* (A virtual environment is a simulation of a physical world, not necessarily our own and usually much less complex.) The latter type encompasses most original computer games, such as Nolan Bushnell's Pong (Atari, 1971, admittedly an *extremely* simple virtual environment). Sometimes the environments are minimalist and abstract, such as with the ever-popular Tetris (Alexei Pajitnov, 1986). As computer technology has become better and more powerful, so have the games expanded and grown in complexity to fill the technological potential. Also, the complexity of the virtual environment seems to be relative to the size of the game's program code, and most commercial games of recent years have large, complex virtual environments, whether 2D (third-person, map view), such as Heroes of Might and Magic, or 3D (first-person, subjective view), such as x—Beyond the Frontier or Return to Castle Wolfenstein.

The fact that game evolution seems to go in the direction of ever larger and more detailed, complex, virtual environments clearly justifies this as a valid, descriptive category, named by its most important common feature. If we adopt games in virtual environments (rather than computer games, digital games, or video games) as the super-category of our investigation, then the extremely vague and overused term *games* has been usefully narrowed down.

Yet, in connection with our current topic, narrative, even further demarcation is needed. Sports games, for instance, such as Tony Hawk's Pro Skater 3 (Gearbox, 2001) are games of pure skill. They have little or no relevance to a discussion of games and narrative discourse. Similarly, open-ended simulation/construction games such as Sim City or The Sims (Will Wright, 1987 and 2001) are all about mastering the rules of the system and using them creatively. So, we need to focus on those virtual environment games in which mastery of the environment or the rules of the simulation is not the primary purpose of playing but in which these elements are secondary to highly specific achievements and goals. Discussions about "the narrative in Tetris" or "the function of back story in Space Invaders" are, quite frankly, an intellectual waste of time. We should be discussing the games that are most problematic and difficult to dismiss from an antinarrativist point of view. What we should be looking for are games with highly idiosyncratic ways of winning, in which the environment has been reduced to a scenic path of difficult but conquerable obstacles. Why? Because these are the ones that are most typically used as examples of "narrative games." But are they?

Problems in Adventure Game Poetics

From a humanist, aesthetic perspective, computer games have always been seen in terms of other artistic genres, rather than as a genre in its own right and with its own standards. Early attempts to discuss adventure games (starting with Niesz and Holland; and Buckles) have mostly looked at games from a literary perspective—not surprisingly, since the games they preferred to look at were text based. As the games developed visually, and especially into 3D, theater and film criticism have been used. Although these early attempts had little influence (with the exception of Brenda Laurel's work), the general approach, to discuss games as though they were something else, is nevertheless still dominant today. The "games-as-narratives" approach is clearly so attractive to scholars that nearly twenty years of insignificant results do not influence their choice of method.[4]

While there undoubtedly exists some structural and thematic affinity between adventure games and stories, it is therefore not self-evident that the former genre really "is" the latter. An equally reasonable hypothesis would be that there is a common cultural impulse that motivates both types. Similar cultural themes are usually found across media and across different forms of expression—for example, film and fashion, without a similar tendency to claim that fashion is film, or vice versa. Likewise, the similarities of structure between adventure games and stories could be ascribed to a certain common source of inspiration, namely life itself.

Like people in real life, readers of stories and players of games rely on interpretable elements to make sense of the situations they encounter. These elements can be conflicts, adversaries and allies, desirable objects, overcoming obstacles and tackling challenges, winning and losing. The fact that these basic elements are present in all three phenomena does not make the game use of them tertiary, just because the narrative use is secondary.

On the contrary, in games, just as in life, the outcomes (winning, losing) are real and personal to the experiencer, unlike in stories.

The mere fact that an adventure game adaptation of a novel, say, Melbourne House's The Hobbit (1982), tries (in a frightfully feeble way) to reenact some of the events of Tolkien's story does not make the game a story, just as the recent *Tomb Raider* movie cannot be mistaken for the game. Yet many theorists do not shy away from calling games stories, and even the more thoughtful ones, like Henry Jenkins, use unfocused terms such as *emergent narratives.* Of course, games can be derived from stories (or the cultural mythologies that produce stories, such as espionage), but so can paintings. Surely, games can use stories as inspiration for the gameplay, but this does not mean that the games are derivative the way a movie adaptation of a novel would be. Tchaikovsky's *1812 Overture* does not tell the story of Napoléon's fatal battle in Russia; it merely scores it. By imitating some key events of Tolkien's story, the Hobbit adventure game uses the story to motivate and structure the gameplay to a certain extent, but it does not retell it.

Even if we adopt the widest (and weakest) possible notion of narratives—that they could be architectural rather than sequential, enacted rather than related, experienced personally and uniquely rather than observed collectively and statically—an ontological difference would still remain. This difference is probably best described with the word *choice.* In a game there must be choice. Even in games of "pure" chance there is choice: what to bet on, how much to bet, and so on. Not only that, but the choices would have to be crucial. In a game everything revolves around the player's ability to make choices. If the choices presented to the player are so limited that they clearly seem to lead the action in one unavoidable direction, they become quasi-choices, and the game becomes a quasi-game. Or to use a less loaded phrase: the story disguises itself as a game, using the game technology to tell itself. An example of this are the "game books," often called Choose Your Own Adventures, detective fiction text games in which simple tree structures are navigated by the user/reader/player. In these games, like the early computer adventure games, a dominant plot is "discovered" by the reader, but in reality it has been there all along. These games are not about choice but about rediscovering the one acceptable path. Typically, and unlike any other game type, they can only be played through once.

Since computer games are simulations, contained in a machine that is capable of emulating any other kind of media machine, it should not surprise us that a game can be used to narrate. A good example is the opening sequence of Half-Life (Valve, 1998), in which the player-avatar is transported in a monorail compartment through an underground tunnel. The player can move freely within the cabin and look out in any direction, but the ride continues its predetermined course, uninfluenced by any action the player might attempt. This opening is the perfect allegory of the unicursal structure of "games" such as Half-Life: there is a perfect path or "ideal sequence" that must be realized, or the game/story will not continue. Half-Life has been praised for its well-designed story, but, as Jesper Juul points out, "Much of the vast journey that it takes to complete Half-Life would be excruciatingly dull if retold in any detail."

Games such as Half-Life are structured like a string of pearls: within each pearl (or microworld) there is plenty of choice, but on the level of the string there is no choice at all. And between the pearls there are often beads of a different sort: cut scenes (short, animated movies) that explain and motivate the coming action. It is interesting to note that the early text adventure games did not have this structure or the cut scenes. There you could often wander all the way back to the beginning—not that it helped you much if you did. The reason is, of course, that the fairly complex 3D worlds of games such as Half-Life are so demanding that the computers they run on cannot deal with the whole world at once. So, the current state of gaming technology actually rewards the episodic string-of-pearls structure over the much more demanding possibility of having the complete gameworld in one model. Thus, what may seem like a narrative structure is also an economic one.

Not all 3D games follow the string-of-pearls structure; in massively multiplayer games such as Sony's EverQuest, the pearls are laid out in two dimensions, with connections between some of them. Also notably different is the absence of cut scenes, probably because the borders between zones in EverQuest are repeatedly crossed in both directions during gameplay.

While many adventure games are clearly attempts at telling stories, cleverly disguised as games, the limited results they achieve (poor to nonexistent characterization, extremely derivative action plots, and, wisely, no attempts at metaphysical themes) should tell us that the stories are hostage to the game environment, even if they are perceived as the dominant factor. We might even speculate that we are no longer looking at stories but hollow shells that are gutted of artistic value. But that would be unfair, because games like Half-Life and The Hobbit are clearly appreciated by their players.

Like the introduction in Half-Life, there is nothing to stop a game from being almost completely storylike. In a visual game environment this

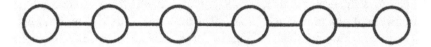

Figure 13.1. Half-Life.

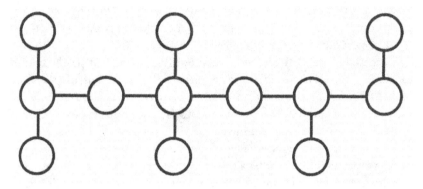

Figure 13.2. Everquest.

would simply be an animated movie, and game engines such as Id's Quake series have indeed been used to produce such movies. But it would, of course, no longer be a game. So, in order to remain playable, the games can never achieve their ambitions of storytelling. Instead, they must engage and motivate their users by other means than those that narratives use. But what means are these?

If we examine a number of adventure games, they all seem quite similar in terms of form: the player-avatar must move through a landscape in order to fulfill a goal while mastering a series of challenges. This phenomenon is called a quest. The purpose of adventure games is to enable players to fulfill quests. This, not storytelling, is their dominant structure.

In a very illuminating essay on MUDs and performance, Ragnhild Tronstad discusses the relationship between act and meaning in questing, using Felman's speech act analysis of Molière's *Don Juan:* "A conflict between act and meaning is present in the activity of quest solving too. To do a quest is to search for the meaning of it. Having reached this meaning, the quest is solved. The paradox of questing is that as soon as meaning is reached, the quest stops functioning as *quest.* When meaning is found, the quest is *history.* It cannot be done again, as it is simply not the same experience to solve a puzzle quest for the second time." Tronstad argues for the difference between quests and stories as a difference between performatives and constatives:

> Stories in general belong to the order of meaning, together with the constatives, and not to the order of the act. Quests, on the other hand, are basically performative: they belong first and foremost to the order of the act. As soon as they are solved, though, they turn into constatives. The reason quests can be easily be confused with "stories" is that we are normally analyzing the quest in retrospective, after we've already solved it. To ignore the performative aspect of quests this way is fundamentally to misjudge questing as a practice. Being acts before they are meaning, we must focus on the way quests *act* to understand the way they work. (Pt. 4.1)

Although we certainly also "analyze" (if that is the correct word) quests while doing them, the in medias res analysis is restricted by the lack of complete knowledge, so we need to distinguish between strategic and reflective analysis. Researchers usually analyze games *after* playing them, and, if Tronstad is correct, then this would obscure the performative dimension in favor of the constative one. Since stories are constatives already, as Tronstad points out, a similar eclipse does not obstruct the analysis of stories.

If we take quests and questing as a key to understanding games, then several questions pop up. Are all quests structurally similar? Are there quests in all kinds of games? Is it possible to come up with a typology of quests, or a grammar? These are big questions, and perhaps a better strategy, at least for the moment, is to analyze games with quests, to find out more about them.

Tentatively, however, it seems clear that there are quests in many types of games. Metaphorically, quests could come to mean any kind of goal orientation, such as the quest to get your initials on the high-score list in Pac-Man. If, however, we define *quest* to mean the hunt for a specific outcome, rather than just winning the game, then there are games that do not qualify, such as a standard Quake-type multiplayer death match game or games such as Tetris. In Tetris there is no final solution, just harder and harder situations, until the player makes one mistake too many. And in a Quake death match, like in chess, there are no specific ways to progress; you win by killing your opponents any which way you can and more times than they.

Space Quest: Beyond the Narrative Frontier

x—Beyond the Frontier (Egosoft, 1999) is a simulation of a galaxy, far, far away, with various alien races and a large number of solar systems connected by "jump gates." The player commands a spaceship that can be extended with all sorts of equipment—the more advanced, the more expensive. To get money for the equipment the player can trade, freight cargo, hunt pirates, or be a pirate. The most lucrative career move, however, is to become a factory owner and produce sellable goods. By exploring the galaxy and establishing trade relations and setting up factories, the player can rise in the galaxy's hierarchy from a lowly pilot to a wealthy magnate with a fleet of space ships. The game is open-ended, so there is no specific winning scenario; the way to lose is to get your ship shot to pieces. As a first-person shooter, role-playing, strategy game, it also consists of quests ("missions"), which the player selects freely.

A cut scene at the start of the game introduces the situation (experimental pilot stranded in alien galaxy), and then you are on your own. Learn to pilot the ship, then learn to trade, build, fight, and so on, and finally learn to manage a business empire or just choose to explore the galaxy. Of the handful of alien races only one is completely hostile, so one goal might be to wage an all-out war on them, if you feel strong enough.

This universe is rather large, so be prepared to spend many hundred hours in it. While you are doing your thing in some corner, the rest of the universe goes about its business (perhaps preparing an attack on you), so there are no prearranged events waiting for the player to come and trigger them. This automation also means that, if you dock in one of your space stations and leave the simulation running while you sleep or do something else, the universe will continue to evolve. When you come back to the game some hours later, you may find your funds have increased from trade and sales at your factories, or perhaps pirates have wiped out a large part of your property.

The voluntary quests are discovered as you explore the solar systems. You might get information about a special technology that is only available at a certain secret space station deep in enemy territory, or there might be an area rich in special natural resources that will give you a trade advantage. In the sequel to x, Xtension (2000), quests were added after the game was released.

In x the quests are a kind of holiday; they are mystery tours you can take when you need a change from the daily business of pursuing a galactic career. They are not necessary but easily afforded by the simulation and its rules. In addition, the player can invent personal quests, such as challenging one of the alien races, or taking over the entire galaxy's production of a certain commodity.

The quests in x do not follow a particular pattern or structure. They are as varied as the rest of the potential events in the game, and they may be dropped, put on hold, and taken up again at will. They are perhaps best described as a special subtype of the exploration that the game, above all, invites.

What is the story in x? The answer must be that you can write your own but only if you want. Players and fans of the game have written stories set in the x universe, so-called fan fiction, and there is also a graphic novel under development, called *Pirate's Gambit.*[5]

I Did It My Way: Playing against the Plot

Many types of games (for example, turn-based strategy, real-time strategy, adventure games, and role-playing games) follow the pearl chain structure described earlier. In some of them the actions taken inside each pearl are simple and generic, but in others the particular subgoals inside are planned and governed by complicated scripts. But the events that go on inside a pearl are sometimes not so easy to plan for the game designers. Warren Spector and Harvey Smith, the lead designers for the first-person role-playing game series Deus Ex (Ion Storm, 1999 and 2002), report their astonishment when they found out that players were using attachable bombs ("LAMS") to climb walls![6] The players would have their avatar place a bomb on the wall, jump onto it, place another a bit higher up, and so on. In this way they could reach places and do things the game designers had not intended them to do, at least not in that way. After having discovered this, the players sent a screen snapshot of their exploit to the surprised designers. Although Deus Ex is a fairly closed adventure game, it is also a simulated world, and here the players subverted the quest design by exploiting the mechanical logic of the simulation. The resulting pleasure is probably much greater than the one they would get by simply solving the game the way it was intended.

This mode of playing is actually very common. In Richard Bartle's classic typology of multiplayer types, this is clearly the explorer type, which Bartle characterizes as players who "try to find out as much as they can about the virtual world. Although initially this means mapping its topology (i.e., exploring the MUD's breadth), later it advances to experimentation with its physics."

In a quest game with specific goals, such as Bungie's Myth II: Soul-blighter, a 3D real-time combat game, subverting the intended solution structure can be quite easy, since the complex scripting required to control the simulation can easily break. In one of the scenarios in Myth II the goal is to conquer a castle by means of a special, invisible dwarf, who can sneak in undetected and open the main gate for your army waiting outside. The dwarf is supposed to do this by throwing a grenade (of which he has an inexhaustible supply) at the drawbridge mechanism. After that, your main force will enter and clean out the opposition. (This is still quite difficult, especially because the thirty to forty soldiers you command must all be controlled in real time.) The dwarf is quite a capable fighter, however, and, by using him alone, I tried to take out all the castle's forces without outside help. By keeping the dwarf on the battlements and having him grenade-bomb the approaching soldiers from above, I actually managed to take out all the enemies while my main force waited outside the gates. The hardest part was to dodge the arrows of a line of archers on one of the walls, but by running zigzag toward them while throwing grenades (and after much saving and reloading) this was actually accomplished.

In other Myth II scenarios there are similar possibilities for the subversive explorer, including killing main villains, who are not supposed to be killed at that point, because they reappear in the next scenario as if nothing had happened to them. In games like this, in which a quest script is put on top of a simulation, the scripters are never safe from explorers who want nothing more than to beat the game by subverting its rules. The top-down, narrative intentions of the scenario designers are subject to the bottom-up laws of the simulation.

The Multiplayer Duplex Quest: Beach Invasion

Quests are by no means limited to single-user games. In the first Multi-User Dungeon (Trubshaw and Bartle, 1979–80), just like the Dungeons and Dragons board games that inspired them, quests were meant to be cooperative. Several players would team up in search of a treasure guarded by a dragon, and they could only kill the dragon by seeking strength in numbers. This ensured friendly cooperation and contributed to the social, helpful atmosphere that characterizes many of the multiplayer games. In the big, commercial, graphical MUDs of the late 1990s, guilds and clans formed to organize players and help beginners.

Lately, a new form of multiplayer quest has appeared, in team-based first-person shooter games such as Quake Team Arena (2000), Counter-

Strike (2000), and Return to Castle Wolfenstein (2001). Here is a narrated retrospective of one performed quest in the latter game:

> *I'm an engineer.* I run zigzag between the barbed wire and the machine-gun sprays from the forward bunker, and I hope my allied comrades will give me cover while I plant and arm the dynamite at the bunker door. Dynamite planted, I run for the breach in the sea wall, and plant a second charge there. Then I wait while the fuse burns, and watch for enemy engineers who might defuse the charge before it blows. Then, in a sudden cascade of light and sound, I am dead, in limbo, hit by an enemy air strike. The engineering job is done, so I switch roles to *medic,* and wait for resurrection, watching the battle rage through the frenzied eyes of a team-member. 4 seconds, 3, 2, 1, there, I am back at the beach landing, while a fierce fight goes on up at the forward bunker door.
>
> Several of my teammates are down, but I ignore their cries for help and run for the breach. There are still six minutes left, the attack has just started, so there is still an element of surprise. Not too many people are defending the German bunker, so I might break through if I sneak in alone. I pass the breach and climb the ladder to the upper bunker, someone snipes at me as I enter the doorway to the back stairs, I am hit, but not down, and as a medic I heal myself quickly while I continue to run down the stairs. In the basement I meet no one, and head straight for the war room. Still no enemies; they are all upstairs fighting. I go for the documents on the table. Objective Taken! I carry the secret documents, and the game changes. The German soldiers now have to stop me from reaching the radio room, where the documents will be transmitted to the Allied Headquarters the moment I enter. Now what?
>
> I could go back up the long way I came, or I could head straight for the radio stairway, the shortest route. But this is also what they will expect. Instead, I sneak into the barracks room at the end of the basement corridor, and peek around the corner, where I can see the radio stairway. Then I wait. The German soldiers should be in a state of panic by now, expecting me to make a run for the radio room but not knowing from what direction. After ten seconds, a gray-clad soldier bounces down the stairs, heading for the war room. He does not see me, so the coast is clear. It is now or never. My comrades are still fighting in the forward trenches. I run to the stairs, and up the flights, expecting hand grenades, gunfire, or worse, a Panzerfaust rocket. That would be the end of me. Nothing. There is no one there! My strategy has paid off: after someone went down to check, they all expect me to come from

the other direction. Ha! As I enter the radio room at the top of the stairs, I allow myself a brief pause, hit "V-5–7" on the keyboard, and smile as my "Yeehaw!" shout coincides with the "Allies Win!" message on everybody's screens. My teammates cheer, while from the Axis side several disappointed voices cry "Nein!"

In this game two teams oppose each other in a typical World War II scenario: the Normandy beach invasion. The Allied team has four objectives in their quest: (1) to break through the bunker wall using explosives; (2) to capture the forward bunker; (3) to steal the secret documents from the war room deep in the basement; and (4) to transmit them by getting them to the radio room. The Axis team has the opposite, mirror image quest: to hinder and stop the Allies every step of the way. If they can do this for eight minutes, they will win by default. Unlike unidirectional quests, this duplex quest game can be played over and over; the only (but crucial) difference is that the individual team members might be totally different from game to game. On each team players choose between the roles of engineer, soldier (with special weapons such as rocket launcher, sniper rifle, and flame thrower), medic (heals wounded teammates), and lieutenant (supplies the others with ammo). When player-avatars get killed, they reappear in the game (which typically lasts four to eight minutes) after a predetermined penalty period. A well-balanced team will consist of different combinations of roles at different stages in the game: snipers and engineers dominate in the beginning, lieutenants and medics in the end stages.

Even if this clearly is a quest game, the duplicity ensures that no two games are the same. Like chess, the moves and strategies can be varied an infinite number of times, although the world and the rules are quite simple.

So, although the goals of the Beach Invasion scenario are as simple as in any quest, the duplex structure makes this type of game very different in terms of player experience and replaying enjoyment. We could argue that the game cannot be replayed, since every game is different and, therefore, in Tronstad's terms, the meaning of the game is endlessly deferred. "But as meaning is also the death of the quest, it is frequently breaking this promise, in order to prolong the questing experience" (Tronstad).

To act is all. Unlike checkers, which ceased to be a serious game when Arthur Samuel's AI player beat all human opponents and showed the game's determinate nature, duplex quests such as Beach Invasion have no meaning, so play goes on forever.

Conclusion: Beyond Narrative—Toward a Quest Game Theory

In this empirical essay I have tried to show how the complex and unpredictable event structures afforded by entertainment simulations need to be divorced from narratological thinking in order to be understood. Instead of looking at games as stories, we might benefit from looking at some games (games with specific goals) as *quest games.* As we have seen, this is not an easily defined genre, but it solves the problematic question of whether games are narrative while also pointing the way to a more useful terminology. In identifying these games as quest games, we can, following Tronstad, explain why they are mistaken for narratives and also be better placed to rescue those aspects of narratology that continue to be of use in our analysis.

Are there "narrative games" that are not also quests? If not, the current focus on storytelling in computer game theory might be replaced by a more productive focus on questing. Clearly, games and game engines can *also* be used to tell stories, but this is probably an extreme end of a spectrum that runs between narration and free play, with rule-based games and quest games somewhere in between. When we take phenomena such as multiplayer and "massively multiplayer" games into account, the likelihood that the narrative end of the spectrum will come to dominate games seems very small.

But only time will tell.

Notes

1. Per Castronova.
2. About "narrativism," see Aarseth, "Genre Trouble."
3. The list is taken from <*http://gamespot.com*> (October 14, 2002).
4. For a thorough discussion of this literature, see Aarseth, *Cybertext.*
5. <*http://www.egosoft.com/X/xnews/200202_44News.html#top6*> (October 14, 2002).
6. <*http://www.themushroom.com/20q/warrenspector.html*> (October 14, 2002).

References

Aarseth, Espen. *Cybertext: Perspectives on Ergodic Literature.* Baltimore: Johns Hopkins University Press, 1997.
———. "Genre Trouble: Narrativism and the Art of Simulation." *First Person.* Ed. Pat Harrigan and Noah Wardrip-Fruin. Cambridge: MIT Press, 2004.
Bartle, Richard. "Hearts, "Hearts, Clubs, Diamonds, Spades: Players Who Suit MUDS" (1996). <*http://www.mud.co.uk/richard/hcds.htm*> (October 14, 2002).

Buckles, Mary Ann. "Interactive Fiction: The Storygame 'Adventure.'" Ph.D. diss., University of California–San Diego, 1985.

Castronova, Edward. "Virtual Worlds: A First-Hand Account of Market and Society on the Cyberian Frontier" (2002). *<http://papers.ssrn.com/sol3/papers .cfm?abstract_id=294828>* (October 14, 2002).

Jenkins, Henry. "Video Games on the Threshold of Art." Paper presented at the Game Cultures conference, University of the West of England, Bristol, June 2001.

Juul, Jesper. "Games Telling Stories? A Brief Note on Games and Narratives." *Game Studies* 1.1. *<http://gamestudies.org/0101/juul-gts>* (October 14, 2002).

Laurel, Brenda Kay. "Toward the Design of a Computer-Based Interactive Fantasy System." Ph.D. diss., Ohio State University. University Microfilms International, 1986.

———. *Computers as Theatre.* Reading MA: Addison—Wesley, 1991.

Niesz, Anthony J., and Norman N. Holland. "Interactive Fiction." *Critical Inquiry* 11.1 (1984): 110–29.

Tronstad, Ragnhild. "Semiotic and Non-Semiotic MUD Performance." Paper presented at the COSIGN conference, Amsterdam, September 11, 2001. *<http://www .kinonet.com/conferences/cosign2001/pdfs/Tronstad.pdf>*.

14

The Myths of Interactive Cinema

Peter Lunenfeld

Charlie Chaplin and Leni Riefenstahl still strike me as odd figures to sell the masses on computers, but then again, I am not, nor have I ever been, an ad man. And so it was in the first half of the 1980s, when computers underwent a makeover, that I watched the Little Tramp morph into a corporate pitchman and the athletic Valkyries from *Olympiad* (1938) recast as digital "revolutionaries." At the very moment when tech marketers discarded mainframe mandarins in favor of "empowered" populations of personal computers users, the two biggest PC manufacturers—IBM (desperate to shed the sober white coats with which they had built their fortune) and Apple (the very embodiment of the computer "revolution")—both chose to invoke the cinema directly in their most important advertising campaigns. In 1981 IBM licensed Charlie Chaplin's image as spokesperson for its new line of PCs and used a Chaplin impersonator to sell the concept of an IBM for the little guy in both print and television ads. That the impersonator was female was weird enough but not half so odd as the decision to hire the Little Tramp—an icon of the battle between the romantic spirit and the brutalism of the machine age—to sell the portal to the information era. Like the robber barons who built mechanized factories while stocking their Victorian era houses with all manner of preindustrial decorative arts, IBM was counting on the lag between technology and aesthetics to sell their machines.

Three years later, in 1984, Apple's television commercial for the first Macintosh computer took direct aim at IBM's PC, and Apple, too, referenced the cinematic. Helmed, as they say in *Variety,* by Ridley Scott—one of England's most accomplished directors of commercials as well as the man who had just created *Blade Runner* (1982), inarguably the most influential film of its era—it premiered during the Super Bowl, the United States's single most important and expensive venue for advertisements, and made a huge impact. A young woman bursts into a totalitarian screening room, IBM's Big Blue conflated with Orwell's Big Brother. She runs down the aisle hefting a sledgehammer in both hands, lets it fly, shatters the screen, and liberates the enslaved audience from the tyranny of command line interfaces and c//: prompts with the power of Mac's GUI (graphical user interface). Gifted bricoleur that he is, Scott also lifted freely from a range of totalitarian cinematic imaginaries, from Orson Welles's *Citizen Kane* (1941) to Riefenstahl's other fascist masterpiece, *Triumph of the Will* (1936).

These two seminal advertising campaigns can serve as fodder for any number of discussions, from a debate about Marshall McLuhan's provo-cation that the content of any new medium is an old one to an earnest condemnation of advanced capitalism's willingness to enlist any and every aesthetic to accomplish consumerist needs. But I bring up Charlie and Leni as a way to literalize the connection between computers and the cinema, a relationship that, when analyzed, too often fuzzes out into aesthetic banalities, technological generalities, and market futurism. Of course, the computational and the cinematic are now such massive and intertwined cultural and economic forces as to make a general discussion of them all but impossible. So, perversely, I choose to discuss not one of the endless successes of this marriage—everything from computer-generated special effects (CGFX) to DVDs to digital filmmaking—but a failure: "interactive cinema," a much-hyped hybrid that never did quite make it. Interestingly, however, the failure of this form has never dampened the enthusiasm of its proponents, and its very lack of success has occasionally inspired even greater fervor to "get it right."

In this, interactive cinema has ascended into the realm of the mythic. There are seminars on interactive cinema from San Francisco State to the University of Southern California; tool development workshops from the University of Washington to Princeton; scholarly conferences from NYU to Brown to MIT; and festivals from Telluride's International Experimental Cinema Exposition to the Rotterdam Film Festival to the so-called first Interactive Film Festival in the Portugal Media 2001 program. In the sum-mer of 2001 a random search engine pulls up over two thousand hits for the phrase *interactive cinema* on the World Wide Web. And journalists continue to a spout a dewy sort of techno-optimism when they cover all of this, as witnessed by a recent story out of Sydney, Australia: "Imagine a cinema screen surrounding you, showing a panoramic scene from which you can pick which action you want to watch, zooming in on certain events and viewing something different from that being viewed by the person next to you." Indeed, *imagine* is the operative word. In the pages to follow, I hope to explore the myths of interactive cinema in order to come up with a kind of abject insight into our contemporary technocultural moment.

First, however, a discussion is in order of what interactive cinema actually looks like. From the medium's short history I offer three examples. The first is an experiment by Glorianna Davenport, director of MIT's Interactive Cinema Group and without a doubt the foremost proponent of the form in the world. On the screen a flock of birds appears, pecking at the ground. As the spectator approaches, the birds take flight. Another screen offers an Indian dancer going through her complex choreography. As the spectator turns to leave, the image cuts to a close-up of the dancer, her nostrils flaring with anger at the effrontery of the spectator daring to turn away from her performance. Davenport characterizes her approach to interactive cinema storytelling as follows: "A novel approach . . . celebrates electronic narrative as a process in which the authors, a networked presentation system, and the audience actively collaborate in the co-construction of meaning . . . A spreading-activation network is used to select relevant story elements from a multimedia database and dynamically conjoin them into an appealing, coherent narrative presentation . . . Connected to the narrative engine through rich feedback loops and intuitively understandable interfaces, the audience becomes an active partner in the shaping and presentation of story."[1] This narrative stresses novelty, the database, and the empowerment of the viewer. All these are ideas that cohere perfectly with the Media Lab's commitment to fostering university/industry ties and to the goal of convergence, a virtual mantra there under the reign of founding director, Nicholas Negroponte.

In the longer, more aesthetically compelling works of the artist Grahame Weinbren, including *The Erl King* (1986) and *Sonata* (1990), existing stories are retold using many classical cinematic tropes but under the "cloak" of the interactive cutaway, a signature grammar that allows the user to control the movement from one scene to another. This is most memorable in *Sonata,* Weinbren's retelling of Leo Tolstoy's most nihilistic story, "The Kreutzer Sonata." A husband is tormented by thoughts that his violinist wife is having an affair with her accompanist. The climactic scene of both the originating tale and the interactive cinema comes when the husband rushes in to the music room and stabs his wife to death. Weinbren offers the prelude to this shocking violence with a view of the wife playing and the husband in torment outside the door. The user can "slide" either perspective however far "over" the other he or she chooses. This allows for a kind of simultaneity that the classic montage between the two scenes would not allow for. Weinbren offers the following analysis of his own practice:

The basis of the interactive cinema is that the viewer has some control over what is on-screen. He or she knows that what is there will change if she or he acts, that it would have been different if he or she had acted differently earlier. Thus, the viewer is aware of a fundamental indeterminacy . . . the viewer must be kept always aware that it is *his, her* action on a particular image that has produced these new sounds or pictures, and techniques to foster this awareness must be developed. In my judgment, the most immediately available techniques can be found in the language of montage. A deliberate use of film editing strategies can keep reconvincing the viewer of the non-arbitrariness of connection between old and new elements, between the elements already there and those produced by viewer action. ("In the Ocean," online)

This artist's narrative also stresses the viewer's sense of control but begins to delve into the formal strategies that would make such work compelling and offers a different strategy for content—less like coherent storytelling and more akin to the condensation of the dream work.

If Davenport's and Weinbren's comments underlie two of the originary myths of interactive cinema—engineering and aesthetic—what of that given by the market? Max Whitby, an interactive media producer, offers the following: "Something happens to people, especially people who come from a film or television background when initially exposed to the idea of interactive multimedia. When you first realize that computers are not just tools, but a new medium through which information can be delivered in completely new ways, a light bulb goes on—it certainly went on in my head and I've seen it go on in lots of other people's heads. Instead of the high priests in their ivory towers deciding what a TV programme will be, you can hand over your programme material to your audience and they can construct their own experiences." Whitby goes on, however, to offer this demurral: "Now that basic premise is very exciting. The trouble is it doesn't sustain. When you actually get in there and try to make things in an interactive way, the premise falls apart" The restraining power of the market, the digital dialectic in action: the flights of theory balanced against the constraints of practice in the world.

This becomes clear when you take a look at my third example, *I'm Your Man,* directed by Bob Bejan, which claimed to be the "The World's First Interactive Movie" when it premiered in a select number of movie theaters in 1992. It is a short interactive movie—each version of the film runs only fifteen minutes—in which viewers, pushing buttons on their armrests, decide at specific points in the narrative to follow a specific character and the trajectory of that character's movements. *I'm Your Man* is ostensibly the tale of a female whistle-blower, her corrupt boss, and an FBI agent who inserts himself between them. Depending on the viewer's choices, however, the story can evolve differently, and various aspects of the character's backgrounds reveal that choosing an alternate path would indeed lead to very different conclusions.

Yet how interactive is such a proposition—such a product—and, more to the point, how radical is its notion of interactivity? As Lev Manovich points out in *The Language of New Media,* "all classical, and even more so modern art is 'interactive'" in any number of ways (56). However, as computers moved out of the workplace and into the home, their capacity for nonlinear assemblage—linking, if you will—disrupted their users' expectations of linearity and fueled a hunger for interactivity as an end unto itself, rather than simply a means. The privileging of the interaction between user and machine became a grail of computer-based media, and the quest for this interaction generated a potent combination of technological, cultural, and economic narratives.[2]

And what of the cinema's own mythologies? Film is more than a medium; it is a system that is inseparable from the myths that drive it and which the cinema forms in turn. There are the myths that surround the industry—the myths of stardom, the gilded dreams and wretched excess of wealth, and the lottery of luck. There are the myths of the technology of cinema itself, from the apocrypha surrounding its origin—the notions that Brazilians shot at screen villains and that Parisians ducked as a locomotive passed over them—all the way through André Bazin's myth of total cinema.[3] It's worth mulling over Bazin's notion that the cinema has striven since its very inception to become the totalizing art form, replacing opera as the culture's supreme *Gesamtkunstwerk.* Yet Bazin wrote this at the very tail end of the classical age of the cinema, just before the onslaught of the medium that would supersede the cinema and, indeed, totalize all manner of consumption—television.[4] Of course, less than a half-century after television as a medium bested the cinema, TV was in turn challenged by the computer. As noted earlier, when the computer moved into the home, that previously unchallenged realm of the color console, new myths—myths of usability, connectivity, and personal empowerment—emerged.

At this point I could offer some sort of nostrum about how all that is needed to prove the viability of the myths is for someone, someday, to make a successful intervention. I could say this, but I won't, for, as the pioneering Russian "net.artist" Olia Lialina noted about her own medium, "saying that net art is just beginning isn't very different from saying it's dead."[5] But it is precisely within the realms of myth that beginnings and endings coexist in an eternal presence. The new myths that emerged revolved around the notion that the narrative impact of film could be grafted to the networked nonlinearity of the digital to create a liberatory new interactive cinema.

It is farcical to speak of a single interactive cinema when in point of fact there were interactive cinemas. From computer science came projects that pushed boundaries in interface, intelligent agency, and computational expertise. On the European media festival circuit one could encounter the more aesthetic explorations, the results of solitary artists toiling away in whatever the digital equivalent of a garret might be or those who had scored a residency at a place such as Canada's Banff Centre for Computing and the Arts. Finally, and for the shortest time, one could even wander into the multiplex (at least in my hometown of Hollywood) and pay money to see an "interactive movie" such as *I'm Your Man* complete with hackneyed plot and a technological updating of the entertainment industry's obsessional story arcs and plot points.

That few have heard of these actual instantiations of interactive cinema, much less actually experienced them, has not been an impediment to people waxing philosophic, and even utopian, about them. This is because, like its technological cousin, virtual reality, the interactive cinema functions best in the realm of myth. And there will be no definitive unmasking, for the myths of interactive cinema fill creative, technological, and even financial needs. Take the greatest flights of executive fantasies about Silliwood—that much-ballyhooed melding of Silicon Valley and Hollywood fostered by computer techies and film business sharpies in the mid-1990s. The triumph of Silliwood would have done much to justify the faith of venture capitalists and other investors in the notion of a technologically deterministic aesthetics, that myth that the machine would somehow give birth sui generis to a new medium that would transform authorship and experience.

So what, then, indeed transcends the realm of fantasy and exists in the real? I would say that the answer lies in shifting from the fixation on interactivity within the narrative object to thinking, instead, about a system-wide application of new technologies of augmentation and communication. This would follow my own interest in the digital media's aesthetics of unfinish and move the discussion from hypertexts to hypercontexts. As more and more contemporary cultural production follows a Duchampian arc—in which the presentation of the object defines that object's function within culture—the shaping and molding of context comes to the fore. This is not news, and, in fact, a quarter of a century's work on defining the differences between the high modern moment and that which followed it hinged precisely on this elevation of context to parity with the text itself. The term *telematic* has been around for almost as long as this debate, but it's only been within the last decade that the combination of computers and communication networks has shown how it can contribute to the creation of context. This context takes many forms, especially in relation to popular media: there is the preplanned marketing of tie-ins from music CDs to television spin-offs to lunch boxes, and there is the efflorescence of fan-generated discursive communities. In certain cases all of these combine to create something far more interesting than backstory and more complicated than synergistic marketing. This is what I call "hypercontext," a rhizomatic and dynamic interlinked communicative community using networks to curate a series of shifting contexts.

If we recast the interactive cinema around the concept of hypercontualization, then, rather than the mythic grail of nonlinear narrative, a phenomenon such as *The Blair Witch Project* (Daniel Myrick and Eduardo Sánchez, 1999) functions as an unusually successful instantiation of the interactive cinema.[6] When the film arrived in theaters, it was presented as if it were a documentary and began with a title card informing the audience that what was to follow consisted of footage found in the Maryland woods a year after the disappearance of three young filmmakers who had gone in search of a legendary local supernatural presence. The genre, the specific treatment of the subject, the pseudorealism of the delivery, and some very convincing improvisational acting (the three stars of the film were indeed isolated and terrified by the directors for a week in those real Maryland Woods) all combined to create what Brenda Laurel speaks of as the "affordances" a narrative object offers to the development of fandom.[7]

Shot for very little money, the film was a huge commercial success, and the dominant cinema has been chasing its hypercontextual strategies ever since. Central to the impact of this project—surely it was and remains more than a "film"—was the choice to use a new communications medium to play off the spectatorial tension of the false documentary. The hypercontext was established a full year in advance of the release of the film itself. A poster campaign across college campuses, aimed at the target demographic group, asked for help from anyone who might have information about the "missing" student filmmakers. Meanwhile, the directors and their small studio put up a Web site that contained the kernel of the film's narrative and created a set of interlinked pseudomentary elements—video clips, news reports, audio fragments—that engage that sense that, while information wanted to be free (to use a 1990s cliché), it didn't seem to have any corollary imperative to be accurate. Here the communicative potential of the Net was deftly deployed to create a hypercontext of remarkable depth, something both pre- and post-, extant to the film itself. The Web site primed the target audience and survived after the film left theaters and moved to video and DVD. The DVD's links back to the Web complete the circuit while simultaneously opening up new layers of hypercontext, as *The Blair Witch Project* main site features links to noncommercial fan sites built from the affordances of the narrative object and its explicitly commercial hypercontexts.

That said, *The Blair Witch Project,* and whatever its progeny in the dominant—or even the sham that passes for the "independent"—cinema today will hardly be developing every facet of hypercontextualization, and, indeed, the phenomenon is as much a function of entertainment's capacity within networked capitalism to co-opt anything to its promotional agenda. In any case, the hypercontextual explosion *The Blair Witch Project* instantiated has not really manifested itself in full bloom again since 1999. The attributes of the interactive cinema we have been searching for in other modes really find their apotheosis in the "expanded" DVD, in which the linear narrative object is embedded in a system of ever-expanding self-reflexive media. Again, such an extratextual and ever-expanding cocoon is the real future of the hopes invested in the interactive cinema.

The "expanded" hypercontextual DVD is part of a historical narrative of home-based playback technology. This begins with the commercial release of videotaped films in the 1970s and that market's subsequent explosion in the 1980s. In that same decade videophiles, as they came to be known, started to become interested in laser discs because of their superior picture and sound. They also offered, for the first time in commercial formats, randomized, nonlinear access to the material and the ability to have alternate audio tracks and ancillary materials such as stills and even written articles attached to the filmic "object" at their center. At that time a new product emerged on the market—the expanded laser disc, especially as perfected by the Criterion Collection, which was a joint venture of Janus Films, one of the oldest distributors of what once went by the name "art films," and the Voyager Company, run by pioneering multimedia publisher Bob Stein. Stein then built upon the success of the Criterion Collection to release early multimedia CD-ROMs. Now there are Criterion Collection DVDs, the fourth technological substrate for this kind of augmented narrativity.

What goes little questioned in all of these "added features" is their promotion of the intentionalist fallacy. The pleasures of expanded hypercontextual DVD are manifest, but they foster an ever stronger authorial voice on theorists and audiences alike. One of the most routine features on DVDs is the addition of a soundtrack featuring the director commenting on the action, sometimes with the addition of interviews with stars and other crew. While fascinating in and of themselves and marketed as a way for viewers to expand their understanding of and appreciation for the art of cinema, these augmentations can also tend to circumscribe the audience's readings of a film text, using the technological novelty of the hypercontext to calcify the director's version as the definitive way to read a film.

Filmmakers will be driven primarily by an impulse toward raw promotion, building in the greatest number and variety of affordances to hook an audience, while the audiences that do latch onto these products and systems are more likely to engage in a relatively unreflexive fandom than the transgressive bricolage so beloved of cultural studies. One of the myths of the interactive cinema that was particularly intoxicating was that which promised, through the combination of technology and aesthetics, to liberate the cinema from the narrative ruts into which it had fallen. This was the idea that new technologies would generate not just new stories but also new ways of telling those new stories. The record on the screen, however, indicates that the real impact of digital technologies was not to strengthen narrative—linear or not—but to contribute to its decimation.

The contemporary blockbuster has been noted for its departures from the normative narrative model developed during the classical Hollywood period. There has been an evacuation of narrative from contemporary media, but that is as much a reflection of the surfeit of narrative as it is a sign of its demise. Indeed, it would be ludicrous to claim some sort of "death of narrative" in the midst of its ever-broadening triumph. The more that television extends its sway around the globe, the more the human race is suffused in story, bathed in narrative. From the thirty-second advertising spot to the half-hour sitcom to the ninety-minute film to the two-hour-plus sporting event, the televisual experience is equally a telenarrative experience. It should strike no one as shocking that the dominant Hollywood cinema, especially in its blockbuster mode, should seem to care less and less about narrative convention and coherence. When Bruce Willis, the star of Luc Beson's *The Fifth Element* (1997), was confronted at a press event about the amiably shambling incoherence of that digital effects–driven film, he laughed and let the scribes know that nobody cares about story anymore. While we do not generally expect our action heroes to moonlight as narratologists, Willis's observation was at least partially accurate.[8]

We simply have so much narrative surrounding us that it is often enough merely to reference it. Like sampling within contemporary music and so much of our endlessly referential advertising culture, the reference to an established and overflowing narrative tradition is sufficient. In other words, the movement toward a referential rather than developmental narrative strategy is an outgrowth of the sheer plentitude of narrative, figured most emblematically by the glowingly accessible archive of everything. Indeed, the Web's "24/7" access promises to make the video store seem as archaic as the repertory theater. But let us not forget that the art of cinema, and film culture itself, flourished far more healthily in the era of the rep theater than it does now. The very proliferation and ubiquitizing of narrative, even the highest-quality narrative, can have the paradoxical effect of making it seem that much less important—Willis's sense that "nobody cares." This is the effect of communications technology on freedom of access and even discourse: when the samizdat culture of Eastern Europe and the Soviet Union during the 1970s mutated into the Western-style market of the post-1989 era, something both ineffable and important was lost. The Web offers a marvelous explosion of access, but the law of unintended consequences could usher in a world in which anything can be obtained but nothing is special.

This would be a dour essay indeed if we were to stop here: myths of interactivity slain, the death of a certain kind of film culture bemoaned, the forces of hypercontextualization firmly under the control of Hollywood studio flacks, narrative coherence as anachronistic as Tin Pan Alley's well-crafted popular lyrics. If we want surcease from this barrage, I would suggest we move away from the cinema and start to think about art. Alfred Barr, the famous curator from the Museum of Modern Art's glory days in the middle of the last century, used to speak confidently of the "art of our time" to refer to the painting, sculpture, and photography that so defined his institution—from Pablo Picasso to Walker Evans to Jackson Pollock. Barr could count on, and indeed was personally responsible for, the sense of a coherent narrative of the "avant-garde arts." And, though we live in what I have characterized as a period of ferocious pluralism, I am intrigued by the concept of proposing the "media of our times."

The past ten years have seen the flowering of a rich body of large-scale video art installations, and it is to these I turn as the next step in this mythopoesis. I will discuss the work of artists Sam Taylor-Wood and Jane and Louise Wilson in relation to the myths of interactive cinema, as these artists offer a range of approaches to the "surfeit" of narrative. I made reference to this plentitude earlier, noting how the Hollywood blockbuster offers one way to confront this deluge of story: simply ignore it and its conventions and learn to create a ninety-minute cinema of attractions, this time around with bankable stars. The few attempts at a computer-driven interactive cinema failed to prove themselves capable of offering a viable nonlinear narrativity to compete with the standard models. The video artists I'm interested in offered a third strategy: they accept the omnipresence of narrative and up the ante, creating installations that distill narrative while at the very same time confounding plentitude.

Sam Taylor-Wood's *Atlantic* (1997) is a three-screen space that condenses the narrative trope of romantic trouble into a short, endless loop of feeling without narrative substrate. Installed in a large rectangular gallery, the viewer enters to face the largest of the three walls, and there confronts an establishing shot of an upscale restaurant. Redolent with the kind of obsessive details the art world has come to expect from the photographic tableaux of Andreas Gursky, Taylor-Wood's restaurant becomes exactly the kind of theater that high-ticket restaurateurs invoke in their descriptions of their own spaces. There is, however, little in the way of drama taking place on this exquisitely rendered stage, at least if we think of drama as evolving over time and involving at least a modicum of narrative. What Taylor-Wood offers here, instead, is a nod to drama, a condensation of the cinema's romantic arc, distilling it down into two looped scenarios playing opposite each other on the walls perpendicular to the projection of the restaurant space. One is a close-up of a woman's teary-eyed face, the other an extreme close-up of a man's hands, wringing nervously.

The room is suffused with a soundtrack seemingly more ambient than scripted, with the woman's voice plaintively imploring, "Why?" as the three loops cycle in an eternal present. From 1977 to 1980 Cindy Sherman made a series of *Untitled Film Stills,* which perfected a certain semiotic reference to the cinematic imaginary—with the artist herself taking on a variety of pitch-perfect incarnations of the Office Girl, the Femme Fatale, and the Moll, all deployed in subtly art-directed environments. Taylor-Wood's piece can be seen to have dynamized the Sherman film stills to a certain degree, spatializing and slightly temporalizing them without going all the way toward actually making a film. If anything, the Sherman stills are turned into a weird variety of animatic by Wood's installation. Here the plentitude of narrative is so much taken for granted that the artist can assume we know precisely that thing to which we refer when invoking the Latin phrase *in medias res.*

If Taylor-Wood is following Sherman's reference to the narratives we know so well as to obviate the need for their presence, Jane and Louise Wilson practice a reference to the narrative that we have lived through but—at least in the West—have not yet internalized enough to understand fully. The Wilsons are twins, fully aware of the inherent freakishness of a collaboration between the mostly identical. In pieces such as *Stasi City* (1997), *Proton, Unity, Energy, Blizzard* (2000), and *Star City* (2000) they use their natural affinity for the intertwined to deal with the intersection of space and politics inherent in the big story of the past twenty years—the dissolution of the Berlin Wall and the end of the Soviet Union. This is a story that, as mentioned earlier, everyone knows but no one really understands, at least not yet. The Wilson sisters have been taking these strategies and applying them to one of the central questions of our time: what becomes of art after the great divide between communism and capitalism is so abruptly sundered in 1989? It is a narrative that cries out to be regarded as central but which is drowned out by the triumphalism of booboisity, the din of celebrity culture that bubbles along in a rich, peaceful, easily distracted West. The Wilsons create multiscreen environments that destabilize the act of spectatorship, upping the ante on celebrity culture's premium on distraction while at the very same time concentrating on the spaces and objects redolent of history and its narratives. They catalogue the spaces and objects of the structuring narrative of the second half of the twentieth century—the Cold War. They have been inside Stasi headquarters in the former East Berlin, in the abandoned missile silos of Norad in Wyoming, and in the cavernous environs of Star City, the former Soviet Union's cosmonaut training center. The spaces they render have both the menace and sterility of security installations, but the technological artifacts they uncover offer a poignant historicism. Here we confront the electronics of the Cold War, not the sleek and streamlined consumerism of the Sharper Image catalogue. They fetishize the clunky apparatuses of spies who never came in from the cold. This is electronics as raw wires and wood-housed transformers, a backstory to our present fascination with the embedded and seamless—the PDAs, Web-enabled cell phones and wireless modems that form our fluid-free notion of sexy. The Wilson sisters treat this as a kind of the return of the politically repressed. After all, it was only a few decades ago that the impulse toward civil defense, a narrative that culminated in thinking the unthinkable, in the complete end, was dominant. The Wilsons make it impossible to lay claim to a single vantage point to take all of this in. The spectator moves from place to place in the installation, and the totality of the visual experience is, just like the totality of the historical narrative, always impossibly and implausibly beyond us. They create a cinema interactive with history, defeat, fear, and triumph. Yet these spaces of eviscerated history and depleted power offer such sheer visual seduction and interactive immersion that they become as enthralling as the celebrity-addled pop culture that forms their overall cultural context.

Sam Taylor-Wood and the Wilson sisters do not make interactive cinema, but they do capitalize upon the doomed genre's aspirational myths, the best hopes of the digital to reanimate the art forms that preceded it. I've written elsewhere that it was precisely because video as a medium moved through its utopian phase that the past decade's video installation artists were able to come into their own; they were freed of the psychic burdens imposed by the impossibly lofty expectations of video's early years. In like measure, when technologists, artists, and Hollywood luftmenschen work through the totalizing myths of interactive cinema, compelling syntheses of film and the digital could come into being.

Notes

1. Glorianna Davenport's comments are from an article cowritten with M. Murtagh entitled "Automatist Storyteller Systems and the Shifting Sands of Story," originally published in the IBM *Systems Journal* in 1997. It can be accessed through the Interactive Cinema Group's copiously documented Web site. <*http://ic.media.mit.edu/Publications/Journals/Automatist/html*>.

2. See also John Caldwell's analysis of the myths of interactivity in *Televisuality.*

3. In this context it is interesting to note Bazin's offhand comment in that essay that "the cinema owes virtually nothing to the scientific spirit" (17).

4. Simon Frith succinctly describes television's hegemony: "In the western world, television has been the dominant medium of the second half of the twentieth century . . . The other mass media—radio, the cinema, recorded music, sport, print—feed off television" (33).

5. Olia Lialina posted her comments to the seminal <nettime> listserve on February 18, 2001, archived at <*http://nettime.org*>.

6. In his discussion of *The Blair Witch Project* J. P. Telotte goes into some detail on the BWP's hypercontexts.

7. Don Norman popularized the term *affordances* within interface design, drawing from the work of the perceptual psychologist J. J. Gibson, in "The Theory of Affordances." Brenda Laurel discusses affordances in relation to narrative systems and fan culture in *Utopian Entrepreneur.*

8. The Bruce Willis press conference at Cannes in 1997 is described at <*http://www.citypages.com/databank/18/860/article3513.asp*>.

References

Bazin, André. "The Myth of Total Cinema." *What Is Cinema?* Vol. 1. Ed. and trans. Hugh Gray. Berkeley: University of California Press, 1967.

Caldwell, John. *Televisuality: Style, Crisis, and Authority in American Television.* New Brunswick NJ: Rutgers University Press, 1995.

Cameron, Andy. "Dissimulations: Illusions of Interactivity." *Millennium Film Journal* 28 (Spring 1995).
    <*http://mfj-online.org/journalPages/MFJ28/Dissimulations.html*>.
Davenport, Glorianna, and M. Murtagh. "Automatist Storyteller Systems and the Shifting Sands of Story."
    <*http://ic.media.mit.edu/Publications/Journals/Automatist/html*>.
Frith, Simon. "The Black Box: The Value of Television and the Future of Television Research." *Screen* 41.1 (Spring 2000): 33–50.
Gibson, J. J. "The Theory of Affordances." *Perceiving, Acting, and Knowing.* Ed. R. E. Shaw and J. Bransford. Hillsdale NJ: Lawrence Erlbaum, 1977.
Laurel, Brenda. *Utopian Entrepreneur.* Cambridge: MIT Press, 2001.
Manovich, Lev. *The Language of New Media.* Cambridge: MIT Press, 2001.
Telotte, J. P. "*The Blair Witch Project:* Film and the Internet." *Film Quarterly* 54.3 (Spring 2001): 32–39.
Weinbren, Grahame. "In the Ocean of Streams of Story." *Millennium Film Journal* 28 (Spring 1995). <*http://mfj-online.org/journalPages/MFJ28/GWOCEAN.html*>.

Coda

Textual Theory and Blind Spots in Media Studies

Liv Hausken

Do new media, genres, and textual formats require new textual theories? Do we have to throw away everything we know about texts and media every time a new medium is invented and start all over again? Media studies is still a young field of research, one that is wrestling with a legacy of often inadvertently borrowed theories. The field is quite heterogeneous in terms of subjects and methodology, and its objects of study—the various media— are in constant change. This situation poses considerable challenges. I would suggest that the most important, at this point, is not keeping pace with the latest developments but keeping an even keel and allowing oneself time for reflection.

Any perspective has blind spots, and a certain degree of blindness is necessary. Seeing something entails neglecting something else. Some blind spots become salient *as such* the moment one starts to examine a culture, discipline, or object of study other than that with which one is normally preoccupied, that is, the moment one decides to study *something else,* something puzzling or out of the ordinary. To study something that falls beyond the parameters of the available theoretical frameworks may, of course, be frustrating, unless one deliberately chooses to explore new territories. In this case frustration with the theoretical inheritance and with the multifarious and ever-changing quality of the objects of study may be turned into an opportunity for adjusting or modifying the existing theoretical frameworks. A frustration that results in a heightened awareness of the set of problems associated with theoretical import, with heterogeneity and change, may actually prove to be an asset. A number of theoretical challenges may be revealed if one approaches the various objects of study with two objectives in mind: first, to accomplish an optimally sensitive analysis of whatever one intends to analyze; and, second, to draw on the results of this analysis in order to tidy up one's toolbox of theories.

The toolbox of textual theory contains instruments for seeing and thinking (*theôria:* "contemplation," "speculation"; from *theôros:* "spectator") that may seem useful. Our habitual ways of seeing, however, might deceive us. If one proceeds pointedly and analytically, it seems possible to identify the text theoretical challenges of media studies in relation to two forms of blindness: medium blindness and text blindness. This rather rough division corresponds to an equally rough division between medium and text. The term *medium* will here cover the materiality of communication and art as well as the expressive resources represented by the different technologies and apparatuses that support the text. On the other hand, the term *text* will be used in a general, and not exclusively linguistic, sense, referring to any expression that can be read or otherwise experienced as meaningful. Concepts such as discourse and genre will here be associated with the questions concerning the text. These simplifications make it possible to focus on two broad but interrelated categories of blindness.

Medium Blindness

It might seem strange that a state of medium blindness should afflict the field of media studies. Yet most media scholars have read analyses of news items in newspapers or on television that are entirely devoid of any reflection regarding the significance of the nature of the medium for a comprehension of the object of analysis. This type of medium blindness is always embarrassing for the blind scholars when sight is restored to them. There is, however, a different kind of medium blindness that is more difficult to pinpoint. This is a form of blindness that is intrinsic to our conceptual apparatus, our theories and perspectives. It manifests itself in two different ways that can, tentatively, be called *total medium blindness* and *nonchalant medium blindness.*

Total Medium Blindness
Total medium blindness can be found in theories and perspectives that are presented as medium independent. That the medium itself matters is simply neglected, but at the same time a particular medium is also silently presumed. In short, theories that are seemingly independent of the medium are usually implicitly tied to a particular medium.

Nonchalant Medium Blindness
Nonchalant medium blindness is endemic to theories and analyses that are

unreflectively based on the theoretical premises of *other* media. This nonchalant blindness is most readily apparent in those approaches that uncritically borrow ideas from medium-specific or medium-sensitive studies of media other than the medium under consideration. Nonchalant medium blindness may be harder to trace and easier to condone than total medium blindness, because it is often the result of negligence—something that can happen in the best of families—but its effects can be just as harmful, especially when the investigator borrows concepts from a theoretical field that is itself characterized by *total* medium blindness.

In the discussion to follow, this rather sketchy presentation will be filled out and concretized by an examination of various aspects of narrative theory. I have chosen the case of narrative for several reasons: narrative can be presented in most media, be it older media such as printed literature, younger media such as film, radio and television or new media such as CD-ROMs and the Internet. Furthermore, narrative may be mediated by most genres and forms of expression, it may be grand or small, and it may represent fictional as well as factual events. This heterogeneity notwithstanding, modern narrative theory often tries to pass as independent of both medium and genre. Theories derive from several disciplines but particularly from comparative literature, folkloristics, and anthropology. Just as different theoretical traditions are transdisciplinary and any one discipline may accommodate a diversity of theoretical approaches, the field of narrative theory has also become increasingly complex. Since the 1970s the circulation of theories across traditions has proliferated. From around 1980 this field of research has expanded considerably, embracing disciplines that traditionally have not been associated with narrative theory, such as economics, law, psychology, and sociology. At the same time, narrative theory has received increasing attention as a transdisciplinary field. This situation is a breeding ground for all kinds of medium blindness.

Within media studies two areas of research have been preoccupied with narrative analysis: film studies and research on news, particularly on television. These two areas have generally been inspired by different traditions of narrative theory. Research on narration in the news is primarily associated with a tradition dominated by the work of Anglo-American literary scholars, such as Henry James, Percy Lubbock, and Wayne C. Booth. Film studies, particularly in Europe, has been inspired by the French structuralist approach to narrative theory, whose main representatives are Roland Barthes, Claude Bremond, and Algirdas Julien Greimas. Both of these theoretical traditions have been a major influence on comparative literature.[1] But the fact that stories can be represented in most media and that the field of narrative theory—and analysis—transcends disciplines does not mean that the theories and strategies of analysis developed for the case of literary narrative can be automatically imported to narratives of other media. Narrative theory, it appears, does not possess medium independence to the extent that has been typically assumed.

The problem of medium specificity has been particularly pressing in research on film narratives, especially in the kind of studies founded on, or including elements of, the Anglo-American theoretical tradition. One of the issues that epitomizes this problem is the controversy surrounding the relevance of the term *narrator* in film.

The American film scholar David Bordwell is among those who have voiced the harshest objections to the use of the term *narrator* in film studies (62). He grants that the term may be applied to voice-over narration and to cases in which a character in the film tells other characters a story, but none of these narrators, Bordwell argues, can take responsibility for the entire film narrative. A narrator has a voice, and the voice belongs to a person who mediates the story by way of verbal language. According to Bordwell, neither the idea of a narrating person nor the emphasis on verbal mediation are very relevant to a medium such as film.

Seymour Chatman, one of Bordwell's most diligent critics, argues that a general theory of narrative cannot accept the idea that some texts include narrators and others do not. If there exist narrators in literary narratives, there must be narrators in all narratives irrespective of the medium (Chatman, *Coming to Terms* 133). To justify his position, Chatman frees the term *narrator* from embeddedness in verbal language and from the idea of a narrating person. The concept of narrator that emerges from this operation is a comprehensive designation for everything that contributes to the viewer's activity of producing meaning. Chatman's insistence on applying the term to film narratives, despite its undeniable vagueness, is symptomatic of a certain change of direction in Anglo-American narrative theory. This theoretical tradition was originally developed to account for a type of discourse for which the term *narrator* was obviously relevant, namely the modern novel—or, to be more precise, verbal, written, narrative prose fiction presented in book form. Anglo-American narrative theory was narrowly focused on literary narrative, and it was not its ambition to propose a general theory of narrative. This changes with Chatman. His argument for applying the term *narrator* to film narratives illustrates the danger of trying to base a media-independent theory on a medium-specific object of research.

Chatman's use of Anglo-American narrative theory set the tone for the study of narrative in media other than the book. His comparative studies of fictional stories in printed literature and in film have been an important point of reference for analysts of narrative within the field of media studies.

Compared to the focus of Anglo-American narrative theory on communication and verbally mediated narrative actions, the emphasis of French narratology on narrative as a discursive mediation of a course of events was more readily transferable to film narrative. The French narratology of the 1960s had admittedly its share of language-oriented terminology. Yet, unlike the kind of narrative theory practiced by Anglo-American critics, French narratology was developed with broad purposes in mind. The leading narratologists were also involved in other segments of the comprehensive structuralist project of the 1960s. Roland Barthes, for instance, theorized not only verbal narrative but also the image. Furthermore, film semiology emerged within the same research community. All this stimulated an awareness of medium-specific conditions.

It has been generally easy to transfer theories and analytical strategies inspired by literary scholarship to narratively oriented research on news. The mediation of radio news is first and foremost verbal. As for printed news, it is, like literature, presented in a medium based mainly on writing. Television news, on the other hand, is conveyed by an audiovisual medium similar to that of film. In order to avoid medium blindness, narrative analyses of television news would have to employ a more medium-sensitive conceptual apparatus than the one traditionally offered by Anglo-American narrative theory. Still, the use of the verbally oriented terminology of Anglo-American narrative theory has posed fewer problems for research on television news than for research on film, because this research has considered its object in a communicational perspective that focuses on ways of speaking, message, power, and legitimacy rather than on visual features.

The conceptual apparatus of the Anglo-American tradition of narrative theory has also caused problems in the analysis of so-called interactive digital texts. A case in point is the treatment of computer-based adventure games proposed by Espen Aarseth in his book *Cybertext: Perspectives on Ergodic Literature*. The analysis rejects all the concepts of Chatman's narrative communication model (92–128), whether they refer to entities external to the text, such as *real author* and *real reader*, or to parameters internal to the text, such as *implied author, implied reader, narrator,* and *narratee*. Unlike Bordwell, Aarseth does not abandon the term *narrator* on account of its verbal connotations. The texts Aarseth examines are on the whole verbal. Rather, it appears to be the notion of a narrating person, as well as the relationship between the narrator and the other entities in Chatman's model, that explains why the term *narrator* is considered useless for adventure games. Aarseth's solution is not to eliminate Chatman's model of communication but, instead, to fill its parameters with alternative concepts. Without inviting too many problems, he is able to substitute the terms *programmer* and *user* for *real author* and *real reader.* Problems arise when it comes to the terms internal to the text.

Initially, he introduces the term *intrigue,* which he borrows from drama theory, in which it normally designates the complications that lead to a crisis resolved either in catastrophe (tragedy) or in a happy ending (comedy) and which with regard to adventure games is meant to replace *story,* a term that is of secondary importance in Chatman's communication model. But, where the dramatic term indicates the troubles that befall the characters in the drama, Aarseth's term specifies the troubles the user is subject to in the adventure games. He furthermore introduces the term *intriguee,* the target of the intrigue, as a parallel to both *narratee, implied reader,* and the *main character,* and the term *intrigant,* which corresponds in part to Chatman's *narrator* and in part to his *implied author.* But the parallel to Chatman's conceptual apparatus is bungled, among other things, by the fact that the user, who takes a strategic responsibility for the success or failure of the main character, plays an active part in the text in a far more radical way than does the reader of a book or the viewer of a film. Aarseth himself is of the opinion that the parallel between Chatman's concepts and his own is of limited value, and he ends up claiming that, strictly speaking, computer-based adventure games are not narratives. My point here is that Aarseth's discussion of Chatman's model harbors a *potential* critique of the medium blindness afflicting not only Chatman's model but to a certain extent Anglo-American narrative theory in general. In contrast to the reader or viewer, the user cannot be treated analytically as an entity external to the text.

Transferring Anglo-American narrative theory to the field of media studies exposes the medium blindness of the tradition. Yet the degree of this blindness varies among the practitioners of the approach. If we stick primarily to the term *narrator* in the previous examples, we may contrast the approaches taken by Aarseth and Chatman. Whereas Chatman blindly tries to adapt the term *narrator* to film, an audiovisual medium that combines several semiotic systems, Aarseth, who studies a verbal type of text, suggests an alternative term that accommodates his own object of research. A third possibility would be to abandon not only the term *narrator,* as Aarseth does, but also the search for substitutes. This step may be necessary for the development of a truly medium-free narrative theory, which is Chatman's objective. But, since the concept of narrator is certainly relevant for certain language-supported media, one should remain able to invoke Anglo-American narrative theory within the limits of its validity, as long as one recognizes it for what it is: a medium-specific theory of narrative among a host of others.

I do not mean by this discussion that we should reject the notion of a general narrative theory. On the contrary, I believe that we should aspire to narrative theories that are independent of medium, while recognizing that the development of such theories demands a certain level of abstraction. Furthermore, I believe that we need medium-specific theories of narrative, theories with a conceptual apparatus sufficiently specialized to define the actual differences between narratives in the various media. In addition to this, we need to be aware of the difference between the two types of narrative theories. The comparative study of narrative in different media, either at the same time or one after the other, is one of the most efficient ways to expose both the common narrative features and the medium-specific aspects of the objects of study.

Let me briefly state my position: it is not only possible but also imperative to pursue medium-independent text theories for the simple reason that it is necessary to clarify what it is that concerns the text and what it is that concerns the medium. It is, furthermore, both possible and necessary to operate with medium-specific textual theories both in order to correct *apparently* medium-independent theories and to operate with a well-suited theoretical basis for methods and strategies of text analysis. A text exists by necessity in a particular medium. A specific text analysis shouldn't therefore neglect the medium in question. The analytical challenge is thus to develop an acute sense of the difference between textual and medial conditions. Only then is it possible to conduct textual analyses that are medium sensitive.

Text Blindness

In media studies text blindness is probably as endemic as medium blindness. The most conspicuous occurrences of text blindness are found in studies that purport to analyze a text but neglect those features of the object of analysis that involve textual conditions. A study of a particular topic may, for instance, fail to see how particular textual features such as style and rhetoric play a crucial part in the comprehension of the topic in question. There is, however, a different kind of text blindness that is more difficult to pinpoint and which will be the subject of my discussion. This form of blindness is intrinsic to our conceptual apparatus, our theories and perspectives. We may tentatively distinguish two types that parallel our categories of media blindness: *total text blindness* and *nonchalant text blindness*.

Total Text Blindness

Total text blindness can be found in theories and perspectives that claim to be independent of particular textual conditions while implicitly relying on a certain type of text. A well-known example is the tendency of treating classical Hollywood cinema as if it represented film as such. Film, of course, is a medium that encapsulates very diverse forms of expression. When one's point of departure is the conventions of a specific film tradition for mediating fictional narratives and when one at the same time explicitly claims to address the medium of film as such, it becomes quite difficult not to confuse the particular characteristics of the medium with particular narrative and aesthetic conventions. Other examples of total blindness is the use of the term *fiction* to denote narrative or the use of the term *text* to refer to the physical inscription of signs on a page, a notion of text that was generally abandoned in the wake of the invention of the printing press and the progressive dematerialization of the conception of the text (see, for instance, Ginzburg 93).

Nonchalant Text Blindness

Nonchalant text blindness is represented by theories and analyses that are based on the theoretical premises of other kinds of texts than the type in question. Here I will discuss two types, though a complete typology would include several other categories. The first one is exemplified by studies that borrow their conceptual apparatus from *text-specific* theories or *text-sensitive* studies of types of texts other than those in question. The second type of nonchalant text blindness is a result of applying theories characterized by *total* blindness to the text. Let me give two examples of the first kind and one example of the second.

Type 1, First Case

Again, we may for examples draw upon narrative-analytical news research based on the Anglo-American tradition of narrative theory. In this kind of research there is an inclination toward considering any speech act as a narrative act. Consider, for instance, the tendency in narrative-analytical research on television to describe the hierarchy of authority found in newscasts as a hierarchy of narrators. At the top of the hierarchy is the news anchor, who is often characterized as an authoritative narrator, that is, as an observer who recounts the events from a position outside the sphere of action. In the various news reports the right to speak is delegated from this anchor to so-called narrators located in the field. These narrators may be both authoritative or personal, depending on whether they take part in the events recounted. They will often interview persons at the scene. The interviewees might also be characterized as narrators but typically as personal and subjective ones. This hierarchy is one of authority in which ultimately no narrator is permitted to speak unless sanctioned by the anchor. The anchor thus maintains authority on behalf of the institution. This is how the standard account goes. But why refer to all these persons as "narrators"?

The study of narrators in Anglo-American narrative theory is implicitly based upon the notion that the objects of study are acts of narration as they are expressed in *narrative* discourses. Yet a news discourse is not necessarily narrative—it might just as well be descriptive, prescriptive, or argumentative. The description of every speech act as an act of narration ignores the differences between various kinds of discourses. By relying on theories borrowed from studies of types of text other than the one under examination, narrative-analytical news research tends to be blind to those textual conditions that define its own object of analysis.

Type 1, Second Case

My second example of nonchalant text blindness is, in principle, of the same type as the preceding one, but it is somewhat more intricate. I mentioned earlier Espen Aarseth's attempt to establish a conceptual apparatus intended as an alternative to that of Chatman, and I noted that such an apparatus represents a potential critique of the media blindness that besets the theoretical tradition to which Chatman belongs. Here I should point out, however, that Aarseth does not arrive at such a critique. As already mentioned, Aarseth believes that the parallel between Chatman's conceptual apparatus and his own is of limited value. His reason for saying this is that he views computer-based adventure games as basically nonnarrative texts. His most important argument for this view appears to be that such games do not offer a structured presentation of an already set course of action. Whether or not, or to what degree, these texts are narrative is something I will not determine here. This would require an analysis of each particular game. The point, however, is that Aarseth's line of reasoning seems to be based on the idea that narratives cannot exist without a sequentially organized discourse, that is, a discourse designed to proceed along one single and fixed order from beginning to end.

If Aarseth had, instead, adopted the French narratology of the 1960s, the case would have been very much the same. Certainly, if asked whether adventure games—with treasure hunts, monsters to be slain, and damsels in distress—can be narrative, I believe that the answer would be different if narrative models other than Chatman's communication model were consulted. The models of both Anglo-American and French theoretical traditions are, however, developed on the basis of the idea of *sequentially organized discourses.* Furthermore, both traditions have embraced the thesis that texts are *semantically autonomous.* From the point of view of the Anglo-American tradition, this is a legacy from New Criticism; from that of the French, from the principle of immanence as laid down by Ferdinand de Saussure's linguistics. As a consequence, the narrative competence brought in by the player, reader, or spectator is neglected in both traditions. Let me embark on a short detour to demonstrate why this point is relevant here.

Wim Wenders was once invited to give a lecture for a colloquium on narrative technique. He was originally trained in the visual arts, as a painter, but had reached a point where he felt that painting lacked something. To say that it was lifeless would be too simple, he says; "I thought that what was missing was an understanding of time." So, when he began filming, he considered himself to be "a painter of space engaged on a quest for time" (51). The problem was that, as a filmmaker, he could not avoid telling stories: "I was only combining time and space; but from that moment on, I was pressed into telling stories" (52). This can hardly be explained unless one takes into consideration the fact that viewers are equipped with *narrative competence* and a confidence in relation to the *semantic structure of the action,* the *symbolic resources* of the culture, and the *temporal properties of action,* to use Paul Ricoeur's terminology (54–64).

Narrative competence is in my view a precondition for narrativity. It is evidently not the only one, but we easily forget that people are able to establish narrative connections not only vis-à-vis sequentially organized discourses such as novels and mainstream fictional films but also in relation to historical source material, events that take place on the street, and blocks of text *not* organized in sequences, in which one either actively participates (ergodic) or does not (read only). In my opinion this ability should be included in the very definition of narrative. If we attempt to carry out a narrative analysis (even if the aim is simply to demonstrate that such an analysis is impossible) without taking into account people's narrative competence—that is, their ability to construct stories out of a text or out of observed events in the absence of a sequentially organized discourse—we will blind ourselves to the text's *potential* for narrative signification.

The visual impairment in Aarseth's approach to computer-based adventure games is indeed an intricate example of nonchalant text blindness. Compared to the nonchalant text blindness of narrative-analytical news research sketched out earlier, it is more difficult to trace and easier to explain away. In both cases we are faced with received theories from a theoretical tradition that was preoccupied with a type of text different from the one under examination, theories that, in addition, had an intrinsic tendency toward medium blindness. As if this point of departure were not difficult enough, in the case of the adventure games we are faced with a field of research in which a sufficiently precise conceptual apparatus has yet to be developed. Aarseth is among those who have tried to remedy this situation. Perhaps we ought to accept a certain degree of blindness.

Type 2

As mentioned earlier, there is also a different type of nonchalant text blindness that is harder to trace and easier to justify than the first type. It results from the uncritical use of received theories characterized by a total blindness toward the text.

As an example, I would here like to mention certain studies of hypertext that seem to have inherited a type of theoretical text blindness in which material conditions are treated as if they were textual conditions. This can be seen in the attempts to establish a concept of "nonlinear text" on the basis of, and in contrast to, the idea of a "linear text," understood as "a text in which all of the particles of inscription—the letters—can be placed successively along one line." [2] This is a concept of text that, in addition to being based in writing and verbal language, involves particular material conditions. But, if the term *text* really denotes the physical manifestation of writing, what, then, is a nonlinear text? Would not all writing based on verbal language, regardless of the medium and the logistics of reading, physically emerge as linear?

As an alternative to the term *nonlinear text,* attempts have been made to introduce the term *multilinear text.* This term also seems to involve material conditions, but, unlike the former, it does not give the impression of being meaningless. If by *text* one really understands the spatial lines of graphic marks, one may rightly assume that the term *multilinear text* designates a material expression composed of several lines of written text that do not form a single chain. This will make sense in the case of the physical manifestation of writing in a verbal hypertext on a CD-ROM. As far as I can tell, however, the term *multilinear* would be equally relevant for the written entries of a phone book. Neither the phone book nor language-based hypertext is organized sequentially. The phone book is arranged alphabetically, but not for the purpose of being read in any particular order from beginning to end. Certain hypertexts, especially those on CD-ROM, are meant to be approached in the same way as phone books: as reference works. But in other verbal hypertexts—for instance, those of narrative fiction—the physical manifestation of writing is supposed to be read and not merely consulted like a database. To avoid text blindness one should recognize that: (1) all language-supported texts are linear in their manifestation to the reader; and (2) a multilinear organization occurs both in the print and the digital medium. One should also develop concepts capable of distinguishing the "database" mode of looking up individual items from the sustained reading called for by narrative discourses.

Closing Remarks: An Invitation

The point of this essay has not been to map out all the different categories of blindness but, rather, to illustrate some of the theoretical challenges in the field of media studies in general and in the study of narrative across media in particular. The theoretical challenge may first and foremost be to identify the blind spots in existing theories, correct these theories if necessary, and try to improve the theoretical foundations on which analysis is based. Let me further emphasize that these text-theoretical challenges do not only involve those preoccupied with texts. As incongruities and conflations concerning text and medium indicate, the blind spots focused on here also represent a more general challenge in media studies. One recurring problem in all the examples of blindness and visual deficiencies described earlier, be it medium blindness, text blindness, or a combination of the two, is the absence of a sufficiently high level of precision. I write this not so much in order to indict a certain practice as to stress the need for slowing down and allowing ourselves time for reflection. Jean-François Lyotard once said that "in a world where success means gaining time, thinking has a single, but irredeemable, fault: it is a waste of time" (36). While we are wasting time, we may take delight in the fact that there is still something into which all the remaining aspects of thought can be put to use.

Notes

A longer version of this article, with a more detailed typology of types of blindness, was originally published as "Tekstteoretiske utfordringer i den medievitenskaplige disiplin," *Norsk medietidsskrift*, no. 1 (2000): 99–113. The present text was translated by Asbjørn Grønstad.

1. As with any field of study, narrative theory and analysis can be divided into traditions and subfields in several ways. This is not the issue here. The rough division between the two traditions presented here is based on some theoretical tendencies in narrative analysis of film and television news.

2. I quote from a randomly chosen text on so-called nonlinear texts (see Aarseth, "Fra I Ching" 59). Aarseth has since abandoned the concept of "nonlinear texts."

References

Aarseth, Espen. "Fra I Ching til Cyberspace. Den ikkelineære tekstens retorikk" (From I Ching to Cyberspace: The Rhetoric of the Non Linear Text). *Fortellingens retorikk* (The Rhetoric of the Narrative). Ed. Gisle Selnes et al. Senter for Europeiske Kulturstudier (SEK), University of Bergen, 1993.

———. *Cybertext: Perspectives on Ergodic Literature.* Baltimore: John Hopkins University Press, 1997.

Booth, Wayne C. *The Rhetoric of Fiction.* 1961. Reprint. Harmondsworth: Penguin Books, 1991.

Bordwell, David. *Narration in the Fiction Film.* 1985. Reprint. London: Routledge, 1997.

Chatman, Seymour. *Coming to Terms: The Rhetoric of Narrative in Fiction and Film.* Ithaca: Cornell University Press, 1990.

Ginzburg, Carlo. "Clues: Morelli, Freud, and Sherlock Holmes." *The Sign of Three: Dupin, Holmes, Peirce.* Ed. Umberto Eco and Thomas A. Sebeok. Bloomington: Indiana University Press, 1983. 81–118. Reprint of "Spie. Radici di un paradigmo indizario." *Crisi della ragione.* Ed. Aldo Gargani. Torino: Einaudi, 1979. 59–106.

Lyotard, Jean-François. "Missive on Universal History" (1984). *The Postmodern Explained.* Minneapolis: University of Minnesota Press, 1993. 23–37. Reprint of *Le postmoderne expliqué aux enfants.* Paris: Editions Galilée, 1988.

Ricoeur, Paul. *Time and Narrative.* Vol. 1. Trans. Kathleen McLaughlin and David Pellauer. Chicago: University of Chicago Press, 1984. Trans. of *Temps et récit.* Paris: Éditions du Seuil, 1983.

Wenders, Wim. "Impossible stories: Talk Given at a Colloquium on Narrative Technique." *The Logic of Images: Essays and Conversations.* Trans. Michael Hofmann. London: Faber and Faber, 1991. Reprint of "Unmögliche Geschichten. Vortrag auf einem Kolloquium über Erzähltechniken." *Die Logik der Bilder. Essays und Gespräche.* Frankfurt am Main: Verlag der Autoren, 1988.

Contributors

Espen Aarseth is a professor at the IT University, Copenhagen, and the author of *Cybertext: Perspectives on Ergodic Literature* (1997) as well as numerous essays on hypertext aesthetics, online culture, and computer games. In 2001 he founded the online journal *Gamestudies,* devoted to the scholarly study of computer games (*http://www.gamestudies.org*). He directs the CALLMOO project (see *http://www.cmc.uib.no*), using MOOs in foreign language learning. Currently he is writing a book on digital culture for the Norwegian Research Survey of Power and Democracy.

David Bordwell is Jacques Ledoux Professor of Film Studies in the Department of Communication Arts at the University of Wisconsin–Madison. His books include *Narration in the Fiction Film* (1985), *Making Meaning: Inference and Rhetoric in the Interpretation of Cinema* (1989), *On the History of Film Style* (1997), *Planet Hong Kong: Popular Cinema and the Art of Entertainment* (2000), *At Full Speed: Hong Kong Cinema in a Borderless World* (2001), and, coedited with Noël Carroll, *Post-Theory: Reconstructing Film Studies* (1996).

Justine Cassell is a member of the faculty at MIT's Media Laboratory, where she heads the Gesture and Narrative Language Research Group. She has coedited *From Barbie to Mortal Kombat: Gender and Computer Games* (1998) and *Embodied Conversational Agents* (2000). She has published extensively in journals as diverse as *Poetics Today* and *Computer Graphics.*

Kamilla Elliott, Ph.D., Harvard University, specializes in relations between the Victorian novel and film/television. She is currently assistant professor at the University of California–Berkeley. Her book, *Rethinking the Novel/Film Debate,* was published in 2003.

Jeanne Ewert is an independent scholar living and working in Gainesville, Florida. Her primary research is in the intersection of narrative theory and cultural studies, and she is currently working on a study of American hard-boiled detection. She has published articles on Raymond Chandler, Vladimir Nabokov, Mary Roberts Rinehart, Art Spiegelman, and metaphysical detective fiction.

Cynthia Freeland's interest in horror dates back at least to the time she was forbidden by her parents to see *Psycho* when it came out in 1960. She did finally get to see it, and her ambivalent interest in the genre culminated in her book *The Naked and the Undead: Evil and the Appeal of Horror* (1999). Trained in classics and currently Professor of Philosophy at the University of Houston, she is an active participant in Houston's art community. Her most recent book is *But Is It Art? An Introduction to Art Theory* (2001).

Liv Hausken is an associate professor in the Department of Media and Communications at the University of Oslo. Her dissertation focuses on slide-motion film, narrative, and photography. She is the coeditor, with Peter Larsen, of *Medievitenskap* (1999–), a four-volume textbook in media studies. She has published numerous articles in Norwegian on such topics as "The Riddle of the Crime Series: Crime and Police Television Series" (1996), "The Temporality of Slide-Motion Films" (1997), "The Woman Does Not Exist—Does the Woman's Film?" (1997), and "Textual Theoretical Challenges in Media Studies" (2000).

David Herman is a professor in the English Department at North Carolina State University, where he teaches discourse analysis, narrative theory, and modern and postmodern literature. The editor of *Narratologies: New Perspectives on Narrative Analysis* (1999), *Narrative Theory and the Cognitive Sciences* (2003), and the Frontiers of Narrative book series at the University of Nebraska Press, he is the author of *Universal Grammar and Narrative Form* (1995) and *Story Logic: Problems and Possibilities of Narrative* (2002). His contribution grows out of ongoing research on a corpus of North Carolina ghost stories.

Emma Kafalenos teaches comparative literature at Washington University in St. Louis. She has published extensively on narrative theory, often in relation to the visual arts or music, in journals including *Poetics Today, Comparative Literature, 19th-Century Music, Visible Language, Studies in Twentieth Century Literature,* and *Narrative.* She is the editor of the May 2001 issue of *Narrative,* devoted to contemporary narratology.

Peter Lunenfeld is director of the Institute for Technology and Aesthetics (ITA) and teaches in the graduate Media Design Program at Art Center College of Design in Pasadena, California. He is the author of *Snap to Grid: A User's Guide to Digital Arts, Media and Cultures* (2000) and editor of the *The Digital Dialectic: New Essays in New Media* (1999). From 1998 to 2002 he was a columnist for the international journal *artext.* He is editorial director of the highly designed Mediawork pamphlet series for the MIT Press. These "theoretical fetish objects" cover the intersections of art, design, technology, and market culture (*mitpress.mit.edu/mediawork*).

David McNeill has taught at Harvard University, the University of Michigan, and the University of Chicago, where he has been professor of psychology and linguistics since 1969. His research on the speech-gesture nexus started in 1980 and has focused on spontaneous gestures in narrative discourse. Current work emphasizes "growth points" in speech and gesture production, cross-linguistic differences in thinking for speaking, the gestures of world leaders, and a system of motion detection and measurement to recover three-dimensional gesture, speech, and gaze cues for discourse segmentation, the latter project in collaboration with computer engineers. His publications on gestures include *Hand and Mind: What Gestures Reveal about Thought* (1992) and the edited collection *Language and Gesture* (2000).

Peter J. Rabinowitz, professor of comparative literature at Hamilton College in Clinton NY, divides his time between music and narrative theory. He is the author of *Before Reading: Narrative Conventions and the Politics of Interpretation* and coauthor, with Michael Smith, of *Authorizing Readers: Resistance and Respect in the Teaching of Literature;* he is also coeditor, with James Phelan, of *Understanding Narrative.* His published articles, which have appeared in such venues as *Critical Inquiry,* PMLA, *Modern Philology, The Cambridge History of Literary Criticism,* and *19th-Century Music,* cover a wide range of subjects, from Dostoevsky to Mrs. E. D. E. N. Southworth, from detective fiction to the ideology of musical structure, from speech-act theory to second-person narration, from Mahler to Scott Joplin. An active music critic for more than twenty-five years, he is currently a contributing editor of *Fanfare* as well as a regular contributor to the British journals *International Piano Quarterly* and *International Record Review.*

A native of Geneva, Switzerland, where she studied under some of the founders of the Geneva school of criticism, **Marie-Laure Ryan** is an independent scholar based in Colorado and a former software consultant. She is the author of *Possible Worlds, Artificial Intelligence, and Narrative Theory* (1991) and *Narrative as Virtual Reality: Immersion and Interactivity in Literature and Electronic Media* (2001), which received the 2001 Jeanne and Aldo Scaglione Prize for Comparative Literature from the Modern Language Association. She has also edited the collection *Cyberspace Textuality: Computer Technology and Literary Theory* (1999). The recipient of a Guggenheim fellowship, she is currently at work on a book project tentatively titled *Literary Cartography.*

Wendy Steiner is founding director of the Penn Humanities Forum and past chair of the English Department at the University of Pennsylvania, where she holds the Richard L. Fisher Professorship. Her special interests are modern literature and visual art, contemporary American fiction, and ethical issues in the arts. Her most recent books are *The Scandal of Pleasure: Art in an Age of Fundamentalism* (1995), named by the *New York Times* as one of the "100 Best Books of 1996"; and *Venus in Exile: The Rejection of Beauty in Twentieth Century Art* (2001). In addition to scholarly work, her cultural criticism has appeared in the *New York Times, London Independent, London Review of Books,* and *Times Literary Supplement.*

Eero Tarasti received his Ph.D. degree at the University of Helsinki after studies abroad in Vienna, Paris (with A. J. Greimas, among others), and Rio de Janeiro. He has been professor of musicology at Helsinki University since 1984. He is also director of the International Semiotics Institute at Imatra, Finland. He received honorary doctorates from Indiana University (Bloomington) and Estonian Music Academy. The author of about three hundred articles on musical semiotics, aesthetics, and general semiotics, he has also published several books, including *Myth* *and Music* (1979; in French, 2000), *Heitor Villa-Lobos* (1995), *A Theory of Musical Semiotics* (1994; in French as *Sémiotique musicale,* 1996), *Existential Semiotics* (2000), and *Le Secret du Professeur Amfortas* (a novel, in French, 2000).

A 1999 fellow of the Swedish Collegium for Advanced Studies, **Katharine Young** is an independent scholar in Berkeley. She is the author of *Taleworlds and Storyrealms: The Phenomenology of Narrative* (1986) and *Presence in the Flesh: The Body in Medicine* (1997). Her current research is on narrative and the body in somatic psychology.

Index